Palgrave Macmillan Asian Business Series

Series Editor: **Harukiyo Hasegawa** is Professor at Doshisha Business School, Kyoto, Japan, and Honourable Research Fellow at the University of Sheffield's School of East Asian Studies, where he was formerly Director of the Centre for Japanese Studies.

The Palgrave Macmillan Asian Business Series seeks to publish theoretical and empirical studies that contribute forward-looking social perspectives on the study of management issues not just in Asia, but by implication elsewhere. The series specifically aims at the development of new frontiers in the scope, themes and methods of business and management studies in Asia, a region which is seen as key to studies of modern management, organisation, strategies, human resources and technologies.

The series invites practitioners, policy-makers and academic researchers to join us at the cutting edge of constructive perspectives on Asian management, seeking to contribute towards the development of civil societies in Asia and further afield.

Titles include:

Claes-Göran Alvstam, Harald Dolles and Patrik Strom (*editors*)
ASIAN INWARD AND OUTWARD FDI
New Challenges in the Global Economy

Glenn D. Hook and Harukiyo Hasegawa (*editors*)
JAPANESE RESPONSES TO GLOBALIZATION IN THE 21st CENTURY
Politics, Security, Economics and Business

David Marutschke
CONTINUOUS IMPROVEMENT STRATEGIES
Japanese Convenience Store Systems

Hiroaki Miyoshi and Yoshifumi Nakata (*editors*)
HAVE JAPANESE FIRMS CHANGED?
The Lost Decade

Hiroaki Miyoshi and Masanobu Kii (*editors*)
TECHNOLOGICAL INNOVATION AND PUBLIC POLICY
The Automotive Industry

Diane Rosemary Sharpe and Harukiyo Hasegawa (*editors*)
NEW HORIZONS IN ASIAN MANAGEMENT
Emerging Issues and Critical Perspectives

Sten Söderman (*editor*)
EMERGING MULTIPLICITY
Integration and Responsiveness in Asian Business Development

Chikako Usui (*editor*)
COMPARATIVE ENTREPRENEURSHIP INITIATIVES
Studies in China, Japan and the USA

Oliver H.M. Yau and Raymond P.M. Chow (*editors*)
HARMONY VERSUS CONFLICT IN ASIAN BUSINESS
Managing in a Turbulent Era

Tan Yi
THE OIL AND GAS SERVICE INDUSTRY IN ASIA
A Comparison of Business Strategies

Palgrave Macmillan Asian Business Series

Series Standing Order ISBN 978–1–403–99841–5

You can receive future titles in this series as they are published by placing a standing order. Please contact your bookseller or, in case of difficulty, write to us at the address below with your name and address, the title of the series and the ISBN quoted above.

Customer Services Department, Macmillan Distribution Ltd, Houndmills, Basingstoke, Hampshire RG21 6XS, England

Asian Inward and Outward FDI

New Challenges in the Global Economy

Edited by

Claes G. Alvstam
Centre for International Business Studies (CIBS),
School of Business, Economics and Law, University of Gothenburg, Sweden

Harald Dolles
Molde University College, Specialized University, Norway
and Centre for International Business Studies (CIBS),
School of Business, Economics and Law, University of Gothenburg, Sweden

and

Patrik Ström
Centre for International Business Studies (CIBS),
School of Business, Economics and Law, University of Gothenburg, Sweden

First published 2014 by
PALGRAVE MACMILLAN

Palgrave Macmillan in the UK is an imprint of Macmillan Publishers Limited, registered in England, company number 785998, of Houndmills, Basingstoke, Hampshire RG21 6XS.

Palgrave Macmillan in the US is a division of St Martin's Press LLC, 175 Fifth Avenue, New York, NY 10010.

Palgrave Macmillan is the global academic imprint of the above companies and has companies and representatives throughout the world.

Palgrave® and Macmillan® are registered trademarks in the United States, the United Kingdom, Europe and other countries.

ISBN 978–1–137–31220–4

This book is printed on paper suitable for recycling and made from fully managed and sustained forest sources. Logging, pulping and manufacturing processes are expected to conform to the environmental regulations of the country of origin.

A catalogue record for this book is available from the British Library.

A catalog record for this book is available from the Library of Congress.

Typeset by MPS Limited, Chennai, India.

Contents

List of Figures vii

List of Tables ix

Foreword x

Preface and Acknowledgements xii

Notes on Contributors xiv

1 Asian Inward and Outward FDI: New Challenges
in the Global Economy – An Introduction 1
Claes G. Alvstam, Harald Dolles, and Patrik Ström

2 Changing Faces of MNCs in China: Subsidiary Strategy
in Corporate Strategic Reorientation 17
Yu Zheng

3 Sponsoring as a Strategy to Enter, Develop, and
Defend Markets: Advertising Patterns of the Beijing
Olympic Games' Sponsoring Partners 36
Harald Dolles and Sten Söderman

4 Global Innovation and R&D for Knowledge Creation:
The Case of P&G, Unilever and Kao 65
Chie Iguchi, Takabumi Hayashi, and Atsuho Nakayama

5 The New Face of Talent Management in Multinational
Corporations: Responding to the Challenges of Searching and
Developing Talent in Emerging Economies 87
Christian Schmidt, Sebastian Mansson, and Harald Dolles

6 Preferences and Intercultural Networking for Globalizing
Practices of Successful Leaders in the Intercultural Workplace 115
Rolf Schlunze, William W. Baber, and Weiwei Ji

7 Foreign Direct Investment and Economic Revitalization
in Japan: The Role of the Foreign Firm in Niseko 137
Andrew Staples

8 Exploring Thick Description in Business System Analysis:
The South Korean Business System from a European
Corporate Perception 153
Flora Bendt, Joakim Sanne, and Harald Dolles

9 Samsung Electronics: From 'National Champion'
   to 'Global Leader'   179
   Sang-Chul Park, Claes G. Alvstam, Harald Dolles, and Patrik Ström

10 A Business Tale on Marriage, Divorce and Remarriage in
   the Corporate World: A Conceptual Framework of Firms'
   Disintegration Process   201
   Roger Schweizer and Katarina Lagerström

11 The 'Hybrid' Emerging Market Multinational
   Enterprise – The Ownership Transfer of Volvo Cars to China   217
   Claes G. Alvstam and Inge Ivarsson

12 Concluding Remarks on Asian Inward and Outward FDI;
   New Challenges in the Global Economy   243
   Claes G. Alvstam, Harald Dolles, and Patrik Ström

Index   249

List of Figures

3.1 The means–objective framework 39

3.2 Yili's longitudinal advertising pattern
(means–objective combinations) 51

3.3 Yili's Olympic advertisements (sample selection) 52

3.4 Advertisements by the two Chinese breweries:
Yanjing and Tsingtao 53

3.5 Two longitudinal advertising patterns
(means–objective combinations) 54

3.6 Advertisements by UPS 55

3.7 Advertisements by Volkswagen brands 56

4.1 Different types of R&D laboratories in this research 70

4.2 The ratio of individually written and papers written
jointly with other organizations (universities and
research institutions) – Kao, P&G and Unilever 75

4.3 The number of national origins-of-affiliations among
authors contributing to Unilever, P&G and Kao research 76

4.4 Ratios of jointly written papers with authors belonging
to overseas organizations 78

4.5 The ratio of research papers by authors belonging
to MNEs subsidiaries 79

4.6 Ratios of jointly written papers by authors belonging
to subsidiaries or local organizations in a host country
external to the MNE subsidiary 80

5.1 National and corporate culture 92

5.2 Leadership dynamics and culture 93

5.3 Interaction between two cultures' leadership dynamics 104

5.4 The global approach to leadership development
within talent management 106

6.1 Standard model in academic conversation 116

6.2 Detailed practitioner's model 117

6.3 Combined network of co-leaders 128

7.1 Japan's inbound and outbound FDI (flow), 1995–2011 138

7.2   Japan's inbound FDI (stock), 1995–2011   140

7.3   FDI stock as a per centage of gross domestic product,
      1995–2011   141

7.4   Niseko: number of foreign visitors and overnight
      stays, 2001–2010   144

7.5   Niseko: foreign tourists by nationality   145

8.1   A framework for business system analysis   161

8.2   Characteristics and linkages of the South Korean
      business environment   164

9.1   R&D expenditures of Samsung Electronics, 1991–2011   187

9.2   Patents assigned to Samsung Electronics by US Patent and
      Trademark Office, 1991–2011   188

11.1 The ownership structure of Volvo Car Corporation   227

11.2 Location of the production and management units of
      Volvo Car Corporation in China: approximate distances
      between separate units   228

List of Tables

3.1   Means–objectives patterns and their codes   46
3.2   Sponsorship involvement and appearance   49
3.3   Dominant means–objectives combinations   50
4.1   Overseas sales ratio of Kao, P&G and Unilever   72
4.2   National origins of affiliations of authors, 1981–1983   82
4.3   National origins of affiliations of authors, 2006–2008   82
5.1   Sample characteristics   96
6.1   Mr J's network   125
6.2   Mr F's network analysis   126
6.3   Results of network analysis   129
6.4   Synthesis of network and preference analysis   130
8.1   Research sample: Main characteristics   156
9.1   Globalization strategies of Samsung Electronics   191

Foreword

Foreign direct investment (FDI), whether inward or outward, reflects the stage of economic development in a national economy. Regionally, Asia is now a venue for various kinds of inward and outward flows of capital, and has come a long way since its first wave of FDI, in Japan in the mid-1970s. This was hailed at the time as a sign of Japan's economic maturity, as well as a way of deflecting criticism of its massive export activity. In the 1980s and 1990s, other Asian economies also became part of this wave of FDI, decreasing Japan's relative importance. Today, a new wave of FDI, much of it centred on China, has grabbed attention not only because of massive inward investment to the region, but also more recently through the outward FDI put into motion by China's own multinational corporations, reflecting the country's unique compressed economic development.

What FDI is, and why and how it is practised, have long been important theoretical topics and are a day-to-day issue of the global geography of business, as shown in this anthology. Five of the chapters herein concern China, while of the others, three discuss Japan and two Korea; this broadly reflects current academic interest in the situation of FDI in Asia, stimulated as it has been in recent decades by globalization. FDI is a catalyst, critical in transforming business and management in both host and home country, and is thus an appropriate coordinate to be chosen by editors of this volume.

As yet there has been little research into Asian business and management from path-dependent and contextual perspectives. However, politics, culture and societal preferences are strong contextual components, which business and management need to adopt and adapt to. Such contextual conditions generate a most interesting reality where FDI is concerned and create unique variations in Asian management systems, as can be seen in Japan, Korea and China.

This is a two-part anthology, the first part focusing on issues of FDI's strategic and managerial implications, and the second part discussing its locational implications. These issues are seen mainly from a Euro-Asian perspective, which both reflects the origin of this anthology, and expresses its particular strength. The editors' mission – to 'capture and elucidate aspects that have been less observed and assessed in the scholarly debate up to now' – is important and been very well realized in this collection. Each chapter provides an interesting narrative on an aspect of business and management in Asia within the rich contextual realities of FDI, and here I would like to congratulate the editors, who have so well collected not only contributions of great individual quality, but contributions that are a pleasure to read.

As a whole, this volume will lead us toward the larger question of where this process of globalization, as manifest in FDI in Asia, will lead in coming decades and what impacts it may have upon the rest of the world.

Harukiyo Hasegawa
Honorary Fellow, White Rose East Asia Centre
The University of Sheffield

Preface and Acknowledgements

Since the 1970s, but especially during the early 1980s, the expansion of Japanese firms into Western countries rapidly increased, and the Western world was fascinated but threatened at the same time by the 'Japanese miracle' and its supporting structures, such as the intensive collaboration between state and industry, the industrial structure (*keiretsu* system), and the 'art of Japanese management'. European researchers and business executives who had been closely observing this development held a workshop entitled 'Transferability of Japanese Management' in Berlin in 1984. This was followed by workshops in London on the 'Internationalization of Japanese Enterprises' (1985), in Rotterdam on 'Industrial Collaboration between Europe and Japan' (1986) and in Tokyo on 'Comparative Studies on International Adaptability of Japanese and European Management' (1987). As a matter of this growing interest into Japan and later Asia in a broader sense the foundation of the Euro-Asia Management Studies Association (EAMSA) was only a natural consequence.

Since the 1980s Asia – its markets, industrial structure, and its firms – has not lost its appeal to Western managers and researchers, but the focus of attention has switched between different topics, starting from the impact of Japanese activities in Europe and North America, looking into the specifics of Japanese management and production as well as investigating the possibilities of transferring elements of Japanese management (key words among others: flexible job organization, implicit communication and shared values, group decision-making methods) and the way that Japanese industrial production is organized into the Western world (key words, for example: lean production, *kanban* system). Today the activities of Chinese firms and new multinationals from Asian emerging markets are catching our attention. Various locations in Asia compete for foreign direct investment not only from the Western world but also from neighbouring countries in Asia.

The Centre for International Business Studies (CIBS) at the School of Business, Economics and Law, University of Gothenburg (Sweden) hosted the 28th EAMSA conference, with a main theme of 'The Changing Competitive Landscape in Euro-Asia Business Relations'. The presentations and discussions during four days in November 2011 focused on one of the most interesting phenomena that have recently emerged in international business. Multinational companies from emerging and developing economies in Asia are becoming important players in the globalized world economy and have embarked upon rapid globalization processes targeting industrialized economies, particularly in North America, Australia, and Europe. Host European countries increasingly face an array of challenges and opportunities arising from the activities of Asia's emerging economies' multinationals. The chapters in this volume originated from being presented at the conference, but were substantially amended afterwards based on the reviewers' comments received. We applied strict selection criteria so as to develop a concise focus of the volume on 'Asian inward and outward FDI: New challenges in the global economy'.

We are grateful and indebted to many people who supported us to make this anthology possible. The conference was supported by Volvo Cars Corporation, Palgrave Macmillan, the City of Gothenburg, and the School of Business, Economics and Law at the University of Gothenburg. More directly toward the publication we would like to express our gratitude to Professor Harukiyo Hasegawa for his offer to include this volume in the Asian Business and Management Series, as well as to Virginia Thorp, Senior Commissioning Editor Business and Management at Palgrave Macmillan, for her encouragement and patience. Last but not least we would like to thank the reviewers engaged in this publication project and the contributing authors for their responses to the comments.

Gothenburg, August 2013
Claes G. Alvstam, Harald Dolles, and Patrik Ström

Notes on Contributors

Claes G. Alvstam holds the Ragnar and Torsten Söderberg rotating chair in economic sciences and is Professor in International Economic Geography at the School of Business, Economics and Law at the University of Gothenburg, Sweden. He is at present acting director at the Centre of International Business Studies (CIBS) at the School. Claes' research has concerned foreign trade, foreign direct investment, regional economic integration in Europe and Asia, external trade policy, the internationalization process of the firm, technology and knowledge transfers between transnational enterprises and local host-market suppliers, and has published numerous books and articles in international journals, most recently *The Changing Competitive Landscape in Euro-Asia Business* (Focussed Issue *Asian Business and Management*, 2013, with Dolles and Ström).

William W. Baber is Associate Professor at Kyoto University, Japan and a leading member of the research group Spaces of International Economy and Management (SIEM). His educational and research interest is in the field of intercultural business communications. William's work focuses on synergistic effects of communications, corporate governance, and impact of expatriates on the Japanese workplace.

Flora Bendt completed her MSc in International Business and Trade at the School of Business, Economics and Law at the University of Gothenburg, Sweden and she holds a BSc in business economics at Luleå University of Technology, Sweden. Her research has focused on foreign market entry strategies of SMEs and the impact of Free Trade Agreements. Flora currently works as fashion demand planner Europe for The Nuance Group, a company in the travel retail industry.

Harald Dolles is Professor in Sport Management at Molde University College, Specialized University in Logistics, Molde (Norway) and Professor in International Business at the University of Gothenburg, Centre for International Business Studies (CIBS), School of Business, Economics and Law (Sweden). From 2001 to 2006 he was assigned by the German Ministry of Education and Science to serve in official mission as expert on Japan and China at the economic section of the German Institute for Japanese Studies in Tokyo and taught as Visiting Professor at Chuo University (Tokyo, Japan). Harald has served on the Board of the Euro-Asia Management Studies Association for more than ten years and frequently contributes to scientific development in the fields of international business, innovation and entrepreneurship, Asian studies and sports management. In this regard, he has a publication stream of articles and books, most recently *The Changing Competitive Landscape in Euro-Asia Business* (Focussed Issue *Asian Business and Management,* 2013, with Alvstam and Ström); *Handbook of Research on Sport and Business* (2013, with Söderman), *Sports Management and Mega Events: J-League Soccer and Mega-Sports Events in Asia* (in Japanese; 2012, with Takahashi, Hayakawa and Söderman); *Sport as a Business: International, Professional and Commercial Aspects* (2011, with Söderman).

Takabumi Hayashi is Professor of Global Business and Management at Graduate School of Business and Management at Kokushikan University, Tokyo, Japan. His research topics include Strategic management on innovation and intellectual property rights, intercultural management and innovation, competitive advantage and knowledge management strategy, theory of internationalization of R & D activities in multinational companies. Recently his topic concentrates on BOP strategies of MNEs. Currently he is Dean of Graduate School of Business and Management at Kokushikan University. Takabumi also serves as a board member of the International Federation of the East Asian Management Association.

Chie Iguchi is Associate Professor of International Business at the Faculty of Business and Commerce at Keio University in Tokyo, Japan. She was awarded a PhD in International Business from University of Reading, Business School, UK. Her research is focused on Global R&D Strategy by MNEs in South East Asian countries, looking at subsidiaries' competence level and spillover effects by MNEs' global R&D to host countries. Chie serves on the Board of Euro-Asia Management Studies Association, European International Business Academy and the Association of Japanese Business Studies. Chie has published articles on MNEs subsidiaries in Asia, most recently 'Globalisation of R&D by TNC subsidiaries: The case of South-East Asian countries' (*Asian Business and Management,* 2012).

Inge Ivarsson is Professor of Economic Geography at the School of Business, Economics and Law at the University of Gothenburg, Sweden, and is affiliated to its Centre of International Business Studies (CIBS). He has published extensively in international journals within the fields of globalization and the role of transnational corporations, foreign direct investment in Europe and Asia, location strategies of R&D activities in TNCs, international technology, and knowledge transfer between transnational corporations and host-market suppliers in emerging markets. In 2012 Inge received, together with a co-author, the 'Best Paper Award' in *International Business Review* by the European International Business Academy. He is also Board Member of the Euro-Asia Management Studies Association.

Weiwei Ji is a lecturer at Academy of Overseas Chinese Studies in Jinan University, China. He also works for Overseas Chinese Affairs Office of the State Council in China. He received his Master's and Ph.D. in management at the Faculty of Business Administration of Ritsumeikan University. His research interests include topics on globalization, locational preferences, network and cross-cultural management in Asia. He is a member of the Euro-Asia Management Study Association (EAMSA) and International Association for Chinese Management Research (IACMR). His book, *Exploring Cross-Cultural Competence in East Asia* was recently published by Palgrave Macmillan.

Katarina Lagerström, PhD, is Associate Professor in International Business at the Department of Business Studies, Uppsala University, Sweden and Associated Researcher at the Centre for International Business Studies (CIBS), School of Business, Economics and Law, University of Gothenburg, Sweden. Katarina's research interests include firms' internationalization process, business strategies, and knowledge management in MNCs. She has published papers in academic journals such as *International Business Review*, *Journal of World Business,* and *International Journal of Project Management.*

Sebastian Mansson holds a Masters Degree in International Business and Trade from the School of Business, Economics and Law, University of Gothenburg, Sweden. His Master's Thesis (co-written with Christian Schmidt) titled 'Talent Management and Leadership Development at Western multinational companies and the transfer of practices to China' was awarded with the Malmsten Award for Best Thesis in international business in 2011. Since then, they have co-authored several publications within talent management. Sebastian currently works as an international tax consultant.

Atsuho Nakayama is Associate Professor of Department of Business Administration at Graduate School of Social Sciences at Tokyo Metropolitan University, Japan. The topic of his recent research is the analysis of the influences of in-store marketing, advertisement placement, and word-of-mouth communication on consumer's purchase behaviours. He is a board member of the Behaviormetric Society of Japan and Japanese Classification Society.

Sang-Chul Park has received PhD degrees in political science in 1993 in Germany and economics in 1997 in Sweden. He is currently Full Professor at Graduate School of Knowledge based Technology and Energy, Korea Polytechnic University and Adjunct Professor at the Center for Science-based Entrepreneurship, Korea Advanced Institute of Science and Technology (KAIST), South Korea. Sang-Chul is also a Private Dozent at Justus Liebig University in Giessen, Germany and Visiting Professor at Gothenburg University, Sweden. His research interests concern industrial policy and regional development, and studies on innovation systems and on science parks and innovative clusters in particular. Currently Sang-Chul's research areas are expanded towards energy policy, sustainable development strategy, high technology ventures, and international business and trade.

Joakim Sanne has a Bachelors degree in Industrial Economics with majors in Industrial Organization, Quality Management, and Logistics from the University of Gavle. After several years of working within the automotive industry, he started studying again at the University of Gothenburg. He graduated from the University of Gothenburg with an MSc in International Business and Trade. Joakim also studied Korean language and culture at Korea University in Seoul.

Rolf D. Schlunze is Professor of Intercultural Management in the Department of International Business Administration at Ritsumeikan University. He focuses his research on the adjustment process of managerial systems and expatriate managers. Co-leading the international research group Spaces of International Economy and Management (SIEM), his academic endeavour is to introduce contextual management appraisals to scholars and international business people. Rolf has served on the Advisory Committee of the Euro-Asia Management Studies Association for several years.

Christian Schmidt holds a Masters Degree in International Business and Trade from the School of Business, Economics and Law, University of Gothenburg, Sweden. His Master's Thesis (co-written with Sebastian Mansson) titled 'Talent Management and Leadership Development at Western multinational companies and the transfer of practices to China' was awarded with the Malmsten Award for Best Thesis in international business in 2011. Since then, they have co-authored several publications within talent management. Christian currently works with organizational development and change management in the automotive industry.

Roger Schweizer is an Associate Professor at the Centre for International Business Studies, Department of Business Administration, School of Business, Economics and Law at the University of Gothenburg. His current research interests are international strategy issues in general and, in particular, firms' internationalization processes, international entrepreneurship, the relationship between headquarters and subsidiaries, and mergers and acquisitions.

Andrew Staples is currently Director of the Economist Corporate Network in Japan and formerly Associate Professor of International Business at Doshisha Business School, Kyoto, Japan. He was awarded a Daiwa Anglo-Japanese Foundation/Japanese Foundation Endowment Committee PhD Scholarship (2000–2003) and a Japanese Ministry of Education, Culture,

Sports, Science and Technology (MEXT) Research Scholarship (Hitotsubashi University, Tokyo, 2001–2003). Andrew's publications include *Responses to Regionalism in East Asia: Japanese Production Networks in the Automotive Sector* published as part of the Palgrave Macmillan Asian Business Series and chapters in edited volumes and textbooks. He was also a Senior Editor for the internationally peer-reviewed journal *Asian Business and Management*.

Patrik Ström is Associate Professor of Economic Geography at the Centre for International Business Studies (CIBS), School of Business, Economics and Law, the University of Gothenburg, and holds PhD degrees in Business administration at Roskilde University, Denmark, and in economic geography at the University of Gothenburg. Patrik's main research has centred around the service industry within the field of internationalization. He is currently President of RESER, The European Network on Research in Services, and chairs a working group within the European Commission on the future of service industry. Most recently Patrik published *The Changing Competitive Landscape in Euro-Asia Business* (Focussed Issue *Asian Business and Management*, 2013, with Alvstam and Dolles).

Sten Söderman is Professor of International Business at Stockholm University, School of Business (Stockholm, Sweden). Previously he was a professor at Luleå University of Technology and a business consultant specializing in startups (in Manila, Geneva, and Brussels). His research has focused on market strategy development and implementation and more currently on the international expansion of European firms in Asia and the global entertainment economy. He is the author and editor of many books, case studies and articles, most recently: *Handbook of Research on Sport and Business* (2013, with Dolles), *Emerging Multiplicity: Integration and Responsiveness in Asian Business Development* (2006). Sten serves at the Advisory Committee of the Euro-Asia Management Studies Association since several years.

Yu Zheng is Lecturer in Asian Business and International Human Resource Management at the School of Management, Royal Holloway University of London. Yu's research interests are in international human resource management, cross-country transfer of management practices, and comparative employment relations. Her research monograph *Managing Human Resources in China: The View from Inside Multinationals* was published in 2012.

1
Asian Inward and Outward FDI: New Challenges in the Global Economy – An Introduction

Claes G. Alvstam, Harald Dolles, and Patrik Ström

1.1 Trends and developments in Asian inward and outward FDI

It has long been conventional wisdom that the re-entrance of Asia has been one of the most remarkable events in the international economy during the last half century. Asia today contains almost 28 per cent of the global GDP in nominal values and 33 per cent when measured in purchasing-power parity terms.[1] It is less commonly discussed, though, that we presumably have only witnessed the first chapters in this massive global shift, and that the increasing influence of Asian nations in general and of Asian firms in particular will take many new features and forms in the foreseeable future.[2] The Asian realm was the dominant economic powerhouse in ancient times, with an estimated two-thirds of the global GDP five hundred years ago, but was thereafter pushed into relative insignificance during the eras of Arab, Portuguese, Dutch, French and British colonial expansion.[3]

The continent as a whole hit its all-time economic low during the years after the Second World War. The spectacular turnaround we have witnessed since then commenced with the rapid recovery of the Japanese economy in the 1950s and 1960s, and the subsequent growth of foreign trade and outward foreign direct investment related to Japan. The outward foreign direct investment (OFDI) from Japan followed initially the classical gradual dispersal of resource-seeking, in parallel with market-seeking, investment, beginning with the East Asian neighbouring region, and now, a few decades later, has circumvented the globe, with iron ore exploitation in Brazil and automotive manufacturing 'transplants' in North America and Europe, to take a few examples. Since the Japanese OFDI was not balanced by an equal expansion of inward foreign direct investment (IFDI), the country built up a huge surplus stock of OFDI during the following decades. This development ran in parallel with an equally massive surplus in Japan's trade balance.

The Asian 'tiger' nations, on the other hand, followed a different internationalization pattern, characterized by an initially higher trade intensity,

1

built on a limited home base, and a more aggressive export-oriented growth, built mainly on imported capital in massive flows of IFDI in subsequently more advanced manufacturing sectors. In both Japan and the 'NIE-tigers', the development followed generally the well-established 'Investment Development Path' (IDP) model, which stipulates a certain level of economic development, together with a certain level of firm-specific advantages in the home market to commence an increase of outward investment (Dunning, 1986; Dunning and Narula, 1996; UNCTAD, 2006). While the ratio of outward/inward FDI stock ratio has now declined to about 4 (2011 figure) in the case of Japan, compared to 20 in 1990, Singapore's O/I-stock ratio amounted to about 0.6 in 1980, and fell to around 0.25 in 1990, and thereafter, with the rise of OFDI, grew to around 0.65 in 2011.[4]

A similar development of initially growing IFDI, followed by rising OFDIs at a certain level of economic development and domestic firm-specific advantages, has been recorded in Hong Kong, Taiwan and South Korea. The new development of rapidly growing OFDI flows from these economies was furthermore complemented by a gradually changed composition of both the geographical destinations and the sectorial content of the OFDI stock. In all cases, geographic dispersal of the OFDI continued in parallel with continuous upgrading of the composition of exports. The larger countries in Southeast Asia – Malaysia, Thailand, Indonesia, the Philippines and Vietnam – have thereafter, with some variations of individual path-developments, subsequently followed the same pattern in a 'flying-geese'-stylized way.[5] A new phenomenon, however, that has become even more obvious during the last decade is a return to a more concentrated geographic pattern of their OFDI as a consequence of the emergent Asian regionalization process, manifested by rapidly growing intra-Asian trade as well as direct investment patterns (Baldwin, Kawai and Wignaraja, 2013).

A major change that pushed the 'Asia-turn' of the 1960s and 1970s into a new phase was the opening up of Mainland China from 1978 to economic and cultural exchanges with capitalist countries to learn from and draw on 'advanced' capitalist management methods, in order to connect China economically to international markets (the open door policy). Those reforms were based on plans of the four modernizations (namely, to modernize Chinese agriculture, industry, science/technology and defence). This development was even more remarkable, given the rapid shift from one extreme to another – from an almost non-existent foreign trade turnover three decades ago to becoming the world's largest exporter of goods today; this was in parallel with a rapid growth of IFDI from a virtual zero-level, since the early 1980s, followed by an equally rapid growth of OFDI, from 2005 and onward. Still, it is of a modest size, due to its late start. China's IFDI stock is today roughly 10 per cent of GDP, to be compared to Singapore, where it exceeds 200 per cent of GDP. Looking at China's O/I stock ratio, it amounted to about 0.14 in the year 2000, grew to around 0.25 in 2006, and at the time of writing is about 0.5. The spectacular re-emergence of China as the major economic power in Asia has, through its sheer extent, also overshadowed the successful transition of composition of trade and investment in the neighbouring economies. Even though the previously dominant Japan has recently been surpassed in economic terms by the population-wise eleven times larger China, it is crucial not to underrate the strength of Japan's continuing economic power and influence in the region, despite two decades of relative stagnation, although at a high level.

The Japanese industrial organization, i.e. organization of companies to large industrial groups (*keiretsu*) with their linkages upstream and downstream in the value-chain, has been frequently described during the 1980s as complex, cumbersome, costly, confusing, inefficient, archaic and as a major obstacle to FDI in Japan (see e.g. Dolles, 1997; Dolles and Kumar, 1996; Hemmert, 1993 for a comprehensive overview). Although it was possible to build up wholly owned subsidiaries in Japan after a change in Japanese legislation in 1980, foreign firms doing business in Japan faced extraordinary difficulties during the period of high economic growth in that country. These hardships were attributed to intangible market barriers such as a lack of understanding of the Japanese industrial system (particularly distribution and manufacturing). In the 1990s, after the end of the 'bubble economy', the following 'lost decade' was experienced by Japanese corporations as an economic crisis, in conditions of persistently low economic growth, continuously declining asset prices and the holding up of household consumption during this period (cf. Horioka, 2006; Ishizaki et al., 2010). Initially this has also deterred many foreign companies from expanding FDI in Japan, but soon the Japanese government recognized that FDI not only brings capital to Japan, but can also exert a positive influence in technology, management, on the labour market and as a supporting factor in Japan's efforts to reform (Dolles, 2010).

Since 1995 IFDI in Japan has increased, whereas Japanese OFDI peaked at the end of the bubble economy and since then has never reached those levels again. The Japan External Trade Organization (2012) reported a outflow of Japanese FDI of US$ 115.7 billion in 2011, reflecting large-scale M&A deals, a string of new business bases established and investments to support existing operations abroad. As of the end of 2000, North America, Europe and other developed economies accounted for 70 per cent of the total Japanese OFDI stock. With the fast growth of investment in emerging countries, however, the share of developed countries declined at the end of 2011, with Asia and Central and South America increasing their shares. In the figure reported for 2011 the Asian region was setting a new all-time high with US$ 39.5 billion OFDI, with a focus on China and the ASEAN countries (ibid.). It is also stated that the rate of return on Japan's OFDI to Asia is higher than that to Europe and the US, an indicator that the 'era of profiting from Asia has begun for Japan' (ibid.: 6). This development lies behind, for instance, Japanese automakers setting up new production plants or investing in new equipment one after another in a race to capture fast-growing demand in emerging countries.

When it comes to Japanese IFDI, for 2011 the Japan External Trade Organization (2012) calculated a net outflow (withdrawal) of US$ 1.7 billion, the second consecutive net outflow, affected by massive net outflows (US$ 4.11 billion, mostly by the US) in the non-manufacturing sector, such as telecommunications and finance/insurance. However, this is claimed to be only a short-term effect as at the beginning of 2012, a net inflow of US$ 920 million was posted in increased investment from Asia (mainly Singapore and Taiwan), Switzerland and the US. While North American and European firms remain the main actors in IFDI in Japan, the presence of Asian firms is rising steadily. Particularly noteworthy are moves of Taiwanese and Chinese firms to buy in resources of Japanese companies and strengthen their business bases by acquiring equity stakes and/or setting up joint ventures. This might in turn enable Japanese companies to expand business operations in China and other parts of Asia.

The likewise impressive development and transformation of the South Korean economy, and the immense potential of ASEAN-10, with its half a billion inhabitants, should also be given better prominence, and not only be viewed in China's shadow. South Korea, compared to Japan, has received relatively little attention by foreign scholars (Hemmert, 2012: 4), which is remarkable, given the fact that the relatively small Korean home base, compared to Japan, makes it a more suitable model for export-oriented industrialization than Japan. Of particular interest is the analysis of Japan's economic transformation as an early model for South Korea, and its later ambition to define its own strategy, using lessons from Japan's economic stagnation since the early 1990s. Hemmert (2012: 21) has summarized the Korean business model in terms of four elements: Confucianism, the Japanese influence, the American influence and military-led industrialization. It is evident that the mix of American influence, symbolized by the high number of Korean senior decision-makers with an American educational background, and the military influence, represented by a 'command culture' and a quick execution of plans, has been a decisive explanation behind the more rapid transformation of the Korean economy, and the success of Korean companies in the global market (Hemmert, 2012: 18–21).

The even larger challenge when it comes to the interpretation of the internationalization processes of Asian economies is inbuilt in the future scenario of South Asia, where India, Pakistan and Bangladesh together record a volume of foreign trade in goods amounting to US$ 922 billion, slightly larger than that of Singapore (US$ 792 billion) and with a trade volume per capita amounting to US$ 580, to be compared with US$ 148,000 in Singapore, US$ 22,000 in South Korea, US$ 14,500 in Malaysia, US$ 13,500 in Japan and US$ 3,000 in China.[6] The shares of foreign trade in services in relation to the total turnover of trade in goods and service are usually below world average in the larger Asian countries, with the notable exception of India. This underrepresentation constitutes another important challenge and opportunity, and it is likely that the service industry in its diverse representations will be the next great engine of change in Asia. Both the Southeast Asian and South Asian countries moreover feature a more favourable demographic composition, measured by the dependency ratio, and on this perspective are better positioned for future economic growth and transition than China.

Foreign trade in goods and services, and FDI, should be viewed as two sides of the same coin, in a dialectical relationship, and as mutually leveraging each other in a global economy characterized by increasingly fragmented patterns of division of labour and specialization, and the transformation from 'trade in products' to 'trade in tasks'. This gradual change, which has very accurately been labelled 'globalisation's second unbundling' (Baldwin, 2012, has even more emphasized the importance of the long-term 'global shift' of production of goods and services from Europe and North America to Asia (Dicken, 2011). The use of the concept of global production networks should rather be viewed in a regional context in the sense that these networks in reality comprise a limited number of countries of production, and that the majority of new entrants in the GPNs have been situated in Asia (Baldwin et al., 2013; Inomata, 2013). This is not to overlook the likely possibility that production networks in the future will become more global, but the main part of the dispersal of economic activities is hitherto in reality concentrated in a few regions, making the term 'semiglobalization' appropriate to illustrate the processes of global shift during recent decades (Ghemawat, 2008).

At the same time as trade in goods and services can be seen as a twin to foreign direct investment, it is relevant to note that the rules and regulations that comprise these activities are entirely different. While international trade in goods early became subject to a multilateralized regime of supranational regulations and mutually binding liberalization of tariffs and non-tariff barriers to trade within the GATT-based system, trade in services was a laggard, and it was not fully integrated into the multilateral order until the mid-1990s with the creation of the World Trade Organization and the General Agreement of Trade in Services (GATS). Nonetheless, after almost two decades in operation, the progress of a complete implementation of cross-border transactions of services in the multilateral system lags behind trade in goods, despite unanimous commitments by the almost 160 member-strong WTO, comprising more than 95 per cent of world trade. Economies in Asia are rapidly being transformed into becoming more dependent on production and consumption of services. Advanced economies such as Japan and Singapore generate more than two-thirds of their total value-added within service production (Jensen, 2013). Emerging economies are rapidly following their development path. The ability to develop and upgrade the Asian service economy is one of the most important challenges for the region, according to the Asian Development Bank (2012). Further liberalization of trade and FDI is necessary, but also to deregulate and integrate markets. A successful shift of the economy to generate bigger incomes from the service industry is vital not to risk ending up in the so-called middle-income trap for emerging economies (Noland, Park and Estrada, 2012; Park and Shin, 2012). Accordingly, the further internationalization of service activities, and the creation of new forms of service concepts within the global value-chain, as well as a more visible and transparent measure of the service content in the value-chain, will constitute a crucial challenge for Asian economies in the future. Services should therefore be given a more prominent role in international business research than has so far been the case (see also, among others, Kirkegaard, 2012; Merchant and Gaur, 2008). The lack of service-related research within international business has also been put forward as a challenge for the future. This development has consistently been labelled 'the second global shift' (Bryson, 2007), and will be an important feature in this volume.

Even more striking is the gap between trade and investment when it comes to attempts to create common rules and regulations at the supranational level. Investments have generally been looked upon from a bilateral perspective, and the ambitions to convergence of rules in the, in many respects, mutually contradictory bilateral investment agreements into a more coherent and transparent general global framework have so far enjoyed limited success. Bilateral investment agreements between nations are furthermore affected by the different attitudes and policies towards FDI – inward as well as outward – between the parties involved. The ongoing project within UNCTAD to coordinate and consolidate international investment policy-making has until now resulted in a number of regional International Investment Agreements (IIAs), comprising the same type of problems as regionalism within trade in goods and services (UNCTAD, 2013a). The commonplace, but nevertheless often overlooked, observation to be always kept in mind is that decisions to commence cross-border activities, exports/imports as well as investments, are made by individuals in firms, not by politicians or states, but the role of the state as a 'container' of laws, regulations, and practices, as well as an active 'regulator', is equally relevant to understand the dynamics of competitive advantages of nations, and of the business environment perceived by the decision-maker.

It is in this context relevant to distinguish between supporting and restricting FDIs – inward and outward – as seen from the government policy perspective, and, in addition, to make a distinction between different grades of active support or restrictions. The Asian cases are in this respect particularly illustrative, since it is usually argued and acknowledged that state interventions to support or restrict FDI have been stronger than in Europe or North America, and that the People's Republic of China by all means represents the most extreme case of an initial near prohibition of FDI in both directions, via a strong policy support for IFDI during the 1980s and 1990s, to an even more active and efficient policy for supporting OFDI during the last decade. The recent attitudes of a more restrictive policy versus IFDI, and the active support for national champions to compete with foreign firms in the domestic market, reflects a new stage of maturity in economic development, and merits a careful and balanced scrutiny from the domestic perspective (inside) as well as from the foreign (outside). In particular, these new trends are important to follow up in times of a shift of Chinese IFDI from being dominated by large transnational corporations to a larger share of small and medium-sized niche companies, which not only act as follow-source suppliers, but also actively seek new market opportunities in China.

The changing processes of FDI policies should furthermore be seen in parallel to the opening up of China for foreign trade through its application to join the WTO, and its final inclusion in the multilateral family in 2001. The rapid export expansion from China was to a large extent a direct effect of IFDI, and initially was export-dominated by foreign firms. This imbalance has gradually shifted in the direction of domestic firms, who combine exports with OFDI. There is at the same time also a shift of the shape of those global production networks, where companies located in China so far have been particularly represented in the final assembly element of the chains, but where a larger share of the total value-added is going to take place in China. On the other hand, there is also a trend to relocate low-end assembly activities to other countries in Asia, as well as to non-Asian destinations, given the rising labour costs in China. Furthermore, the examples of 'reshoring' of manufacturing activities to Europe and North America should also not be underrated, despite their so far relative insignificance.

1.2   About the content of this volume

The starting-point of this volume – which emanated from research within the network of the *Euro-Asia Management Studies Association* (EAMSA) and its 28th annual conference, hosted by the Centre for International Business Studies at the University of Gothenburg, School of Business, Economics and Law, comprising scholars in international business, economic geography, and management, mainly from Europe and Asia – is to explore new forms and features of foreign direct investment related to emerging Asian countries, in order to increase our general understanding of the complexity of the internationalization process of Asian firms and commercial relations between Europe and Asia. It is in this context particularly important to investigate differences and varieties of Asian business internationalization, to find out in which aspects there is a need to extend and to revise traditional Western-based theories and interpretations, based on empirical findings in emerging economies in general and in Asia in particular.

One basic pre-understanding behind this volume is that there are indeed a number of crucial gaps between mainstream theories and Asian realities, although these should not be exaggerated either. The focus of the separate contributions to this volume moves between OFDI and IFDI on the one side, and between the Asian and non-Asian perspective on the other. This is to stress that the investment pattern should always be seen as a mutual process, where decisions to invest abroad are mirrored in the circumstances around receiving investment in the host country. There has also been an explicit aim to adopt the business firm perspective in the majority of the contributions in an attempt to point at the still remaining deficit of company-based studies compared to more general macro-oriented descriptions and analyses of country-to-country investment patterns. The previously mentioned historical imbalance between inward and outward FDI in Japan can be viewed from both the macro perspective as an effect of government policies, but can also be seen as a micro-level cultural and mental phenomenon.

The chapter by *Andrew Staples* brings about both the general development of a liberalized view on IFDI in Japan – in many respects an effect of the long-term stagnation of the Japanese economy – and at the same time also the growth of new types and sectors of IFDI. The example of the investments in the northern ski-resort of Niseko by foreign actors from Australia, Hong Kong, and Malaysia illustrates the shift from manufacturing-based to service-based investment, specifically to new service sectors in the tourism and leisure industries, as well as the shift from investment in big Japanese urban conglomerations to the rural periphery. It is also an example of the new geographical origins of investment, including capital from outside the larger financial centres inside and outside Asia.

Also Japanese investment abroad has historically been large and extensive, but heavily concentrated in manufacturing and underrepresented in services. Recently, however, there are signs of an increasing activity in location overseas of R&D facilities related to manufacturing as well as to services, and also to increased multinational research cooperation with non-Japanese companies. R&D functions have so far been cautiously kept at home, but this traditional wariness to protect its companies from insight by foreigners might also have contributed to a stagnating development in exploring new fields of innovation, and there is thus an increasing interest in Japan to investigate the opportunities of various forms of international research collaboration.

In the contribution by *Chie Iguchi, Takabumi Hayashi* and *Atsuo Nakayama*, the objective is to investigate knowledge-transfers and various kinds of technological cooperation in the consumer sectors, using the Japanese company Kao Corporation, manufacturer of personal care, toiletries, cleaning products, and specialty chemicals, together with the transnational giants and competitors Unilever and Procter & Gamble as an illustrative example of how cross-national scientific research takes place and how different nationalities are affiliated to each other. Kao is by far the least internation-alized company of the three cases, with only one-fourth of its sales outside Japan, and it has also most to learn from how further dispersal of R&D activ-ities can be managed. The study shows that to become a critical source of dynamic capabilities in the global market, firms need to look beyond a reli-ance on the kind of in-house central research that Kao has concentrated on. There is a need not just to maintain central laboratories but to look abroad for knowledge creation, as P&G and Unilever have successfully managed.

A related aspect of the slow adaptation of the Japanese business sector to not only invest in overseas manufacturing with the entire control of the technical processes, product development, and management and opera-tions in Japanese hands, but also to become more involved in intercultural communication in the daily life of the company, at home and abroad, is explored by *Rolf D. Schlunze, Weiwei Ji* and *William W. Baber*. In their in-depth interviews of European managers in Tokyo, and Japanese managers with experience of working abroad, both groups involved in co-leadership with a foreign partner, the authors demonstrate the challenges and limita-tions of the creation of 'global managers' as an ultimate representation of globalization, and how deepened knowledge about the cultural mindset of decision-makers and key actors in internationally organized companies is essential to understand the new phases of internationalization that many Asian companies are entering through the accelerated investment abroad, in other parts of Asia, and not least in developed Western economies.

The issue of intercultural co-leadership in the Japanese context is closely related to how to cope with global talent management as a whole, not only in Japan, but to an even larger extent in other Asian countries. The chapter by *Christian Schmidt, Sebastian Mansson* and *Harald Dolles* focuses on the lack of skilled talent to cope with the rapid importance of emerging markets for multinational corporations. The lack of experience of international manage-ment is particularly acute in China, owing to the late internationalization and the limited number (measured in relative terms) of young persons who have had the opportunity to study abroad and/or work for foreign companies in China. Even though there has been a rapid development of both career opportunities for Chinese managers abroad and within foreign companies in China, it will take a long time to reach a global standard of Chinese management experience and also to cope with the rising number of acquisitions abroad by Chinese firms and other OFDI-related effects. The group of 'sea turtles', returning to China after having completed higher busi-ness education overseas and having pursued a professional career abroad in international companies, may only partly cover the urgent need of manage-ment competence in these new Chinese multinationals or for foreign mul-tinationals seeking Chinese entrants to their talent pools. The interviews carried out by these authors with large multinational corporations across different industries in China confirm that adaptions of talent identification and development processes are limited but do exist. The endeavour by foreign multinationals to implement a global and universal talent management approach at the higher level of managerial responsibility should be more systematically taken into consideration when assessing the future growth of new emerging Chinese multinationals in the global arena.

With a growing number of foreign companies investing in China over the years, there is also a growing need for more in-depth analysis of the various subsidiary strategies that have been adopted. Previous research has often judged strategy in MNCs as an internally consistent set of policies and practices that fit with the environmental contingencies, industrial/sector or organizational attributes. In the chapter by *Yu Cheng*, it is shown, however, how subsidiary managers deploy local resources to address the subsidiary strategic concerns to move away from being a low-cost production base. Contrary to existing research that studies MNCs as a coherent whole, this study has focused on a single unit (a subsidiary). The findings reveal complementarities and contradictions in corporate as well as subsidiary strategy, which is a common scenario of strategic reorientation in MNCs. The study also identified a multicentric power structure within MNCs, and political struggles by the managers had significant impact on the subsidiary management policies and practices. These findings challenge the conventional wisdom that strategy in MNCs is about centralized strategic planning and decentralized practice to operationalize corporate strategy. It turned out that management policies and practices were quite subsidiary-specific, which endorses the idea that strategy enactment at the subsidiary level manifests a dynamic process of segmentation and reconstruction of strategies, policies, and practices, rather than a top-down application of central strategy.

Even though IFDI to China has attracted the largest attention during the last decades, the growing OFDI has given rise to a new field of study, namely, the intricate relationship between inward and outward flows, adopting an actor-based approach. The assumption behind this approach is that the same actors are involved in both directions. The existing debate has so far mainly concerned the issue of 'round-tripping' – outward capital flows directed at Hong Kong, various Caribbean tax havens and elsewhere, which at the next stage are transformed into inward investment. Such an order is typical in a heavily regulated monetary/financial regime, also characterized by large differences in policy regulations between domestic and foreign capital, and it is evident from numerous empirical studies that these 'loops' of capital flows have played an important role in the total IFDI volumes in China's manufacturing sector. It has in this respect been argued that the internationalization of China's economy has been strongly exaggerated, given that a fair share of the recorded investment volumes in reality emanate from domestic sources, and are directed at domestic purposes.

However, despite 'round-tripping', the main forceful new trend is, once again, the accelerated process of internationalization of Chinese enterprises and the aggressive acquisitions of large, global companies, as well as green-field investments in both advanced and developing economies around the world, which will gradually make the round-tripping issue less significant. The most spectacular recent examples of foreign bids by Chinese companies have been Haier's greenfield investments in the United States in 1999–2001, SAIC's acquisition of South Korea's Ssangyong in 2004, Lenovo's taking over of IBM's PC business in 2005, the TCL–Thompson Electronics deal, Wanxiang Group's cross-border M&As in the US, Zhejiang Geely's acquisition of Swedish Volvo Car Corp. from Ford Motor Corp. in 2010, and, most recently, Shuanghui International Holdings' bid for American Smithfield Foods, the world's largest pork processor and hog producer, in 2013. All these deals merit deep investigation from the academic community, since they most likely represent just the beginning of a far larger 'deluge' of Chinese investment overseas. We will address those issues with three contributions in the collection, taking three different perspectives on this phenomenon.

The chapter by *Harald Dolles* and *Sten Söderman* takes a marketing approach, and explores how Chinese firms use new forms of marketing to enter new markets or to prove themselves as being ready for the world market. So far sponsorship, product placement or other new approaches have been considered as emerging interesting areas at the intersection of advertising and entertainment. However, over the past two decades sponsorship-linked marketing growth has outstripped conventional advertising growth, and successful corporate marketers integrate sponsorship and advertising to cross-promote the two media and multiply the effect of the marketing investment. By linking advertising and sponsorship Chinese firms aim at increasing national as well as international awareness among consumers, thus increasing their brand equity. In that respect the Olympic Games and other mega-events have developed as one of the largest international marketing platforms in the world (Dolles and Söderman, 2008), and those events have been used by established multinational enterprises and brands such as GE, VW or Coca-Cola. Most sport sponsorship research has focused on the markets in North America, Europe or Australia, thus covering a different economic development and representing dissimilar market conditions.

This research aims to fill the gap by describing and analysing the advertising behaviour of the Chinese as well as foreign sponsoring partners to the Beijing Olympic Games in 2008. A means–objective framework of sponsoring focusing on six factors was applied in a longitudinal analysis of 739 advertisements, articles, and press releases between 2001 and 2008. By applying a qualitative content analysis the authors discovered eight dominant means–objectives combinations leading to different sponsor advertising strategies, depending mainly on the lead time to the Olympic Games, strategic purpose, and the level of internationalization of the sponsoring company.

Another far less observed aspect in the internationalization strategy of Chinese firms, though, is the disintegration process that either forgoes an acquisition in the sense that the acquired company has been open for external bids, or runs in parallel with the change of ownership. It is in this regard relevant to distinguish between hostile and friendly takeovers. In the chapter by *Roger Schweizer* and *Katarina Hamberg Lagerström*, the neglected issue of disintegration following a demerger is discussed in conceptual and theoretical terms, using the change of ownership of Volvo Car Corp. (VCC) from Ford Motor Corp. to Chinese Zhejiang Geely Holdings as an empirical example. During the roughly twelve years of Ford's ownership of VCC, the Volvo brand was technically and commercially deeply integrated in the Ford family. The process of disintegration, including a negotiation phase, took more than two years, and continued for another couple of years in remote parts of the organization, e.g. in the joint assembly plant in Chongqing, China. It should be noted that this example represents a 'friendly' bid to a company that had declared its subsidiary open for external sales, but nevertheless the disintegration process was far from painless. Therefore, the contribution of this chapter is the building up of a solid platform for describing and analysing similar cases of disintegration followed by a demerger and an external acquisition, most likely often originating in China, and its impact on the internationalization process as a whole.

The Volvo–Geely case is also interesting, viewed from another aspect, namely, the fact that it represents a new phenomenon, where private Chinese firms, which are registered and floated in foreign stock markets, usually Hong Kong, and incorporated somewhere else, usually in the Cayman Islands or British Virgin Islands, acquires a large Western-based well-established multinational firm, possessing a globally recognized brand and the latest technological capabilities, in order to strengthen its competitive advantage in the Chinese home market. *Claes Alvstam* and *Inge Ivarsson* argue in their chapter, in which they follow this acquisition in a detailed longitudinal 'online' study through frequent interviews over time with representatives of VCC, both in Sweden and China, that this move has created a new category between being 'foreign' and being 'domestic', and suggest that VCC in China has become a 'hybrid' in this twilight zone between different, difficult to interpret, regulatory frameworks. Furthermore this particular acquisition is based on a mix of private and public financial sources, where three cities in China on a formal minority basis have been involved in the financial platform behind the purchase, and expect reasonably some kind of return in form of local manufacturing and service sector employment, which has made the issue even more complex. VCC has in different respects been treated by national and local authorities as 'foreign', and in other aspects as 'domestic', thereby giving rise to the 'hybrid' label. It remains to be seen whether this is a transitory situation where VCC gradually will become treated like any other domestic company, or, as is argued by these authors, that Chinese authorities are confident of keeping these newly acquired foreign multinationals in a twilight zone, making it possible to adopt different rules on an *ad hoc* basis. In the latter scenario the hybrid phenomenon is well worth continued research efforts.

It was previously noted that countries like South Korea should not be over-looked, despite the imminent risk of being overshadowed by its large neigh-bours. The FDI outflows have long been much larger than the inflows, and the O/I-ratio exceeded ≥1 for the first time in 2008, and is now about 1.20 (UNCTAD, 2013b). The rapid growth of OFDI in South Korea has been very much concentrated to the large conglomerates, the *chaebols*, which received a special boost to successful internationalization through a concerted and sustained government policy to create strong national champions over the years. One of the best examples of the success of this policy is the Samsung Group, and even though Samsung is a fairly well-explored case, both in Korea and abroad, many underlying factors behind its global conquest are still to be revealed, and it is also a good example in the effort to focus more on the corporate level to better understand the competitive advantages of nations. Samsung is not only the main actor behind South Korea's soaring OFDI, it is also by far the largest exporter of goods from South Korea, account-ing roughly for one-sixth of the total export value, exceeding the entire exports from a medium-sized emerging market economy, such as South Africa, Argentina or Chile. In their chapter *Sang-Chul Park, Claes Alvstam, Harald Dolles* and *Patrik Ström* focus specifically on factors that explain how Samsung Electronics became a 'national champion' and, thereafter, a 'global leader', but also on how it sought to maintain and strengthen global leader-ship. The creation of a global R&D platform, the capability of the company to use the business rather than the product as a guiding strategy, and the ability to attract talent on the global market are some of the lessons to learn for other Asian companies that aim at repeating the Samsung saga.

South Korean successes on the world market should also be seen in the view of the perspective of the 'old industrial core' countries. In 2011, the Free Trade Agreement between the EU and South Korea (KOREU FTA) was finally implemented, and there is an eternal debate in political as well as in business circles around the benefits and possible drawbacks of such liberali-zation schemes. The EU currently carries out similar free trade negotiations with India, Singapore and a number of other ASEAN countries, and will in the near future commence similar talks with Japan. At the same time, the lack of formalized bilateral trade relation with China has led to acute prob-lems in a number of industrial sectors, which has affected business on both sides negatively. There is accordingly a great need to make deeper empirical investigations related to the impacts of FTAs on trade investment flows at the sectorial and the corporate level.

The chapter by *Flora Bendt, Joakim Sanne* and *Harald Dolles* contributes to filling this vacuum by making an extensive survey of managers and sales representatives in European firms with responsibility for trade and other contacts with South Korea. The platform of research was the description and understanding of the Korean business system, and the results demonstrate the need to go beyond pure economic factors, measured by tariff reduction and revealed comparative advantages in separate industries.

Summarily, this volume as a whole aims at highlighting phenomena that are considered to be underrepresented in research regarding the internationalization process of Asian economies – both advanced economies with a 'lagged' internationalization in different respects, like Japan, and new emerging economies at different stages of economic development. Outward and inward FDI should be seen as a compound phenomenon with several actors involved, and should likewise be viewed as closely interrelated with other representations of international economic interaction.

Notes

1. Asia is defined in this collection as the 34 countries/territorial units in the following IMF classification: Developing Asia (28), Advanced economies (4), plus Pakistan and Afghanistan. IMF *World Economic Outlook Database*, April 2013 (2012 figures).
2. Another recently coined term for this development is 're-polarization', to note how the gravity centre of world economic affairs has moved in the direction of Asia (Oxelheim, 2012; Lindberg and Alvstam, 2012).
3. The famous backward extrapolations of the regional composition of the world economy between the years 2000 and 1000 by the late Scottish economist Angus Maddison (Maddison, 2007) do indeed not claim to be an exact estimate, but have nevertheless been accepted as a reasonable approximation, given fairly well-established accounts of the geographical distribution of world population during different periods of time, and through assessments on the general welfare level in different parts of the world.
4. Calculated from UNCTAD, *World Investment Report*, various issues.
5. Although many objections can be raised regarding the theoretical foundation of Akamatsu's (1961 [1937]) famous metaphor, the empirical evidence of his predictions of a gradual dispersal of economic take-off in the East Asian realm cannot be denied. See also the revisitation of Akamatsu's contribution by Kojima (2000).
6. IMF *Direction of Trade and International Financial Statistics, Databases*, 2012 figures [accessed 10 June 2013].

References

Akamatsu, K. (1961 [1937]) 'A Theory of Unbalanced Growth in the World Economy', *Weltwirtschaftliches Archiv*, 86(1): 198–209.

Asian Development Bank (2012) Asian Development Outlook 2012 Update. Services and Asia's Future Growth. Manila: ADB.

Baldwin, R. (2012) 'Trade and Industrialisation after Globalisation's Second Unbundling: How Building and Joining a Supply Chain Are Different and Why It Matters', in Robert C. Feenstra and Alan M. Taylor (eds), *Globalization in an Age of Crisis: Multilateral Economic Cooperation in the Twenty-First Century* (Chicago, IL: University of Chicago Press) draft of 11 October 2012, www.nber.org/chapters/c12590.pdf, accessed 21 August 2013.

Baldwin, R., M. Kawai and G. Wignaraja (eds) (2013) *The Future of the World Trading System: Asian Perspectives* (London: Centre for Economic Policy Research).

Bryson, J. (2007) 'The "Second" Global Shift: The Offshoring or Global Sourcing of Corporate Services and Distanciated Emotional Labour', *Geografiska Annaler*, Series B, 89 (Supplement): 31–43.

Dicken, P. (2011) *Global Shift: Mapping the Changing Contours of the World Economy*, 6th ed. (London: SAGE).

Dolles, H. (1997) *Keiretsu: Emergenz, Struktur, Wettbewerbsstärke und Dynamik japanischer Verbundgruppen [Keiretsu: Emergence, Structure, Competitive Strengths and Organizational Dynamics of Corporate Groupings in Japan]* (Frankfurt am Main: Peter Lang).

Dolles, H. (2010) 日本における失われた10年と外国企業―その含意と結果 [The Lost Decade and Foreign Companies in Japan – Implications and Consequences], in T. Ishizaki, Y. Takahashi, H. Tanaka, H. Umehara and M. Tatebe (eds), 失われた10年 – バブル崩壊からの脱却と発展 *[The Lost Decade – Departure and Development Since the Collapse of the Bubble Economy]* (Tokyo: Chuo University Press): 201–226.

Dolles, H. and Kumar, B.N. (1996) 'Überlegungen zur strategischen Führung und Wettbewerbsstärke japanischer Untenehmen' [A New Approach to Strategic Leadership and Sustained Competitive Advantages of Corporate Groupings in Japan], in J. Engelhard (ed.), *Strategische Führung internationaler Unternehmen. Paradoxien, Strategien und Erfahrungen [Strategic Leadership in International Corporations: Paradoxes, Strategies and Experiences]* (Wiesbaden: Gabler): 39–68.

Dolles, H. and Söderman, S. (2008) 'Mega-sporting Events in Asia: Impacts on Society, Business and Management – An Introduction', *Asian Business and Management*, 7(1): 1–16.

Dunning, J.H. (1986) 'The Investment Development Cycle Revisited', *Weltwirtschaftliches Archiv*, 122(4): 667–675.

Dunning, J.H. and Narula, R. (1996) 'The Investment Development Path Revisited: Some Emerging Issues', in J.H. Dunning and R. Narula (eds), *Foreign Direct Investment and Governments: Catalysts for Economic Restructuring* (London: Routledge): 1–41.

Ghemawat, P. (2008) 'The Globalization of Business Education: Through the Lens of Semiglobalization', *Journal of Management Development*, 27(4): 391–414.

Hemmert, M. (1993) *Vertikale Kooperation zwischen japanischen Industrieunternehmen [Vertical Cooperation between Japanese Industrial Firms]* (Wiesbaden: Deutscher Universitätsverlag).

Hemmert, M. (2012) *Tiger Management. Korean Companies on World Markets* (Abingdon: Routledge).

Horioka, C.Y. (2006) 'The Causes of Japan's "Lost Decade": The Role of Household Consumption *Japan and the World Economy*, 18(4): 378–400.

Inomata, S. (2013) 'Trade in Value-Added: An East Asian Perspective', in: R. Baldwin, M. Kawai and G. Wignaraja (eds), *The Future of the World Trading System: Asian Perspectives* (London: Centre for Economic Policy Research – VoxEU.org eBook): 29–37.

Ishizaki, T., Takahashi, Y., Tanaka, H., Umehara, H. and Tatebe, M. (eds) (2010) 失われた10年 – バブル崩壊からの脱却と発展 *[The Lost Decade – Departure and Development since the Collapse of the Bubble Economy]* (Tokyo: Chuo University Press).

Jensen, J.B. (2013) *Overlooked Opportunity: Tradable Business Services, Developing Asia, and Growth*, ADB Economics Working Paper Series, No. 326 (Manila: Asian Development Bank), http://www.adb.org/sites/default/files/pub/2013/economics-wp326.pdf [accessed 29 July 2013].

Japan External Trade Organization (JETRO) (2012) *JETRO Global Trade and Investment Report: Companies and People Move Forward towards Globalization*, http://www.jetro.go.jp/en/reports/white_paper/trade_invest_2012.pdf [accessed 29 July 2013].

Kirkegaard, J.F. (2012) *Transactions: A New Look at Service Sector Foreign Direct*, ADB Economics Working Paper Series, No. 318 (Manila: Asian Development Bank), http://www.adb.org/sites/default/files/pub/2012/economics-wp318.pdf [accessed 29 July 2013].

Kojima, K. (2000) '雁行型経済発展論・赤松オリジナル' [Akamatsu's Original Contribution – The Flying Geese Type of Economic Development], 世界経済評論 *[World Economic Essays]*, 44 (3): 8–20.

Lindberg, L. and Alvstam, C.G. (2012) 'Interregional Trade Facing Re-Polarization: The EU Trade Negotiations with ASEAN Countries', in: L. Oxelheim (ed.), *EU–Asia and the Re-Polarization of the Global Economic Arena* (Singapore: World Scientific Press): 55–94.

Maddison, A. (2007) *The World Economy: A Millennial Perspective/Historical Statistics, Vol. 1–2* (Paris: OECD, Development Centre Studies).

Merchant, H. and Gaur, A. (2008) 'Opening the "Non-Manufacturing" Envelope: The Next Big Enterprise for International Business Research', *Management International Review*, 48(4): 379–396.

Noland, M., Park, D. and Estrada, G.B. (2012) *Developing the Service Sector as Engine of Growth for Asia: An Overview*, ADB Economics Working Paper Series, No. 320 (Manila: Asian Development Bank), http://www.adb.org/sites/default/files/pub/2012/economics-wp320.pdf [accessed 29 July 2013].

Oxelheim, L. (ed.) (2012) *EU–Asia and the Re-Polarization of the Global Economic Arena* (Singapore: World Scientific Press).

Park, D. and Shin, K. (2012) *The Service Sector in Asia: Is it an Engine of Growth?*, ADB Economics Working Paper Series, No. 322 (Manila: Asian Development Bank), http://www.adb.org/sites/default/files/pub/2012/economics-wp322.pdf [accessed 29 July 2013].

United Nations Conference for Trade and Development (UNCTAD) (2006) *World Investment Report. FDI from Developing and Transition Economies: Implications for Development* (Geneva: UNCTAD), http://unctad.org/en/Docs/wir2006_en.pdf [accessed 29 July 2013].

United Nations Conference for Trade and Development (UNCTAD) (2013a) 'The Rise of Regionalism in International Investment Policymaking: Consolidation or Complexity?' *IIA Issues Note*, June (3) (Geneva: UNCTAD), http://unctad.org/en/PublicationsLibrary/webdiaepcb2013d8_en.pdf [accessed 29 July 2013].

United Nations Conference for Trade and Development (UNCTAD) (2013b) *World Investment Report. Global Value Chains: Investment and Trade for Development* (Geneva: UNCTAD), http://unctad.org/en/PublicationsLibrary/wir2013_en.pdf [accessed 29 July 2013].

Statistical sources

International Monetary Fund (IMF), *Direction of Trade Statistics, Database* (Washington, DC: IMF).

International Monetary Fund (IMF), *World Economic Outlook* (Washington, DC: IMF).

United Nations Conference for Trade and Development (UNCTAD), *World Investment Report*, various issues 2001–2013 (Geneva: UNCTAD).

2
Changing Faces of MNCs in China: Subsidiary Strategy in Corporate Strategic Reorientation

Yu Zheng

2.1 Introduction

China is in transition. So are the multinational corporations (MNCs) in China. For many MNCs, the rationale for relocation to China used to be overwhelmingly to capture low-cost production. This has been supplanted by market access and research and development (R&D) reasons in recent years. While much has been written about changes of MNCs' strategies in terms of entering and operating in China (Child, 1994; Child and Tsai, 2005; Cooke, 2008; Luo, 2007, 2001; Sun, Zedtwitz and Simon, 2008), limited attention has been given to understanding how subsidiaries cope with corporate-level strategic changes. This study aims to fill this gap by considering how corporate strategies get translated and executed innovatively at subsidiaries, which have conventionally been seen as 'strategy implementers' (Bartlett and Ghoshal, 1989).

Contrary to a coherent approach in understanding MNCs as possessing mono-power-centric unity with congruent functional units playing well-defined roles, this study endorses the view that MNCs are more like federal networks (Andersson, Forsgren and Holm, 2007). Corporate strategies are enacted at subsidiaries (Boisot and Child, 1999), and strategies also emerge from subsidiaries (Birkinshaw and Hood, 1998; Birkinshaw and Ridderstrale, 1999). This is because actors at subsidiaries take initiatives to pursue subsidiary-specific advantages which, from a resource-based view, are critical for subsidiaries' survival within MNCs (Garcia-Pont, Canales and Noboa, 2009). Such distinctive and subsidiary-specific advantages can be transferrable or non-transferrable within the MNCs (Rugman and Verbeke, 2001). Also, actors at subsidiaries have the capacity to mobilize resources embedded within and outside the MNCs in order to overcome the organizational constraints on subsidiaries taking initiatives to pursue subsidiary strategy (Birkinshaw and Ridderstrale, 1999; Edwards, Colling and Ferner, 2007; Kristensen and Zeitlin, 2005). Resources at subsidiaries' disposal, especially those developed locally, give rise to the attainment of subsidiary strategy.

17

In this sense, subsidiary strategy is a social construct, which evolves as actors manipulate their knowledge and access to embedded resources, negotiate for power within MNCs and generate subsidiary-specific advantages.

The transitional nature of the Chinese economy and the scale and economic diversity of China offer a site for the investigation of emerging subsidiary strategy. Since the Chinese government launched the policy to reform the economy and open up to foreign investments in the late 1970s, China has witnessed drastic industrial restructuring, relaxed regulations on individual mobility and fast-growing consumer markets. MNCs are faced with a more open environment and less restraints on choosing collaborative partners, sourcing a local workforce and exploring the Chinese markets. In the meantime, however, some critical resources are still controlled or directed by the central and regional governments. Relations with key officials remain important for accessing some locally embedded resources. This institutional setting allows considerable space for actors at subsidiaries to develop management practices that address subsidiary strategic concerns (Zheng, 2012).

This research is based on detailed multiple case studies. The rationale of conducting case studies is based on the limited theoretical frameworks that could be applied to analyse a subsidiary in its own account. Research of subsidiary strategy in MNCs has often been drawn from the HQ's perspective, explaining the designated roles of subsidiaries from above. (This point will be further discussed in the following section.) Subsidiaries, in contrast, have often been viewed as functional or operational units and with limited strategic contribution. A case study approach enables us to move away from such HQ-centred thinking, to appreciate emerging patterns and new observation, and to explore the meaning of subsidiary strategy.

Findings based on case studies will also enrich our understanding of the reality of managing subsidiaries in MNCs. Existing empirical studies tend to take a quantitative approach to test the strength of the relationship between certain management practices, corporate performance and the contingency factors that mediate the relationship. However, as Scandura and Williams (2000) noted in their review, the rigidity of research design associated with quantitative methods limits the number and types of variables to be studied, rendering the usefulness of the research findings questionable. Subsidiary strategy, defined as an active process by which actors develop subsidiary-specific advantages, needs to be understood in its context. Case studies help to uncover the 'black box' between an MNC's international strategy, the actual policies and practices exercised in various units (HQ or subsidiaries) and the complex forces that shape corporate and subsidiary strategies.

The chapter is organized as follows: first, a theoretical review shows the gaps in the existing literature on subsidiary strategy within MNCs. This is followed by a section which discusses the contributions and limitations of using multiple case studies with mixed research methods. The next section discusses the research findings from the case studies, and propositions that can be developed from these studies. The final section concludes the chapter by summarizing the emergent subsidiary strategies and the implications for corporate-level strategic reorientation.

2.2 Literature review: Subsidiary strategy, power structure and subsidiary upgrading

Dunning's influential OLI (ownership, location, internalization) frame-work (1980) underpins MNCs with their ability to mobilize and synergize resources. Such a HQ-centred view of MNCs has long dominated the inter-national business literature. Most attention has been given to understand-ing the corporate strategy of managing across countries. Corporate strategy is often considered as a formalized process that produces a consensus system of rational decisions at HQ. Subsidiaries management, by contrast, is seen as concerned with operational issues, and subsidiaries' influence on corporate strategy has long been underestimated or simply ignored as a realistic area of research. More recent work has considered subsidiaries' ability to shape both the planning and enacting of corporate strategy; this study is particularly concerned with the enacting side, and demonstrates how subsidiary-specific strategy emerged during a period of corporate strategic reorientation.

2.2.1 Subsidiary strategy

Initially developed by international business scholars in order to explain dif-ferent ways MNCs coordinate cross-country operations, subsidiary strategy is more or less an abbreviation of 'the strategic value of subsidiaries to the MNCs.' Inspired by the work of Porter (1986), Prahalad and Doz (1987) and Bartlett and Ghoshal (1989), earlier scholars generally took a 'coherence approach' in viewing subsidiary strategy as part of MNCs' endeavour to address the tension between integrating international operations and achieving local responsiveness (Andersson, Björkman and Forsgren, 2005; Birkinshaw and Hood, 1998; Roth and Morrison, 1992; Taggart, 1997). Many studies of MNCs have focused predominantly on how the corporate HQs allocate resources, designate subsidiary roles and coordinate knowledge transfer among subsidiaries across different countries. While a small amount of research has attempted to explain how subsidiaries may redefine their own roles (Birkinshaw, 1997; Birkinshaw, Hood and Jonsson, 1998; Birkinshaw and Ridderstrale, 1999), the definition of what accounts for sub-sidiary strategy remains vague.

To explore the broader meanings of subsidiary strategy, the assumption that different units of an MNC serve a homogenous corporate strategy to gain competitive advantage has to be abandoned. While overarching corporate strategy affects resource allocation, performance targets as well as the establishment and closure of subsidiaries, subsidiaries are not simply the passive implementers of corporate strategy. Subsidiary strategy can derive from corporate strategy, provided that HQ and subsidiaries have the interests in and capacity to explore transferable competitive advantage (Bartlett and Ghoshal, 1989). However, subsidiary strategy is also locally embedded, aiming to generate non-transferable and subsidiary-specific competitive advantage so that they can outperform other subsidiaries and local firms (Rugman and Verbeke, 2001). Subsidiary strategy can also be generated by taking part in international production and service networks or production clusters (Kristensen and Zeitlin, 2005). Considering the heterogeneity of strategy within MNCs allows us to redefine subsidiary strategy to reflect the contested process of strategy development in MNCs.

2.2.2   Power structure in MNCs

Corporate-level strategic orientation often has implications for the power structure between HQ and subsidiaries, which restrains the development of subsidiary strategy. The meaning of power in MNCs here is threefold. From a structuralist view, power concerns the legitimacy of authority in decision-making (Weber, 1968 (1922)). Within MNCs, the connotation of a dyadic HQ–subsidiary hierarchy gives rise to HQ's power in deciding subsidiary matters. The structural power of subsidiaries (or subsidiary autonomy) comes from a HQ delegation. In other words, subsidiaries can legitimately make their own decisions only when the HQ allows them to do so. While such a mono-power-centric approach offers justification to HQ authority, the reality is that the nexus of HQ–subsidiary relations in today's MNCs is much more complicated. Power at subsidiary level cannot merely be explained by HQ delegation.

An alternative source of power comes from possession and access to critical resources such as capital, technology and knowledge (Pfeffer and Salancik, 1978). From a resource dependence view, HQ's power over subsidiaries relies on its being a primary allocator of resources. Since resources are embedded within and beyond the parameter of MNCs; subsidiaries are able to seek alternative source of power, by building up relationships with powerful agents of local or international institutions (Edwards, Colling and Ferner, 2007). Collaboration and conflicts between subsidiaries also shape the power structure of MNCs. Information sharing and learning between sister subsidiaries can reduce the level of resource reliance on the HQ. Competition with sister subsidiaries, on the other hand, can discourage resistance to HQ influence (Elger and Smith, 2005). To further our understanding of subsidiary strategy under corporate strategic reorientation, the implications of such a multi-centric power sources have to be addressed.

Finally, from a strategic choice perspective, power is subject to managers' contestation and construction (Child, 1997). The link between corporate strategy and the management outcomes at subsidiaries is moderated by managers at different levels of the MNC (Boisot and Child, 1999; Edwards, Colling and Ferner, 2007; Ferner, Edwards and Tempel, 2012; Geppert and Williams, 2006; Kristensen and Zeitlin, 2005). Individual interests, concerns and agendas with regard to their assignments will be reflected in managers engaging in purposive actions, exerting formal and informal control, and dealing with conflicts to realize corporate, group and individual goals. Kristensen and Zeitlin's (2005) case studies show how corporate strategies can be hazardous for subsidiaries in realizing such organizational objectives as gaining operational efficiency and competitive advantage. Their work reveals that HQ's decisions to reduce the number of employees on economic grounds lead to the loss of members who were originally recruited to enhance the HR competence. This is because the corporate HR strategies are implemented in such a way as to advance subsidiary managers' interests rather than to serve the intended strategic objectives designated by the HQ. This wide range of actors' influence has to be reflected in the study of the link between China's transition, MNCs' strategic reorientation and subsidiary strategy.

2.2.3   Global industrial structure and subsidiary upgrading

The impacts of global industrial structure on MNCs are reflected in both corporate-level strategic reorientation and subsidiary-level strategy development. At corporate level, global industrial structure is a key indicator to the operation and management of MNCs' cross-country networks. Many existing studies concerning the relationship between MNCs and global industrial structure have revealed MNCs' capability of dividing production (or services) process into functional segments, allocating different segments across countries and thereby creating a spatial division of labour at a global scale (Frobel, Heinrichs and Kreye, 1980). Some relevant studies examine how MNCs make use of international labour markets by analysing the organization of global commodity chains (Gereffi, 1999), global value chains (Kaplinsky, 2000) or global production networks (Ernst and Kim, 2002). These researchers move attention from the segmentation of production functions within MNCs to the coordination of different production and services providers across countries. They argue that MNCs run a chain or a network of functional units in order to effectively develop, manufacture and deliver products and services to consumers worldwide. Although MNCs' ownership of functional units varies in different types of commodity chains or production networks, a hierarchy (or a 'grading' of various units) is used to describe the technological complexity and labour intensity of the specific functional units. They further contend that firms performing lower-end functions need to develop the capability to move up the hierarchy (or 'upgrade') by accumulating necessary capital, knowledge and human resources.

   In spite of the insights offered by these analyses, limited empirical evidence has illustrated how subsidiary upgrading has been achieved. Observing that

MNCs tend to keep core functions in the home country and relocate peripheral functions overseas, some scholars suggest the relationship between the parent plants and the overseas subsidiaries reflects a core–periphery division of labour at international level (Dicken et al., 2001; Gertler, 2004; Nadvi and Halder, 2005). Since cross-country difference in labour market institutions persist, corporate strategic reorientation can be understood as a process in which MNCs continuously stratify production and service processes into functional units and relocate these units to the countries that offer the best possible cost and return combination. In particular, the labour-intensive segments, which are characterized by standardized production/service processes and low skill requirements, are more likely to be relocated to countries where there is a sufficient supply of a disciplined and low-waged local labour force. Such conflicting interests between HQ and subsidiaries in corporate strategic reorientation, restructuring and relocation have to be addressed in the study of subsidiary strategy.

In summary, to study subsidiary strategy is not to deny that HQ's influence persists and that subsidiary managers have had to coordinate with the HQ to develop subsidiary-level strategy, policies and management practices. But we do need to renew our understanding of subsidiary strategy in the light of the collision of goals and concerns between HQs and subsidiaries, multi-centric power relations within MNCs, and the political actions of managers at different levels. Researchers have to move away from a 'coherence approach' in theorizing MNCs and consider how various units of MNCs manage to gain critical resources, such as the accessing a local knowledge base, building relationships with industrial and national institutions, as well as evolving/generating subsidiary specific strategy. We must also capture the contested process through which strategic decisions are interpreted, evaluated, negotiated and exercised at different units of the MNC (Edwards, Colling and Ferner, 2007; Ferner, Edwards and Tempel, 2012). In other words, we have to take seriously managers in subsidiaries as actors whose choices have a crucial input into the process of creating, developing and implementing strategies.

2.3   Research methodology

Four Japanese companies located in China were carefully selected and researched with the purpose of bringing the subsidiary level into sharper focus. Japanese MNCs have the reputation of being ethnocentric in their international management orientation (Harzing, 1999). Chinese subsidiaries were set up as low-cost production plants: most strategic planning and decision-making was centralized at the HQ and only a limited number of Chinese managers sat on the corporate board. However, the managerial superiority of Japanese MNCs had been seriously challenged over the past decades, partly due to the decline of the Japanese economy. Japanese MNCs have taken steps to restructure their global networks and to localize subsidiary management in order to improve operational efficiency. Such a strategic reorientation gave rise to subsidiaries' search for more structural power, including gaining more autonomy in deciding subsidiary matters and taking part in corporate strategic planning. In the meantime, China has become an indispensable part of many MNCs' global thinking, either as a key production base, a growing (yet diverse) consumer market, or a potential research and development (R&D) hub (The Economist Intelligence Unit, 2011). This transition allows subsidiaries to develop strategies locally, which can include gaining ownership of valuable assets, knowledge and/or access to local networks (Birkinshaw and Ridderstrale, 1999). Such an empirical setting, therefore, enables the investigation of possible subsidiary strategy in corporate strategic reorientations.

The case studies were based on two white-goods manufacturers (referred to as WG-A and WG-B in this chapter) and two synthetic fibre manufacturers (referred to as SF-A and SF-B). Each set of companies shared company size, age, parent companies' international experiences, product range and production mode. In terms of the location of these subsidiaries, they are sited in the Yangtze delta set of industrial clusters. The first round of fieldwork was conducted in 2007. To get the feel of the experiences of managers at subsidiary level, I adopted mixed qualitative research methods: semi-structured interviews, formal and information discussions with the managers and employees at various venues, observation at the workplace, attending company meetings and off-work activities, and collecting company documentations. I spent a month living in the factory dormitories of the four companies—these are typical of MNCs in China (Smith, 2003)—and thereby gained lengthy access to the managers, engineers and workers through these extended ethnographic encounters. Such combined research methods allowed me to be open to unanticipated events and to gain a holistic view of the multiple realities in the field (Gephart, 2004). The companies were revisited in 2010 for follow-up interviews. In total, 225 individuals were interviewed, and the length of interviews varied from 40 to 90 minutes.

2.4   Findings and discussion

2.4.1   Corporate strategic reorientation: Localization as an overarching corporate strategy

All four Chinese subsidiaries included in this study are facing strategic reorientation owing to the restructuring in Japan and rising importance of the Chinese consumer market for the HQ's global strategy. Both WG-A and WG-B relocated semi-automated assembly lines to China in the mid-1990s. The Chinese subsidiaries manufactured lines of standard products, more than 90 per cent of which were distributed and sold locally. Since the Japanese household white goods brands were well recognized by Chinese consumers, both companies achieved their growth targets soon after incorporation.

By 2000, however, their dominant position in China had been shaken by the rising power of Korean, Taiwanese and Chinese manufacturers. In the face of this competition, both companies were pressed to tighten cost and quality control, expand product range and upgrade product profiles. In the mid-2000s, both firms announced mid-term localization plans, which included sourcing production material from local suppliers, launching local product development programs, reinforcing local sales and customer services and integrating more local managers into the regional management teams.

The synthetic fibre industry had a different path of development in China. Relocation was characterized by restructuring of the product range and reinforcement of innovative capacities at the HQ. Both SF-A and SF-B were set up with export-centred production bases, supplementing their parent plants in Japan and sister plants in ASEAN countries. During the 1990s, their products were mainly exported to the international market, predominantly Japan. But a shrinking textile industry and rising labour costs in Japan forced SF-A and SF-B's parent companies to terminate some lines of textile fibre manufacturing and to close down a number of production plants in Japan. The Chinese subsidiaries' exports to Japan also shrank but their domestic sales expanded. The Chinese synthetic fibre industry grew dramatically over the past two decades, especially in the Yangtze delta area. The output of synthetic fibre manufacturing in China has accelerated since the mid-1990s. By the end of 2006, China contributed more than half of the total output of textile synthetic fibre worldwide. While acknowledging the pressure of cost control, managers of SF-A and SF-B shared the view that the Japanese fibre manufacturers could not win a 'price battle.' Rather, they needed to differentiate their products or services to survive in the Chinese market.

From the late 1990s, the Japanese HQs launched their global restructuring plans and started to consolidate their overseas subsidiaries. Some chose to decentralize decision-making and delegate control and coordination to the regional level. Among the cases, WG-A, SF-A and SF-B's ownership was partly transferred to the Chinese holding companies, which played the role of regional HQ. Except for large-scale investment decisions, the Chinese holding companies were designated to play the central role for strategic planning, financing and coordinating subsidiary management. WG-A further divided China into three sub-regions—north-east China, south-east China and west China—each with subsidiaries specialized in production, sales and customer services. All these subsidiaries reported to the regional offices, which were directly controlled by the Chinese HQ. WG-B's parent company had not set up a Chinese HQ at the time this study was conducted. The Chinese representative office in Beijing played a regional HQ role and reported back to the HQ. SF-A's Chinese holding company was set up in Shanghai, with North China and South China offices, taking care of subsidiaries in the respective regions. SF-A reported directly to the Chinese holding company. SF-B's parent company also set up a holding company in Shanghai, which controlled the subsidiaries in South China. Subsidiaries in North China reported to the parent companies' Beijing representative office.

The Chinese holding companies were not fully functioning owing to certain policy restraints set by the Chinese government. Under the Foreign Currency Control Regulations, non-financial institutions could not have either internal or external financing functions, which meant that the Chinese HQ's proposed financing function was not legally feasible. Foreign-invested companies were prohibited from bridging international and domestic trade, which restrained the ability of the Chinese holding companies to centralize international trade for the subsidiaries. The Chinese HQ prioritized improving the consistency of local policies and practices. The companies launched standardized recruitment policies and selection criteria, centralized some in-house training and career development programs, and introduced more unified performance appraisal and promotion procedures. This created tension and resistance from the subsidiaries, who were concerned that their control over many subsidiary management issues was technically weakened.

2.4.2   Subsidiary strategy

Existing literature on subsidiary strategy tends to emphasize the roles of subsidiaries *within* the MNCs (Bartlett and Ghoshal, 1989; Birkinshaw and Hood, 1998), and subsidiaries' ability to construct their roles (Birkinshaw and Ridderstrale, 1999; Ferdows, 1997; García-Pont, Canales and Noboa, 2009). However, under corporate restructuring, subsidiaries have the opportunity to change their roles, voluntarily or involuntarily. Restructuring also means that subsidiaries are at risk of being marginalized, sold off or closed, especially those that take the lower-value-added functions, such as the standard product manufacturing plants in this study. It is therefore equally important for subsidiaries to develop an 'exit' strategy, in case HQ withdraws from certain sectors, relocates to other low-cost countries or goes bankrupt in the home country. What evolves is a portfolio of subsidiary strategy.

In the past decades, Japanese MNCs had experienced large-scale restructuring. On the one hand, a stagnant domestic consumer market and rising labour costs forced Japanese MNCs to slim down domestic operations and review their global business strategy. On the other, the rise of China as a competitive production site and a potential consumer market made them reassess the leverage of the Chinese business. In the case studies, the Japanese HQ intended to strengthen the coordination role of the regional HQ, redistribute production and service functions among subsidiaries, and enhance operational efficiency through a *localization* strategy. Concerned with the vulnerable position in the corporate restructuring process, subsidiaries were keen to upgrade the portfolio of products and engaging in higher-value-added functions (such as R&D), though, as shown later, these attempts were often in conflict with the corporate restructuring plans. At the same time, subsidiaries were also concerned with the possibility of being made redundant—HQ could relocate manufacturing standard products to inner China or other low-cost countries. Becoming more independent and able to look after their future was also an indispensable aspect of subsidiary strategy.

2.4.2.1   'Climbing' strategy: Upgrading the product profile

The adoption of a 'climbing' strategy meant that subsidiaries took steps to move from low-end to high-end products, which included improving the product quality, expanding the range of products and manufacturing more technologically sophisticated products. MNCs offer a wide range of products, which can be graded in a hierarchy according to the technological complexity and labour intensity required for manufacturing them (Gereffi, 1999). Moving production that requires relatively less technological sophistication and high labour intensity offshore is one way that MNCs stay competitive. For subsidiaries that were set up to implement strategic relocation of low-end products, upgrading can be achieved through building up capital, technological capacity and management know-how (Coughlan and Brady, 1996; Ferdows, 1997; Taggart, 1998; Wedcofa, 2007).

In the four cases, subsidiary management saw the corporate localization strategy as allowing space for a *climbing* strategy. In WG-A, for example, consolidation and restructuring of the Chinese networks left the subsidiary limited space to build their own distribution, sales and customer support networks. A majority (60 per cent) of local business transactions were coordinated by WG-A Trade Co., a wholly owned subsidiary of the Japanese parent company. Another 20 per cent of the sales were channelled through franchised stores. R&D was highly centralized at the corporate HQ in Japan, and WG-A Research in Beijing conducted model modification and product development. Technological support and customer services were offered by WG-A Services, again, owned by the Chinese HQ. Overall, WG-A was designated to be a cost-effective manufacturing plant in the corporate strategic blueprint.

However, managers in WG-A were by no means content with a 'low-value added production function,' which was taken as too much of a 'marginal function' by the local employees. The local managers initiated a climbing strategy by first developing alternative sales routes. They managed to channel some line of products by obtaining bulk purchase orders from a number of local real estate developers. These real estate developers targeted the rising middle-class households in the cities by offering renovated and serviced apartments. WG-A's new, stylish and reliable products matched the image of these apartments, which were pre-installed with household white goods. Securing contracts from the local real estate developers supported WG-A's negotiation to upgrade their product profile, taking on more technologically advanced product models. Also, WG-A out-performed its sister plants and became a supplier to the US market, which strengthened its position in the company's global production networks.

Existing literature emphasizes the production technology–management process fit. That is to say, subsidiaries need to develop the management practices that can support the production technology adopted (Coughlan and Brady, 1996). However, upgrading the product profile is far from a straightforward process as a consequence of technical and management sophistication at subsidiary level (Wilkinson et al., 2001). The pursuit of a climbing strategy often involves negotiation with the HQ and competing against sister subsidiaries. Subsidiaries' leverage in such negotiation and competition often depends on their relationship with local stakeholders, such as suppliers, clients, government officials and union representatives, who can be mobilized to lobby for the interest of subsidiaries. Developing the management practices that facilitate the access to local stakeholders is, therefore, critical to subsidiary's climbing strategy as well.

2.4.2.2 *'Bundling' strategy: Undertaking higher value-added functions*

The 'bundling' strategy meant subsidiaries striving to engage in performing multiple value-added functional activities. Given the risk of technology spill-over, MNCs have the tendency to retain functions with strategic concerns at HQ (Cannice, Chen and Daniels, 2003). Relocation overseas often means setting up subsidiaries to perform certain functional segments. As subsidiaries develop, these functional segments sometimes become overlapping and inefficient. For the HQ, restructuring involves identifying the core competence of individual subsidiaries and coordinating among subsidiaries more effectively. Tension arose since subsidiaries' attempt to incorporate higher-value-added functional activities was in conflict with the corporate restructuring plan to decentralize and specialize in different functional segments. WG-B is an example of the hard battle subsidiaries had gone through when their pursuit of uniqueness in the local market clashed with the HQ's intention to specialize its subsidiary functions.

WG-B was relatively independent in terms of sales and customer services. Distribution channels were diversified and largely controlled by the local sales managers. More than 70 per cent of sales were channelled through local superstores, with which the local managers maintained strong personal connections. They also employed a team of technicians to offer technical support and customer services. WG-B remained dependent on the Japanese parent company for new product models, although product model modification and production prototypes were sometimes made. WG-B engaged in long negotiations with the HQ to conduct R&D locally in order to speed up new product development, tailor the new products to local clients and reduce the cost of new product design. When the Japanese parent launched a mid-term strategy to localize its overseas operation, WG-B's concern was naturally to undertake R&D locally:

> We are the only one among all the Japanese joint ventures in China that centralized the functions of manufacturing, sales, and customer services.

These functions are effectively connected and coordinated here. There is not much time wasted with communication. This gives our factory a major [competitive] advantage. Our next step will be to start developing new models here ... R&D in Japan takes a long time. They over invest in quality. Models are over-priced, expensive to manufacture and don't really suit the Chinese market. (Head of the Department of Sales, WG-B, Chinese, 42, male)

However, the Japanese side was reluctant to relocate R&D to a factory, arguing that the quality standard might go down without central control, and WG-B's economic interests would jeopardize the sharing of new model information among subsidiaries. They often emphasized that WG-B needed to make better use of services offered by other sister companies to facilitate the mid-term strategy to develop a more efficient local operation:

We are a manufacturing plant without a marketing function. The [Japanese] HQ handles product design, development, and commercialisation. That is why we would prefer to use a specialized trading company – a wholly owned subsidiary of our parent company – to extend our market share in China. Meanwhile, the factory can concentrate on improving product quality, enhance production efficiency and adjusting products based on market feedback. (Chief Accounting Officer, Japanese, 52, male)

The parent companies' intention to expand WG-B's manufacturing capacities and WG-B's wish to take on R&D locally produced a long-running conflict. In 2005, the Japanese parent company set up a trading house in Shanghai, aimed at coordinating the distribution of products of the various subsidiaries. Most Chinese managers of WG-B were highly sceptical about the ability of a foreign-invested trading company to handle domestic sales, especially since the existing supply–production–sales–customer service network was functioning well. However, in exchange for the sales of some lines of products, they were hoping that WG-B would be in a better position to negotiate for the localization of R&D. By the time WG-B was revisited in 2010, it was still unclear whether an R&D centre would be set up in the subsidiary.

The *bundling* strategy evolved as subsidiaries take initiative to create new products, generate novel knowledge or develop innovative management practices, which could either be transferrable within the MNCs or subsidiary-specific. In this sense, a bundling strategy differs from a climbing strategy in that subsidiaries have to find their own niche in undertaking higher value-added functions rather than repositioning themselves in a chain of pre-designated functions. Tapping into local resources can build up subsidiaries' capacity to undertake higher value-added functions. But what was equally important was to gain consent from HQ to perform such functions, because HQ's intention to retain strategic functions or allocate it to another subsidiary can block subsidiaries' initiatives (Birkinshaw and Ridderstrale, 1999). A critical management issue for subsidiaries that used to undertake low-end production functions was the access to decision-making within the MNCs.

2.4.2.3   'Fledging' strategy: The future without an HQ

The 'fledging' strategy concerns subsidiaries becoming an independent business entity. Under corporate-level restructuring and reconsolidation, subsidiaries often have to deal with HQ's exit, which can take different forms. It is not unusual for MNCs to relocate subsidiaries within or across host countries. Changes in labour costs, promulgation and removal of preferential policies or the rise and decline of consumer markets are all possible causes for relocation. This type of relocation was observed in the textile industry, where Japanese garment manufacturers left China to set up factories in countries like Vietnam, Bangladesh or Cambodia. Diplomatic and political instability can also trigger reviews of the risks in investing in the host countries. Japanese products boycott, anti-Japan demonstrations and recent riots have forced Japanese MNCs to reconsider their future in China (JETRO, 2006; 2012). HQ's exit arrangements can range from short-term production suspension or permanent termination of business. HQ's exit may also be forced by financial difficulties in the home country. The withdrawal of Japanese mobile phone manufacturers from the Chinese market was largely due to the parent companies' lost competitiveness in the industry. Fledging strategy particularly concerns how to manage HQ's exit to the benefit of subsidiaries.

The impact of HQ's exit on subsidiaries varies. For some subsidiaries, especially those standard product manufacturers in deficit, HQ exit can lead to closure. One of the managers explained their situation as follows:

> Japanese companies will not give us endless investment. Many of the factories in Japan have been shut and so has the Thailand factory. If we don't make enough money, they will close this factory as well. I mean, why not? Putting the lot of money in the bank can earn more interest than running this factory. But the local government will not let a factory with such scale to be shut. So what we could do is to make sure that the factory can keep running without the Japanese. (Production Manager, SF-A, Chinese, male, 35)

The fledging strategy to the SF-A here is based on a possible crisis, assuming that HQ would stop putting resources into incompetent subsidiaries. Avoiding competition with the HQ's distribution networks led by the Shanghai trade house meant that SF-A set up sales offices in Shenyang, Wenzhou, Guangzhou and Chongqing to handle their products directly. In terms of suppliers, they gradually moved from importing to sourcing from local firms. Their policy to recruit directly from local vocational schools and universities made them major employers of the local young population aged between 18 and 22. SF-A also actively took part in many local government-led accreditations. They had been nominated with the 'workplace safety award' every year from 2000 to 2008. They welcomed local unions' inspections and were named a 'harmonious workplace.' They collaborated with the environment protection bureau to set up a water recycling project, which won them a title of 'environmental friendly factory.' As noted by the general manager of SF-A, their target was to become a '*model* local factory.'

HQ's exit also created opportunities for subsidiaries to inherit tangible or intangible assets. In this study, SF-B was a case that illustrates how subsidiaries managed to become a successor of a business section, from which the HQ had gradually stepped down. As explained earlier, the global structure of synthetic fibre industry had experienced a major shift over the past decades. China had become the largest producer of and market for textile fibre, which was accompanied by shrinking production capacity and consumption of textile fibre in Japan, the EU and the US. Reflected in corporate mid-term global strategy, SF-B's parent company aimed to focus on industrial fibre business in Japan and leave the textile fibre business to overseas subsidiaries. Compared to these sister plants, SF-B's advantage included its access to China's largest textile industry cluster in the Yangtze delta, long-term collaborative relations with the only textile research institution in Shanghai, and their alliance with nearby sister plants that offered complementary product range and supplementary manufacturing capacity:

> We [sister plants in the vicinity] do help each other out in emergency. But it wasn't like an interdependent relationship. When the HQ decided to marginalize the whole range of textile fibre business, it became ever clear to us that we were in this together. We needed the collective efforts to persuade the HQ that we were the best place to carry on the textile fibre business. (Head of Administration and HR, SF-B, Chinese, male, 42)

SF-B had expanded its production capacity, handled a range of standard and high-end textile fibre products and diversified sales channels. In 2008, a Chinese R&D centre was set up in the factory compound, in charge of developing two lines of textile fibre. An additional line of fibre was brought to the R&D centre in 2009. By then, SF-B had secured a core position in textile fibre section, linking the local R&D, manufacturing and distribution.

Subsidiary strategy comprises a portfolio of subsidiaries' reactive and proactive choices in the face of corporate strategic reorientation. Corporate restructuring often led to reshuffling and reshaping of functional activities performed at different levels of the MNCs. Three types of subsidiary strategy have been identified: *climbing up* the segments of stratified functions, *bundling* together different functional activities, and *fledging* into relatively independent and functional units. The attainment of subsidiary strategy, however, depends on the ability of subsidiaries to access and mobilize local resources, to influence decision-making at different levels of MNCs, and to collaborate and compete with rival plants.

2.5   Conclusion

The research findings reported in this chapter are an attempt to add to existing literature by showing the complexity of subsidiary strategy as it emerged during a period of corporate strategic reorientation. Unlike previous research that judges strategy in MNCs as an internally consistent set of policies and practices that fit with the environmental contingencies, industrial/sector or organizational attributes, this study considered how subsidiary managers deploy local resources to address the subsidiary strategic concerns to move away from being a low-cost production base. Contrary to existing research that studies MNCs as a coherent whole, this study focused on a unit (subsidiary) and conducted more micro-level analysis. It revealed complementarities and contradictions in corporate strategy and subsidiary strategy, which is a common scenario of strategic reorientation in MNCs. It also identified a multi-centric power structure within MNCs, and managers' political struggles had significant impact on subsidiary management policies and practices.

These findings challenge the conventional wisdom that strategy in MNCs is about centralized strategic planning and decentralized practice to operationalize corporate strategy. This chapter showed that management policies and practices were quite subsidiary-specific, which endorses the idea that strategy enactment at the subsidiary level manifests an emergent dynamic process of segmentation and reconstruction of strategies, policies and practices, rather than a top-down application of central strategy.

As for the argument that more sophisticated management policies and practices will be adopted in subsidiaries undertaking high value-added activities (Fernandez-Stark, Bamber and Gereffi, 2011), the case studies offered mixed results, which reflected the global-wide industry changes. The case studies were located in industries that were experiencing structural changes. The conventional leaders in the household white goods industrial and synthetic fibre industries, such as the Japanese MNCs, had gradually moved away from the products and services. China, in contrast, had become a major site of these industry sectors, both in terms of production and consumption. Subsidiaries were therefore where the loci management policies and practices were constructed, where a repertoire of management practices exercised by the Japanese parent companies, competitive international MNCs and local companies informed subsidiary managers' choices.

More importantly, the results suggested that subsidiary managers actively formulated new policies and reshaped existing management practices in order to address their own strategic concerns. The study revealed that there were at least three aspects of subsidiary strategy, which were not necessarily mutually exclusive. Subsidiary strategy stemmed from concerns of being part of the MNCs as well as being a self-sufficient business unit. On the one hand, subsidiaries can strengthen their leverage within the MNCs by performing functions with higher added values (the climbing strategy) or generate new values (the bundling strategy). On the other hand, subsidiaries could also take the opportunities offered by corporate restructuring and seek to become a relatively independent entity (the fledging strategy). Whatever the subsidiary strategy pursued, it required subsidiary managers to effectively organize a workforce, whose skill profiles might differ significantly from the parent company. They also needed to nurture a subsidiary management team with the knowledge and experience to deal with the local workforce, the ability to take initiatives and search for opportunities, and the tactics to deal with power relations with the stakeholders from within and outside the MNCs. Subsidiary strategy is therefore the construction of functions, policies and practices to manage locally embedded skills, knowledge and access.

Given that the focus of this study was at the subsidiary level, it was not possible to test whether subsidiary strategy could influence the direction of strategic planning at the corporate HQ. However, as was observed in the cases, the MNCs studied were in the process of developing a more regionally based structure, and strategies were often formed at the regional HQ. Being involved in strategic planning at the regional HQ level meant it was important for subsidiaries to influence the direction of regional strategies that were directly relevant to them.

The empirical focus of this study has been on Chinese subsidiaries of Japanese MNCs. Locating the research context in declining parent companies and rising subsidiaries allowed the study to highlight the conflict in managing subsidiaries in the changing global industry structure. Also the capacity of subsidiary managers to deploy their knowledge and access to local resources in order to achieve subsidiaries strategies could be demonstrated. All these findings highlight the real need for more workplace-based case studies and micro-level analysis to understand the social reality and diversity of strategy in MNCs. In particular, comparative case studies could be located in a mature and robust host country setting to investigate dynamic process strategy emergence at various levels of MNCs.

References

Andersson, U., Björkman, I. and Forsgren, M. (2005) 'Managing Subsidiary Knowledge Creation: The Effect of Control Mechanisms on Subsidiary Local Embeddedness,' *International Business Review*, 14(5): 521–538.

Andersson, U., Forsgren, M. and Holm, U. (2007) 'Balancing Subsidiary Influence in the Federative MNC: A Business Network View,' *Journal of International Business Studies*, 38(5): 802–818.

Bartlett, C.A. and Ghoshal, S. (1989) *Managing Across Borders: The Transnational Solution* (Boston, MA: Harvard Business School Press).

Birkinshaw, J. (1997) 'Entrepreneurship in Multinational Corporations: The Characteristics of Subsidiary Initiative,' *Strategic Management Journal*, 18(3): 207–229.

Birkinshaw, J. and Hood, N. (1998) 'Multinational Subsidiary Evolution: Capability and Charter Change in Foreign-Owned Subsidiary Companies,' *Academy of Management Review*, 23(4): 773–795.

Birkinshaw, J. and Ridderstrale, J. (1999) 'Fighting the Corporate Immune System: A Process Study of Subsidiary Initiatives in Multinational Corporations,' *International Business Review*, 8(1): 149–180.

Birkinshaw, J.M., Hood, N. and Jonsson. S. (1998) 'Building Firm-Specific Advantages in Multinational Corporations: The Role of Subsidiary Initiative,' *Strategic Management Journal*, 19(3): 221–242.

Boisot, M., and Child, J. (1999) 'Organizations as Adaptive Systems in Complex Environments: The Case of China,' *Organization Science*, 10(3): 237–252.

Cannice, M., Chen, R. and Daniels, J. (2003) 'Managing International Technology Transfer Risk: A Case Analysis of U.S. High-Technology Firms in Asia,' *Journal of High Technology Management Research*, 14(2): 171–187.

Child, J. (1994) *Management in China during the Age of Reform* (Cambridge: Cambridge University Press).

Child, J. (1997) 'Strategic Choice in the Analysis of Action, Structure, Organizations and Environment: Retrospect and Prospect', *Organization Studies* 18(1): 43–76.

Child, J. and Tsai, D. (2005) 'The Dynamic Between Firms' Environmental Strategies and Institutional Constraints in Emerging Economies: Evidence from China and Taiwan,' *Journal of Management Studies*, 42(1): 95–125.

Cooke, F.L. (2008) *Competition, Strategy and Management in China* (London: Palgrave).

Coughlan, P. and Brady, E. (1996) 'Evolution towards Product Development in Subsidiaries of Multinational Enterprises,' *International Journal of Technology Management*, 12(7/8): 733–747.

Dicken, P., Kelly, P., Olds, K. and Yeung, H.W. (2001) 'Chains and Networks, Territories and Scales: Towards an Analytical Framework for the Global Economy,' *Global Networks*, 1(2): 89–112.

Dunning, J.H. (1980) 'Toward an Eclectic Theory of International Production: Some Empirical Tests,' *Journal of International Business Studies*, 11(1): 9–13.

Edwards, T., Colling, T. and Ferner, A. (2007) 'Conceptual Approaches to the Transfer of Employment Practices in Multinational Companies: An Integrated Approach,' *Human Resource Management Journal*, 17(3): 201–217.

Elger, T. and Smith, C. (2005) *Assembling Work: Remaking Factory Regimes in Japanese Multinationals in Britain* (Oxford: Oxford University Press).

Ernst, D. and Kim, L. (2002) 'Global Production Networks, Knowledge Diffusion, and Local Capability Formation,' *Research Policy*, 31(8–9): 1417–1429.

Ferdows, K. (1997) 'Making the Most of Foreign Factories,' *Harvard Business Review*, 2: 73–88.

Fernandez-Stark, K., Bamber, P. and Gereffi, G. (2011) 'The Offshore Services Global Value Chain: Economic Upgrading And Workforce Development,' Duke Centre on Globalisation, Governance and Competitiveness, Duke University.

Ferner, A., Edwards, T. and Tempel, A. (2012) 'Power, Institutions and the Cross-National Transfer of Employment Practices in Multinationals,' *Human Relations*, 65(2): 163–187.

Frobel, F., Heinrichs, J. and Kreye, O. (1980) *The New International Division of Labour: Structural Unemployment in Industrialised Countries and Industrialisation in Developing Countries* (Cambridge: Cambridge University Press).

Garcia-Pont, C., Canales, J.I. and Noboa, F. (2009) 'Subsidiary Strategy: The Embeddedness Component,' *Journal of Management Studies*, 46(2): 182–214.

Gephart, R.P. (2004) 'Qualitative Research and *The Academy of Management Journal*,' *Academy of Management Journal*, 47(4): 454–462.

Geppert, M. and Williams, K. (2006) 'Global, National and Local Practices in Multinational Corporations: Towards a Socio-Political Framework,' *International Journal of HRM*, 17(1): 49–69.

Gereffi, G. (1999) 'International Trade and Industrial Upgrading in the Apparel Commodity Chain,' *Journal of International Economics*, 48(1): 48–70.

Gertler, M. (2004) *Manufacturing Culture: The Institutional Geography of Industrial Practice* (New York: Oxford University Press).

Harzing, A.W. (1999) *Managing the Multinationals: An International Study of Control Mechanisms* (Cheltenham: Edward Elgar).

Japan External Trade Organization (JETRO) (2006) *Japanese Corporate Activity in New Growth Markets and the Emerging East Asian Free Trade Zone*, 2006 JETRO White Paper on International Trade and Foreign Direct Investment, http://www.jetro.go.jp/en/reports/white_paper/2006.pdf [accessed July 29, 2013].

Japan External Trade Organization (JETRO) (2012) *JETRO Global Trade and Investment Report: Companies and People Move Forward towards Globalization*, http://www.jetro.go.jp/en/reports/white_paper/trade_invest_2012.pdf [accessed July 29, 2013].

Kaplinsky, R. (2000) 'Globalisation and Unequalisation: What Can Be Learned from Value Chain Analysis?,' *Journal of Development Studies*, 37(2): 117–146.

Kristensen, P.H. and Zeitlin, J. (2005) *Local Players in Global Games: The Strategic Constitution of a Multinational Corporation* (Oxford: Oxford University Press).

Luo, Y.D. (2001) *Strategy, Structure and Performance of MNCs in China* (Westport, CT: Greenwood).

Luo, Y.D. (2007) 'From Foreign Investors to Strategic Insiders: Shifting Parameters, Prescriptions and Paradigms for MNCs in China,' *Journal of World Business*, 42(1): 14–34.

Nadvi, K. and Halder, G. (2005) 'Local Clusters in Global Value Chains: Exploring Dynamic Linkages between Germany and Pakistan,' *Entrepreneurship & Regional Development*, 17(5): 339–363.

Pfeffer J. and Salancik, G. (1978) *The External Control of Organizations*. (London: Harper & Row)

Porter, M.E. (1986) *Competition in Global Industries* (Boston, MA: Harvard Business School).

Prahalad, C.K. and Doz, L.Y. (1987) *The Multinational Mission: Balancing Local Demands and Global Vision* (London: Collier Macmillan).

Roth, K. and Morrison, A.J. (1992) 'Implementing Global Strategy: Characteristics of Global Subsidiary Mandates,' *Journal of International Business Studies*, 23(4): 715–735.

Rugman, A.M. and Verbeke, A. (2001) 'Subsidiary-Specific Advantages in Multinational Enterprises,' *Strategic Management Journal*, 22(3): 237–250.

Scandura, T.A. and Williams, E.A. (2000) 'Research Methodology in Management: Current Practices, Trends, and Implications for Future Research,' *Academy of Management Journal*, 43(6): 1248–1264.

Smith, C. (2003) 'Living at Work: Management Control and the Chinese Dormitory Labour System,' *Asia Pacific Journal of Management*, 20(3): 333–358.

Sun, Y., von Zedtwitz, M. and Simon, D.F. (eds) (2008) *Global R&D in China* (London: Routledge).

Taggart, J. (1997) 'Autonomy and Procedural Justice: A Framework for Evaluating Subsidiary Strategy,' *Journal of International Business Studies*, 28(1): 51–76.

Taggart, J. (1998) 'Determinants of Increasing R&D Complexity in Affiliates of Manufacturing Multinational Corporations in the UK,' *R&D Management*, 28(2): 101–110.

The Economist Intelligence Unit (2011) 'Multinational Companies and China: What Future?' Available: http://www.managementthinking.eiu.com/multinational-companies-and-china.html [accessed July 4, 2012].

Weber, M. (1968) *Economy and Society: An Outline of Interpretive Sociology*. (New York: Bedminster Press. (originally published in 1922)).

Wedcofa, J.W. (2007) 'Subsidiary Technology Upgrading and International Technology Transfer, with Reference to China,' *Asia Pacific Business Review*, 13(3): 451–469.

Wilkinson, B., Gamble, J., Humphrey, J., Morris, J. and Anthony, D. (2001) 'The New International Division of Labour in Asian Electronics: Work Organization and Human Resources in Japan and Malaysia,' *Journal of Management Studies*, 38(5): 675–695.

Zheng, Y. (2012) *Managing Human Resources in China: The View from Inside Multinationals* (Cambridge: Cambridge University Press).

3
Sponsoring as a Strategy to Enter, Develop, and Defend Markets: Advertising Patterns of the Beijing Olympic Games' Sponsoring Partners

Harald Dolles and Sten Söderman

3.1 Sponsoring and mega-sporting events

The Olympic Games are an event that attracts the focus of the media and the attention of the entire world for two weeks every four years. The Games are one of the largest international marketing platforms in the world. From the opening ceremony of the XXIXth Olympiad in Beijing 2008 to the moment that Beijing bade farewell, this mega-sporting event was the biggest broadcast event in history. The Beijing Olympic Games were made available across the world, with broadcasts in 220 territories and an estimated potential TV audience of 4.3 billion people. The sporting performances helped drive not only television audiences, but also internet and mobile phone downloads, to new levels. The Beijing Olympics Global Television and Online Media Report (IOC, 2008a) announces that a total of more than 61,700 hours of dedicated Beijing 2008 television and 72 per cent of coverage (44,454 hours) were aired on free-to-air terrestrial channels (all other coverage was aired on either pay TV cable/satellite platforms or free-to-air digital channels). According to the report, the region to enjoy the most dedicated TV coverage in 2008 was Europe with 21,292 hours of coverage. This represents a 46 per cent increase over the 14,602 hours of broadcasting that were reported to have been aired in 2004 during the Athens Games in the European time zones. It is also stated that of the 6.7 billion people globally there was a total of 4.3 billion people who had home access to dedicated Beijing 2008 TV coverage aired by official broadcasters. This represents 63 per cent of the world's population. Projections indicate that 3.6 billion people watched at least one minute of dedicated Beijing 2008 TV coverage, thus representing 83 per cent of the total potential TV audience and 53 per cent of the world's population. The projected number of people in Asia who saw at least one minute of coverage was 2.1 billion, about 60 per cent of those who saw at least one minute of TV coverage globally. The average minute of Beijing 2008 TV coverage was seen by 160 million viewers (ibid.).

Apart from investigating the impact of mega-sporting events in Asia, which could be considered as a large field of research in itself (Dolles and Söderman, 2008; Takahashi et al., 2012), the obvious question to ask is whether sponsoring such kind of a mega-sporting event is a wise investment and/or effective international marketing strategy. Sponsorship is not only a vital and rapidly expanding revenue source for sport organizations—its share in financing the Olympic Games has risen dramatically (see e.g. Preuss, 2004)—but also has become a core marketing activity that often comple- ments advertising endeavours for many organizations. Sponsoring is thus a rapidly growing phenomenon in marketing, but it is linked with uncertainty and many pitfalls. With increasing marketing budgets previously unidenti- fied risks were often encountered, and were difficult to predict both for the event organizer and the sponsoring company. Sponsoring of persons and individual athletes is probably more risky despite its popularity in endorse- ment advertising (Kambitsis et al., 2002; O'Reilly and Forster, 2008; Yang, Sparks, and Li, 2008). Sponsoring of mega-sporting events like the Olympic Games seems less risky, thus making it a more appealing option.

Despite an increasing academic interest in research on sport sponsorship, the emerging or developing market context has been little examined in research. There have been very few attempts to analyze how sponsorship works in an emerging market context, as for example in the Chinese culture and market (see Berkowitz et al., 2007; Davies, 2008; Fan and Pfitzenmaier, 2002; Geng, Burton, and Blakemore, 2002; Heslop, Nadeau, and O'Reilly, 2010; Jin and Bu, 2010; Söderman and Dolles, 2008, 2010, 2012; Yang, Sparks, and Li, 2008). Most sport sponsorship research has focused on the markets in North America, Europe or Australia, thus covering a different economic development and representing dissimilar market conditions. As a result it might be concluded that mainstream sponsorship theories are built upon the foundation of a highly developed and commercialized mar- ket context. China, with its own form of market organization and cultural background, however, provides a very different market for sport sponsor- ship. Research that addresses the uniqueness of an emerging market context and identifies the ways in which international and domestic corporations perceive and act on the opportunities for sponsorship investment in China is therefore needed.

The purpose of the present research is to describe and explain Olympic sponsor advertising behaviour and sponsorship in an emerging market context. First, we develop the 'means–objectives framework', thus link- ing sponsorship to brand equity factors, means, and objectives based on current research. The means factors are: co-branding (1), revenue streams (2), and new customers (3). The objectives factors are: product image (4), corporation image (5), and regional image (6). The next section introduces the methodology—sampling strategy, sample data, and the method of data analysis. Finally, eight combinations of sponsorship patterns are identified in the analysis, thus providing insights into the strategic aims related to sponsorship advertising, which are dependent on the level of internationalization of the sponsoring firm.

3.2   Developing the framework for research

Sponsorship has not only become an important emerging field of study, commensurate with its increasing significance in the field of marketing (Amis and Cornwell, 2005; Cornwell, 2008; Cornwell and Coote, 2005; Walliser, 2003). Also for many firms sport sponsorship today is a key element of an integrated marketing communication strategy (Cornwell, Weeks, and Roy, 2005; Hartland, Skinner, and Griffiths, 2005). Sponsorship can be characterized as a promotional practice that has moved from its roots as a tool for corporate donations to a highly developed marketing discipline where both the sponsors and the sponsee benefit in a marketing relationship (Polonsky and Speed, 2001).

The emerging strategic view of sponsorship is seen as a potential source of competitive advantage by Fahy, Farrelly and Quester (2004), and their research concludes that conceptual theories should be further developed, especially in the area of international marketing. These authors' arguments also demonstrate the breadth of the resource mix that underpins successful sponsorship and delineates the nature of the relationship between sponsorship-related resources and superior performance in the marketplace. They claim that it is important and significant to develop contributions toward 'understanding the mechanics of sponsorship management and that this should be further developed ... and tested empirically in future research' (ibid.: 1026). The literature review undertaken by Cornwell, Weeks, and Roy (2005) deals primarily with the exploration of theoretical explanations of how sponsorship works and open questions for research, bringing together variables such as individual (and group) factors, as well as market and management factors, with the aim of understanding their influence on sponsorship-processing mechanics and related outcomes. The fact that sponsors rarely pursue a single sponsoring objective presents further difficulties when determining the value of a sponsor's engagement.

The perceived fit between a sponsoring brand and an event is considered to be a key sponsorship requirement (Söderman and Dolles, 2008), but little is known about the variables that are related to the perceived fit (Roy and Graff, 2002). Data from 260 event managers in Australia, Norway, Sweden, and UK are compared by Andersson et al. (2013) with respect to their events' revenue sources, ownership, and other factors thought to influence revenue. In this survey statistical tests reveal that event size (i.e. attendance), professionalism (as measured by staff members), and the 'fit' between event and sponsor (as measured by type of event correlated with different sponsors and grant sources) significantly affect festival revenue. Andersson et al. argue in their conclusion that by applying certain strategies festival managers can enhance their external revenue generation and support. It is concluded that professionalism, including the employment of development staff to source revenue and manage the relationships, is vital to this process, but the next question becomes valid: how should these vital relationships be managed for long-term event viability (ibid.). O'Reilly et al. (2007) assert that a need exists for continued development of theory and practitioner's tools applied in the evaluation of sponsorships. Sophisticated, grounded theoretical models are required.

In order to focus on empirical work it is necessary to delimit the number of important factors. Since there are a few conceptualizations already mentioned (e.g. Cornwall, 2008; Crompton 2004) but no dominant model hitherto reported in the research, our approach was to identify key variables based on literature to develop our framework. We identified the following six variables constructing brand equity factors in international sponsoring activities: the sponsor needs to consider three image factors, and there are three strategic means associated with its Olympic sponsorship engagement (see Figure 3.1).

In the 1980s, brand equity grew to become one of the most important and central concepts in marketing. However, there has been some confusion as to what the term actually means, since there are a number of different definitions of the concept. Keller (2003) argues that most scholars, including Aaker (1996), agree that brand equity is a marketing effect that can only be ascribed to the brand. This means that the result of a marketing campaign will differ for a specific product or service depending on the brand it derives from. Thus, the brand equity shows the part of a company's assets that can be ascribed to the brand, its name, and its symbols: 'Brand equity is a set of assets (and liabilities) linked to a brand's name and symbol that adds to

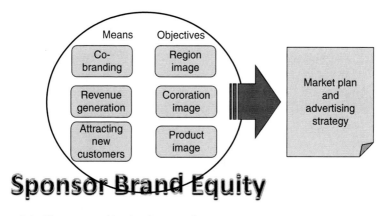

Figure 3.1   The means–objective framework

(or subtracts from) the value provided by a product or service to a firm and/ or that firm's customers' (Aaker, 1996: 7; also Eisenhardt and Galunic, 2000). Many executives consider their brand an important asset (Melin, 1999; Keller, 2003), and it is argued that a company's reputation has the same risk and returns as a company's financial situation (Laforet and Saunders, 1999, 2005). Therefore, the link to a partner through sponsorship can become a strategic issue, especially as solid awareness among consumers increases the brand equity. Awareness, according to Aaker (1996), is one out of four assets (together with perceived quality, brand associations, and brand loyalty) that can be linked to a brand name or symbol, also referred to as brand equity. The relevance of consumer awareness is also emphasized by Smolianov and Shilbury (2005) in their conclusion that successful corporate marketers and event managers integrate sponsorship and advertising to cross-promote the two media and multiply the effect of the marketing investment. We conclude that a solid awareness among consumers increases the brand equity, and advertising and sponsorship are the most common link where effective integration and cooperation lead to awareness.

The strength of a conventional advertisement lies in its propensity to send a direct and specific message. Sponsorship of an event, on the other hand, facilitates an opportunity to indirectly deliver a message, for example, increasing brand awareness and enhancing brand image, which could lead to increased sales. The sponsor normally aims at strengthening her/his brand equity or strives for a reciprocal strengthening. Of course, sponsorship is only one of the marketing communication channels that can be used in a company's marketing mix. The results of market research indicate the potential of top sport sponsorship in increasing awareness of brands (Johan and Pham, 1999; Lardinoit and Derbaix, 2001; Rifon et al., 2004; Speed and Thompson, 2000).

To make the marketing strategy more effective, sponsorship should be integrated with other channels—not only advertising but also sales promotion, the internet or word of mouth. According to Kotler (2003), integrated marketing communications is a way of looking at the whole marketing process from the viewpoint of the customer:

> It is therefore important that the external, internal and interactive communications carry the same clear message to avoid confused positioning. The message that the audience receives from the host of the Olympic Games via the sponsor must be the same as the one it received directly from the sponsor. Otherwise the message can be perceived as indistinct and lose its impact. (Söderman and Dolles, 2008: 98)

In this sense co-branding is considered to be another way of gaining benefits from intangible assets and a brand leverage strategy (James, 2006). The first factor in our framework reflects this relationship: the sponsor associated with the Olympic Movement and the Olympic Games, that is, the *co-branding factor*, constructed as a symmetrical brand alliance between two established brands for mutual benefit. In our case, this relates to whether and how the sponsor's name is associated with the Beijing Olympic Games.

The brand's associations are those that can be connected to the company and its brands. Association means what is directly, or indirectly, linked in the consumer's mind to a specific brand. Aaker (1996) and Cornwall and Coote (2005) implies that associations create value for the company by helping the consumer to understand information and to differentiate the brand, which subsequently gives the consumer reasons to buy and thus to create revenues, induce positive feelings/attitudes toward the brand and facilitate brand extensions. Overton (2007) also mentions that sponsorship is an investment that is in cash or in kind, and the reward can exploit business potential related to an event. We operationalize those thoughts as the next factor in our framework: *revenue generation*.

Sponsorship can heighten the firm's brand and create awareness of a business and products in the minds of a new set of customers. Sports fans have a high emotional solidarity, and therefore they are often characterized as exercising a loyal consumer behaviour (for example, purchasing tickets and merchandising products). Schlesinger (2013) points out that fans consume their sport clubs' products on a regular basis, admitting that price and quality only play a secondary role.

> It is therefore inconceivable that fans with high emotional solidarity are likely to change to another club only because tickets are cheaper, the stadium is nicer or there is a wider range of merchandising products offered. Even the attractiveness of the athletic performance or the success of a team/club does influence the fans' loyalty only insignificantly. (ibid.: 435)

We might conclude that sports fans are a highly attractive target group for marketers, in the same sense that O'Guinn and Muniz (2001) write that people in a brand community can be considered as 'active loyalists', consumers who are 'committed, conscientious—almost passionate.' A problem, however, is the extent to which this consumer behaviour can be transferred to products indirectly associated with the sport and the event, such as the sponsors' products. Companies certainly plan in their sponsorship activation strategy that the passion fans feel toward a sport team or club is transferred to or 'rub off' on their brand (Madrigal, 2004). We operationalize this as a factor in our framework: *creating new customers*.

By assuming that the image of a firm strengthens its brand value, we construct the three image-factors of our framework. Advertising normally conforms to one of the two basic types: product-orientated or corporation-orientated (Berkowitz et al., 2003). A product-orientated advertisement focuses on the product or the service being offered, and its prime task is to support the sales of the product in achieving the market plan. The traditional brand contract of 'one brand = one product = one promise', however, has been displaced to 'one brand = one promise = several products' (Kapferer, 1992). Firms therefore prefer to use their existing brand when introducing new products (Filipsson, 2008). Usually a company seeks to communicate the unique benefits that distinguish the product and give it its competitive edge. In a sponsorship relation, however, we propose that the advertisement is emphasizing the special features of the product or brand plus highlighting sponsor relationship to outsell the competition. This is addressed in our framework by asking whether the focus of the advertisements is on the sponsors' products and which sponsor associations are used in the advertisements. We construct ***product image*** as the next factor in our framework.

By contrast corporation-centred advertising and corporation branding is not product-specific. It aims to build a sound reputation and image for the whole organization to achieve a wide range of objectives with different target audiences (e.g. the development of Levono, as discussed by Chao, Samiee, and Yip (2003) or Doebele (2002)). These could include financial stakeholders, government, and customers. Corporation-centred advertising may be undertaken for many reasons, for example, pioneering, in the sense of presenting new developments within the organization or image building in general. Corporate-centred advertising might be linked with corporate social responsibility activities by presenting the corporation as caring and responsible. These marketing strategies are designed to inform or reinforce positive images in target audiences. Corporate-centred advertising also covers the growing interest for the brand's internationalization (Vallaster and Chernatony, 2005) and its international marketing strategy. In this sense it can be read as the process of developing a firm's brand equity that appeals to overseas target customers' positive attitudes about the brand (Bennet, 1995). Not least based on Hollensen (2007), we see advertisements focusing on the corporation as a form of market plan to increase awareness and to establish a position in new foreign markets. The ***corporation image*** is operationalized to cover this argument.

The sixth and last factor, ***region image***, follows this argumentation as well but takes a different viewpoint. Companies that are looking to expand their customer base internationally face challenges that are different from those encountered in domestic markets. Decisions have to be made about how much adaptation of the marketing package is necessary to achieve the desired positioning in the context of local needs and foreign customers' expectations. This fundamental conflict is known to be constituent for every problem in international management and might be considered as a 'classical problem.' It deals with the fundamental question of whether business operations abroad should 'conform to the host business system or attempt to inject some degree of change into the prevailing pattern' (Fayerweather, 1978: 8). The logic of thinking in such terms stems basically from the expected differences between parent-country and host-country environments and business patterns in international management, and is about balancing local demands and a global vision (see e.g. Dolles, 1997; Kumar, Steinmann, and Dolles, 1993; Prahalad and Doz, 1987; Dolles and Takahashi, 2011). Some corporations choose to ignore any differences and market in the same way globally, but other corporations modify their marketing carefully to suit local conditions.

3.3   Sample characteristics and methodology

3.3.1   The Olympic Games' sponsors

There were five sponsorship levels at the Beijing Olympic Games:

1. **The Olympic Partners** (named the TOP Program) (12 sponsors): Created in 1985 and managed by the International Olympic Committee (IOC), the TOP Program is the only sponsorship with exclusive worldwide marketing rights to the use of the Games' Marks for both Winter and Summer Games. The global marketing rights include partnerships with the IOC, all active National Olympic Committees (NOCs) and their Olympic teams, the two Organizing Committees of the Olympic Games (OCOGs) and the Games of each quadrennium. The following companies were the TOP Partners for the 2008 Beijing Olympic Games: Atos Origin, Coca-Cola, General Electric, Johnson & Johnson, Kodak, Lenovo, Manulife, McDonalds, Omega, Panasonic, Samsung, and Visa.

   In addition to the global TOP Program, the Olympic Games are supported by a domestic sponsorship program, which grants marketing rights by using the Games' marks within the host country. The domestic Olympic Sponsorship Program, which includes sponsors, suppliers, and providers, is managed by the respective OCOG under the direction of the IOC. Domestic sponsorship programs are primarily focused on fulfilling the many specific operational needs of the OCOG during the planning and staging of the Games. In addition, domestic sponsors also support the host nation's NOC and Olympic team (IOC, 2008b, 2008c). For the Beijing Olympic Games the following corporations were selected by the Beijing Organizing Committee for the Olympic Games (BOCOG) on four sponsorship levels:

2. *Beijing 2008 partners* (11 firms): Bank of China, CNC, Sinopec, CNPC, China Mobile, VW, Adidas, Johnson & Johnson, Air China, PICC, and State Grid.

3. *Beijing 2008 sponsors* (10 firms): UPS, Haier, Budweiser, Sohu.com, YiLi, Tsingtao, Yanjing Beer, bhpbilliton, HéngYuánXiáng, and TongYi.

4. *Beijing 2008 exclusive suppliers* (15 firms): Great Wall, Kerry Oil & Grains, Gehua Ticketmaster Ticketing, MengNa, BEIFA, HuáDi, YADU, Snickers, Qinxihe, Sinian, TechnoGym, Royal, Staples, Aggreko, and Schenker.

5. *Beijing 2008 co-exclusive suppliers* (17 firms): Taishan, Sunglo, EF, Aifly, Crystal CG, Yuanpei Translation, Der Floor, Aokang, Liby, PricewaterhouseCoopers, Dayun, Capinfo, Unipack, Microsoft (China), Kokuyo, Newauto, and Mondo.

The sponsors' fees are different for different levels: in the first level, sponsors pay at least US\$ 65 million; in the second level, the lowest fee was US\$ 30 million; sponsors in the third level had to pay at least 0.1 billion RMB [≈US\$ 14.7 million]; and in the fourth level, the suppliers had to pay at least 16 million RMB [≈US\$ 2.35 million], with the exclusive suppliers paying a fee of at least 41 million RMB [≈US\$ 6 million]. The rights and benefits awarded to sponsors were convoluted and differed at each level of sponsoring according to sponsors' specific contributions to the Beijing Olympic Games. Sponsors provided direct and significant support to the Beijing Organizing Committee for the Olympic Games (BOCOG), the Chinese Olympic Committee (COC), and the Chinese Olympic Team in the form of cash and/or value-in-kind. In return, sponsors received the corresponding rights and benefits as designated by BOCOG. The rights and benefits were differentiated between each tier in proportion to the specific contributions made by the partners, sponsors, and suppliers to the Beijing 2008 Games (IOC, 2008b, 2008c).

3.3.2   Sample characteristics

The data used for this research was collected during three different periods by three different Chinese teams comprising of two master's students each. It covers the period from the announcement that Beijing had won the bidding process to host the Olympic Games on July 13, 2001 until the beginning of the Games on August 8, 2008. It therefore might be considered as longitudinal. In detail we collected the following data:

2006: 200 randomly collected excerpts from clippings: 120 Chinese national newspaper articles, press releases, advertisements, and 80 Chinese Web articles and advertisements from Beijing 2008 sponsors and Beijing Olympic activities. The advertisement clippings covered January to July 2006, whereas the articles and press releases covered the period back to 2001. The data was gathered in June/July 2006 in Beijing libraries. In addition, internet sources were pursued using English and Chinese keywords. The collected material was written 75 per cent in Chinese. The number of officially announced sponsors was 36.

2007: The same search design was used: 292 excerpts and advertisements clippings from 44 newspapers and magazines; 80 per cent of the data was written in Chinese. The data gathering took place in July/August 2007 in libraries in Shanghai. The investigated number of officially announced sponsors grew to 67.

2008: The same search design was applied during May to July 2008 in Shanghai ahead of the beginning of the Olympic Games: 247 excerpts and advertisements clippings—again more than 80per cent in Chinese—were collected. The number of sponsors was 65.

The longitudinal analysis is therefore based on 739 advertisements, articles, and press releases covering the period 2001 to 2008. The longitudinal research method is used to discover relationships between variables that are not related to various background variables. This observational research technique involves studying the same group of individuals over an extended period of time. There is a limitation in the sampling since we do not have exactly the same newspapers in all three data collection times, but they are close to being the same. The sponsors continued to be the same, although the number of sponsoring companies increased over time. The data selection was limited to Chinese newspapers and magazines at the Chinese National Library in Beijing; the Library of the Graduate School of Chinese Academy of Social Sciences (CASS) in Beijing; the National Shanghai Library and local universities' libraries in Shanghai. The newspaper and magazine collection in the Chinese National Library in Beijing is considered to be one of the largest available in China, covering all major domestic newspapers and magazines. A compiled list of the newspapers and magazines that were searched in 2006, 2007, and in 2008 can be found below.[1] The analysis is based on a selection of advertisements in the printed media and also does not cover other marketing channels such as TV, radio, etc.

3.3.3 Applying the framework in research

By applying the six factors (see Figure 3.1) of the proposed means–objective framework, we divided our sample into nine patterns, each associated with a different code (see Table 3.1). A qualitative content analysis was applied to match the advertisements with the means–objective framework of sponsoring. Content analysis has a long history in research and, according to Rosengren (1981), it dates back its origins in Scandinavia. Research using qualitative content analysis focuses on the characteristics of language as communication with attention to the content or contextual meaning of the text (Budd, Thorp, and Donohew, 1967; Lindkvist, 1981; McTavish and Pirro, 1990). Weber (1990) points out that the specific type of content analysis approach chosen by a researcher needs to vary with the theoretical and substantive interests of the researcher and the problem being studied. In our case, we chose a directed approach to content analysis. Potter and Levine-Donnerstein (1999) and Mayring (1995) might categorize this as a deductive use of theory based on their distinctions on the role of theory. The advantage in our case is that a content analysis based on this directed approach allowed for a more structured process than would be possible in a

Table 3.1   Means-objectives patterns and their codes

Pattern	Means/Factor 1–3	Objectives/Factor 4–6	Code
1	Co-branding	Region Image	*P14*
2	Co-branding	Corporation Image	*P15*
3	Co-branding	Product Image	*P16*
4	Revenue Generation	Region Image	*P24*
5	Revenue Generation	Corporation Image	*P25*
6	Revenue Generation	Product Image	*P26*
7	Attracting New Customers	Region Image	*P34*
8	Attracting New Customers	Corporation Image	*P35*
9	Attracting New Customers	Product Image	*P36*

conventional content analysis approach, as argued by Hickey and Kipping (1996). Our analysis also uses Creswell's (2003) suggestion to code indications extracted from qualitative data. All 739 excerpts and advertisements were examined and labelled with single dominant 'pattern.' The qualitative content analysis of the clippings and web articles was done by a Chinese master's degree student and afterwards the same examination was conducted by a second Chinese master's degree student. Both coders received several hours of instructions and training by the authors ahead of the coding process. The final coding, however, was done independently by both coders, without consultation or guidance.

Intercoder reliability between both codings was introduced as a measure to ensure reliability. As Neuendorf (2002: 141) notes, 'given that a goal of content analysis is to identify and record relatively objective (or at least intersubjective) characteristics of messages, reliability is paramount. Without the establishment of reliability, content analysis measures are useless.' Lombard, Snyder-Duch, and Bracken (2010) refer to intercoder reliability as the standard measure of qualitative research quality. Other analysts mention that 'High levels of disagreement among judges suggest weaknesses in research methods, including the possibility of poor operational definitions, categories, and judge training' (Kolbe and Burnett, 1991: 248). Lombard, Snyder-Duch, and Bracken (2010) suggest that coefficients of 0.90 or greater are nearly always acceptable, 0.80 or greater is acceptable in most situations, and 0.70 may be appropriate in some exploratory studies for some indices. They recommend that higher criteria can be used in analysis for indices known to be liberal (i.e. per cent agreement) and lower criteria can be used for indices known to be more conservative. Achieving in our research an intercoder reliability for the full sample to be coded above 80 per cent, we consider the results as reliable and a descriptive statistical analysis as an appropriate methodology.

In those few cases when the two coders had different opinions about labelling the clippings with single dominant 'pattern' joint decisions were taken together with the authors. This procedure followed the recommenda-tion by Lombard, Snyder-Duchy, and Bracken (2010: 4) that

> depending on the characteristics of the data and the coders, the disa-greements can be resolved by randomly selecting the decisions of the different coders, using a 'majority' decision rule (when there are an odd number of coders), having the researcher or other expert serve as tie-breaker, or discussing and resolving the disagreements.

As the clippings and advertisements were more than 90 per cent written in Chinese, it needs to be mentioned for this process that the first author of this chapter studied in China and speaks, reads, and writes Mandarin Chinese.

Potter and Levine-Donnerstein (1997) note that for latent content the coders must provide subjective interpretations based on their own mental schema, and that this

> only increases the importance of making the case that the judgments of coders are intersubjective, that is, those judgments, while subjectively derived, are shared across coders, and the meaning therefore is also likely to reach out to readers of the research. (ibid.: 266)

We therefore introduced as an additional step to increase validity a discus-sion round with local experts (Chinese marketing managers with experience of Western business practices) to avoid cultural bias explanations. There was very little expressed need during this discussion round to amend the initial coding. The overall benefit of this exercise was on a different level, as we received many comments on how to interpret the data and on marketing practices in China in general terms. Following the suggestion by Ghauri (2004) for conducting qualitative research in international management, we also applied several measures of data triangulation such as to consult printed interviews taken from the website of the BOGOC as well as from the sponsoring companies to check and validate the information from different perspectives. In addition we also conducted two interviews with sponsoring companies.

3.3.4   Limitations

We are aware that the analysis is based on a selection of advertisements in print media and also does not cover other marketing channels, like TV, radio etc. Data collection was also limited to a period in 2006, 2007, and again in 2007, focusing on printed Chinese media available in Beijing and Shanghai universities' libraries. However, as Simons (2003) notes, China is the most complex media market, with more than 3,000 television chan-nels, some 1,800 radio stations, over 1,000 newspapers, more than 7,000 magazines, and numerous internet portals. Given the size of the country, there are also various regional variations found, complicating marketing research even further. All advertisements in China also need to be approved by the official China Advertising Association, with regulations varying according to region (ibid.).

3.4   Findings and analysis

Only 26 (2006), 45 (2007), and 25 (2008) of the sponsors appeared in the collected clippings. The figure for 2008 might be explained for companies that focused their marketing efforts by other means, such as on-site displays, etc., but this does not explain why only 45 out of the 65 sponsors appeared in our 2007 sample (see Table 3.2).

Our analysis discovers eight dominant means–objectives combinations in sponsorship (patterns) leading to different patterns of sponsor advertising strategies depending on the *lead time* to the Olympic Games and the level of internationalization of the sponsoring firm (see Table 3.3).

One advertising strategy pattern emerges in 2001–2003, three domi-nating pattern in 2004–2006, four patterns in 2007, and four patterns in 2008—altogether *eight advertising strategy patterns*. Initially, all sponsors mainly focused on co-branding marketing efforts (2001–2003). In the sec-ond stage (2004–2006), global Olympic sponsors of the TOP Program linked co-branding with corporation image (Pattern code: P15). Chinese brands focused on product/corporation image and new customers (P35 and P36). In the third stage (2007), global Olympic sponsors focused more on local markets and new customers in their advertising (P36). Our analysis reveals that the Chinese brands tended to keep an activation strategy based on revenue generation and a focus on the product image (P26). Only a few local sponsors placed emphasis on leveraging their sponsorship investment toward co-branding and creating an international image for the corporation (P15), as did Yili Industrial Group (referred to as Yili thereafter). Unknown to the world market and at the sponsorship announcement in 2005, Yili invested in Olympic advertisements and employed numerous sports stars to draw public attention and demonstrate the unique identity of the Olympic dairy sponsor.

We distinguish four-stages in Yili's marketing strategy in the longitudinal analysis (see Figure 3.2). In the first stage (2001–2005), prior to its engage-ment as an Olympic sponsor, Yili developed new and improved existing products, 'For Health,' to achieve the high-quality requirements set by the standards of the BOCOG focus. With the sponsorship announcement in 2005 Yili invested heavily in the next stage of Olympic advertisements with its new products by engaging sports stars to draw public attention and to showcase the unique identity of the Olympic dairy sponsor (P16). For example, Yili signed a contract with Olympic champion Liu Xiang (the

Table 3.2 Sponsorship involvement and appearance

No.	Name	2006 No.	2007 No.	2008 No.	2007 Added sponsor	2008 Added sponsor
1	Worldwide Olympic Partners	11	12	12	Johnson-Johnson	0
2	Beijing 2008 Partners	11	11	11		0
3	Beijing 2008 Sponsors	9	10	10	TongYi	0
4	Beijing 2008 Exclusive Suppliers	5	15	15	Great Wall, Kerry Oil& Grains, Gehua Ticketmaster Ticketing, Qinxihe, Sinian, TechnoGym, Royal, Staples, aggreko, schenker	0
5	Beijing 2008 Suppliers	0	17	15	Taishan, Sunglo, EF,Aifly, Crystal CG, Yuanpei Translation, Der Floor, Aokang, Liby, PricewaterhouseCoopers, Dayun, Capinfo, Unipack, Microsoft(China), Kokuyo, Newauto, Mondo	Sunglo Der Floor Reduced –2
6	**Total**	**36**	**65**	**63**	29	–2
7	Actual No. of sponsors appeared in the sample	26	45	25		–20 (2007–2008)

Note: Sole co-branding as the main factor according to our examined excerpts during the preparatory stage 2001–2003 is not mentioned here.

first Olympic champion of the 110m men's hurdles in Chinese history) as spokesperson (Faines, 2007; see Figure 3.3). In the next stage (2006–2007), 'For the health of Olympic Games,' Yili promoted healthy and nutrient products for high-performing athletes to attract new customers (P36). In the last stage (during and after 2008), 'For the health after Olympic Games,' Yili promised to continue producing high-standard dairy products by emphasizing its commitment to the Olympic Games (P16). By being appointed as a sponsor of World Expo 2010 in Shanghai Yili continued its marketing efforts

Table 3.3 Dominant means-objectives combinations

Pattern code	Pattern type	Survey in 2006 Rank (in %)	Example firm (2006)	Survey in 2007 Rank (in %)	Example firm (2007)	Survey in 2008 Rank (in %)	Example firm (2008)
P36	Attracting New Customers – Product image	1(64.5)	YiLi	1(32.4)	Coca Cola		
P26	Revenue Generation – Product Image			2(23.5)	China Mobile	2(16.0)	China Mobile
P15	Co-branding – Corporation Image	3(4.7)	Coca Cola	3(17.6)	Héng Yuán Xiáng	1(36.0)	UPS
P35	Attracting New Customers – Corporation Image	2(30.8)	CNPC	4(11.8)	UPS		
P25	Revenue Generation – Corporation Image					2(16.0)	Tsingtao
P16	Co-branding – Product Image					2(16.0)	Sohu

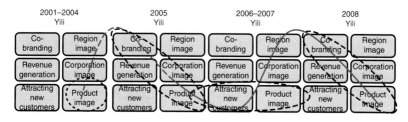

Figure 3.2　Yili's longitudinal advertising pattern (means–objective combinations)

to develop markets built on world-class event sponsoring. In 2013 it still proudly announced on the Yili website:

> Inner Mongolia Yili Industrial Group Co., Ltd. is the market-leading dairy products manufacturer with the broadest product line in China. As the only dairy producer that can meet the requirements of the Olympic Games and World Expo. Yili Group was appointed as dairy products provider of Beijing Olympic Games and Expo 2010 Shanghai. (http://www.yili.com/en/about_yili/background.shtml [accessed July 20, 2013]

The fourth stage (2008 ahead of the Olympic Games) is dominated by the co-branding and corporation image pattern (P15). Foreign large sponsors in particular were still trying to establish a sustainable basis in China, aiming in their advertising strategy to be broadly recognized by Chinese customers as supporting the 'joint national effort'. Well-known foreign and Chinese brands did not change their advertising strategy and continued with the pattern of focusing on revenue generation and product image (P26). Two new patterns also emerged during this period, namely, the co-branding and product image pattern (P16) and the revenue generation and corporation image pattern (P25). The latter pattern was practiced by well-known Chinese companies, who wanted to emphasize in their marketing that they were also connected to the Olympic Games and to local customers, and to respond to competitors on the Chinese market. Tsingtao Brewery Co. Ltd (referred to as Tsingtao thereafter) is an example of this strategy (see Figure 3.4).

Tsingtao is the oldest existing brewery in China, tracing its roots back to 1903 when its predecessor, Tsingtao Brewery Factory, was first established. Tsingtao signed a sponsorship agreement to be a 'domestic beer sponsor' in August 2005. Before that, and already in October 2004, Anheuser-Busch's Budweiser (referred to as Budweiser thereafter) had become the official 'international beer sponsor' of the Beijing Olympic Games. And only days before the agreement with Tsingtao, Beijing Yanjing Brewery Co. Ltd (referred to as Yangjing thereafter) became an official 'domestic beer

„Empower your inner strength!   "Make dreams come true!
With me, China will be stronger"   One cup away from my dream"

„ Honour China – Energy source behind gold medals"   „Yili yogurt – bring out the best in champions"

Figure 3.3   Yili's Olympic advertisements (sample selection)

sponsor'. The motives of these three companies to be associated with the Beijing Olympic Games were different. Yanjing was targeting the Beijing Olympic Games as an important strategic step to make itself an international brand name in the beer brewing industry worldwide, thus applying the co-branding and corporation image pattern (P15). Budweiser expected its sponsorship with the BOCOG to reinforce its commitment to supporting the communities where it does business and sponsoring, but surprisingly we did not find any Budweiser advertisements in our sample. For Tsingtao Beer the Beijing 2008 Olympic Games were an integral move in achieving its 'globalization dreams' through the international platform of the Beijing 2008 Olympic Games (BOCOG, 2005a). It also needs to be mentioned that this was the first time in the history of the Olympic Games that three companies had non-exclusively shared sponsorship rights in the same product category.

Figure 3.4   Advertisements by the two Chinese breweries: Yanjing and Tsingtao
Note: Advertisement on the left (2008), on the right top (2008), right bottom (2007).

Taking the longitudinal perspective into account we see that advertisements were aligned with management's strategic intentions toward market development in China. The following patterns of advertising strategies emerged (Figure 3.5).

In the first example United Parcel Service of America, Inc. (referred to as UPS hereafter) displayed a sequential logic: a co-branding/corporate image focus, then acquire new customers before coming back to the pattern of co-branding/corporation image in advertising. UPS is a business-to-business concept, which began to operate in China in 1988 and invested constantly to expand its Chinese business. In 2001 UPS became the first package delivery company to begin direct flights from the US to China, and in 2005 UPS was the first global delivery company to take direct control of its operations in major metropolitan centres within China. David Abney, President of UPS International, was quoted when signing the agreement with the BOCOG: 'This sponsorship is another important step in strengthening our brand presence in one of the fastest growing markets in the world,' and Ken Torok, President, UPS Asia Pacific, said: 'UPS is honoured and excited about being part of delivering the world's greatest sporting event to China, and are committed to helping the organizing committee reach its vision of *One*

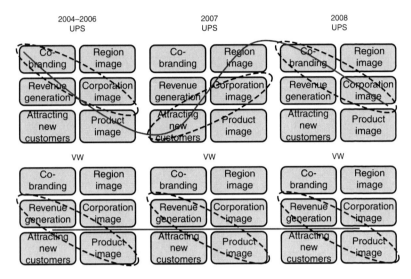

Figure 3.5   Two longitudinal advertising patterns (means–objective combinations)
Note: The lines are only used to link the patterns and to visualize the strategy over time.

World, One Dream' (BOCOG, 2005b). The rationale behind the advertising campaign might be understood as to showcase how UPS's global network, expertise, and technology could help companies in China to enhance their business, in the same way that UPS was doing for the BOCOG to help stage the world's most successful Games (see Figure 3.6 for advertising examples). The changes in advertising strategy in 2007 was timed to coincide with the 500-day countdown to start the Beijing Olympics, and featured the renowned Chinese actor Zhang Fengyi in TV commercials (Murphy, 2007)—and thus was not within the scope of our sample. Targeted at new customers, including Chinese professionals, executives, and managers, the advertising also used familiar Chinese idioms to signify UPS's commitment to the Olympic Games, such as delivering with pinpoint accuracy and completing a task successfully to communicate the reliability of UPS's express delivery capability (UPS, 2007).

In the second example the Volkswagen group followed the same 'profit max strategy' throughout their sponsoring activities in the years leading up to the Beijing Olympic Games: revenue generation with different products. Volkswagen, together with, for example, China Mobile, was already a well-known brand in China. Volkswagen group's advertising strategy, comprising the VW, Audi, and Skoda brands, therefore targeted the product and specific product features to further strengthening its already prominent position in the Chinese automotive market (see Figure 3.7). Volkswagen was the first

Figure 3.6   Advertisements by UPS
Note: Advertisement on top (2006), bottom left and right (2008).

Western automobile manufacturer to enter China when it opened its first office in 1985. There followed a successful joint-venture partnership and a near monopoly in government and taxi sales for nearly twenty years. VW was the undisputed leader of the Chinese passenger car market until the early years of the new millennium. VW was able to sell high volumes —taxis and official car fleets—and thus harness economies of scale, while acquiring credibility at the same time. In 2003, one year before the sponsorship agreement was announced, the Volkswagen Group held a market share of over 30 per cent but was coming under increasing threat from Asian and European competitors. VW announced on its corporate website:

> For the first time in history of the Olympic Games, this mega sports event is being held in the People's Republic of China. Four million visitors are expected. Participation as a national main sponsor is an important component in the Volkswagen Group's strategy for successful involvement in Asia's most important car market. (VW, 2008)

Figure 3.7   Advertisements by Volkswagen brands
Note: Advertisement on top left (2005), top right (2006) and bottom (2008).

Chen Zhixin, the general manager of Shanghai VW, further explained in an interview that Shanghai VW and FAW VW would donate about 5,000 cars for the Beijing Olympic Games, revealing also that VW had paid up to US\$ 102 million for its sponsorship (Jiu, 2007).

3.5 Conclusion

There are two central research questions in sponsorship research: first are the 'pre-decisions,' which identify the factors that influenced the selection of sponsors and sponsees; and second, the 'post-decisions,' which include how the sponsors will communicate the sponsorship message to their audiences and lay out the market objectives associated with their sponsorship. This chapter focuses on the second question but the first also needs to be considered at the same time in order to understand the sponsorship involvement. Given the five sponsorship levels available only 25 (45 in 2007, 26 in 2006) of the 63 (65, 36) participating companies appeared in the collected advertisements and articles. This is surprising if we take previous research into account suggesting that Chinese advertising professionals and managers were generally favourable toward advertising as an efficient business tool (Semenik and Tao, 1993; Liu, 2002). This finding might be explained by the limitation of only including print media in our sample, whereas the companies might have chosen to focus on other sponsorship activation strategies. It might also be the fact that their sponsorship was not self-imposed, but government-appointed. The purpose of the government inviting companies to be sponsors might simply be a means of making them share the financial burden of the Beijing Olympic Games 2008. One of the sponsors explained this in a personal interview: 'At that time there was no question of choice, either you accept this "offer" or there is the likelihood of being forced out of business in the future.' We might therefore conclude that sponsorship in an emerging market context might serve different purposes, and activating the sponsorship investment by designing an focused advertising strategy is therefore not necessarily needed—but would allow the sponsor to leverage the investment.

Another challenge with sponsorship in an emerging market context is the risk associated with the event. In 2008 the Tibetan uprising escalated owing to the authoritarian government style and the existing political climate in China. In March 2008 the European Union foreign ministers rejected the call to boycott the opening ceremony of the Beijing Olympic Games, although a few days later thousands of protesters and counter-protesters lined the planned route of the torch relay in London. As this and further protests (see Institute for Defense Studies and Analyses, 2008, for a chronology of events) happened shortly ahead of the Games and human-rights activists also started to criticize the sponsors of the Beijing Olympic Games for partnering with China, this constituted one of many issues creating uncertainty among existing sponsors and potential investors. For example, Adidas expressed concern about Tibet and also addressed boycott calls in a AFP press release (AFP, 2008):

> We are concerned about the recent situation in Tibet. We hope that the situation will calm down very soon, ... We believe that a boycott of the Beijing Olympic Games would be counter-productive and we have therefore reiterated our commitment to the 2008 Beijing Olympic Games.

In the same statement it was claimed that privately the sponsors were worried, had appointed crisis management teams, increased their budgets for media consultants, and had been talking privately to the BOCOG, which had invited sponsors to Beijing for talks in that matter. In the same context Volkswagen was quoted in a German newspaper:

> The torch relay is accompanied exclusively by Volkswagen vehicles. So, did the company ever consider withdrawing its sponsorship in light of the protests in Paris, London and San Francisco? 'China is our most important market,' is the answer. If we had withdrawn from the torch relay, we would not have sold another car here, not a single one. (Nass, 2008: 3)

Is sponsoring a mega-sporting event like the Beijing Olympic Games a wise investment and/or effective marketing strategy? The question is difficult to answer, when only investigating printed media and advertisements. The Beijing 2008 Olympic Games were truly significant in Olympic history since they were the most watched, most participated in, and the most record-shattering Olympic Games to date, and it all took place in an emerging market. This in itself adds a new dimension into research on the impacts of mega-sporting events in Asia (Dolles and Söderman, 2008; Takahashi et al., 2012). The sponsoring companies contributed to this success story in many ways. We also might assume that the huge expectation and support resulted in a higher level of recognition and positively changed consuming behaviours during that time, which were influenced by the marketing of the BOCOG. Tom Doctoroff, CEO of J. Walter Thompson (JWT) Greater China, explains that 'many Chinese individuals use the nation's status as a surrogate identity for themselves' (Faines, 2007). That is to say, citizens equate China's development and the national ambition by hosting the Olympic Games with their own. Advertising campaigns that capture a spirit of victory might therefore be considered to have a larger impact and a higher chance to make their brand more meaningful to the Chinese consumer.

But the question remains whether there was a sustainable marketing and business impact created by the sponsorship. If the sponsorship of the Beijing Olympics was used as a marketing tool and promotional instrument to increase brand awareness and enhance corporate image, so that corporate sponsors could obtain pre-defined benefits from sponsorship, as claimed by Sleight (1989) and Meenaghan (1991a, b), the question still is how to measure a seemingly possible increased brand awareness and enhanced corporate image ahead of and after the Games. How to differentiate between the different activation strategies chosen by the sponsors? What kind of follow-up strategies were applied by Chinese and foreign sponsoring firms after the Beijing Olympics to build upon the initial sponsorship investment? Those sponsoring partners not following up might have lost the opportunity to gain benefit from their Olympic sponsorship investment.

Notes

This chapter is a slightly revised and extended version of our article "Mega-sporting events and international marketing in emerging markets: Advertising patterns and market strategies of Beijing Olympic Games' sponsoring partners" originally published in the "Essays in Commemoration of the Seventieth Birthday of Professor Yoshiaki Takahashi" (Shōgaku Ronsan [The Journal of Commerce], ISSN 0286-7702, vol. 54 (2013), no. 3–4 (March), pp. 41–77). We would like to thank Yoshiaki Takahashi and the Society of Business and Commerce in Chuo University (Tokyo, Japan) for granting permission to use the text. Finally, thanks to the companies who granted us permission to reproduce the advertisements in the text. Every effort has been made to trace and acknowledge ownership of copyright. The publisher would be pleased to make suitable arrangements to clear permissions with any copyright holders of the advertisements whom we have not been possible to contact.

1. **Newspapers:** *People's Daily, People's Daily Overseas Edition, China Business Post, China Economic Times, 21st Century Business Herald, Beijing Daily, Beijing Times, Economic Daily, Guangming Daily, The Economic Observer, Beijing Evening, Elite Reference, Chengdu Business, China Business Times, China Commercial Times, China Petrochemical News, China Quality Daily, Chinese Business, Chinese Customer, Economic Daily, First Financial Daily, Global Times, Health Paper, International Business Daily, Jiefang Daily, Jinghua Times, People's Post and Telecommunication News, Shandong Business, Southeast Business, Sports Weekly, Talents Market, The First, Tsingtao Daily, Tsingtao Evening, Xinjing Newspaper, 21st Century Business Herald.*

    Magazines and Journals: *Beijing Youth Message, Caijing Magazine, CEO & CIO, Chinese & Foreign Entrepreneurs, China Entrepreneur, China Quality, China's Foreign Trade, China Telecommunication Trade, Chinese National Geography, Chinese Sports, Computer Space, English Salon, Fashion Shopping Guide, Global Entrepreneur, International Airlines, Lifeweek, Outlook Weekly, Marketing China, Nanfeng Chuang, New Economy Weekly, New Fortune, Personal Computer, Sino-Foreign Management, Sports Pictures, The Investors, Tendermag, Tennis, Total Sports, World Broadcasting & TV.*

References

Aaker, D.A. (1996) *Building Strong Brands* (New York: The Free Press).

AFP (2008) 'Olympics: Jittery Sponsors Stay Loyal to China, But Worry in Private,' http://afp.google.com/article/ALeqM5ixanOb_pWv9TtCyg0vYAUAJnQ3XA [accessed September 10, 2009].

Amis, J., and Cornwell, B. (2005) *Global Sport Sponsorship: A Multidisciplinary Approach* (Oxford: Berg).

Andersson, T.D., Getz, D., Mykletun, R.J., Jæger, K., and Dolles, H. (2013) 'Factors Influencing Grant and Sponsorship Revenue for Festivals,' *Event Management* (in press).

Bennett, P.D. (ed.) (1995) *AMA Dictionary of Marketing Terms*, 2nd ed. (Chicago: American Marketing Association).

Berkowitz, E., Crane, F., Kerin, R., Hartley, S., and Rudelius, W. (2003) *Marketing*, 5th ed. (Toronto: McGraw-Hill Ryerson).

Berkowitz, P., Gjermano, G., Gomez, L., and Schafer, G. (2007) 'Brand China: Using the 2008 Olympic Games to Enhance China's Image,' *Place Branding and Public Diplomacy*, 3(2): 164–178.

BOCOG (2005a) 'Tsingtao Beer Becomes Sponsor of Beijing 2008 Games,' http://www.china.org.cn/english/olympic/138617.htm [accessed September 10, 2009].

BOCOG (2005b) 'UPS is Named Official Sponsor of the Beijing 2008 Olympic Games,' http://en.beijing2008.cn/26/96/article212029626.shtml [accessed September 10, 2009].

Budd, R.W., Thorp, R.K., and Donohew, L. (1967) *Content Analysis of Communications* (New York: Macmillan).

Chao, P., Samiee, S., and Yip, L.-S. (2003) 'International Marketing and the Asia-Pacific Region: Developments, Opportunities, and Research Issues,' *International Marketing Review*, 20(5): 480–492.

Cornwell, T.B. (2008) 'State of the Art and Science in Sponsorship-linked Marketing,' *Journal of Advertising*, 37(3), 41–55.

Cornwell, T.B., and Coote, L.V. (2005) 'Corporate Sponsorship of a Cause: The Role of Identification on Purchase Intent,' *Journal of Business Research*, 58(3): 268–276.

Cornwell, T.B., Weeks, S.C., and Roy, D.P. (2005) 'Sponsorship-linked Marketing: Opening the Black Box,' *The Journal of Advertising*, 34(2): 21–42.

Creswell, J.W. (2003) *Research Design: Qualitative, Quantitative and Mixed Methods Approaches* (Thousand Oaks, CA: Sage).

Crompton, J.L. (2004) 'Conceptualization and Alternate Operationalizations of the Measurement of Sponsorship Effectiveness in Sports,' *Leisure Studies*, 23(3): 267–281.

Davies, J. (2008) *The Olympic Game Effect—How Sports Marketing Builds Strong Brands* (Singapore: John Wiley & Sons (Asia)).

Doebele, J. (2002) 'No A for Asia,' *Forbes*, April: 35–37.

Dolles, H. (1997) *Keiretsu: Emergenz, Struktur, Wettbewerbsstärke und Dynamik japanischer Verbundgruppen [Keiretsu: Emergence, Structure, Competitive Strengths and Organizational Dynamics of Corporate Groupings in Japan]* (Frankfurt am Main: Peter Lang).

Dolles, H., and Söderman, S. (2008) 'Mega-sporting Events in Asia: Impacts on Society, Business and Management—An Introduction,' *Asian Business and Management*, 7 (1): 1–16.

Dolles, H., and Takahashi, Y. (2011) 'The "Lost Decade" and Changes in the Japanese Business Environment: Consequences for Foreign Direct Investment and Human Resource Management in Foreign Subsidiaries in Japan,' in S. Horn (ed.), *Emerging Perspectives in Japanese Human Resource Management* (Frankfurt am Main: Peter Lang): 165–190.

Eisenhardt, K.M., and Galunic, D.C. (2000) 'Coevolving: At Last, a Way to Make Synergies Work,' *Harvard Business Review*, 78(1): 91–101.

Fahy, J., Farrelly, F., and Quester, P. (2004) 'Competitive Advantages through Sponsorship—A Conceptual Model and Research Propositions,' *European Journal of Marketing*, 38(8): 1013–1030.

Faines, A. (2007) 'Beijing Games 2008—Advertisers Try to Capture the Spirit,' *CNBC* (06.12.) http://www.cnbc.com/id/20162221/Beijing_Games_2008_Advertisers_Try_To_Capture_The_Spirit [accessed July 28, 2008].

Fan, Y., and Pfitzenmaier, N. (2002) 'Event Sponsorship in China,' *Corporate Communications: An International Journal*, 7(2): 110–116.

Fayerweather, J. (1978) *International Business Strategy and Administration* (Cambridge, MA: Balinger).

Filipsson, D. (2008) *In-between Brands: Exploring the Essence of Brand Portfolio Management* (Stockholm: Stockholm University, School of Business).

Geng, L., Burton, R., and Blakemore, C. (2002) 'Sport Sponsorship in China: Transition and Evolution,' *Sport Marketing Quarterly*, 11(1): 20–32.

Ghauri, P. (2004) 'Designing and Conducting Case Studies in International Business Research,' in R. Marschan-Piekkari and C. Welch (eds), *Handbook of Qualitative Research Methods for International Business* (Cheltenham: Edward Elgar): 109–124.

Hartland, T., Skinner, H., and Griffiths, A. (2005) 'Tries and Conversions: Are Sports Sponsors Pursuing the Right Objectives?,' *International Journal of Sport Marketing and Sponsorship*, 6(3): 164–173.

Heslop, L.A., Nadeau, J., and O'Reilly, N. (2010) 'China and the Olympics: Views of Insiders and Outsiders,' *International Marketing Review*, 27(4): 404–433.

Hickey, G., and Kipping, C. (1996) 'Issues in Research. A Multi-stage Approach to the Coding of Data from Open-ended Questions,' *Nurse Researcher*, 4(1): 81–91.

Hollensen, S. (2007) *Global Marketing: A Decision Oriented Approach* (Hemel Hempstead: Prentice Hall).

Institute for Defense Studies and Analyses (eds) (2008) 'Tibetan Uprising and the 2008 Beijing Olympics: A Chronology,' http://www.idsa.in/chronology/TibetanUprisingandthe2008 BeijingOlympics?q=print/3275 [accessed July 21, 2010].

IOC (eds) (2008a) 'Games of the XXIX Olympiad, Beijing 2008: Global Television and Online Media Report,' http://www.olympic.org/Documents/IOC_Marketing/Broadcasting/ Beijing_2008_Global_Broadcast_Overview.pdf [accessed July 20, 2013].

IOC (eds) (2008b) 'Olympic Marketing Fact File 2008,' http://www.olympic.org/Documents/ fact_file_2008.pdf [accessed July 20, 2013].

IOC (eds) (2008c) 'IOC Marketing Media Guide. Beijing 2008,' http://multimedia.olympic.org/ pdf/en_report_1329.pdf [accessed December 19, 2008].

James, D.O. (2006) 'Extension to Alliance: Aaker and Keller's Model Revisited,' *Journal of Product and Brand Management*, 15(1): 15–22.

Jin, H., and Bu, T. (2010) 'Studies on Beijing Olympic Games' Spiritual Legacy: Brand Value,' *Journal of Sustainable Development*, 3(2): 255–260.

Jiu, J. (2007) 'VW to Expand Operations by Sponsoring Beijing Olympics,' http://autonews.gasgoo.com/AutoNews/Autobiz_print.aspx?id=3061 [accessed June 27, 2008].

Johan, G.V., and Pham, M.T. (1999) 'Relateness, Prominence and Constructive Sponsor Identification,' *Journal of Marketing Research*, 36(4): 299–313.

Kambitsis, C., Harahousou, Y., Theodorakis, N., and Chatzibeis, G. (2002) 'Sport Advertising in Print Media: The Case of 2000 Olympic Games,' *Corporate Communications: An International Journal*, 7(3): 155–161.

Kapferer, J.N. (1992) *Strategic Brand Management* (London: Kogan Page).

Keller, K.L. (2003) *Strategic Brand Management: Building, Measuring, and Managing Brand Equity*, 2nd ed. (Hemel Hempstead: Prentice Hall).

Kolbe, R.H., and Burnett, M.S. (1991) 'Content Analysis Research: An Examination of Applications with Directives for Improving Research Reliability and Objectivity,' *Journal of Consumer Research*, 18(29): 243–250.

Kotler, P. (2003) *Marketing Management*, 11th ed. (Hemel Hempstead: Prentice Hall).

Kumar, B.N., Steinmann, H., and Dolles, H. (1993) 'Das Management in Niederlassungen deutscher Unternehmen in Japan—eine empirische Untersuchung unter besonderer Berücksichtigung von Klein- und Mittelbetrieben [Subsidiary Management of German Small- and Medium-Sized Companies in Japan],' *Diskussionsbeitrag des Lehrstuhls für Betriebswirtschaftslehre insbesondere Internationales Management (Prof. Dr. Brij N. Kumar)*, no. 2 (Erlangen-Nürnberg: Friedrich-Alexander-Universität).

Laforet, S., and Saunders, J. (1999) 'Managing Brand Portfolios: Why Leaders Do What They Do,' *Journal of Advertising Research*, 39(1): 51–66.

Laforet, S., and Saunders, J. (2005) 'Managing Brand Portfolios: How Strategies Have Changed,' *Journal of Advertising Research*, 45(3): 314–327.

Lardinoit, T., and Derbaix, C. (2001) 'Sponsorship and Recall of Sponsors,' *Psychology & Marketing*, 18(2): 167–190.

Lindkvist, K. (1981) 'Approaches to Textual Analysis,' in K.E. Rosengren (ed.), *Advances in Content Analysis* (Beverly Hills, CA: Sage): 23–41.

Liu, W.-L. (2002) 'Advertising in China: Product Branding and Beyond,' *Corporate Communications*, 7(2): 117–125.

Lombard, M., Snyder-Duch, J., and Bracken, C.C. (2010) 'Practical Resources for Assessing and Reporting Intercoder Reliability in Content Analysis Research Projects,' http://matthewlombard.com/reliability/#Neuendorf [accessed September 15, 2012].

McTavish, D.-G., and Pirro, E.-B. (1990) 'Contextual Content Analysis,' *Quality and Quantity*, 24: 245–265.

Madrigal, R. (2004) 'A Review of Team Identification and its Influence on Consumers' Responses Toward Corporate Sponsors,' in L.R. Kahle and C. Riley (eds), *Sports Marketing and the Psychology of Marketing Communication* (Mahwah, NJ: Erlbaum): 241–258.

Mayring, P. (1995) *Qualitative Inhaltsanalyse. Grundfragen und Techniken [Qualitative Content Analysis. Basic Questions and Techniques]*, 5th ed. (Weinheim: Deutscher Studienverlag).

Meenaghan, T. (1991a) 'The Role of Sponsorship in the Marketing Communication Mix,' *International Journal of Advertising*, 10(1): 35–47.

Meenaghan, T. (1991b) 'Sponsorship: Legitimising the Medium,' *European Journal of Marketing*, 25(11): 5–10.

Melin, F. (1999) *Varumärkesstrategi—om konsten att utveckla starka varumärken [Branding—The Art of Developing Strong Brands]* (Malmö: Liber Ekonomi).

Murphy, J. (2007) 'Zhang Stars in UPS Olympic Ads,' *Asia's Media & Marketing Newspaper* (May 18): 9.

Nass, M. (2008) 'A Balmy Evening's Conversation Highlights Lasting Friction between China and the West,' http://www.german-times.com/index.php?option=com_content&task=view &id=6911&Itemid=99 [accessed September 15, 2012].

Neuendorf, K.A. (2002) *The Content Analysis Guidebook* (Thousand Oaks, CA: Sage).

O'Guinn, T.C., and Muniz, A.M. (2001) 'Brand Community,' *Journal of Consumer Research*, 27(4): 412–432.

O'Reilly, N., and Forster, G. (2008) 'Risk Management in Sports Sponsorship: Application to Human Mortality Risk,' *International Journal of Sports Marketing and Sponsorship*, 10(1): 45–62.

O'Reilly, N., Nadeau, J., Séguin, B., and Harrison, M. (2007) 'In-Stadium Sponsorship Evaluation of a Mega-sponsee: The 2004 Grey Cup,' *International Journal of Sports Marketing and Sponsorship*, 8(2): 179–198.

Overton, R. (2007) *Sponsorships: Finding and Selling Marketing Partnerships* (Murwillumbah: Martin Books).

Polonsky, M.J., and Speed, R. (2001) 'Linking Sponsorship and Cause Related Marketing,' *European Journal of Marketing*, 35(11/12): 1361–1385.

Potter, W.J., and Levine-Donnerstein, D. (1999) 'Rethinking Validity and Reliability in Content Analysis,' *Journal of Applied Communication Research*, 27(3), 258–284.

Prahalad, C.K., and Doz, Y.L. (1987) *The Multinational Mission* (New York: The Free Press).

Preuss, H. (2004) *The Economics of Staging the Olympics—A Comparison of the Games 1972–2008* (Cheltenham: Edward Elgar).

Rifon, N.J., Choi, S.M., Trimble, C.S., and Li, H. (2004) 'Congruence Effects in Sponsorship,' *Journal of Advertising*, 33(1): 29–42.

Rosengren, K.E. (ed.) (1981) *Advances in Content Analysis* (Beverly Hills, CA: Sage).

Roy, D.P., and Graff, T.R. (2002) 'Influences on Consumer Responses to Winter Olympics Sponsorship,' *International Journal of Sports Marketing and Sponsorship*, 4(4): 355–375.

Schlesinger, T. (2013) 'A Review of Fan Identity and its Influence on Sport Sponsorship Effectiveness,' in S. Söderman and H. Dolles (eds), *Handbook of Research on Sport and Business* (Cheltenham: Edward Elgar): 435–455.

Semenik, R.J., and Tao, D. (1993) 'Chinese Managers Attitudes towards Advertising: Before and After the Tiananmen Square Incident,' *International Journal of Advertising*, 13(3): 243–255.

Simons, C. (2003) 'Marketing to the Masses,' *Far Eastern Economic Review*, 166(35): 32.

Sleight, S. (1989) *Sponsorship: What Is It and How to Use It?* (London: McGraw Hill).

Smolianov. P., and Shilbury, D. (2005) 'Examining Integrated Advertising and Sponsorship in Corporate Marketing Through Televised Sport,' *Sport Marketing Quarterly*, 14(4): 239–250.

Söderman, S., and Dolles, H. (2008) 'Strategic Fit in International Sponsorship. The Case of the Olympic Games in Beijing,' *International Journal of Sports Marketing and Sponsorship*, 9(2): 95–110.

Söderman, S., and Dolles. H. (2010) 'Sponsoring the Beijing Olympic Games—Patterns of Sponsor Advertising,' *Asia Pacific Journal of Marketing and Logistics*, 22(1): 8–24.

Söderman, S., and Dolles, H. (2012) '北京オリンピック・スポンサー企業のブランド訴求―スポンサー企業の広告パターンの比較研究―' [Brand Appeal of the Sponsoring Companies of the Beijing Olympics: A Comparative Research on the Advertising Patterns of the Sponsoring Companies],' in Y. Takahashi, H. Hayakawa, H. Dolles, and S. Söderman (eds), スポーツ・マネジメントとメガイベント：Jリーグ・サッカーとアジアのメガスポーツ・イベント [Sports Management and Mega Events: J-League Soccer and Mega-Sports Events in Asia] (Tokyo: Bunshindo): 223–245.

Speed, R., and Thompsen, P. (2000) 'Determinants of Sports Sponsorship Response,' *Journal of the Academy of Marketing Science*, 28(2): 226–238.

Takahashi, Y., Hayakawa, H., Dolles, H., and Söderman, S. (eds) (2012) スポーツ・マネジメントとメガイベント：Jリーグ・サッカーとアジアのメガスポーツ・イベント [Sports Management and Mega Events: J-League Soccer and Mega-Sports Events in Asia] (Tokyo: Bunshindo).

UPS (2007) 'UPS Showcases Role in Beijing 2008 Games in New Ad Campaign,' http://www.ups.com/content/cn/en/about/news/press_releases/04122007.html [accessed July 31, 2012].

Vallaster, C., and de Chernatony, L. (2005) 'Internationalisation of Service Brands: The Role of Leadership during the Internal Brand Building Process,' *Journal of Marketing Management*, 21(1–2): 181–203.

VW (2008) 'Volkswagen Sponsors the 2008 Olympic Games,' http://www.volk swagenag.com/   content/vwcorp/info_center/en/news/2008/03/volkswagen_ sponsors_the_2008_olympic_games.html [accessed October 10, 2009].

Walliser, B. (2003) 'An International Review of Sponsorship Research: Extension and Update,' *International Journal of Advertising*, 22(1): 5–40.

Weber, R.P. (1990) *Basic Content Analysis* (Beverly Hills, CA: Sage).

Yang, X.S., Sparks, R., and Li, M. (2008) 'Sport Sponsorship as a Strategic Investment in China: Perceived Risks and Benefits by Corporate Sponsors Prior to the Beijing 2008 Olympics,' *International Journal of Sports Marketing and Sponsorship*, 10(1): 63–78.

4
Global Innovation and R&D for Knowledge Creation: The Case of P&G, Unilever and Kao

Chie Iguchi, Takabumi Hayashi, and Atsuho Nakayama

4.1 Introduction

The objective of this chapter is to identify a directional shift toward the decentralization of scientific technological knowledge-creation by Multinational Enterprises (MNEs) in the global market and to determine the extent to which MNEs leverage local knowledge. Therefore, we investigate how firms can retain competitive advantages from the viewpoint of global knowledge-creation. In doing so, we seek to overcome intrinsically static views in the resource-based view and clarify sources of contemporary MNEs' dynamic capabilities (Cantwell, 1995; Dunning, 1996; Teece, 2009: 136–175; Wernerfelt, 1984). We also examine the dynamic capabilities of contemporary MNEs, which can be seen as MNE-specific from our analysis of the roles of overseas subsidiaries' R&D capabilities. In particular, we clarify the relationship between the mechanisms of innovative activities and knowledge creation by MNEs and sources of global competitive advantage.

Scholars have recently focused on the role of knowledge in MNEs. Large MNEs exist not as a response to market failure in buying and selling knowledge, but as a consequence of their ability to organize the generation and transfer of knowledge worldwide. They are described as repositories of knowledge able to create unique capabilities. Since these capabilities are fostered through firm-specific social-learning processes, they are easier to transfer within an MNE than across organizations, and constitute the true ownership advantages of the MNE as a group (Cantwell, 1989, 1991, 1994; Kogut and Zander, 1993, 1995). As much existing literature on globalization and decentralization of R&D has suggested, MNEs have aimed to innovate through knowledge-creation processes by utilizing subsidiaries' resources of R&D facilities in the host country. In rapidly changing competitive environments, MNEs have been under considerable pressure to respond to competitors not only in their home country, but also in host countries. MNEs have been seeking new products with global scale, and it is more critical than ever to generate new technological knowledge and high-demand concepts in order to develop such products. To raise global sales figures through successful new-product development, pre-1990s R&D strategy was generally to invest in R&D facilities and human resources, and raise R&D capabilities within the organization. However, changes in the global competitive environment and shorter product lifecycles have meant that strengthening in-house R&D activities has often led to further decline in R&D investment efficiency.

Although R&D has been the least-globalized function of MNEs (UNCTAD, 2005), the more global the company, the more pressure it has to deploy R&D human resources strategically, regardless of nationality. Traditionally, R&D decentralization was from developed home country to developed host countries; where undertaken in developing countries, it was for adapting products or processes to local conditions. The production process is no longer driven only by the need for local adaptation; R&D by MNEs is required to respond to increased competition, access foreign research-talent pools, reduce costs and accelerate technology development (UNCTAD, 2005). As a result, global companies can retain multicultural knowledge resources as part of their institutional capability, and in consequence, theoretical arguments on R&D globalization have evolved (Hayashi, 2004). In the 1970s and 1980s, theoretical discussions of R&D globalization centred on MNEs from the USA and Europe. However, a backdrop of difficulty in maintaining global competitive edge and global decentralization of the production of scientific technological knowledge has motivated even highly globalized companies to shift away from closed innovation systems toward the principle of 'metanational innovation' (Asakawa, 2006; Doz, 2006; Doz, Santos and Williamson, 2001).

We also investigate to what extent the national origin of engineers or scientists working in R&D has diversified, and to what extent MNEs in culture-specific industries leverage local R&D personnel and construct regional R&D networking within the region to develop new products for growing regional markets. Previous research on various aspects of subsidiaries' R&D activities in culture-free industries (e.g. electrical and electronics) indicates how competence-creating subsidiaries have established R&D laboratories to utilize local knowledge and creative inputs, including technology, to develop new products aimed at expanding the global-market scope of their MNE. Research in such industries also suggests that R&D globalization has evolved (Hayashi and Serapio, 2006; Iguchi, 2006, 2008; Serapio and Hayashi, 2004). This study focuses on MNEs in culture-specific industries such as toiletry, food and beverages to clarify if MNEs in this area show similar results. To develop our research, we chose to analyse subsidiary-specific R&D capabilities on the mechanisms of knowledge transfer and creation through global R&D networking by MNEs.

We look at three cases of MNEs in culture-specific industries, in which sensitivity to local consumer preference is necessary. We consider subsidiary evolution in a host country, attending specifically to R&D activities in host-country subsidiaries. The aim is to analyse MNE-specific global knowledge-creation mechanisms as innovation systems within the MNE group, through analysing R&D by subsidiaries in both developed and developing host countries. To clarify how MNEs create knowledge strategically during new product development for global or regional markets, we analyse research papers as outcomes of R&D and knowledge-creating activities by MNEs. We collected 2,893 technical and scientific research papers considered competitive in developing new products in culture-specific industries by researchers and engineers associated with Kao, P&G and Unilever, and categorized them into the departments within the targeted MNEs to which authors and co-authors belonged, and the national origin of affiliation. This information was used to assess the evolution of global mechanisms of knowledge-creation in these companies. The periods selected for study were 1981–1983, 1991–1993, 2001–2003 and 2006–2008. Technical and scientific research papers were limited to those published in the UK, USA and Netherlands, major hubs of scientific journals. As a statistical methodology, we used two-way ANOVA without repetition to test if differences in MNE and number of years relate to the incidence of national origin among authors, and a multiple comparison by the Bonferroni method to test if differences between time-period and between MNEs exert significant influences.

The chapter is structured as following: after brief surveys of the concepts of dynamic capabilities, R&D laboratories and a discussion of how R&D is managed by MNEs in culture-free versus culture-specific industries, respectively, four hypotheses relating to strategic behaviours of MNEs in culture-specific industries in a global competitive environment with a high likelihood of significant influence from cultural factors in the targeted market or region are tested and analysed. The results of the tests are finally discussed and assessed in the concluding paragraph.

4.2 Dynamic capabilities of MNEs

Issues of inter-organizational linkages between subsidiary capabilities and MNE home-country headquarters have been discussed in terms of subsidiary evolution (Birkinshaw and Hood, 1998), dynamic capabilities, home-base-augmenting or -exploiting R&D (Kuemmerle, 1997) and R&D globalization. Scholars have also suggested supply-side factors such as obtaining R&D human resources and access to new technology (Florida, 1997), competence-creating and competence-exploiting subsidiaries (Cantwell and Mudambi, 2005) for linkages, and dynamism of enhancement of R&D capabilities at overseas subsidiaries and MNE headquarters (Asakawa, 2001a, 2001b, 2004). Although the focus has been largely on MNEs in general or subsidiaries in the USA or Europe, recent research evolution has shifted attention toward subsidiaries in host developing countries, such as ASEAN countries (Iguchi, 2006, 2008).

Large MNEs such as Kao, P&G and Unilever exist not as a response to market failure in the buying and selling of knowledge, but as a consequence of their ability to organize the generation and transfer of knowledge world-wide. Such firms are repositories of knowledge able to create unique capabilities which, being fostered through firm-specific social learning processes, are easier to transfer within the MNE than across organizations, and constitute the true ownership advantages of the MNE as a group (Cantwell, 1989, 1991, 1994; Kogut and Zander, 1993, 1995). A subsidiary's responsibilities, roles and functional scope in the host country will vary, depending on the inputs available. However, with changes in subsidiaries and their history of operations in host countries, subsidiaries have become aware that parent organizations are not the sole source of competitive advantage for the MNE.

In recent years, some subsidiaries have acquired a more creative role linked to the closer integration of subsidiaries into global networks within the MNE. These subsidiaries are characterized as having a competence-creating role; others continue to be competence-exploiting (Cantwell and Mudambi, 2005). Therefore, increasing research attention is given to subsidiaries that reflect recent phenomena, specifically competence-creating subsidiaries, who use local knowledge and creative inputs to develop new products aimed at expanding the global market scope of their MNE group (Burgelman, 1983a, 1983b; Cantwell, 1987; D'Cruz, 1986; Dunning, 1996; Pearce, 1992, 2001; Rugman and Verbeke, 1992; White and Poynter, 1984). Competence-creating subsidiaries have their autonomy and creative scope supported by the home-country headquarters, allowing some element of asset-seeking or knowledge-seeking behaviour based on their ability to affect the MNE's competitiveness and the creative assets of the host or regional economy. In order to function effectively, the MNE must rely on the area in which it is located for existing local technology, unique elements of research capacity in the local science base, and sufficiency in human capital. Therefore, the emergence of competence-creating subsidiaries is a crucial manifestation of an increasingly decentralized approach to the generation and application of knowledge. This approach attaches importance to the role of a subsidiary's capabilities and emphasizes that it is part of a network (Birkinshaw and Hood, 1998).

Conducting global collaborative R&D is necessary for new product development and the innovations required to develop new products to meet consumer demand. We examine whether we can identify inherently different knowledge-creation mechanisms in MNEs through analysing the R&D activities of Kao, P&G and Unilever. We note that a directional shift toward decentralizing scientific technological knowledge-creation on a global scale implies cross-border knowledge-creation strategies in order for MNEs to leverage globally dispersed excellence. We also clarify to what extent MNEs in culture-specific industries decentralize R&D and construct R&D networks to leverage locally specific knowledge in the target region so as to develop products appropriate to the regional market. Finally, we analyse global knowledge creation by MNE groups, via the innovation system of particular MNEs.

4.3   Definitions and evolution of R&D laboratories

When we discuss R&D facilities, laboratories and functions, we need to address several levels. According to international guidelines (those of OECD, National Science Foundation Network (NFS) and Ministry of Internal Affairs and Communications of Japan (MIC)), **R&D** comprises creative work 'undertaken on a systematic basis in order to increase the stock of knowledge, including knowledge of man, culture and society, and the use of this stock of knowledge to devise new applications' (OECD, 2002: 30).

Firms' research activities start with **basic research** – the objective of basic research is to gain a more comprehensive knowledge or understanding of the subject under study without specific applications in mind; in industry, basic research is defined as research that advances scientific knowledge, but does not have specific immediate commercial objectives – representing fundamental investigations in the broad area of science relevant to the firm. Basic research is not to solve a specific problem, or meet a currently perceived commercial objective; thus, the basic research phase ends when a particular piece of scientific output is perceived as providing an idea holding important commercial possibilities.

The next stage is **applied research** – the objective of applied research is to gain the knowledge or understanding to meet a specific recognized need; in industry, applied research includes investigations to discover new scientific knowledge that has specific commercial objectives with respect to products, processes, or services – in which the basic research is picked up and moved forward toward what should become an increasingly clear commercial possibility.

In our research typology, the applied research phase ends with the definition of the broad outlines of the new product concept. In its conventional application, this typology then concludes with a **development stage** – development is the systematic use of the knowledge or understanding gained from research directed toward the production of useful materials, devices, systems, or methods, including the design and development of prototypes and processes – in which the product concept derived from applied research is refined into a commercially innovative product (along with its associated production process).

However, in the context of approaches to innovation in a MNE, two alternative paths can occur at the development stage. In one, the innovation process is essentially centralized, with the definitive product derived and implemented in the home country through the efforts of centralized R&D, marketing, engineering and management personnel. This sequence, in the

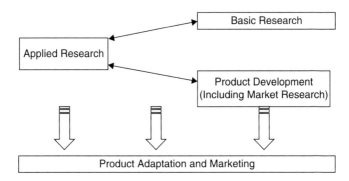

Figure 4.1   Different types of R&D laboratories in this research
Source: Pearce (1999, 2002).

context of a contemporary MNE, implies an additional process, **adaptation**: overseas subsidiaries may find it necessary to adapt the product and/or production process, in minor or peripheral ways, to meet host-country needs or aspects of the production environment. The relationship between basic research, applied research, product development and product adaptation is illustrated in Figure 4.1. In this path, overseas subsidiaries carry out adaptation development as necessary. In the second path, the development/ innovation stage itself is **decentralized**, to make the process responsive to global-innovation strategy.

4.4   R&D by MNEs in culture-free industries

Although research has been lacking on different types of R&D laboratory in different types of industry, previous research has targeted culture-free industries (electrical and electronics industry) in Malaysia, Thailand and Singapore, and culture-specific industries in Thailand and Singapore. Interviews were carried out for 10 Japanese MNE subsidiaries, and questions centred on (1) what type of R&D laboratories they have, (2) what type of R&D activities they have, (3) the reasons behind the R&D level in the host countries, and other relevant questions (Iguchi, 2012). Analysing various aspects of subsidiaries' R&D activities in culture-free industries indicates that competence-creating subsidiaries have established R&D laboratories to utilize local knowledge and creative inputs, including technology, to develop new products aimed at expanding the global scope of their MNE. If a subsidiary has basic research laboratories, it tends to pursue collaborative research by linking inter-organizationally with entities such as universities and public research institutes – although based on a small sample size, there are indications that in culture-free industries, a positive relationship exists between basic research and collaborative R&D (Iguchi, 2012). Since basic research is defined as that which advances scientific knowledge but does not have specific immediate commercial objectives, those performing basic research do so on projects that have nothing directly to do with what they produce or offer in host countries. We can assume that basic research laboratories in culture-free industries are carrying out 'seed' research utilizing local research inputs, but that in culture-specific industries, collaborative research is present, even though host-country laboratories may not have a specific product-development role.

There are differences between culture-free and culture-specific industries. Findings also suggest a grouping pattern of R&D by an MNE (MNE parent) in decentralizing R&D to Southeast Asian countries (Iguchi, 2012). Some subsidiaries acknowledge that the driving forces of their R&D are influenced by parent MNEs in home countries. As already mentioned, until recently basic research was carried out mainly at home and developed in host countries. Whether MNEs decentralize higher competence-level R&D (basic research) to host countries such as Malaysia, Thailand and Singapore is determined by the MNE parent. The results also suggest that once subsidiaries become competence-creating, their roles in R&D and production networking are further enhanced, e.g. from product development laboratory to applied research laboratory, with resultant higher autonomy.

In order to develop products with brand-new concepts, it is necessary to integrate multiple ideas by organizing a wide variety of research members with diversified cognitive approaches. We focus our study on culture-specific industries, identifying how subsidiary R&D contributes to MNE product development in the global market.

4.5   R&D by MNEs in culture-specific industries

We focus on R&D by three MNEs in culture-specific industries from various home countries, specifically Kao Corporation (Japan), Procter and Gamble (USA) and Unilever (UK and Netherlands).

Kao was originally founded in 1887 and formally established in 1940 in Japan. In fiscal year 2009, its turnover was US$ 12,993 million, with an operating income of US$ 985.4 million (net income US$ 656.2 million). Kao invested about US$ 519 million in R&D in 2009. In total, Kao has 33,745 employees, with production and sales networking operations in 24 countries. Kao's first foreign direct investment was in Thailand and Taiwan, ROC, in 1964.

P&G was established in 1837 in the USA, and by 2008 had subsidiaries in over 80 countries. In 2008, turnover was US$ 83,503 million, operating income US$ 17,083 million (net profit US$ 12,075 million), and R&D expenditure US$ 2,226 million, with 138,000 employees worldwide. P&G has 24 global brands, with over US$ 1 billion sales. P&G's first foreign direct investment was to the UK in 1930.

Although Unilever was officially established in 1930, the original companies that joined forces to create it were already well established before the twentieth century. In 2008, Unilever's turnover was €40.5 billion, while operating profit was €7,167 million (net profit €5,285 million); it invested €927 million in R&D. It has 174,000 employees in 270 countries and operates 13 brands with over €1 billion in sales.

The three companies have some common characteristics and variables. Firstly, they all manufacture and sell products in culture-specific industries such as toiletries. Secondly, as Table 4.1 shows, they have maintained upward trends in global sales over years. Over half of P&G and Unilever sales are overseas, although Kao's overseas share remains below 30 per cent. While Kao's data shows low dependency on overseas sales compared to P&G and Unilever, these figures imply that all three companies compete globally and regionally through global production and sales networking, as well as R&D networking. From their global business activities, they can launch new products (or product ranges and brands) through a rapid product-development process. Thirdly, their R&D expenditures are high enough to compare with sectors such as pharmaceuticals, implying they each have in-group corporate innovation strategies. In addition, they each started FDI early – as early as 1930 for P&G, while Kao's launch in the 1960s was fairly early for Japanese companies. While there are other global competitors in the industry, these common features are only seen in these three companies from different national origins.

Table 4.1 Overseas sales ratio of Kao, P&G and Unilever

	1983–1985	1993–1995	1998–2000	2003–2005	2008–2009
Kao	n.a.	20.26%	24.67%	27.47%	24.35%
P&G	n.a.	50.49%	50.72%	52.71%	60.68%
Unilever	38.13%	47.00%	58.00%	58.36%	69.83%

Note: Overseas sales ratios of Unilever calculated using sales from Western Europe and outside Western Europe; 1991–1993 ratio of P&G constructed from 1992–1993 data, from 1991–1992 for Unilever due to restrictions.
Source: Online database (http://www.mergentonline.com.kras5.lib.keio.ac.jp:2048/basicsearch.php [accessed January 10, 2011], Kao.

4.6   Research questions, hypotheses and research methodology

Recent shifts toward liberalization of trade and investment and global standardization of products or process specifications have been implemented by bodies such as the World Trade Organization (WTO). Rapid development of ICT (Information and Communication Technology), seen in internet technology, has further accelerated business models across borders. As a result, business activities traditionally carried out within an MNE's home country have been outsourced and parent MNEs have decentralized by utilizing the most efficient specialized inputs in host countries. These trends have further accelerated global competition and product development for globally compatible products. The diverse lifestyles and demands of global markets require firms to take on the higher R&D costs and risks of tailoring products to host-country and global demand. Although MNEs still maintain core R&D functions in the home country, the trend of diversification in markets has led MNEs to consider the necessity for collaborative research with internationally reputable organizations such as universities and public research institutes, not only at home but also in host countries.

We observe how subsidiaries' capabilities may change over time and how rapidly MNEs decentralize R&D. Based on the theoretical discussions above, we assume that decentralization and diversification of R&D activities will have positive effects on knowledge creation for MNE subsidiaries, and hence the MNE group as a whole. Therefore, we propose four hypotheses relating to strategic behaviours of MNEs in culture-specific industries in a global competitive environment with a high likelihood of significant influence from cultural factors in the targeted market or region.

Hypothesis 1:
Firms with higher dependency on overseas markets will diversify research across R&D facilities and become collaborative organizations, and as a result, R&D will shift from individual to collaborative projects as the number of national origins increases.

Hypothesis 2:
Firms with higher dependency on overseas markets will leverage the capabilities of R&D organizations external to the MNE and home country (e.g. universities, research institutes and overseas firms).

Hypothesis 3:
MNEs in culture-specific industries have a higher tendency to leverage the R&D capabilities of subsidiaries in a host country.

Hypothesis 4:
MNE subsidiaries in culture-specific industries have a higher tendency to enhance networking and collaborative research practices with external R&D organizations (such as local universities, public research institutes and local firms) in a host country.

To analyse our hypotheses, we use scientific and technological research papers, since many R&D project outcomes appear in journals as research papers. In order to clarify how MNEs create knowledge strategically during new-product development for global or regional markets, we analyse research papers as outcomes of knowledge creation by MNEs. We searched for technological papers that were instrumental in developing competitive new products in culture-specific industries and were authored by researchers or engineers associated with Kao, P&G, or Unilever. We selected time-periods of 1981–1983, 1991–1993, 2001–2003 and 2006–2008, and used the JSTPlus (database of the Japan Science and Technology Agency) on technological papers. We limited scope to papers published in the UK, USA and Netherlands, major hubs of scientific journals; 2,893 papers were identified, of which 519 were published in 1981–1983, 779 in 1991–1993, 823 in 2001–2003, and 772 in 2006–2008. For the dependent variable, we use 'overseas sales ratios' as proxy for 'dependency on overseas market,' due to data limitations.

4.7   Analysis

This section examines those papers by category, i.e. papers by individual researchers, written jointly within a company, written in collaboration with other organizations, and whose projects were conducted by authors of foreign origin. We aim thereby to assess the extent of the characteristics and globalization of organizational knowledge-creation structures in the three MNEs.

Hypothesis 1:
Regarding Hypothesis 1, we assume that firms with higher dependency on overseas markets will diversify research across R&D facilities and become collaborative organizations. As a result, R&D will shift from individual to collaborative projects as the number of national origins increases. Figure 4.2 shows the ratios of individually and jointly written papers with other organizations, constructed based on the number of papers attributed to researchers belonging to the three MNEs, categorized either individually (one author) or jointly (researchers belonging to external organizations).

In 1981–1983, 17–25 per cent of papers by each MNE were single-author. However, as the figure clearly shows, for each MNE this ratio has constantly declined and for the latest period stood at 1.2 per cent for P&G, 5.6 per cent for Unilever and 6.3 per cent for Kao. Average ratios also declined from 21.1 per cent (1981–1983) to 4.4 per cent (2006–2008). It is notable that P&G's ratio dramatically declined from 24.8 per cent (1981–1983) to 1.2 per cent (2006–2008). The downward path of individually written papers clearly shows a growing trend toward 'knowledge creation through collaborative research' to handle increasing demands for diversified technological and market-specific preferences, rather than 'knowledge-creating activities by individual research' in new-product development research.

Mirroring the decline in single-author works are jointly written papers, that is, outcomes of collaborative research between MNE and external institution. Average ratios here have dramatically increased from 31.7 per cent (1981–1983) to 70.2 per cent (2006–2008). In particular, ratios for P&G and

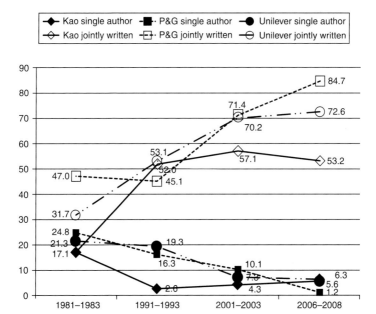

Figure 4.2 The ratio of individually written and papers written jointly with other organizations (universities and research institutions) – Kao, P&G and Unilever –
Notes:
1. Kao1, P&G1 and Unilever 1 represent the ratios of individually written papers; Kao2, P&G2 and Unilever 2 represent the ratios of jointly written papers with other institutions.
2. Individually written papers imply a single author. Jointly written papers are outcomes of collaborative research with researchers in other organizations, e.g. universities, research institutes, other firms. Most of our sample indicates jointly written papers are outcomes of collaborative research with universities.
Source: Compiled by the authors using database of JSTPlus (database of Japan Science and technology Agency)

Unilever rose from 31.9 per cent (1981–1983) to 47 per cent (2006–2008) and 72.6 per cent (1981–1983) to 84.7 per cent (2006–2008), respectively, implying that their R&D activities have shifted from 'individual research within the MNE' to 'knowledge creation through collaborative research' in new-product development – however, when we carefully examine the ratio of jointly written papers through inter-departmental projects within Kao (or P&G), Kao has higher ratios than P&G, that is, in-firm collaborative knowledge-creation has been actively pursued by Kao rather than P&G (Hayashi & Nakayama, 2009).

As Figure 4.3 indicates, the number of national origins-of-affiliation – national origin here implies nationality of author's affiliation, not necessarily nationality as per passport – among authors has consistently increased from 1981–1983 to 2006–2008. The ratios of Kao, P&G and Unilever in 1981–1983

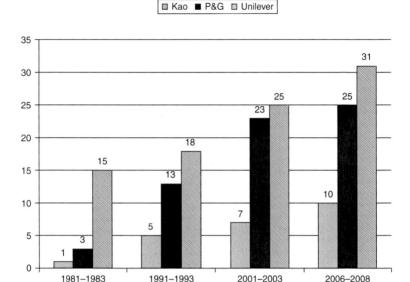

Figure 4.3   The number of national origins-of-affiliations among authors contributing to Unilever, P&G and Kao research
Source: Compiled by the authors using database of JSTPlus (database of Japan Science and technology Agency).

were 1 country for Kao, 3 countries for P&G and 15 countries for Unilever; in 2006–2008 they were 10, 25 and 31 countries respectively.

For our statistical analysis to test whether there are statistically significant differences in the number of national origins between MNEs and between time-periods, we used two-way ANOVA without repetition. We obtained significance probability of 0.000 at firm level and 0.003 at the time-period level at 95 per cent significance level. Therefore, the results suggest that differences in firms and time-periods have positive effects on the number of national origins. However, two-way ANOVA without repetition cannot provide support if significant differences appear between firms. Therefore, we use multiple comparison analysis by the Bonferroni method to test differences between firms and period of years. Between P&G and Unilever, significance probability is 0.071 and the result was not significant at 95 per cent level. These results suggest that P&G and Unilever have a similar number of national origins among authors. However, significant probability of Kao and P&G, and Kao and Unilever, were 0.002 and 0.000 respectively. Therefore, results between Kao and P&G, Kao and Unilever show differences in the number of national origins. When we analyse the year periods, we had significant results for 1991–1993 and 2006–2008 at 95 per cent level, but not for 1981–1983 and 1991–1993.

After carefully testing Hypothesis 1, from the later 1990s there are statistically significant differences in the number of national origins. Newly created knowledge, assessed from paper publications in scientific journals through research projects by authors (where at least one belongs to one of the MNEs) in R&D facilities during the process of developing new products for global markets by our targeted MNEs over the period 1996–2008 has shown an emphasis on jointly researched projects with diverse national origins rather than individual research characterized by a single nationality. As a result, we can conclude that Hypothesis 1 is partially supported (after 1996) for our chosen MNEs.

Hypothesis 2

Our second hypothesis is that firms with higher dependency on overseas markets will leverage the capabilities of R&D organizations external to the MNE and home country. We looked at whether the names of researchers or engineers belonging to overseas R&D facilities (such as subsidiaries, universities, research institutes, firms) were cited as authors to assess whether MNEs were exploiting 'capabilities of R&D organizations external to the MNEs overseas.'

As Figure 4.4 shows, the average ratios of jointly written papers by authors fitting this description consistently increased from 4.9 per cent in 1981–1983 to 34.1 per cent in 2006–2008. Specifically the ratios of internationally co-authored papers by P&G and Unilever dramatically increased from 0.8 per cent (1981–1983) to 46.6 per cent (2006–2008) for P&G, and from 14.0 per cent (1981–1983) to 44.3 per cent (2006–2008) for Unilever. In comparison, Kao, with lower overseas dependency than P&G and Unilever, has maintained lower ratios of internationally co-authored papers, namely zero (1981–1983) and 11.4 per cent (2006–2008).

To test between MNEs and between time-periods for statistically significant differences in MNEs' motivation to collaborate with organizations external to the MNE, we used two-way ANOVA without repetition, obtaining significance probability of 0.008 at firm level and 0.006 at time-period level at 95 per cent significance, suggesting that differences in firms and time-periods have positive effects on MNEs' motivation to collaborate with external organizations. We used multiple comparison analysis (Bonferroni method) to test for differences between firms and periods. Between P&G and Unilever, significance probability is 0.981 and the result was not significant at 95 per cent level, suggesting that P&G and Unilever have similar motivation, statistically. However, the significant probabilities of Kao and P&G, and Kao and Unilever were 0.042 and 0.009 respectively, implying significant differences between Kao and P&G, Kao and Unilever in motivation to collaborate with external organizations. When analysed by period, we found significant results at 95 per cent level for 1981–1983, compared with 2001–2003 and 2006–2008, but not for other periods.

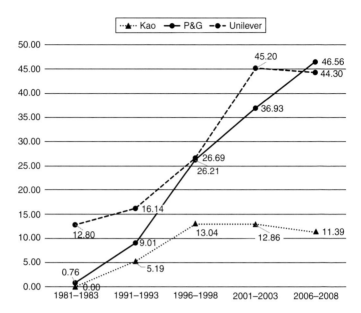

Figure 4.4 Ratios of jointly written papers with authors belonging to overseas organizations

Note: Overseas institutions include overseas subsidiaries, affiliates, universities, research institutes and companies.

Source: Compiled by the authors using database of JSTPlus (database of Japan Science and technology Agency).

After careful testing, from the early 1990s there are statistically significant differences in motivation to collaborate with external organizations for P&G and Unilever. The results clearly suggest that MNEs are increasingly creating knowledge strategically through joint research with researchers in overseas organizations to exploit the diversified knowledge obtainable from overseas organizations as firms expand into new products at global scale. Through the 2000s, P&G and Unilever have registered overseas dependency ratios of over 50 per cent in sales, while Kao's overseas dependency ratio is 20 per cent; and their number of internationally co-authored papers has increased dramatically. Therefore, we can conclude that Hypothesis 2 is supported for our chosen MNEs.

Hypothesis 3

Our third hypothesis is that MNEs in culture-specific industries have a higher tendency to leverage R&D capabilities in host-country subsidiaries, due to the difficulties in developing multi-domestic type products.

Figure 4.5 shows the ratio of research papers by authors working for MNE subsidiaries in host countries. Average ratios have consistently increased,

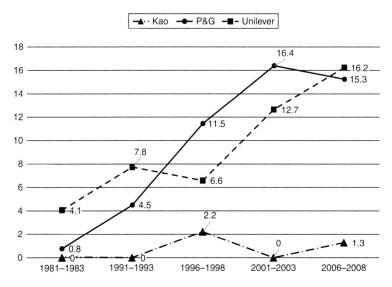

Figure 4.5   The ratio of research papers by authors belonging to MNEs subsidiaries
Note: Papers by overseas subsidiaries mean those written by researchers/engineers belonging to overseas subsidiaries.
Source: Compiled by the authors using database of JSTPlus (database of Japan Science and technology Agency).

from 1.6 per cent in 1981–1983 to 10.9 per cent in 2006–2008. P&G and Unilever, especially, increased from 1981–1983 to 2006–2008 – from 0.8 per cent to 15.3 per cent for P&G, and from 4.1 per cent to 16.2 per cent for Unilever. However, Kao's ratio, 1.3 per cent even in 2006–2008, indicates that it has not fully exploited host-country R&D capabilities, either because its subsidiaries are not competence-creating or its knowledge-creating mechanisms are poorly developed.

Two-way ANOVA without repetition was used to test for statistically significant differences between MNEs and between periods in the tendency to leverage R&D capabilities in host-country subsidiaries. Significance probability of 0.007 at firm level and 0.070 at the period level at 95 per cent significance suggests that differences in firm, but not differences in period, have positive effects on the tendency to leverage subsidiaries' R&D capabilities. We used Bonferroni multiple comparison analysis to test differences between firms. Between P&G and Unilever, significance probability is 1.00 and result was not significant at 95 per cent level, indicating that P&G and Unilever have similar tendencies in leveraging R&D in subsidiaries. However, the significant probability of Kao and P&G, and Kao and Unilever were 0.014 and 0.016 respectively, implying results between Kao and P&G, Kao and Unilever have significant differences in this area.

We can conclude that results support Hypothesis 3 for P&G and Unilever, but not for Kao; therefore, this hypothesis is only partially supported.

Hypothesis 4
Our final hypothesis is that, because of issues involved in developing multi-region or regionally preferred products, MNE subsidiaries in culture-specific industries have a higher tendency to enhance networking and collaborative research practices with external R&D organizations (such as local universities, public research institutes and local firms) in a host country.

Figure 4.6 demonstrates the ratios of jointly written papers by authors belonging to host-country subsidiaries and local organizations in host countries external to the MNE subsidiary.

As Figure 4.6 shows, in 1981–1983 the average ratio of papers written jointly between MNE-subsidiary researchers in a host country and researchers belonging to a research organization external to the MNE in that host country was below 1 per cent for the three MNEs – clear evidence that collaborative research between subsidiaries and local research organizations in a host country was not present. However, from 2001–2003, particularly

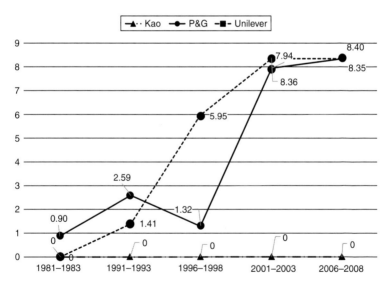

Figure 4.6   Ratios of jointly written papers by authors belonging to subsidiaries or local organizations in a host country external to the MNE subsidiary

Note: Joint paper between overseas subsidiaries and local institutions means those between overseas subsidiaries and local universities, research institutes, or companies.
Source: Compiled by the authors using database of JSTPlus (database of Japan Science and technology Agency).

2006–2008, the ratios for both P&G and Unilever exceeded 8 per cent, indicating that collaborative research between subsidiary R&D and local organizations external to the MNE had been implemented.

In addition to the above, if we include papers written jointly between researchers in subsidiaries and researchers in organizations located in a third country (excluding home country and host country of targeted subsidiary), ratios for both P&G and Unilever exceed 10 per cent. However, even in 2006–2008, we see no evidence of Kao subsidiaries performing collaborative research with organizations external to the host country.

We used two-way ANOVA without repetition for our statistical analysis to test whether there are statistically significant differences in tendency to enhance networking and collaborative research with external R&D organizations in host countries between MNEs and between time-periods, obtaining significance probability of 0.025 at firm level and 0.025 at period level at 95 per cent significance. Therefore, the results suggest that differences in firm have positive effects on the tendency to leverage subsidiary R&D capabilities, but not difference in periods (different time-periods do not affect the tendency). We used Bonferroni multiple comparison analysis to test differences between firms. Significance probabilities of 0.070 and 1.000 were found between P&G and Unilever, and Unilever and Kao respectively; the results, not significant at 95 per cent level, suggest that P&G–Unilever and Unilever–Kao have similar tendencies to enhance networking and collaborative research. However, the significant probability of Kao and P&G was 0.038, and this result suggests significant differences toward networking with external R&D organizations.

For Hypothesis 4, results are supportive for P&G and Unilever, but not for Kao; therefore, the hypothesis is partially supported.

For P&G and Unilever, our analysis suggests that the results support all our hypotheses; while for Kao, the results support Hypotheses 1 and 2 but not Hypotheses 3 and 4.

The number of national origins of affiliation (of authors involved in Unilever, P&G and Kao researchers and engineers) increased from 1981–1983 to 2006–2008. The ratios of Kao, P&G and Unilever in 1981–1983 were 1 country for Kao, 3 for P&G, and 15 for Unilever; in 2006–2008, the figures were 10, 25 and 31 countries respectively. Table 4.2 shows the evolution of national origins.

As Tables 4.2 and 4.3 demonstrate, national origins of affiliation have not merely increased in volume. There is also evidence that R&D output, in terms of number of papers, has been enhanced by variety in research teams, both MNE-subsidiary and university laboratories and other R&D laboratories in host developing countries. In particular, results from both P&G and Unilever suggest a clear evolution of R&D capabilities in subsidiaries in host developing countries such as India and China. On the other hand, results from Kao do not suggest such evolution, even in 2006–2008. Internationally

82

Table 4.2   National origins of affiliations of authors, 1981–1983

	National origin of authors	1981–1983 Unilever	Kao	P&G
1	Australia	(**)		
2	Belgium	*		(*)
3	Canada	*		
4	Switzerland	*		
5	Germany	(*)		
6	Spain	*		
7	Finland	(**)		
8	France	(*)		
9	Ireland	*		
10	Israel	*		
11	Japan	*	***	
12	Netherlands	***		
13	South Africa	*		
14	UK	***		(*)
15	USA	**		***
	Number of national origins of authors	15	1	3

Note: (1) * <4 papers, ** 5–9 papers, *** more than 10 papers. (2) Total number of national origins of authors means that of nationals of affiliations to which authors belonged. (3) Asterisks in parentheses show inclusion of papers written by researchers belonging to the overseas subsidiary; alternately, cases without parentheses show that papers are jointly written between researchers at home and overseas institutions.
Source: Compiled by the authors using database of JSTPlus (database of Japan Science and technology Agency).

Table 4.3   National origins of affiliations of authors, 2006–2008

	National origin of authors	2006–2008 Unilever	Kao	P&G
1	Australia	**		
2	Austria	*		**
3	Belgium	***	*	(***)
4	Bangladesh			*
5	Bulgaria	**		*
6	Canada	**	*	**
7	Switzerland	**	*	(**)
8	China	(***)		(**)
9	Czech Republic			*
10	Germany	(***)		***
11	Denmark	**		*
12	Spain	**	*	*
13	Finland	(*)		*
14	France	(***)		**
15	Greece	*		*

(continued)

Table 4.3   Continued

	National origin of authors	2006–2008		
		Unilever	Kao	P&G
16	Hungary	*		
17	India	(***)		*
18	Iran	*		
19	Italy	***	*	(**)
20	Jamaica	*		
21	Japan	*	***	(***)
22	Kenya	(*)		
23	Korea	(*)		**
24	Lithuania	*		
25	Mexico	*		
26	Netherlands	***	*	**
27	Norway			*
28	New Zealand	*		*
29	Poland	*		
30	Russia			*
31	Singapore			(*)
32	Sweden	***	*	*
33	Turkey			*
34	Taiwan	*		*
35	UK	***	*	(***)
36	Ukraine	*		
37	USA	(***)	*	***
Total number of national origins		31	10	27

Note: As Table 4.2.
Source: Compiled by the authors using database of JSTPlus (database of Japan Science and technology Agency).

co-authored papers have been conducted by Kao, but are limited to work between home-country R&D facilities and overseas universities.

4.8   Conclusion

We have sought to clarify the relationship between mechanisms of global knowledge transfer and creation by MNE groups and the source of global competitive advantages. We have also investigated how far national origins among R&D facilities have diversified and to what extent MNEs in culture-specific industries leverage local R&D personnel and construct R&D networking within the region in developing new products for enlarging regional markets.

Our findings suggest that MNEs' knowledge-creation mechanisms and innovation systems have evolved from an individually centred to organizationally collaborative research approach, from closed in-firm research to inter-organizational open research, and from research in one host country to exploiting global networks. Importantly, MNEs' specific strategic knowledge-creation systems have evolved from global R&D networks centred at home-country headquarters to subsidiary-driven R&D influenced by enhanced R&D capabilities and subsidiary evolution. Thus, MNEs' global strategic knowledge-creation systems have developed from a base of global R&D capabilities networks obtained by the MNE group as a whole. We have thus clarified that 'global mechanisms of strategic knowledge creation' by MNEs are sources of revised 'global competitive advantage' or 'global dynamic capabilities'. This differs from general and conventional views on sources of competitive advantage and dynamic capabilities, which discuss home-country research or global R&D capabilities in general. Here, analysis of R&D capabilities in overseas subsidiaries and mechanisms of knowledge transfer and creation through global R&D networking has been necessary to argue for knowledge-creation capabilities as a source of MNE-specific dynamic capabilities, rather than of firms in general.

Conventional literature on overseas subsidiaries has tried to categorize by level of subsidiary capabilities. We therefore focused on R&D capabilities in both home-country MNE headquarters and overseas subsidiary, and investigated the evolution of global knowledge creation in our selected culture-specific MNEs. We find that knowledge-creation and innovation systems have evolved from individually centred to organizationally collaborative research, from closed in-firm research to open inter-organizational research, and from single (host) country systems to global networks.

MNEs have developed global strategic knowledge-creation systems across a base of global R&D networks, but compared to P&G and Unilever, Kao, though developing its networking of global knowledge-creation, has not really achieved a level of exploitation commensurate with its own overseas subsidiaries' R&D facilities. This is a determinant of differences between MNEs with global innovation systems (e.g. P&G and Unilever) and MNEs without (e.g. Kao).

This research therefore suggests that to become a critical source of dynamic capabilities (i.e. competitive advantage) in the global market, firms need to look beyond a reliance on the kind of in-house central research (for patents, etc.) that Kao has concentrated on; such central research is necessary, but limited in effect. Rather, firms need not just to maintain central laboratories, but to look outward for knowledge creation appropriate to the modern climate of diversified global markets, as P&G and Unilever have successfully managed.

References

Asakawa, K. (2001a) 'Organizational Tension in International R&D Management: The Case of Japanese Firms,' *Research Policy*, 30(5): 735–757.

Asakawa, K. (2001b) 'Evolving Headquarters–Subsidiary Dynamics in International R&D: The Case of Japanese Multinationals,; *R&D Management*, 31(1): 1–14.

Asakawa, K. (2004) 'Co-evolution of National Innovation System and Organizational System: A Situation of Biotechnology Sector in Japan,' *Journal of Asian Business*, 20(3): 9–40.

Asakawa, K. (2006) 'Metanashonaru Keieiron Ni Okeru Ronten To Kongo No Kenkyuu No Houkousei' [Theoretical Issues and Directions in Meta-national Management],' *Sosikikagaku*, 40(1): 13–25.

Birkinshaw, J. and Hood, N. (1998) 'Multinational Subsidiary Evolution: Capability and Charter Change in Foreign-owned Subsidiary Companies,' *Academy of Management Review*, 23(4): 773–795.

Burgelman, R.A. (1983a) 'A Process Model of Internal Corporate Venturing in the Diversified Major Firm,' *Administrative Science Quarterly*, 28: 223–244.

Burgelman, R.A. (1983b) 'A Model of the Interaction of Strategic Behavior, Corporate Context and the Concept of Strategy,' *Academy of Management Review*, 8: 61–70.

Cantwell, J.A. (1987) 'The Reorganisation of European Industries after Integration: Selected Evidence on the Role of Transnational Enterprise Activities,' *Journal of Common Market Studies*, 26: 127–151.

Cantwell, J.A. (1989) *Technological Innovation and the Multinational Corporation* (Oxford: Basil Blackwell).

Cantwell, J.A. (1991) 'The International Agglomeration of R&D,' in M.C. Casson (ed.), *Global Research Strategy and International Competitiveness*. (Oxford: Basil Blackwell): 104–132.

Cantwell, J.A. (1994) 'Introduction,' in J.A. Cantwell (ed.) *Transnational Corporations and Innovatory Activities* (London: Routledge): 1–32.

Cantwell, J.A. (1995) 'The Globalisation of Technology: What Remains of the Product Cycle Model?,' *Cambridge Journal of Economics*, 19(1): 155–174.

Cantwell, J.A. and Mudambi, R. (2005) 'MNE Competence-creating Subsidiary Mandates,' *Strategic Management Journal*, 26(12): 1109–1128.

D'Cruz, J. (1986) *Strategic Management of Subsidiaries: Managing the Multinational Subsidiary* (London: Croom Helm).

Doz, Y.L. (2006) 'Meta Nashonaru Inobeishon Purosesu o Saitekika Suru (『メタナショナル・イノベーション・プロセスを最適化する』)'. *Soshikikagaku* (組織科学), 40(1): 4–12.

Doz, Y., Santos, J. and Williamson, P. (2001) *From Global to Metanational* (Boston, MA: Harvard Business School Press).

Dunning, J.H. (1996) 'The Geographical Sources of the Competitiveness of Firms: Some Results of a New Survey,' *Transnational Corporations*, 5: 1–29.

Florida, R. (1997) 'The Globalization of R&D: Results of a Survey of Foreign-affiliated R&D Laboratories in the USA,' *Research Policy*, 26(1): 85–103.

Hayashi, T. (2004) 'Gijutsukaihatsuryoku no Kokusaiteki Bunsanka To Shuuchuuka' (World Wide Dispersion and Concentration of R&D Capabilities, 技術開発力の国際的分散化と集中化) *Rikkyo Keizaigaku Kenkyu* (立教経済学研究), 57(3): 63–88.

Hayashi, T. and Serapio, M. (2006) 'Cross-border Linkages in Research and Development: Evidence from 22 US, Asian and European MNCs,' *Asian Business and Management*, 5(2): 271–298.

Iguchi, C. (2006) 'Subsidiary Evolution and the Emergence of Competence-creating Subsidiaries in Host Developing Countries,' *Ritsumeikan Business Review*, 45(1): 43–84.

Iguchi, C. (2008) 'Determinants of Backward Linkages: The Case of TNC Subsidiaries in Malaysia,' *Asian Business and Management*, 7(1): 53–73.

Iguchi, C. (2012) 'Globalisation of R&D by TNC Subsidiaries: The Case of South-East Asian Countries,' *Asian Business and Management*, 11(1): 79–100.

JSTPlus (database of Japan Science and Technology Agency available through Keio University's internal access).

Kogut, B. and Zander, U. (1993) Knowledge of the Firm and the Evolutionary Theory of the Multinational Corporation,' *Journal of International Business Studies*, 24(4): 625–45.

Kogut, B. and Zander, U. (1995) 'Knowledge and the Speed of the Transfer and Imitation of Organizational Capabilities,' *Organization Science*, 6(1): 76–91.

Kuemmerle, W. (1997) 'Building Effective R&D Capabilities Abroad,' *Harvard Business Review*, March–April: 61–70

OECD (2002) *Frascati Manual: Proposed Standard Practice for Surveys on Research and Experimental Development* (Paris: OECD).

Pearce, R.D. (1992) *The Determinants of Foreign Direct Investment* (New York: United Nations).

Pearce, R.D. (2001) 'Multinationals and Industrialisation: The Bases of "Inward Investment" Policy,' *International Journal of the Economics of Business*, 8(1): 51–73.

Pearce, R.D. and Papanastassiou, M. (1996) 'R&D Networks and Innovation: Decentralized Product Development in Multinational Enterprises,' *R&D Management*, 26(4): 315–333.

Rugman, A. and Verbeke, A. (1992) 'A Note on the Transnational Solution and the Transaction-Cost Theory of Multinational Strategic Management,' *Journal of International Business Studies*, 23: 761–772.

Serapio, M. and Hayashi, T. (eds) (2004) *Internationalization of R&D and the Emergence of Global R&D Networks* (London: Elsevier).

Teece, D.J. (2009). 'Dynamic Capabilities and the Essence of the Multinational Enterprise'. In: D.J. Teece (ed.) *Dynamic Capabilities and Strategic Management: Organizing for Innovation and Growth* (Oxford: Oxford University Press): 137–181.

UNCTAD (2005) *World Investment Report: Transnational Corporations and the Internationalization of R&D* (New York: United Nations).

Wernerfelt, B. (1984), 'A Resource-Based View of the Firm,' *Strategic Management Journal*, 5: 171–180.

White, R.E. and Poynter, T.A. (1984) 'Strategies for Foreign-owned Subsidiaries in Canada,' *Business Quarterly*, Summer: 59–69.

5
The New Face of Talent Management in Multinational Corporations: Responding to the Challenges of Searching and Developing Talent in Emerging Economies

Christian Schmidt, Sebastian Mansson, and Harald Dolles

5.1 Challenges of identifying and developing talent in emerging economies

In emerging economies, the shortage in the supply of skilled talent is a significant problem for human resources (HR) activities of established multinational corporations (MNCs). This is also true for emerging economies' new multinationals, particularly in filling leadership positions (Lim, Dai and Meuse, 2009; Sanyal, 2007; Schuler, Jackson and Tarique, 2011). When filling global leadership positions MNCs can either choose from acquiring or recruiting external talent, or identifying and developing internal talent (Caligiuri, 2006). It has been widely acknowledged that it is beneficial to invest resources in developing talented employees with the ability to adapt to various situations and fit into global roles. This has motivated MNCs to create talent management programs to develop and nurture their own future leaders (Collings and Mellahi, 2009; Hawser, 2008; Ready, Hill and Conger, 2008), with the ambition to maximize the potential of human capital and gain competitive advantage (Beechler and Woodward, 2009; De Pablos and Lytras, 2008).

It is argued that successful domestic managers cannot necessarily transfer that same level of success into the global arena (Jokinen, 2005). To complicate things further, some scholars argue that there is no universal consensus on a specific model of competencies or criteria for these global managers (Bartlett and Ghoshal, 1992; Baruch, 2002). The challenge for many MNCs has been to adapt traditional talent development practices to the global level and environment (Jokinen, 2005; Ready, Hill and Conger, 2008). This is predominantly true for established MNCs (defined in this chapter as MNCs from North America and Western Europe) operating in emerging markets, as successful practices 'at home' often require significant adaptation to be effective in a different environment (Björkman and Lu, 1999; Dolles and

Wilmking, 2005a, 2005b). It is further recognized that MNCs have a demand for leaders and managers that understand the operational conditions and business environment on the local level, while simultaneously understanding the firm's global strategy (Dolles and Wilmking, 2005a; Harvey, Speier and Novicevic, 1999). Some companies choose to recruit from the global open market, but according to Tan and Wellins (2006) this has yielded less than desirable results in attaining successful global leaders. These negative results are largely due to recruited leaders being poorly prepared and having high turnover. This suggests that it is beneficial for MNCs to develop local talent from subsidiary locations, so that a global mindset grows from a local emerging market perspective, which stays with that talented individual throughout their development (Caldwell and Xiong, 2010).

During the last decade, established MNCs have taken a significant amount of interest in the BRIC economies, and there has been a vast flow of foreign direct investment (FDI) into these countries. Of the BRIC countries, the People's Republic of China (hence: China) has displayed the highest economic growth and is becoming increasingly integrated into the global business environment (see among others Dolles, 2006; Kühlmann and Dolles, 2002). This economic development and the increasing activities of Chinese corporations abroad has led to a higher demand of, and talent management strategies for, Chinese nationals with talent and leadership potential (Caldwell and Xiong, 2010; Tung, 2008). However, many researchers find that China's supply of employees with the competencies and potential to develop into higher-level leaders within MNCs is limited. China's shortage in this talent pool of potential leaders is the largest among all BRIC economies, and it is within the global and executive leadership job function that it is experiencing the highest deficit (Dietz, Orr and Xing, 2008; Farrell and Grant, 2005; Ready, Hill and Conger, 2008; Tan and Wellins, 2006; Teagarden, Meyer and Jones, 2008). In the past, this shortage has forced established MNCs to bring in overseas Chinese and expatriates from Western economies to fill leadership positions. Now, the focus has strongly shifted toward developing local employees within China's domestic talent pool. There is a tendency for the MNCs' Chinese division to neglect or demonstrate indifference to global and strategic thinking. Thus, the development of global leadership skills in Chinese nationals represents an important strategic initiative for MNCs (Caldwell and Xiong, 2010). This focus on developing global leadership skills within Chinese nationals translates into developing local Chinese talents into potential global leaders. The general research question therefore is of high importance: how are MNCs' approaches to global talent identification and development for employees with global leadership potential structured and adapted to fit with the challenges of searching and advancing Chinese talent?

The chapter is structured in four main sections. It begins with developing the theoretical framework for research. Next the methodology is discussed and important sample characteristics provided. Finally, the results of our study are presented and discussed, followed by conclusions, managerial implications and suggestions for future research.

5.2 Theoretical research framework

5.2.1 Talent management

The literature points to a number of recurring themes, and there seems to be a consensus on one central and fundamental goal of talent management: finding the right person, at the right time, to put in the right position (Conger and Fulmer, 2003; Phillips and Edwards, 2009; Stainton, 2005; Watkin, 2007). Commonly talents are referred to as a certain pool of individuals categorized as 'talents' or 'high potentials,' with particular ability or possibility to have an immediate or future positive effect on corporations' performance (Brittain, 2007; CIPD, 2011; Stahl et al., 2007). But each organization has its own definition of talent (CIPD, 2011) and what constitutes a high potential employee (Stainton, 2005). Brittain (2007) argues that there are different levels of talents. High-potential talent concerns managers and leaders within the organization, and involves a small fraction of the entire internal workforce. In contrast, 'key talent' makes up a larger portion of employees and consists of employees that stay in the same positions for a much longer time. It is also argued that talent can be taken to include anyone at any level who can help an organization reach its goals and drive performance (Michaels, Handfield-Jones and Axelrod, 2001: viii).

The purpose of talent management is to develop an employee's potential into performance (Buckingham, 2005), and to maximize her/his potential (Guillory, 2009). Sullivan (2004) adds that the goal of the talent management process is also to increase overall workforce productivity through constantly improving the utilization, retention and attraction of talent. As such the specific goals and objectives of talent management go beyond the traditional, general HRM activities that apply to all employees. In addition, talent management is also considered to be more strategic in scope and integrated with overall corporative strategic goals (Lewis & Heckman, 2006). Furthermore, it seeks to integrate relevant HR practices into a seamless process (Sullivan, 2004). Hence, talent management involves all HR functions striving toward the same objective of managing the top talents within the firm. Talent management programs are usually designed to develop a company-wide, holistic mindset among employees that are seen as potential future leaders within the company by developing skills, competencies and behaviours that will contribute to successful careers (Iles, Chuai and Preece, 2010).

One vital trend in talent management is using internal talent pools to identify promising leaders among existing employees (Collings and Mellahi, 2009; Hawser, 2008). In a study conducted by Ready, Conger and Hill (2010), all of the companies in their sample stated that they purposely identify high-potential managers, and consider it to be one of the most crucial strategies to pursue. There are two essential phases of leadership management – identification and development (Tan and Wellins, 2006). Many large MNCs see benefits in monitoring the internal leadership pipeline for talents that have leadership potential, and there are certain development practices and programs focusing specifically on managing leadership talents (Conger and Fulmer, 2003; Groves, 2007). It is argued that improving internal development practices and programs and focusing on the internal talent will reap more benefits, such as cost advantages, productivity and a higher retention and success rate of actually developing future leaders, compared to bringing in talent from the open market (Crossland, 2005; Tan and Wellins, 2006). In regard to this, investing in the establishment and quality of internal talent pools of high-potential leaders is a key factor for companies that are successful at developing future leaders. This is further seen as a more favourable way of ensuring that companies find the right kind of leadership candidates for filling executive positions (Crossland, 2005; Watkin, 2007).

Conger and Fulmer (2003) state that in earlier times many companies kept their talent management initiatives and succession planning strategies separated. Additionally, many companies look upon succession planning as being equivalent to effective talent management, which is not the case (Kesler, 2002). There is a strong case, however, for companies to combine these two functions as they ultimately have the same final goal (Conger and Fulmer, 2003; Lewis and Heckman, 2006). In addition, Kesler (2002) concludes that companies garner the most benefit from using the entire leadership talent pipeline in the succession planning of managers, rather than limiting the selection to only a few employees. By integrating succession planning and talent management, companies can focus on which competencies need to be developed for certain individuals in the organization, as well as establishing an internal education system that works to develop those competencies (Conger and Fulmer, 2003).

5.2.2   Talent identification and development

The holistic process of talent management is described in the literature with several steps or phases (Boxall, Purcell and Wright, 2007; CIPD, 2011; Farley, 2005; McCauley and Wakefield 2006; Sharma and Bhatnagar, 2009). Some of these talent management phases include: attraction, recruitment, identification, selection, development, education, succession planning, retention and various ways of measuring and reviewing the result and performance of talent management's effectiveness. Generally it is argued that MNCs find greater value in developing a firm-specific definition of what talent management is (CIPD, 2011; Sullivan, 2004). However, Stahl et al. (2007) acknowledge the fact that there is a global convergence of talent practices and programs, and many companies tend to imitate and implement best practices.

Talent identification processes search for employees who are deemed to be high performers with high potential (Blass, 2007). When companies search for talent, one approach is to look for specific competencies. These might differ across companies based on a company's strategies, HR priorities and corporate values. Sample criteria include but are not limited to: leadership, judgment, accountability fulfilment, organization and planning, use of delegation, initiative, decisiveness, professional competence and problem analysis (Edwards and Bartlett, 1983). Another common approach is to look at capability frameworks. These are designed to capture personal traits, specific competencies and the capacity to develop. They typically include: cognitive ability, learning ability, cognitive complexity/capacity, emotional intelligence and personality traits (Corporate Leadership Council, 2003). As to the execution of talent identification, some companies shift the responsibility of talent identification to dedicated members of the HR department who collaborate with executives responsible for the assessments (Fulmer and Conger, 2004: 59). Another identification process that has emerged is known as an organizational talent review (OTR). During an OTR, high potentials go through an evaluation of a number of different criteria, such as their potential, learning agility, people skills and their ability to drive change (Aguirre, Post and Hewlett, 2009). An OTR can be conducted both by internal resources or outsourced for a third-party assessment (Watkin, 2007).

Once talents have been identified and selected within the MNC, the next step is *talent development*. Learning and performance development are cornerstones in this process, although the practices vary from trainee and early orientation programs to leadership development and executive training (Frank and Taylor, 2004). These practices entail the efficient administration of the HR departments' specialty and generalist functions, and different practices target different kinds of development (Lewis and Heckman, 2006). This is a subjective process and there is no common standard that runs true across all companies. Additionally, Barlow (2005) emphasizes that differences in current talents' skills and abilities result in different learning and development potential. It is also argued that in addition to each individual's unique capacity to learn and develop in different ways, development should also be dependent upon that individual's likely career trajectory.

5.2.3 Talent management and culture

MNCs operate in the context of two different types of culture – national culture and corporate culture – where the former refers to the set of common beliefs and values of a nation and the latter to the set of common beliefs and values of a firm. This distinction is important for two reasons. First, the national culture of the home country of an MNC has a significant impact on corporate culture (Derr, Roussillon and Bournois, 2002; Schein, 2009; Dolles and Takahashi, 2011). This is also known as the country-of-origin effect, where the national culture of the MNC has a strong influence on the management style and employment practices of the MNC worldwide (Dolles and Takahashi, 2011; Edwards, 2011). Second, the national culture of an employee has a significant impact on how that employee thinks and operates (Derr, Roussillon and Bournois, 2002). An employee's national culture will influence her/his professional behaviour and shape their expectations of how a company should operate. The different types of behaviour and expectations that result from different cultures influences how well employees function within a specific MNC.

While several models of culture have been developed, Schein's framework (originally presented in 1985) and the interpretation by Derr and Laurent (1989) are helpful to further structure the analysis. Schein (2004: 17) defines culture as

> a pattern of shared basic assumptions that was learned by a group as it solved its problems of external adaptation and internal integration, that has worked well enough to be considered valid and, therefore, to be taught to new members as the correct way to perceive, think, and feel in those problems.

He discusses three different levels (Schein, 2004, 2009): first, *artifacts* refer to visible manifestations of a culture; second: *espoused beliefs and values* are the guiding beliefs and preferences of a culture; third, *basic assumptions* are the invisible, preconscious or unconscious, non-debatable, underlying cognitive structures that determine how people from that culture think, feel and perceive. Basic assumptions are what give meaning to the values and norms. Derr and Laurent (1989) interpret Schein's three levels of culture as a triangle to illustrate how these different levels of culture relate to an MNCs corporate culture, as can be seen in Figure 5.1.

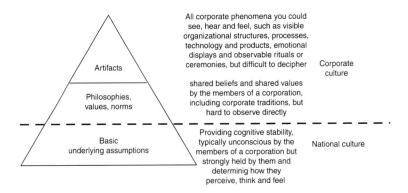

Figure 5.1   National and corporate culture
Source: Based upon Derr and Laurent (1989); Schein (2004, 2009).

Derr, Roussillon and Bournois (2002) argue that leadership development within MNCs must consider the cultural backgrounds of its employees. Rowley et al. (2011) conclude that HRM practices, such as leadership development, that are developed in one context cannot be presumed to be completely functional and appropriate in other regions of the world, where people have significantly different values. This is confirmed by previous studies on expatriation, such as those by Stahl (1997) and Dolles (2002). An individual's cultural background has a strong influence on their cognitive maps, values, demeanour and language (Dolles, 1997; Morlok and Dolles, 2005a, 2005b), which could have impacts on the appropriateness and effectiveness of HRM practices such as leadership development. Taking those arguments into consideration, we need to investigate how Schein's three levels of culture fit into a model that relates culture and leadership development. The proposed model (see Figure 5.2) refers to Derr and Laurent (1989), Derr, Roussillon and Bournois (2002) and builds upon Schein's levels of culture to show how national culture and organizational culture interact in leadership development, as demonstrated by the arrows.

The model builds upon a corporation's national culture or the basic assumptions according to Schein's framework, and indicates that the home national culture influences the corporate culture of an MNC as well as the cognitive maps of its home-country employees. The corporate culture significantly influences how leaders are identified and developed (leadership dynamics). The factor 'individual differences of competencies' takes into account that even within one national culture not all people have the same exact cognitive map, and there are individual differences based on learning and experiences that shape the way individuals behave and operate. Derr, Roussillon and Bournois (2002: xiv) emphasize that 'people are noted for their ability to make personal choices and deviate from family and cultural values. There are diverse personal experiences within any common context.'

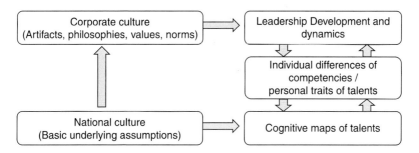

Figure 5.2 Leadership dynamics and culture
Source: Based upon Derr and Laurent (1989); Derr, Roussillon and Bournois (2002); Schein (2004, 2009).

Several authors have argued that culture is a major challenge that needs to be taken into consideration when transferring HRM practices and programs from the home country to China (Easterby-Smith, Malina and Lu, 1995; Warner, 1998). Björkman and Lu argued as early as 1999 that MNCs need to adapt leadership development practices to the Chinese business environment. This can be understood if one considers that the effectiveness of HRM practices largely depend on the degree to which those practices fit the values and beliefs of the host country (Huo and Von Glinow, 1995). This phenomenon is often described in terms of best practices versus best fit, and researchers have generally found that HRM is one of the business functions that attempts to maintain the national flavour of the MNC's home country, while still adjusting to local conditions (Brewster and Mayrhofer, 2011). Empirical findings indicate that this adjustment does take place and that these practices are adapted locally (Björkman et al., 2008). However, a recent qualitative study by Hartmann, Feisel and Schober (2010) found that there is little to no cultural adaptation of talent management practices in China.

We summarize the discussion above, by asking a second – more specific – research question: how are MNCs' talent management and leadership development practices and programs adapted to fit the local Chinese culture, and what are the specific challenges resisting within?

5.2.4   Leadership and culture

Leadership values and the importance of leadership vary across cultures. Effective leadership behaviour or practices in one culture can be completely ineffective in another. For that reason ITAP International (2011) argues that a single global leadership-development approach across an international organization will not work when developing global leaders. Furthermore, Peterson and Hunt (1997), writing specifically on American concepts, state that the common American understanding of the concept of leadership is specific to America and may not be applicable or practical when applied to different cultures, especially to Chinese society. They further argue that the American concept of leadership may be fitting for capturing the American conceptualization of leadership, but transferring this concept globally will pose difficulties. This is not only true for American concepts of leadership, but can be applied to the understanding of other countries' leadership concepts as well.

The GLOBE study revealed that different cultures yield different culturally implicit theories of leadership (House et al., 2004). It was also discovered that certain leadership attributes exist that are universally desirable or undesirable across cultures. This is important to consider for global leadership development within MNCs to decide which leadership competencies are to be developed. In order to operate effectively as a leader, an individual must first be perceived as a leader by the people he/she is leading (Gerstner and Day, 1994). If the leadership competencies developed by leadership development practices and programs in MNCs are not perceived as leadership competencies by employees in the host country, problematic issues could potentially develop (ibid.).

We summarize the discussion above, by asking the third question in our research: to what extent is the corporate framework of how leaders should behave, both at lower and higher levels of responsibilities, transferred and implemented in a globally standardized talent management and leadership development system, and to what extent is this practiced in China?

5.3 Methodology

5.3.1 Research sample

We pursued non-random, purposeful sampling and created a maximum variation sample in order to garner a greater diversity of perspectives even from a relatively small sample. With this in mind, we targeted MNCs from different countries and different industries, and interviewed employees that worked either at the MNC headquarters, in China, or held significant global responsibility for talent management and leadership development. Additionally, we only approached MNCs that employed at least 5,000 employees worldwide, and employed Chinese nationals in China.

We chose to approach most of the largest companies in Sweden, owing to their availability and geographical proximity. Because of this, we were also able to conduct face-to-face interviews with all but one of the respondents located in Sweden. As a measure to control for a Swedish bias in the sample we also developed a non-Swedish control group, selected within the list of Fortune 500 companies. Four MNCs based in USA, Switzerland, The Netherlands and Germany responded positively to our inquiry, enough to allow for some confidence regarding the internal validity of any consequent findings. At the end of this process, we developed a sample of 14 MNCs with operations in China (see Table 5.1 for further sample characteristics). In the beginning we assumed that any significant difference between the Swedish and the foreign sample might be due to country-specific aspects. However, as the analysis showed, there was no significant difference between the practices applied in Swedish and foreign MNCs, except when addressing aspects of organizational culture. We therefore combined both samples within the analysis and only separate both in this chapter when discussing organizational culture.

5.3.2 Data collection, analysis and limitations

The interviews were set up and conducted during spring 2011 (for details refer to Mansson and Schmidt, 2011). To improve the interview protocol's questions, we conducted two shorter pilot interviews and received feedback on the questions from tutors and fellow researchers. A total of 22 interviews were conducted and recorded. Ten interviews were conducted in Swedish,

Table 5.1 Sample characteristics

Metrics / Company	Country-of-origin	Industry	Revenue 2010 (bln$)[3]	Countries active in	Year of entry in China	Employees Worldwide (China)	Interviewee title(s)
Company A	Switzerland / Sweden	Power & Automation Technology	31.6	100	1979	116500 (10000)	Talent Manager Northern Europe, Learning & Dev.; Regional Talent Manager for North Asia Region
Company B	Sweden	Pharmaceuticals	33.3	100	1993/94	60000 (4500)	Global Leadership Talent Development Partner; Global Talent Development Director
Company C	Sweden	Construction & Mining, Power Tools, Assembly Systems, Compressors	11.6	170	1983	33000 (4300)	VP China Investment Company
Company D	Sweden	Home Electric Appliances	17.7	150	1993	52000 (<2000)	Senior Learning & Development Manager; Director Head of HR in China
Company E	Sweden	Tele-communication Services	33.8	190	1892	90400 (12000)	Head of Global Leadership Talent Planning; Head of HR in China & North East Asia; Director for Executive Development

Company	Country	Industry					Position
Company F	USA	Conglomerate	150	100		300000 (14000)	Manager Global Recruiting & Staffing Services; Manager of HRM Organizational Dev. in Asia China
Company G	Sweden	Health Care	1.4	30	2006	7000 (70)	Global HR Director, Leadership and Capability Dev.
Company H	Switzerland	Food & Nutrition	126.9	140	1908	280000 (4000)	HR Operations Manager, Zone Africa, Oceania & Asia
Company I	The Netherlands	Electronics	37.1	100	1920	200000 (1100)	Senior Director Talent Management, Learning & Organizational Development
Company J	Sweden	Global Hygiene & Paper	18.1	100	1998	45000 (950)	VP Management & Organizational Development
Company K	Sweden	Commercial Vehicles	13	100	1996/97	34000 (50)	Head of Competence Development; Product Manager for Leadership Training
Company L	Sweden	Engineering	10.1	130	1916	45000 (4800)	Senior VP Group Demand Chain; Director of Talent Management
Company M	Sweden	Automotive	18.8	100	2006	20000 (100)	VP HR, Talent Management
Company N	Germany	Engineering	19.1	50	1998	70000 (4000)	Deputy General Manager Finance/IT in Shanghai

and 12 were conducted in English. Eleven interviews were conducted face-to-face in Sweden, and the remaining 11 interviews were phone interviews. In order to mitigate disadvantages of phone interviews, such as misunderstandings or lack of focus, we followed the suggestion by Anderson and Arsenault (1998: 192) that the effectiveness of phone interviews can be enhanced by establishing pre-contact with the interviewees.

By using the NVivo 9 software for qualitative data analysis, we applied a qualitative content analysis as described by Mayring (1995) to analyse the transcribed interviews. We also applied measures of data triangulation to increase the validity of our study, such as interviewing more than one person in the MNC (14 companies, 22 interviews) and asking clarifying questions when something was unclear in order to increase the accuracy of the information retrieved. With that said, there is always an issue of how much information the respondents are willing to provide, especially information regarding company challenges. However, based on the recommendation by Strauss and Corbin (1990), we tried to establish an open environment in our interviews, where the respondents felt comfortable speaking about difficulties and challenges.

This study is only focused on established MNCs, and therefore the perspectives of emerging new multinationals from China are missing. We only interviewed the people administering the talent management practices and procedures in MNCs. Speaking with actual talents about their experiences with leadership development would have yielded a different perspective. With regard to the sample size, while 14 MNCs (22 interviews) provides a sufficient sample size for a qualitative study, the next step to be taken up in research might be a quantitative study that uses a larger number of MNCs.

5.4   Empirical findings

5.4.1   MNCs' approaches to global talent identification and development

The findings to our general research question – 'How are MNCs' approaches to global talent identification and development for employees with global leadership potential structured and adapted to fit with the challenges of searching and advancing Chinese talent?' – could be summarized as follows: 11 MNCs (out of 14) clearly stated that the identification process of talent within the company looks the same worldwide. While identification practices take place locally, the same platform and protocol of finding internal talents are used globally. Talents are measured against the same leadership criteria and competencies everywhere within MNCs. In regard to China, decisions as to who is identified and selected for leadership development practices and programs are local responsibilities, but the processes and standards come from headquarters. Only two MNCs explained that although there is a standard identification approach, various degrees of local adaptations exist as of today. For instance, Company H explained that best practices are developed and shared across all its markets. Most HR initiatives are rolled out globally, but Company H is flexible as to the timing the market adopts to implement the global initiatives. This is very much the case in China, where scale can stretch the resources in a growing organization. Additionally, Company L also mentioned that its identification process is currently different depending on where a person is in the organization. However, the same company also mentioned that it is in the midst of creating and implementing a more standardized process worldwide.

MNCs have different approaches to developing talent across their global operations. These approaches range from a high degree of standardization across different countries to high degrees of freedom by local operations to choose which programs and practices they want to use. Also, MNCs differ in the level to which global talent management practices can be adapted to local environments. The majority of MNCs transfer some standardized leadership development programs to China. For example, Company D's leadership programs look exactly the same on a global level, and it has developed a clear manual and instructions on how the instructor should act, what he/she should include, and how the program should be run. The only adaptation is in regard to language on the basic leadership level for newly appointed leaders. Five MNCs have specific programs created for China or the Asia-Pacific region. For example, Company N has a China Leadership Program for developing employees who have the potential to move into a manager role. It needs to be clarified, however, that this is on a lower leadership level, and the next-level leadership development course is global. This trend is common for the other MNCs that have country-specific or China-specific leadership development programs.

Most MNCs stated that the higher and more global level of leadership, the more standardized the practices and programs are. A good example of this is Company K's 'Manager and Leadership Education System.' At lower levels of leadership responsibilities, programs for things such as business acumen and communication are the responsibility of the local HR department, although there are strong guidelines on how they should be structured. Regarding higher-level leadership programs, Company K uses standardized global program offerings in all countries.

With regard to how long each MNC has been active in the Chinese market and its implications for local leadership development, the MNCs in our sample can be split into two broad groups – entry into China before 1921 (five MNCs), and entry into China after 1979 (nine MNCs). There are no strong differentiating trends between these groups when it comes to levels of adaptation in their practices to China. An equal number of both categories have China- or Asia-specific development programs for Chinese or Asian talents. With regard to difficulties in developing talents in China the post-1979 group displayed a higher frequency of retention difficulties than the pre-1921 group. This could perhaps be explained by the fact that the pre-1921 MNCs already had a kind of brand equity in China and therefore the names and products of those MNCs seemed to be more attractive and well known to potential employees. Additionally, the pre-1921 group experienced a higher frequency of difficulty with developing English language capabilities than the post-1979 group. However, although our study was not meant to investigate this question, possible explanations could be the age group of employees attracted to the companies, the general knowledge of English at the time of entry as well as initial location decisions. We need, however, clearly state that between 1941 and 1979 no Western firm had significant operations in China, thus making the potential in-house knowledge about the Chinese market fairly useless. In reality we need to consider that all foreign companies started from 'scratch' in China when economic reform began in the 1980s.

With regard to number of employees in China, some trends within our sample emerged as well. It was much more common for MNCs with 2,000 or more employees in China to have China- or Asia-specific leadership development programs than those with fewer than 2,000 employees. This could potentially be explained by the fact that MNCs must be able to achieve some sort of economies of scale effect in order to make a China- or Asia-specific leadership development program financially viable. With regard to difficulties faced in China, the MNCs with 2,000 employees or less in China cited more frequently that one of the difficulties faced was that Chinese nationals had different perspectives on leadership that differed from their organizational definition of leadership.

5.4.2   Specific challenges of adapting talent identification to the conditions in China

The findings in regard to the second – more specific – research question – 'How are MNCs' talent management and leadership development practices and programs adapted to fit the local Chinese culture, and what are the specific challenges resisting within?' – can be summarized rather coherently in our sample, as none of the MNCs mentioned significant difficulties in transferring the identification processes of their talent management approach. The guidelines of how to identify and select talents for development toward higher-level leadership positions are highly standardized within most MNCs. Only one MNC stated that although the guidelines of what leadership criteria and competencies talents ought to be measured and evaluated against is determined from headquarters, the responsibility of how to implement and adapt the process of finding and selecting talents is local. Additionally, MNCs do not only have internally standardized identification processes; they also display a trend of moving toward an even higher degree of internal standardization and control of reviewing talent. For example, Company L is looking to implement a standardized global identification processes, and Company J states that 'It is not in our philosophy to have a standardized plan for all individuals, but we have exactly the same approach globally of how it [the leadership identification and development process] should look like.'

The use of individual development plans (IDP) and talent reviews encountered no difficulty, and there were virtually no incompatibilities between the organizational culture of the MNC and the Chinese national culture. With that said, MNCs experienced some difficulty in transferring development processes of their talent management approach. For example, MNCs encountered difficulty in sending Chinese nationals on international assignments:

> ... mobility is a big problem. It is not easy to get Chinese to move somewhere else in the world, they want to stay in China. But at the same time, China is so big so why should [I] move somewhere else? ... So this is a tough challenge. (Company J)

These difficulties can be linked to differences in the organizational culture of MNCs and the Chinese national culture. International assignments and job rotations are part of the organizational culture of MNCs, and future leaders are expected to take part in these practices as part of their development. Many MNCs indicated that international assignments are more important practices for the leadership development process of Chinese employees than their Western counterparts. Several MNCs mentioned that Chinese talents face difficulty in succeeding at higher levels of leadership within the MNC, because they can be less accustomed to global interaction with a variety of different cultures and are not as comfortable socializing with colleagues from other countries. This can give the impression that Chinese talents are shy or timid, when in reality there is a language and lack of experience barrier that acts as a speed bump to Chinese talents' climb up the MNC's corporate ladder. Based on this, international assignments give Chinese employees the opportunity to spend time in an international context and gain the international exposure needed to develop a more global mindset. It was stated in the interviews that family ties create a cultural difficulty when MNCs want Chinese nationals go on extended international assignments in order to gain experience so that they can move into higher leadership positions. These family ties make mobility a barrier to develop Chinese global leaders as, for example, emphasized by Company N in our interviews:

> Chinese nationals need to take care for their parents, their parents are not leaving the country so Chinese nationals need to go back to their home town. ... So if they want to move to South America, they need to take their parents. Do they want to go? No. So they do not go.

5.4.3   Specific challenges of transferring leadership values to talent management in China

The third research question – 'To what extent is the corporate framework of how leaders should behave, transferred and implemented in a globally standardized talent management and leadership development system, and to what extent is this practiced in China?' – received mixed answers. The MNCs in our sample demonstrated a clear understanding of what leadership stands for in their company, and that it is important that this perspective is transferred worldwide. For instance, Company J explained that the experience of its organizational culture is that when meeting a group of people from other countries, one can immediately tell who is a Company J employee and who is not. Thus, in order to ensure that a MNC-specific leader follows the same basic principles, and has the fundamental competencies needed to develop toward higher-level leadership positions, it is central that the same identification tool is used globally. In the context of this discussion, it needs to be highlighted that a few MNCs pointed out that the intention of identification, and perhaps even more development, is not to force the MNC's organizational culture upon individuals. Instead, our interpretation is that the ambition for some MNCs is to find individuals who fit in with the MNC's organizational culture. When doing so it is important that all these leadership talents share a common set of competencies and personal traits, regardless of national culture.

MNCs adapt leadership development practices in China to varying extents. The level of the adaptation of leadership development practices varies based on the specific leadership development practice and on the specific MNC. With regard to leadership development programs, there are different degrees of adaptation. The leadership development practices largely adhere to the structure and guidelines established by the headquarters of the MNCs; in some cases no adaptations are made, and trainers from the MNC's headquarters administer the development practices worldwide to ensure that they follow standard protocol. Some MNCs allow these globally standardized programs to be locally adapted in relatively small ways, such as using the local language while keeping the content exactly the same. This is in line with Hartmann, Feisel and Schober's (2010) findings on HRM practices (not necessarily leadership identification and development), that MNCs transfer HRM practices to China relatively unchanged. 'They basically look the same. We have no special processes or documents for China, the same values and foundations are valid there as well' (Company D).

Other MNCs allow greater levels of adaptations based on cultural differences. The greatest adaptations were displayed in the establishment of China-specific leadership development programs. These programs were specifically designed with the development needs of Chinese nationals in mind, and thus are different than any other country-specific leadership development program that may exist in the MNCs. These types of localized programs were recommended by Björkman and Lu (1999). One example of this is Company N's 'China Leadership Program.' After being identified by their managers, talents from different locations in China are sent to participate in this program when they first become managers within the company. The program runs every two years, and is focused on leadership in the China region. With that said, all MNCs indicated that there was a certain core value of principles and guidelines that must be adhered to, regardless of cultural differences.

Additionally, at higher levels of leadership development programs, the level of adaptation to China and Asia decreased significantly. Once leaders were responsible for regional or global operations, there was a certain standard of leadership competencies that had to be met, regardless of whether or not that leader was from China or any other country. Thus, when operating on a global level of leadership, no customization or special attention is given to any country. Company M holds this to be true by stating that regardless of where people are coming from; '... they [have] got to be people who can actually operate globally as leaders in a global corporation.'

5.5   Analysis and discussion

One could argue that when a foreign MNC is establishing operations in China, that the MNC's corporate culture would be influenced by Chinese national culture. This is confirmed by our research for the subsidiary level in China and local levels of leadership, but there was no indication by our interviewees that elements of the local Chinese subsidiary culture could make their way into the home-country corporate culture of the MNCs (see Figure 5.3). On the contrary, our interview partners solely emphasized the role of a strong 'home' corporate culture having an impact on local subsidiary management, and thus the role of the foreign subsidiary to act as a change agent in the Chinese context.

These aspirations to transfer Western organizational leadership principles relates back to Schein's (2004) definition of culture, as Western MNCs have found success with their global leadership styles in the past, and have no reason to believe they will not work in China. Although Rowley et al. (2011) argue that HRM practices developed in one culture cannot be presumed to be effective in other cultures, where people have different values and perspectives, MNCs on the contrary believe this approach to be effective and successful: '[Are these processes completely standardized?] Yes. So far we have had this approach and system for three years and it has worked surprisingly well. We have not done any changes or encountered any problems' (Company A).

The global talent management approach by the companies in our sample is relatively centralized in the form of which and how processes are supposed to be transferred and implemented. The Western perception of a global leader may not be in sync with the Chinese perception of a global

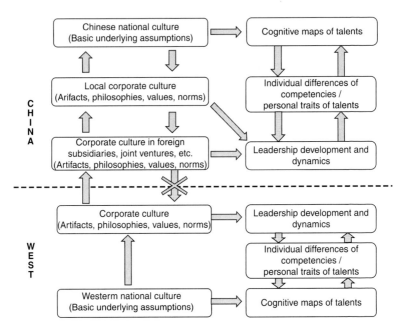

Figure 5.3   Interaction between two cultures' leadership dynamics
Source: Schmidt, Mansson and Dolles (2013: 13).

leader, but the way MNCs are addressing the shortage of Chinese global leaders tends to be to standardize a global talent management approach. So far MNCs have actively been developing Chinese leaders by using this global approach for a limited time. In line with Lewis and Heckman's (2006) research, MNCs stated that it is important to align and integrate talent management goals with their business strategies, and that talent management is a growing priority in China as China is increasingly becoming a key market for many MNCs. Additionally, many MNCs stated that there is a huge leadership talent pool available in China, but that the majority of this talent pool is very young and have not worked for the company a long time.

When discussing the degree to which adaptations are made to talent management processes in China, two of five non-Swedish MNCs explicitly mentioned that at some point, corporate culture is non-negotiable and there comes a point where local adaptation is no longer acceptable for subsidiaries. For example, Company F states that,

> The core of what we do is the same everywhere. It is adapted locally to some degree to fit the culture and to fit the needs of the country, but for the most part, we have a common view of leadership and common training processes. ... I think it's more common than you think.

Swedish companies respond to this same point with more regularity; eight of nine Swedish MNCs mentioned that up to a certain point, corporate culture is non-negotiable. For instance Company B holds that,

> One of our objectives as a company is to ... build local leaders who can lead globally. So at the end of the day we are a global organization, we do have to be able to work across regions and some of those things are not negotiable. ... So there are some things that you just say 'it is.' And that's working for us.

Based on this, our research suggests that Swedish MNCs advocate for stronger adherence to their company standards than others. Overall, we conclude the high emphasis placed by our interview partners on home-country corporate culture supports our findings towards research question two, that while there is a degree of adaptation in leadership development processes, these adaptations are limited and do not supersede the corporate cultural norm for leadership (research question three).

5.6   Conclusions

5.6.1   Adaptation or global standardization

It was our initial assumption, well supported by the literature, that talent management and leadership development practices are adapted locally, and that there is a crucial need for local adaptation in order to work successfully with Chinese counterparts. However, the experiences that MNCs shared with us during the research show that MNCs have limited or no adaptations of the overall approach to talent management in China, and if there are adaptations, that these come at the lowest levels of leadership development (subsidiary level). At higher levels of leadership, there are virtually no adaptations, and all countries, including China, adhere to, and are measured against, the internal global standard set by the individual MNC, deeply rooted in the corporate as well as their home-country culture.

While the identification process of finding and selecting internal talents for leadership development practices and programs is globally standardized within the vast majority of MNCs, the actual development process is slightly adapted. Leadership development practices at lower levels of leadership tend to be adapted to local needs, although there is a consistent emphasis that MNCs do not compromise on their leadership values and principles. Leadership development practices at higher levels of leadership, such as global leadership positions, are globally standardized. When operating at a global level, talents are expected to adhere to global internal standards, and we did not identify any special consideration based on Chinese talents' national culture.

Figure 5.4 describes MNCs' global approaches to leadership development within talent management. The leadership development focus, represented by the y-axis, reflects our finding that on lower levels of leadership development, the focus tends to be on how to lead people and leadership behaviour within the MNC. At higher levels of leadership development, however, our findings indicate that these programs are more focused on strategic and global leadership. In general, the x-axis shows that at higher levels of leadership development there is more focus and strategy-related issues and an overall high degree of standardization. Additionally, the basic level leadership development has different degrees of standardization among the MNCs within our research sample, with some using specific practices and programs for China and others using largely standardized content. The 'X' in the top left corner shows that no MNCs have low degrees of standardization in strategy-focused leadership development.

With this standardized corporate approach to talent management and leadership development, one step that becomes crucial in order to identify and develop internal leadership talents is to have a well-functioning and effective external recruitment system. This is especially true considering that the leadership competencies and personal traits included in the leadership identification framework are rooted in Western MNCs' national culture. Since national cultures are different, it is important to identify leadership talent that fit and match the specific MNC's corporate culture. This is also found by Tarique and Schuler (2009), who contend that the objective of talent management is to find individuals that match the firm's goals in a global environment. The fact that many MNCs stated that the similarities

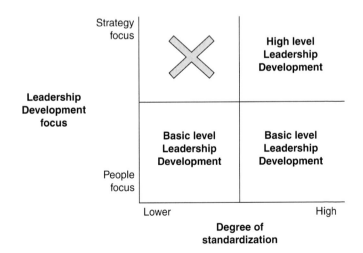

Figure 5.4   The global approach to leadership development within talent management

between Western and Chinese people are larger than the differences might be an understanding that has developed out of having a recruitment system at the subsidiary level that focuses on employing Chinese nationals with Western mindsets. Thus, when MNCs experience that there are relatively few difficulties in identifying or developing Chinese nationals, this may be due to MNCs actively recruiting Chinese talents that have already been exposed to another MNC's Western corporate culture, and therefore are able to more easily transition to a new MNC.

Although the MNCs in the study are acknowledging a shortage of global leaders sourced in China, they do not face any significant difficulties with transferring their talent management and leadership development approach. The companies in our sample are also not experiencing any major difficulties with implementing and executing their global approach. To address this, we would like to suggest two plausible explanations that have emerged from our findings as to why most MNCs do not experience difficulties when transferring a standardized talent management system (Schmidt, Mansson and Dolles, 2013).

The first explanation is that Western MNCs are attracting and recruiting Chinese talents with a Western mindset, and that Chinese nationals are adapting to the Western concept of leadership; not the other way around. The majority of this group is discussed in the literature as 'new argonauts,' 'sea turtles,' or 'cosmopolitans' who return to China after having gained educational and professional experiences abroad – refer, for example, to the 108 success stories of Chinese returnees assembled by Zhang, Wang and Alon (2011); investigations on Chinese high-skilled returnees after taking advanced degrees in Australia by Hao and Welch (2012); the work by Saxenia (2006) on 'new argonauts,' coming from one country, learning the complexities of a foreign technology cluster and taking this knowledge back home, thus becoming strategic agents in the spread of dynamic high technology clusters around the globe; or articles in Chinese media, e.g. *China Daily*, 2008. Further emphasis on high-skilled returnees is placed by the Chinese government, even including this strategic target in middle- and long-term development plans like the National Plan for Medium- and Long-term Scientific and Technological Development (2006–2020), the National Plan for Medium- and Long-term Human Resources Development (2010–2020) and the National Plan for Medium- and Long-term Education Reform and Development 2010–2020 (State Council, 2006, 2010a, 2010b, as cited in Hao and Welch, 2012).

The discussion might be summarized within the context of our research, that this type of returning and emerging Chinese 'cosmopolitans' openly embrace Western managerial individualistic values. Ralston et al. (1996) stress two aspects of Western management styles that Chinese 'cosmopolitans' adapt: first is openness to change – willingness to accept new ideas and ways of doing things; and second is self-enhancement – attaching greater attention to social power than traditional, local Chinese. If this is the type of Chinese leadership talents that MNCs attract, then most likely the difficulties MNCs experience could be perceived as a minor obstacle in talent management and leadership development.

As a second explanation we might consider the time lag responsible for the shortage of global leadership talent in China. Many companies have not actively been transferring their talent management and leadership development systems to China for too long, especially relative to how long they have been implemented in their home countries. Company loyalty is a significant aspect when selecting internal talents for global leadership development practices and programs, and many MNCs stated that they do not want to spend resources on leadership talents that they are not sure will stay at the company. Thus, as of today, relatively few Chinese leadership talents have been exposed to and formally trained in the Western organizational leadership culture and are hence lacking long-term experience with Westernized global leadership values and principles.

5.6.2   Managerial implications

Our research has clearly indicated that MNCs have a defined vision of what leadership encompasses within their own companies. They have also explained that this perception of leadership should be the same worldwide. Thus, it is vital for MNCs that there is a universal understanding throughout the company of what specific leadership competencies and values pervade the corporate culture. Having globally standardized processes of how to identify and develop leadership talents helps to transfer these corporate leadership culture principles worldwide, including to China, and this is the approach that most MNCs use. However, it is also crucial in that sense to analyse how these leadership competencies reveal themselves in different cultures to understand the gaps that need to be filled. The execution and effectiveness of the link between leadership talent identification and development therefore becomes an important part of both talent management and leadership development. Our research indicates that this link is what characterizes individual differences that should have an impact on the leadership dynamics of talents.

Our research has also shown that culture is not a significant barrier when implementing a globally standardized talent management and leadership development process in China, which deviates from previous research. The reason for this may be that MNCs attract Chinese nationals who have developed a Western mindset, i.e. cosmopolitans. Given the fact that MNCs do have certain leadership criteria specific to each MNC's corporate culture, it is also these cosmopolitans that MNCs should try to not only identify within the company, but also recruit and acquire externally.

Another important aspect of our research is that MNCs point out that there is a lack of Chinese leadership talents with enough experience working in a Western organizational context, thereby suggesting a time lag. Thus, we conclude that because of this time lag, MNCs need to have patience with their standardized talent management approach, and be diligent in making sure that the processes are completely universal within their company. There is no need to rush or force the development of Chinese talents for global leadership positions if the MNCs believe and hold their own leadership visions to be as important as we have found in our research. Promoting Chinese talents to higher-level or global leadership positions prematurely without understanding and embodying the MNC's corporate culture could yield significant problems. It does not matter what national culture talents originate from, they all need to share and believe in the same principles and values emphasized by MNCs' unique corporate cultures.

5.6.3 Further research

Our research supports Brewster and Mayrhofer's (2011) finding that HRM is a business function that maintains the home country's organizational culture, while adjusting to local conditions. These practices are not necessarily standard across all MNCs, but might be considered instead as practices most compatible with the MNC's organizational culture. Additionally, our research shows that the adjustment to local conditions is rather weak as MNCs want to have more global control by using a system that allows them to monitor and make its internal talent visible throughout the company. Those findings are, however, based on a rather small qualitative sample of predominantly Swedish MNCs. Further investigations, also including MNCs with their home base in the US or in other European countries, are needed to further validate our findings. One more interesting area would be to compare the contemporary approaches of Western talent management and leadership development with the approach by Chinese large companies to talent management and leadership development. This would allow more direct comparisons between talent management processes and perhaps shed more light on why some difficulties arise when identifying and developing Chinese talents, and also why there is an acknowledged shortage of Chinese global leaders. Furthermore, studies on talent management and leadership development within Chinese new emerging MNCs operating in Western countries would also contribute to the academic literature and offer insight into how Chinese companies structure and adapt their approach globally.

References

Aguirre, D., Post, L. and Hewlett, S.A. (2009) 'The Talent Innovation Imperative,' *Strategy + Business*, 56 (Autumn): 1–13.
Anderson, G. and Arsenault, N. (1998) *Fundamentals of Educational Research*, 2nd ed. (London: Falmer Press).
Barlow, L. (2005) 'Talent Development: the New Imperative?,' *Development and Learning in Organizations*, 20(3): 6–9.

Bartlett, C.A. and Ghoshal, S. (1992) 'What is a Global Manager?,' *Harvard Business Review*, 70(5): 124–132.

Baruch, Y. (2002) 'No Such Thing as a Global Manager,' *Business Horizons*, 45(1): 36–42.

Beechler, S. and Woodward, I. (2009) 'The Global "War for Talent",' *Journal of International Management*, 15: 273–285.

Björkman, I. and Lu, Y. (1999) 'The Management of Human Resources in Chinese–Western Joint Ventures,' *Journal of World Business*, 34(3): 306–324.

Björkman, I., Budhwar, P., Smale, A. and Sumelius, J. (2008) 'Human Resource Management in Foreign-owned Subsidiaries: China Versus India,' *The International Journal of Human Resource Management*, 19(5): 964–978.

Blass, E. (2007) 'Talent Management – Maximizing Talent for Business Performance,' Executive Summary, Chartered Management Institute and Ashridge Consulting, http://www.ashridge.org.uk [accessed 31 January 31, 2011].

Boxall, P., Purcell, J. and Wright, P.M. (2007) '*Oxford Handbook of Human Resource Management*: Scope, Analysis and Significance,' in P. Boxall, J. Purcell and P.M. Wright (eds), *The Oxford Handbook of Human Resource Management* (Oxford: Oxford University Press): 1–16.

Brewster, C. and Mayrhofer, W. (2011) 'Comparative Human Resource Management,' in A. Harzing and A.H. Pinnington (eds), *International Human Resource Management* (London: Sage Publications): 47–78.

Brittain, S. (2007) 'How to Manage Key Talent,' *People Management*, 13(12): 46–47.

Buckingham, M. (2005) 'Managers and Leaders,' *Leadership Excellence*, 22(12): 5–6.

Caldwell, C. and Xiong, J. (2010) 'Narrowing the Gap – Developing Chinese Talent to Operate on a Global Level,' *EuroBiz*, November: 28–29.

Caligiuri, P.M. (2006) 'Developing Global Leaders,' *Human Resources Management Review*, 16(2): 219–228.

China Daily (2008) 'Overseas Chinese Eye Motherland for Jobs,' *China Daily*, December 29, http://www.chinadaily.com.cn/business/2008–12/29/content_7349282.htm [accessed July 23, 2013].

CIPD [The Chartered Institute for Personnel Development] (2011) *Talent Management: An Overview*, http://www.cipd.co.uk/default.cipd [accessed July 23, 2013].

Collings, D. and Mellahi, K. (2009) 'Strategic Talent Management: A Review and Research Agenda,' *Human Resource Management Review*, 19(4): 304–313.

Conger, J.A. and Fulmer, R.M. (2003) 'Developing Your Leadership Pipeline,' *Harvard Business Review*, 81(12): 76–84.

Corporate Leadership Council (2003) *Literature Review: Assessment Methods for Identifying Leadership Potential* (Washington: Corporate Executive Board), http://www.alleanza.cr/docs/Assessment_methods_for_identifying_leadership_potential.pdf [accessed July 23, 2013].

Crossland, R. (2005) 'Who Will Lead Now? Develop Internal Talent,' *Leadership Excellence*, 22(13): 6.

De Pablos, P.O. and Lytras, M.D. (2008) 'Competencies and Human Resource Management: Implications for Organizational Competitive Advantage,' *Journal of Knowledge Management*, 12(6): 48–55.

Derr, C.B. and Laurent, A. (1989) 'The Internal and External Career: A Theoretical and Cross-Cultural Perspective,' in M.B. Arthur, B. Laurence and D.T. Hall (eds), *Handbook of Career Theory* (New York: Cambridge University Press): 454–471.

Derr, C.B., Roussillon, S. and Bournois, F. (2002) *Cross-cultural Approaches to Leadership Development* (Westport, CT: Quorum Books).

Dietz, M., Orr, G. and Xing, J. (2008) 'How Chinese Companies Can Succeed Abroad,' *McKinsey Quarterly*, http://www.mckinseyquarterly.com [accessed 4 February 4, 2011].

Dolles, H. (1997) *Keiretsu: Emergenz, Struktur, Wettbewerbsstärke und Dynamik japanischer Verbundgruppen* [Keiretsu: Emergence, Structure, Competitive Strengths and Organizational Dynamics of Corporate Groupings in Japan] (Frankfurt am Main: Peter Lang).

Dolles, H. (2002) 'Die Qual der Wahl – Personalauswahl für den Einsatz in Japan [The question of choice – Employee selection instruments for international assignments to Japan],' *Journal of the German Chamber of Industry and Commerce in Japan*, 11(4): 13–15.

Dolles, H. (2006) 'The Changing Environment for Entrepreneurship Development: Private Business in the People's Republic of China,' in S. Södermann (ed.), *Emerging Multiplicity: Integration and Responsiveness in Asian Business Development* (Basingstoke: Palgrave Macmillan): 234–254.

Dolles, H. and Takahashi, Y. (2011) 'The "Lost Decade" and Changes in the Japanese Business Environment: Consequences for Foreign Direct Investment and Human Resource Management in Foreign Subsidiaries in Japan,' in S. Horn (ed.), *Emerging Perspectives in Japanese Human Resource Management* (Frankfurt am Main: Peter Lang): 165–190.

Dolles, H. and Wilmking, N. (2005a) 'Trust or Distrust? China's Accession to the World Trade Organization and Its Strategic Implications for Chinese–Foreign Joint Ventures,' in A. Giroud, D. Yang and A. Mohr (eds), *Multinationals and Asia: Organizational and Institutional Relationships* (Abingdon/New York: Routledge/ Curzon): 87–109.

Dolles, H. and Wilmking, N. (2005b) *International Joint Ventures in China after WTO Accession: Will Trust Relations Change?*, German Institute for Japanese Studies Working Paper, No. 05/7, German Institute for Japanese Studies.

Easterby-Smith, M., Danusia, M. and Lu, Y. (1995) 'How Culture-sensitive is HRM? A Comparative Analysis of Practice in Chinese and UK Companies,' *International Journal of Human Resource Management*, 6(1): 31–59.

Edwards, M. and Bartlett, T. (1983) 'Innovations in Talent Identification,' *SAM Advanced Management Journal*, 48(4): 16–24.

Edwards, T. (2011) 'The Transfer of Employment Practices across Borders in Multinational Companies,' in A. Harzing and A.H. Pinnington (eds), *International Human Resource Management* (London: Sage): 267–290.

Farley, C. (2005) 'HR's Role in Talent Management in Driving Business Results,' *Employment Relations Today*, 32(1): 55–61.

Farrell, D. and Grant, A.J. (2005) 'China's Looming Talent Shortage,' *McKinsey Quarterly*, http://www.mckinseyquarterly.com [accessed February 4, 2011].

Frank, F.D. and Taylor, C.R. (2004) 'Talent Management: Trends that Will Shape the Future,' *Human Resource Planning*, 27(1): 33–41.

Fulmer, R. and Conger, J. (2004) *Growing Your Company's Leaders: How Do Great Organizations Use Succession Management to Sustain Competitive Advantage?* (New York: AMACOM).

Gerstner, C.R. and Day, D.V. (1994) 'Cross-cultural Comparison of Leadership Prototypes,' *Leadership Quarterly*, 5(2): 121–134.

Groves, K.S. (2007) 'Integrating Leadership Development and Succession Planning Best Practices,' *Journal of Management Development*, 26(3): 239–260.

Guillory, W.A. (2009) *The Age of Human Potential – Talent Management*, Salt Lake City, UT: Innovations International Inc., http://www.innovint.com/services/talent-management.php [accessed February 1, 2011].

Hao, J. and Welch, A. (2012) 'A Tale of Sea Turtles: Job-Seeking Experiences of *Hai Gui* (High-skilled Returnees) in China,' *Higher Education Policy*, 25(2): 243–260.

Hartmann, E., Feisel, E. and Schober, H. (2010) 'Talent Management of Western MNCs in China: Balancing Global Integration and Local Responsiveness,' *Journal of World Business*, 45(2): 169–178.

Harvey, M.G., Speier, C. and Novicevic, M.M. (1999) 'The Impact of Emerging Markets on Staffing the Global Organization: A Knowledge-based View,' *Journal of International Management*, 5(3): 167–186.

Hawser, A. (2008) 'China Faces Growing Skills Shortage,' *Global Finance*, 22(1): 4.

House, R., Hanges, P., Javidan, M., Dorfman, P. and Gupta, V. (2004) *Culture, Leadership and Organizations: The GLOBE Study of 62 Societies* (Thousand Oaks, CA: Sage).

Huo, Y.P. and Von Glinow, M.A. (1995), 'On Transplanting Human Resource Practices to China: A Culture-driven Approach,' *International Journal of Manpower*, 16(9): 3–15.

Iles, P., Chuai, X. and Preece, D. (2010) 'Talent Management and HRM in Multinational Companies in Beijing: Definitions, Differences and Drivers,' *Journal of World Business*, 45(2): 179–189.

ITAP International (2011) 'Global Leadership Development,' http://www.itapintl.com [accessed February 28, 2011].

Jokinen, T. (2005) 'Global Leadership Competencies: A Review and Discussion,' *Journal of European Industrial Training*, 29(3): 199–216.

Kesler, G.C. (2002) 'Why the Leadership Bench Never Gets Deeper: Ten Insights about Executive Talent Development,' *Human Resource Planning*, 25(1): 32–44.

Kühlmann, T.M. and Dolles, H. (eds) (2002) *Sino-German Business Relationships during the Age of Economic Reform* (Munich: Iudicium).

Lewis, R.E. and Heckman, R.J. (2006) 'Talent Management: A Critical Review,' *Human Resource Management Review*, 16(2): 139–154.

Lim, J., Dai, G. and Meuse, K. (2009) 'Managing Global Enterprises: The Critical Developmental Needs of Chinese Executives,' http://www.kornferryinstitute.com/files/pdf1/Chinese Ldrshp1.pdf [accessed February 17, 2011].

McCauley, C. and Wakefield, M. (2006) 'Talent Management in the 21st Century: Help Your Company Find, Develop, and Keep its Strongest Workers,' *Journal for Quality and Participation*, 29(4): 4–7.

Mansson, S. and Schmidt, C. (2011) *Managing Talents for Global Leadership Positions in Multinational Corporations*, Centre for International Business Studies, School of Business, Economics and Law, University of Gothenburg.

Mayring, P. (1995) *Qualitative Inhaltsanalyse. Grundfragen und Techniken* [*Qualitative Content Analysis. Basic Questions and Techniques*], 5th ed. (Weinheim: Deutscher Studienverlag).

Michaels, E., Handfield-Jones, H. and Axelrod, B. (2001) *The War for Talent* (Boston, MA: Harvard Business School Press).

Morlok, E. and Dolles, H. (2005a) 'Die Auslandsentsendung aus der Sicht der mitrei-senden Familie. Teil 1: Umzug nach Japan [Managing the Overseas Assignment from a Family Perspective. Part 1: Moving to Japan],' *Journal of the German Chamber of Industry and Commerce in Japan*, 14(1) 22–25.

Morlok, E. and Dolles, H. (2005b) 'Die Auslandsentsendung aus der Sicht der mitrei-senden Familie. Teil 2: Verbesserungswünsche und Empfehlungen [Managing the Overseas Assignment from a Family Perspective. Part 2: Requests and Recommendations],' *Journal of the German Chamber of Industry and Commerce in Japan*, 14(2) 22–25.

Peterson, M.F. and Hunt, J.G. (1997) 'International Perspectives on International Leadership,' *Leadership Quarterly*, 8(3): 203–231.

Phillips, J.J. and Edwards, L. (2009) *Managing Talent Retention: An ROI Approach* (San Francisco, CA: Pfeiffer).

Ralston, D.A., Kai-Cheng, Y., Wang, X., Terpstra, R.H. and Wei, H. (1996) 'The Cosmopolitan Chinese Manager: Findings of a Study on Managerial Values across the Six Regions of China,' *Journal of International Management*, 2: 79–109.

Ready, D.A., Hill, L.A. and Conger, J.A. (2008) 'Winning the Race for Talent in Emerging Markets,' *Harvard Business Review*, 86(11): 62–70.

Ready, D.A., Conger, J.A. and Hill, L.A. (2010) 'Are You a High Potential?,' *Harvard Business Review*, 88(6): 78–84.

Rowley, C., Poon, I.H., Zhu, Y. and Warner, M. (2011) 'Approaches to International Human Resources Management,' in A. Harzing and A.H. Pinnington (eds), *International Human Resource Management* (London: Sage): 153–182.

Sanyal, S. (2007) 'China–India and the Global Talent Shortage,' Deutsche Bank, Global Markets Research, Economics Research, March 28, 2007, http://gmr.db.com [accessed January 30, 2011].

Saxenian, A. (2006) *The New Argonauts: Regional Advantage in a Global Economy* (Cambridge, MA: Harvard University Press).

Schein, E.H. (2004) *Organizational Culture and Leadership* (San Francisco, CA: Jossey-Bass).

Schein, E.H. (2009) *The Corporate Culture Survival Guide* (San Francisco, CA: Jossey-Bass).

Schmidt, C., Mansson, S. and Dolles, H. (2013) 'Managing Talents for Global Leadership Positions in MNCs: Responding to the Challenges in China,' *Asian Business and Management*, 12(4): 477–496.

Schuler, R.S., Jackson, S.E. and Tarique, I. (2011) 'Framework for Global Talent Management: HR Actions for Dealing with Global Talent Challenges,' in H. Scullion and D. Collings (eds), *Global Talent Management* (London: Routledge): 17–36.

Sharma, R. and Bhatnagar, J. (2009) Talent Management – Competency Development: Key to Global Leadership', *Industrial and Commercial Training*, 41(3): 118–132.

Stahl, G.K. (1997) *Internationaler Einsatz von Führungskräften* [*International Missions of Corporate Leaders*] (Munich, Vienna: Oldenbourg).

Stahl, G.K., Björkman, I., Farndale, E., Morris, S.S., Paauwe, J., Stiles, P., Trevor, J. and Wright, P.M. (2007) *Global Talent Management: How Leading Multinationals Build and Sustain their Talent Pipeline*, INSEAD Faculty & Research Working Paper (Fontainebleau: INSEAD).

Stainton, A. (2005) 'Talent Management: Latest Buzzword or Refocusing Existing Processes?,' *Competency and Emotional Intelligence*, 12(4): 39–43.

State Council (2006) *National Plan for Medium and Long-Term Scientific and Technological Development (2006–2020)* (Beijing: China Legal Publishing House).

State Council (2010a) *National Plan for Medium and Long-Term Human Resources Development (2010–2020)* (Beijing: China Legal Publishing House).

State Council (2010b) *National Plan for Medium and Long-Term Education Reform and Development (2010–2020)* (Beijing: China Legal Publishing House).

Strauss, A. and Corbin, J. (1990) *Basics of Qualitative Research: Grounded Theory Procedures and Techniques* (London: Sage).

Sullivan, J. (2004) 'Talent Management Defined: Is It a Buzzword or a Major Breakthrough?,' *ERE.net*, September 13, http://www.ere.net/2004/09/13/talent-management-defined-is-it-a-buzzword-or-a-major-breakthrough/ [accessed July 24, 2013].

114   *Christian Schmidt, Sebastian Mansson, and Harald Dolles*

Tan, R. and Wellins, R. (2006) 'Growing Today's Chinese Leaders for Tomorrow's Needs,' *Training + Development*, 60: 20–23.

Tarique, I. and Schuler, R. (2009) 'Global Talent Management: Literature Review, Integrative Framework, and Suggestions for Further Research,' *Journal of World Business*, 45(2): 122–133.

Teagarden, M.B., Meyer, J. and Jones, D. (2008) 'Knowledge Sharing among High-Tech MNCs in China and India: Invisible Barriers, Best Practices and Next Steps,' *Organizational Dynamics*, 37(2): 190–202.

Tung, R.L. (2008) 'The Human Resource Challenge to Outward Foreign Direct Investment Aspirations from Emerging Economies: The Case of China,' *International Journal of Human Resource Management*, 18(5): 868–889.

Warner, M. (1998) 'Culture, Human Resources and Organizations in Asia: Seeking a Model with "Chinese" Characteristics,' *International Journal of Employment Studies*, 6(2): 1–17.

Watkin, C. (2007) 'How to Manage Leadership Talent Strategically,' *People Management*, 13(22): 44–45.

Zhang, W., Wang, H. and Alon, I. (2011) *Entrepreneurial and Business Elites of China: The Chinese Returnees who Have Shaped Modern China* (Bingley: Emerald).

6

Preferences and Intercultural Networking for Globalizing Practices of Successful Leaders in the Intercultural Workplace

Rolf Schlunze, William W. Baber, and Weiwei Ji

6.1 Introduction

Intercultural competence is much needed in international business. However, the working life career of a single Western expatriate may not be sufficient to gain the necessary cultural sensitivity for the achievements demanded in the fast-changing East Asian business world. The authors consulted international managers who are under pressure to prove that their activities lead to a return on investment (ROI) to determine the preferences and networking that might enable them to achieve long-term success overseas. In an initial phase their performance might be evaluated by their network activities extending or stabilizing the international firm's overseas network. Yeung (1997) uses the term 'extrafirm' network to refer to the relationship between firm and institution. From a resources-based perspective, network resources are embedded within the linkages inter-organizational relations (Tang and Xi, 2006) and extrafirm relations, for multinational companies (MNCs). Overseas networks can be described as network resources abroad that are concerned with the overseas operation.

In order to be efficient managers must develop appropriate preferences in the corporate, market and living environments. Their networking activities in these environments need to sustain their business success. Synergy needs to be created in the managerial pipelines connecting global and local corporate and market environments. Frequently individual managers seem overwhelmed by these demands.

In this chapter, we introduce a case study of two international managers who have succeeded in creating synergy with each other, fulfilling the needs of their transnational employer. As co-workers they learned to improve their decision-making by creating internal debates introducing Eastern and Western views to each other. When they later became co-leaders, the debates increasingly shifted focus to corporate governance. While corporate governance definitions and approaches may be converging on some international scenes (Wojcik, 2006), the current definitions are generally focused on corporate structure, rather than being detailed and practical. Daily, Dalton and Cannella (2003) demonstrated that most thinking and practice is based on agent–owner conflict (agency theory). The brief definitions given by Denis and McConnell (2003) as well as that of Larcker, Richardson and Tuna (2007, p. 964) – 'Corporate Governance refers to the set of mechanisms that influence the decisions made by managers when there is a separation of ownership and control' – and the focus of O'Sullivan (2011) on '... governance of corporate resource allocation and its implications for corporate and economic performance,' fit with the point made by Daily et al. These comments reveal a simplified model of corporate governance in academic discussions (Figure 6.1).

On a practical level, we turn to the subjects of this research study, Mr F and Mr J and their combined decades of experience as practitioners. Comments by Mr F recorded on December 1, 2012 expand the limited version considerably to include more top management aspects, middle management and rank-and-file aspects, and a communication strategy that reaches throughout the organization (Figure 6.2). Corporate Social Responsibility (CSR) and Standard Operating Procedures (SOP) are included based on the comments of the co-leaders and other practitioners interviewed.

The striking differences between the academic model and the practitioner model are mentioned by Wojcik (2006), but have not previously been presented in the literature. Recent anthologies such as Fernando (2009) and Mallin (2010) present versions including distribution of power and the five broad points proposed by the Organization for Economic Co-operation and Development (OECD), yet these models remain simplistic in comparison with Figure 6.2. One Tokyo practitioner interviewed in May 2013 for this chapter described the practical scope of corporate governance as 'almost everything.' Academia must therefore delve into the detailed practitioner

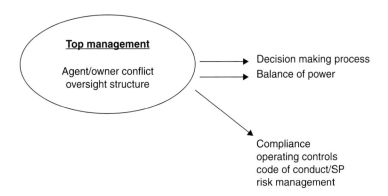

Figure 6.1 Standard model in academic conversation

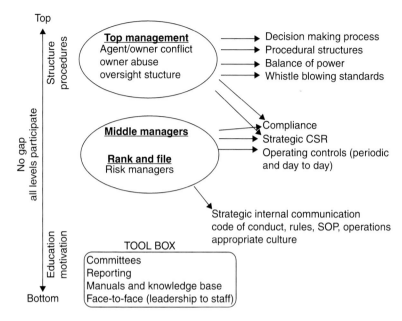

Figure 6.2   Detailed practitioner's model

model to narrow the gap between the academic discussion and the daily landscape of the business world. Further, academia must bring to light the overriding structures and strategies embedded in a practitioner's understanding of corporate governance beyond merely top-level wiring diagrams or legal compliance. Doing so will allow us to see the impact of corporate governance practices on the success of leaders and organizations.

The more complex understanding and practices of corporate governance by the managers in this study have become the main means for developing their skills, mutual thinking and success. In this chapter we have developed and applied a unique management appraisal that investigates individual cultures, differences in preferences and interaction within personal and combined networks. With the results from this case we discuss the complementarity of the co-leaders' preferences and networking activities that added value to the corporate process through corporate governance. Between these co-leaders a valuable debate on corporate governance forged their decisions and ensured their organizational impact. Finally, the mutual inspiration of the co-leaders contributing to corporate success is discussed.

Leadership is defined as the process of influencing employees to direct their efforts toward the achievement of particular goals (Hodgetts and Luthans, 2000: 363). Chen et al. (2007: 331) argued that further study about leadership is necessary specifically regarding the dynamic integration between the individuals involved in a team and the team as a whole. In 1999 the book *Co-leaders: The Power of Great Partnerships* was published by Heenan and Bennis. They were the first to present this new way of thinking about corporate co-leadership, proposing joint selection, complementary skills and emotional orientations, and mechanisms for coordination as the key factors that should be analysed (O'Toole et al. 2002: 82). Johne and Harborne (2003) found that paired leadership was more successful than single leadership. Pare et al. (2007) found that co-leadership has a clear impact among immigrant entrepreneurs in Canada, relating co-leadership to the creation and development of social capital used in the management of ethnic firms. Investigating dual leadership structures such as paired leadership, Zander and Butler (2010: 261) noted that 'co-leadership involves enabling, participative and communicative leadership styles challenging traditional concepts of authority.' In this chapter we show that building trusting relations and leadership qualities for motivating subordinates as well as equals are important aspects of intercultural leadership.

Similar to Japan, France is categorized by Hofstede (1991) as a country that maintains a large 'power distance,' where subordinates are considerably dependent on their leaders. In contrast to changing styles in the Western business world, leadership in Asian societies has long functioned according to clearly defined hierarchies. Western managers leading in Asia may need personal collaboration in order to attain success within Asia. They will need to recruit an equal, not a subordinate, who can in actual fact collaborate. Finding a suitable equal poses a great challenge. It could be seen as problematic or expensive to have two leaders in the same company. On the other hand, it could unlock synergy in a context-driven business environment. We wish to expand the argument that doing business in Japan means not only to build relations with employees, customers, suppliers and other clients (Adler and Gundersen, 2008: 32) but also with equals who can function as advisors in the long term. We will make clear that complementary preferences and network information-sharing are keys to success for foreign expatriate managers who have constraints regarding their intercultural competence.

Studies on preferences have been focused on MNCs' locational requirements (Cox, 1972; Dunning, 2009). Studies in this field have largely been conducted at the firm level (Edgington, 1995; Boston and Ross, 1996; Berköz, 1998). In a similar way to Kahn (1992) we studied the differences of preference in strong family-like business ties. Meester (2004) saw the choice of a location as an investment decision by an individual manager. However, few in-depth interviews have been conducted at the level of the individual on this topic.

Lam and Yeung (2010) showed that expatriate managers rely on the local staff resources to reduce their uncertainty in the host business environment with regard to China. The preferences of managers have an important effect on the business strategy success abroad. MNCs prefer to hire managers who fit the culture, are more cooperative and more experienced (Cohen and Prusak, 2001). It is therefore of significance to investigate cross-border managers' locational behaviours because business action is embedded in social relations (Granovetter, 1985). These managers play a role as a boundary spanner gathering market information, and bridging internal and external contexts of international groups (Aldrich and Herker, 1977; Dowling et al., 2008).

Plattner (2012a) found that expatriate managers can be distinguished as globalizer, networker, embedder and localizer by their preferences in the corporate, market and living environments. Plattner (2012b) also presented an interesting case study investigating to what extent managers with divergent cultural norms contribute to internationalization of business networks, finding that the international manager with intercultural competence or the so-called hybrid manager might contribute most (Schlunze, 2012).

According to the definition provided by Gertsen (1990: 346), intercultural competence is the ability to function effectively in another culture, which can be conceptualized by three dimensions for expatriate success: an affective dimension, a cognitive dimension, and a communicative, behavioural dimension. Through the application of cultural competence, particularly in times of crisis and transition, it is important to create new business opportunities and generate successful strategies.

MNCs may view corporate governance as important because they must navigate multiple compliance codes in international locations. They may seek the development of efficient uniform global practices or localized systems, such as the locally different approaches found by Khanna, Kogan and Palepu (2002). Nonetheless, the reasons for locally crafted approaches are not clear in the literature, though the co-leaders studied were quick to explain the potential for conflict and miscommunication between HQ and branches, particularly when geographical as well as product hierarchies are present.

Culturally fluent agents have an underestimated economic effect on the success of corporate organizations, cooperation between companies, as well as business processes and business models (Kaeppeli, 2006). Essential for good management and control practices is the inclusion of the social perspective. The 'soft facts' of social interaction can be visualized by social network analysis. Objectified this way they convert into 'hard facts' that can be applied to strategy building. Thus, networks become manageable assets. Network measures such as relational density, personal centrality or collaborative cohesion of subgroups help to identify influential roles and critical players in the business network, such as information brokers on the one hand and informational bottlenecks on the other. Consequently, the manager is able to reveal weak and strong ties, communication gaps and underutilized employees in the networking activities of organizations.

Only through the inclusion of network perspectives in every step of the well-known management process of recognition, planning, action and control, is the manager in the position to propose the right action at the right time. Effective network optimization generates several benefits, including fast access to resources, information and knowledge advantages, flexibility and speed to market, as well as credibility and accountability, which lead to higher reputation. In the following, an example of good practice based on networks is illustrated.

The purpose of this case study is to clarify to what extent co-leaders need to have complementary preferences and share information within their networks in the corporate, market and living environments to create cultural synergy in the intercultural workplace by implementing practices such as corporate governance. Therefore, the research questions for this case study are:

Research question 1: Are leaders who can share their information network and adjust their preferences able to innovate satisfactory solutions for their corporate organization?

Research question 2: Can leaders with a clear vision of corporate governance succeed in influencing and motivating the board and employee levels in the organization?

This case study should contribute to further methodological developments for the concept of a contextual management appraisal as introduced initially by Eisenhardt (1989).

6.2   Methodology and material

At the center of the case study are two international managers, one French and one Japanese. They have known each other for more than three decades, building a relationship first as co-workers, then co-leaders, co-CEOs and co-auditors. They first worked together in Hong Kong for a leading US financial institution, eventually becoming co-presidents of a Japanese insurance company purchased by a leading French company. Currently they work as corporate auditors for the second largest French bank in Tokyo. Overall they constructed excellent relationships within the local and global business community while promoting each other's business careers and the application of good business practices including corporate governance.

The two managers were invited to workshops and interviewed together to explain their approach to intercultural management and their business ethics. We followed Kurt Lewin's 1946 call for action research aiming at better intercultural cooperation between international groups, in our case, managers, students and academia. Action research is about the iterative interplay, a spiral (Berg, 2009), of the research and the individuals studied. Therefore it is suitable for educators and businesspeople concerned about students entering a business landscape with frequent, highly visible failures of management, as exemplified by Olympus, TEPCO, Livedoor, Daio Paper, Akafuku and others in recent years. We taught the co-leaders, and other managers, about networks as they revealed their networks to us and our students. The authors may hardly have influenced the co-leaders' intercultural competence as global networkers but they learned from us how to express and comprehend their business network. Their activity within our workshops included self-reflection on their daily work of ensuring good corporate governance while students matched those experiences to readings on theory and the authors developed new theory.

Initially, we focused on intercultural synergy through mutual cultural adjustment alongside complementary preferences and information-sharing in global and local networks, but later discovered the engine of our co-leader's business success: corporate governance. A core idea of the workshops was to understand the interconnectivity of those issues. Our workshops were structured as follows: (1) Intercultural encounters discussing challenges of the intercultural workplace; (2) Intercultural training engaging participants in open-ended role plays; (3) Guided discussion developing some practical advice and implications for both professional and future managers.

In line with the action research process, managers first communicated as potential change agents with the authors. In the second stage a learning process was initiated with role plays to stimulate action planning and proposals of concrete steps to transform the corporate group and its environment. The final stage was to develop and codify some data and results that help to initiate changes in behaviour.

Ripples of the action research continue to spread through the work lives of managers and former students, some of whom have joined SIEM. The researchers hope that the SIEM workshops reported online (http://www.siemrg.org) and the SIEM Linked In presence will encourage a virtual community of good intercultural practices.[1]

Extensive research was necessary in preparation for the cyclical learning processes of the workshops. Accordingly, several interviews with the research subjects were carried out over five years. Most important of these was an in-depth interview about their combined personal network on September 17, 2010 at the Tokyo Campus of Ritsumeikan University. The evaluations control group consists of 34 European managing directors and presidents based in Tokyo. Additional interviews included other managers in order to gain more insight into the business topics of this chapter.

Accordingly, quantitative data from the onscreen analyses was triangulated with the in-depth interviews to confirm validity (Eisenhardt, 1989; Yin, 2003). Additionally, this case study was regarded as the most interesting research case by European Business Council (EBC)-listed managers – such cases are considered to deepen insight into the research objective and inspire theoretical development (Eisenhardt, 1989; Bartunek et al., 2006).

Thus, theoretical sampling of single cases is widely used and case study research exploits opportunities to explore significant phenomena (Weick, 1993; Eisenhardt and Graebner, 2007). Gummesson (2007a) identifies case studies as appropriate for research when knowledge is limited and complex phenomena are the target. This study employs action research (Gummesson 2007a) including the managers, authors and other managers in workshops where all participants interacted to develop understanding of business issues including corporate governance and cultural adjustment.

The action research approach enabled the authors and study targets to jointly understand the vocabulary, learning points, explanations and layers of related issues that might otherwise have gone undetected or been confused. Action research differs from ethnography in that joint knowledge is discussed and created with the intent of developing deep, tacit understanding, which has impact on the work of all participants. Gummesson (2007b: 244) identifies this as involvement and understanding through direct experience. The authors agree with Flyvbjerg (2006) and Gummesson (2007a) that case studies are well suited to presenting complexity in context, and can generate and test theory.

As described in detail by Schlunze et al. (2013), the two research subjects were exposed to a Venn diagram with three sections representing corporate, market and living environments. Each manager needed to state the importance of supporters. We distinguished between male and female individual supporters and institutional supporters, including corporate customers and clients. The strength of the relationship was also indicated by the thickness of the connecting arrow between the interviewee and the supporter. Distance decay helped to distinguish local, national and international spaces in concentric circles in the diagram.

The next step of our analysis was to investigate the preferences of the managers in their corporate, market and living environments. Important in each environment were the variables or characteristics outlined in Table 6.4. Using conjoint analysis both managers were asked to choose one of two sets of business environments that seemed more preferable to their personal approaches to business success. The program randomly and repeatedly produces question sets checking preferences, and cross-checks the most preferred sets before a final manual correction of the ranking by the manager (see also Plattner, 2012a). Finally, the results were compared to the network analysis and were discussed with the managers. These results provide feedback as to whether the manager is balanced or has strong focus on globalizing, global networking, embedding or localizing activities within the intercultural workplace.

The applied contextual management appraisal for research in the field of management geography is outlined in our monograph (Schlunze et al., 2012). Our academic endeavour is to deepen our understanding of the managerial relations needed to create a long-term success in local and global business groups. Since we present only this single case we do not attempt to generalize to all managers working in international groups. Rather we hope to describe characteristics that might be important for theory development and for those practitioners who wish to succeed in the intercultural workplace through collaboration. One central question that we also addressed during our workshops was: How can synergy be created by international managers with different cultural backgrounds? Other researchers may find this case paradigmatic in the way Flyvbjerg (2006) discusses and therefore generalizable, but we leave this to other judges.

6.3   Case study results

As Schlunze and Ji (2012) showed in a previous study on mutual acculturation, both managers entertain a collectivistic view of doing business in Japan. Mr F and Mr J both hold universalistic viewpoints, although their home cultures are categorized as particularistic cultures (Trompenaars and Hampden-Turner, 1998). Both individuals are in fact able to compromise and reconcile their views through open discussion, particularly regarding corporate governance.

6.3.1   Cultural views on corporate governance

One of the international managers comes from France, but he admires German management for strong internal control and maintains a critical stance toward American approaches despite encouraging the implementation of corporate governance. This shows that the simplistic approach of viewing cultural differences as uniform within a country, or even an individual, does not always work.

The interviews reveal that the senior managers as equals initiate a debate process together. Debating corporate governance issues enables them to achieve better decisions. They seem to be opposite to each other in the range of involvement. Mr J emphasizes customer and labour relations, while the French manager, Mr F, keeps back from those clients but demands transparency for those interactions. However, both act in reflection of their corporate environment reconciling their cultural ways. The outcome of the reconciliations of their culturally different decision-making process and their different views on corporate governance can be presented later at board meetings in a harmonious and settled way. Thus, they act and speak as a team and give direction clearly.

During the 2011 and 2012 workshops (SIEM, n.d.) with the co-leaders the research team learned that corporate governance aids survival in the global and local market as shown by their successful turnaround of a Japanese insurance company. Transparency and information-sharing in the intercultural workplace works powerfully toward corporate success because corporate governance boosts top management as well as the entire organization improving teamwork and spirit. The workshops revealed that international managers, like our co-leaders, can successfully span boundaries when they have a clear vision of corporate governance.

It is important to note that both managers originate from cultures where affiliation with an elite educational background has high importance. However, in their professional life they learned to shed this attitude and to adjust for interaction with their stakeholders. Their common career path at an American financial institution helped them take advantage of a universalistic approach appropriate in global finance, heavily influenced by American universalistic thinking. Moreover the globalized business environments favour this approach in Tokyo and Hong Kong where their careers have largely played out. Thus, by adjusting to a globalizing business environment, their approaches merged.

6.3.2 Mutual mechanism

Friendly communication about corporate governance gives the managers freedom to debate each other and thereby improve their corporate decision-making. As a result, they initiate corporate governance measures in their organization systemically to prevent scandals and heighten the credibility of their organization. Thus they have expanded the modern definition of corporate governance, making it 'integrated into companies – top to bottom' according to their presentation at the December 2012 SIEM Workshop. They verbalized it further in this workshop, saying 'navigate the danger zones,' suggesting a strategic corporate governance approach to management of the whole organization.

In interviews, the co-leaders told us, 'We always argue, we never agree with each other!' However, they informed us that they finally do agree before board meetings. They genuinely appreciate each other as mutual advisors in the decision-making process. They have achieved this through decades of work together, including the revival of a Japanese insurance company after its takeover by a French company. Mr F and Mr J ultimately developed a similar way of viewing and resolving business issues, one born of reconciliation of culturally different approaches (Schlunze and Ji, 2012). Their views on corporate governance are much influenced by the globalization of the finance industry, which has changed not only their individual cultures but also the culture of the global cities, Tokyo and Hong Kong, where they have worked and lived. Their collaboration is indeed a success story owing to their capability to perceive and adjust to environmental changes as co-leaders of a corporate organization. They explained their thinking about responsibility: 'We didn't divide responsibilities, his responsibility is my responsibility, and my responsibility is his responsibility. [The] brain can be divided into right and left side, but we didn't divide.' To facilitate knowledge about corporate governance that speaks to an international community, their ambition has created a heterogeneous team of transcultural actors at the board meeting level (Earley and Gibson, 2002). That they replicated their synergy, establishing a board of directors consisting of half international and half host country managers, is a signal of their powerful impact on the host country workplace as international co-leaders.

6.3.3   Network

Taking an actor-centred approach, we interviewed both managers about how their personal networks crucial for their business success. We began with interpreting the ego-network of Mr F and Mr J. The analysis of their networks is summarized also in the following.

6.3.3.1   *Local network in the global city*

Both research subjects insist they are equals but Mr F is very important for Mr J as a mentor in global business, providing a 'somehow' philosophical approach to practical problems. Additionally, two bi-directional linkages to his mentor/family and the alumni network embed him well in the living sphere. Mr J and Mr F were initially employees of competing companies when they met in Hong Kong. After a friendship had developed by discussing business issues, Mr F invited Mr J to work with him for the same company. Thereafter they became a co-worker team. They were co-presidents for an insurance company, and after a brief retirement they continued to work as co-CEOs and finally as corporate co-auditors.

Most of the local interactions done within and outside of the organization that are HR-related are conducted by Mr J, such as dealing with labour unions, local clients and customers. In these relations Mr J's lawyer-network becomes crucial for his business success. However, Mr J always keeps Mr F updated on such dealings. For their common business success Mr J maintains good

Table 6.1   Mr J's network

	Corporate	Market	Living
International	Employer Media/Information	Supporters Swiss College AIESEC (student association) French US Former supervisor	Alumni
National	Clients Media/Information	Supporters College Mentor	Family RU Professor
Local	Clients Supporters Mentor Mr F		

connections to clients and gained many supporters within the local corporate environment.

Mr F's Japanese co-worker is by far the most important element of his business success in the local market of Tokyo. Together with Mr J, he succeeds in producing intercultural synergy that helps him and his mentor to promote their careers from efficient co-workers to become finally respected corporate leaders and auditors. Additionally, he has been able to count on several other corporate supporters within Tokyo. Within the local market environment he keeps close working contact with clients as well as friendly yet task-oriented relations with information providers. Within his living environment there is a cyclist who is a close relatively young friend and also a mentee. Mr F has foreign friends in Tokyo who respect him and consult with him about professional issues including corporate governance.

6.3.3.2   *Networking nation-wide*

At the national level there are only a few relationships in the market environment: clients and media relations. Media relations became important to the co-leaders when the French investor sold the successfully restructured Japanese insurance company to an American company and reporting in *Keizei Shinbun* and the *Wall Street Journal* increased the stature of the co-leaders. Further, Mr J has a good, old friend who visits from Osaka for dinner meetings to consult him and just to enjoy friendship. This Japanese person is indebted to Mr F for helping him overcome serious workplace problems by exposing him to practices for controlling the company with more sophisticated corporate governance. Outside of Tokyo, academic relationships are important in building reputation through a process of educational exchanges communicating corporate governance practices to international business practitioners.

On the national level Mr J is well embedded while Mr F is more selective, since the Japanese financial industry is concentrated in Tokyo. Even for the Japanese co-leader it is sufficient to focus on a network within the global city, Tokyo. For them, the rest of Japan is not greatly important for the finance sector.

Table 6.2   Mr F's network analysis

	Corporate	Market	Living
International	Supporters	Employer	Alumni
	Colleagues	Supporters	Publishing
	Former supervisor	Media	Family
National		Clients	RU Professor
		Media	
Global city Tokyo	Mentor of Mr J	Clients	Cyclist
	Supporters	Information provider	

6.3.3.3 Global network

Mr F built his most important linkage to a French university colleague. The contact, meeting for the first time in thirty years, resulted in his being offered 'the job of his life' in a global insurance company. They had known each other during university years, taking graduate-level business courses at a leading university in Paris. Mr F told us that he is not a fan of alumni meetings. Thus, he even withdrew from the alumni group of a previous employer, a leading American bank. He told us: 'My philosophy is not keeping many, but some important contacts.' His way of networking is – as a result – very straightforward. Here, he differs widely from his friend and co-worker, Mr J., who conducts an indirect networking style that includes a lot of even 'not yet known' acquaintances. Mr F keeps good contacts with three supporters in the UK that help him to connect and communicate financial business globally. Among them is a US lawyer based in London that provides first-class information from the financial markets.

Unlike his mentor Mr F, Mr J appreciates and enjoys his alumni relations. The alumni from his early years of study in Switzerland remain of great importance to his current business activities. During the interview he emphasized that AIESEC (Association Internationale des Etudiants en Sciences Economiques et Commerciales) plays an important role in his daily work. He mentioned that he communicates with members from AIESEC every month and gains valuable detailed information.[2]

It appears those linkages between the local and global business environments are of foremost importance for Mr J's success. Thus, much of the success of the both co-leaders is due to the fact that their place of residence is the global city, Tokyo. Although Mr F worked for US companies, he did not develop a human network in the US. Rather, their joint network is focused on Euro-Asian relations. Mr F emphasized that his philosophy is to keep only some important contacts, revealing that the quality of individuals in the network is an important part of their success. The experience of the two managers described here implies that traditional leadership concepts should be considered as co-leadership approaches capable of creating intercultural synergy.

Local clients of Mr F and Mr J tend to be disconnected from the global financial business. They rely on the co-leaders as a team of brokers connecting them to overseas markets in the EU and US. At the same time, the co-leaders tend to consult their clients about trade with London and other European financial markets where they have additional reliable support. Another reason for favouring the European financial scene is the reliability and the transparency arising from stronger regulation and governmental control, especially since the recent financial crisis.

Regarding support of local clients, Mr J used a Japanese proverb to emphasize his way of thinking: *Nasake ha hito no tame ni narazu.* The meaning is 'A kindness is never wasted.' He applies this kindness to his friends and to his clients, getting the most out of each relationship. In Japan he acts in a complementary and collaborative fashion with Mr F, facilitating the latter's global and local knowledge.

It appears that overseas linkages provided by AIESEC are very important for Mr J's global connectiveness. For these leaders it is crucial to develop their ability through learning from their experiences.

6.3.4   Co-leadership networking

In the following section it is shown how both managers skilfully combined their networking activities to succeed in a local and a global business environment respectively. Their common network activities are mapped by the categories introduced below (also see Figure 6.3 and Table 6.3).

The lines visualize the relation types between ego and alteri and among the alteri. The single solid line means strong relations, the double and triple solid line means mutual strong relations, and the dashed line indicates weak relations.

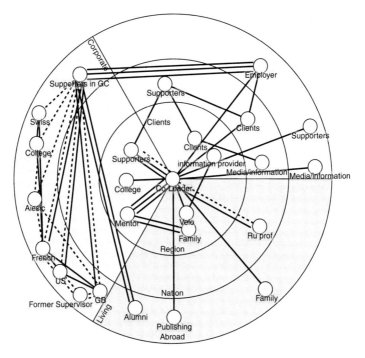

Figure 6.3   Combined network of co-leaders

Note: The map was created during our interview with the co-leaders at the Ritsumeikan Tokyo Campus, September 17, 2009 based on their ego-network, used with permission.

Source: Own data based on interview at the Ritsumeikan University Tokyo Campus (September 17, 2010).

Table 6.3 Results of network analysis

	Mr F	Mr J	Co-leaders
Circle local (Tokyo region)	5	5	7
Circle nation (Japan)	3	4	4
Circle abroad (Global)	12	11	14
Sector market	7	6	8
Sector corporate	8	11	11
Sector living	5	3	6
Total	20	20	25
Density (with ego)	0.086	0.129	0.120

The data presented in the above table support the interview findings that Mr J has excellent access to stakeholder groups within the domestic work and market environments while Mr F maintains strong linkages to fewer business people.

Density reflects the ratio of the number of actual links in a population to the number of possible links in the same population. Actors in a high-density network are likely to have a greater level of contact than those in a low-density network. Thus, information can be expected to flow more freely among members of a high-density network (Scott, 1991). The network density of Mr J is higher than that of Mr F. Combined, the density of the network is 0.12. The network density is the number of existing relations divided by the number of all possible relations. VennMaker differentiates between density with ego and density where ego is not part of calculation. The density of the network map indicates the ratio of the relations present to the possible number of relations.

Mr J has important ties in the local and national markets. Mr F commented on the importance of such weak ties in the domestic market with the following words: 'Supporters exist everywhere and they are most important.' Both command linkages that bridge corporate and market environments. Additionally, both have networks that bridge market and living environments: despite being of retirement age, they function as mentors for young foreign business people and bankers based in Tokyo. Tellingly, their engagement and credibility still generates employment offers. The greatest brokering achievement has been translating US and EU financial banking and corporate governance to the domestic Japanese market and vice versa. With thirty years of work experience in the financial business in Asia they facilitate their personal intercultural synergy to attain leadership roles and remain important consultants in the financial community of practice (COP), professionals who contribute practices and knowledge to build capacity (Wenger, McDermott and Snyder, 2002).

6.3.5   Network and preferences

Local networks are most important, but they can be only facilitated via a global network. Intercultural synergy between Mr J and Mr F is created throughout the process of communication between local and global communities of practice. Mr F is a sophisticated broker for the global financial market, whereas Mr J has the understanding of global processes, and it is he who primarily interacts with the local Corporate Governance COP. In sum, the French national is operating as a visionary but market-oriented leader while the Japanese national operates as a social-emotional but pragmatic leader within the co-leader team. In co-leadership they overcome problems by implementing feasible solutions facilitating the cultural mix to gain efficiency.

In Table 6.4, we suggest that distance should function as a weight for the network data by sector. Data for the preferences and networking activities is distinguished by global (circle abroad), national and local distance degree ('nation' and 'local' circles indicating outside and inside Tokyo respectively). Against our expectations Mr F emphasized human resource access whereas Mr J had a strong preference for cooperation within the multinational enterprise. According to our expectations Mr J was strong in the cooperation with the local customer and clients whereas Mr F showed a preference for market opportunities in general. Mr J had no visible preference in the living environment but Mr F was eager to build a local information network mainly with the help of Mr J.

Table 6.4   Synthesis of network and preference analysis

Manager / Attribute	MrF Prefer	MrF Network Sector	MrF Network Distance	MrJ Prefer	MrJ Network Sector	MrJ Network Distance	Co-leader Network Sector	Co-leader Network Distance
Human resource access	0.115	8	12	0.0	11	11	11	14
Good working atmosphere	0.0			0.115				
Cooperation within the own multinational enterprise	0.076			0.576				
Market opportunity	0.576	7	3	0.230	6	4	8	4
cooperation with customers	0.307			0.346				
Governmental support setting	0.0			0.0				
Manifold city life	0.192	5	5	0.076	3	5	6	7
Local information network	0.307			0.0				
Livable living environment	0.0			0.038				

According to the typology proposed by Plattner (2012a), we expected Mr F to function within the co-leadership team as a globalizer and Mr J. as localizer. However, we did not find such clear-cut roles for the co-leaders. Table 6.4 led us to infer that both co-leaders have a strong network in the corporate environment. Mr J appears to have a stronger preference for cooperation within the own multinational enterprise, while Mr F has a relative strong preference for human resource access, which basically characterizes the cooperative relation with Mr J. Within the market environment the network of Mr J is slightly stronger, although Mr F has a strong preference to seek market opportunities. This derives properly from the fact that Mr J has a stronger preference for cooperation with customers and clients. In the living environment Mr J does not need to make extra effort to find supporters since he is a host country national. Mr F, as a foreigner, needs to focus on the local information network to sustain his satisfaction and wellbeing working and living abroad in working to avoid and overcome lock-in effects (Befu and Guichard-Anguis, 2001) in the foreign business community.

From our preference analysis it appears that Mr F functions as a networker with a strong preference for embedding his visionary thinking locally, while Mr J is a local embedder with a strong preference for global networking. To conclude, both managers hold different, but also similar preferences, which are not only complementary but cause mutual and constant knowledge transfer. Recently, their success as corporate auditors builds on corporate governance knowledge transfers. Their unique approach sustains a dynamic balance between them. From the control group survey and previous research, we found that the ability to stay balanced while evolving in the corporate, market and living environments as well as the existence of a culturally fluent advisor is a key to success for international managers (Schlunze, 2012; Baber, 2012). The co-leaders develop their competences and promote these to each other, initiating a dynamic mutual learning process with respect while leveraging their paired competences.

6.4 Conclusions

The case study found support for the first research question. The co-leaders share their information network and adjust with their preferences to each other, not dividing any responsibilities. We found that an important strategy for success was always making sure that they reach satisfactory solutions by negotiating together about the pro and cons of their decisions. We observed that network synergy increases their creativity, flexibility and problem-solving skills with a potential multiple effect for the organization concerned. The co-leaders create network synergy and function as multipliers impacting their organization's fundamental structure by pursuing better corporate governance. According to Kaeppeli (2006), missing cultural knowledge is the main obstacle of Western managers in Japan. However, the results from this case infer a possible solution for leaders: to find collaborators among local staff to help initiate and conduct a reflective negotiation process about corporate governance and other issues. Thus they may develop solutions for their international team, enabling them to face the challenges of an intercultural workplace in an international organization.

Combining different preferences and networking experiences in a team is an important lesson from the success of these co-leaders. Spatial proximity or co-location with a collaborative co-worker or equal leader enabled them to discover and evaluate different ways of leadership through culturally appropriate yet challenging corporate governance approaches.

Multiple embeddedness in various business environments was achieved by the co-leaders' preference through information exchange. Both co-leaders successfully embed their beliefs on governing a corporation in global and local economic spaces. They function as a team of brokers for the demands of the global business environment, ensuring that the local subsidiary stays connected.

To achieve success as a team and for the organization, they apply to decision-making a well-known but often not thoroughly implemented management process. The process is based on the principle of mutual and interpersonal trust, including such practices as honest and complete information-sharing. This process led them to develop corporate governance as a communication tool throughout all levels of the company, not only top management, permeating the organizational chart and creating social capital. Their systemic evolution of corporate governance stands in stark apposition to the limited view taken by business academia.

Their personal credibility and accountability is deeply transferred to the organization, leading to the good reputation and profitability of the entire organization. This success was recognized publicly in the financial media in Tokyo and New York, thereby attracting new business opportunities to their organizations as well as boosting their own career paths even after retirement. After their initial retirement they became co-CEOs and then co-corporate auditors of a leading international financial institution's subsidiary in Tokyo. Thus, we also gained support from the interview data for the second research question, that the co-leaders enthuse headquarters with a clear vision of corporate governance that enables them to better manage the local workplace and build creditability for the international financial group.

Leaders have to survive recessions and the global economic crisis, and therefore need to rethink existing approaches. The network analysis presented here suggests that co-leaders need to build mutual trust by strong ties based on credibility and professionalism. They need to create a community that helps to integrate the commitment between foreigners with host country nationals. Through their co-leadership approach, they provide a successful pattern to make us rethink how to share power and knowledge in order to create a positive future for the entire organization.

The co-leaders studied emphasized such basic points as 'Know yourself and your culture well. Have a good idea of your strengths, development needs, and avoid preconceptions' as a recipe to lead and to compete in an intercultural business environment successfully.

To conclude, the case infers that the co-leaders are able to make decisions together, and build consensus guiding board meetings by their argument of better corporate governance. Through their complementary preferences and network synergy they leverage knowledge of corporate governance, meeting global as well as local demands. Their call for transparency and other good practices is disseminated in the corporate network, which gives them the competence and credibility to lead people successfully. These findings show us the importance of developing multicultural management (Harvey et al., 1999) for global management teams. Nowadays, however, charismatic omnipotent leaders, as described by House (1977), are not needed so much as leaders who are deeply involved in implementing policy such as corporate governance, thereby raising the credibility of the MNC.

Despite having a larger sample of individuals in the target population, we have presented only one important case study. The results of the analysis make us confident that the case is indeed interesting for the Tokyo-based business community. Furthermore, this case study generates new insights combining a novel framework of preferences and network theory. The approach outlined in this chapter should be replicated with other leaders in other global city locations. We hope that the case presented will help scholars to develop new theories on leadership and sustained competitive advantages created by interculturally sensitive and dynamic synergistic co-leadership in international groups.

Notes

1. See SIEM manager training events at URL http://www.siemrg.org/.
2. AIESEC, an institution represented in some 100 countries and with over 45,000 members, is the world's largest student-run organization. AIESEC alumni are located all over the globe, working in various professions and industries, and playing important roles in their communities.

Acknowledgment: We are grateful for the support we received from Professor Dr Michael Schönhut, who created VennMaker and invited us to present our initial results on this co-leadership case study. We feel indebted for his permission to reprint the map and related text of the combined co-leader network in this book. Many thanks go to Dr Michael Plattner, who introduced this network mapping methodology to our SIEM research group members. The authors are greatly indebted to the two corporate auditors who cooperated with our survey patiently during and after our workshops, enabling us to go beyond mapping their individual networks.

References

Adler, N.J. and Gundersen, A. (2008) *International Dimensions of Organizational Behavior* (Cincinnati, OH: South-Western/Cengage Learning).

Aldrich, H. and Herker, D. (1977) 'Boundary Spanning Roles and Organization Structure,' *Academy of Management Review*, 2(2): 217–230.

Baber, W. (2012) 'Adjusting to a Distant Space: Cultural Adjustment and Interculturally Fluent Support,' in R.D. Schlunze, N. Agola and W. Baber (eds), *Spaces of International Economy and Management: Launching New Perspectives on Management and Geography* (Basingstoke: Palgrave Macmillan).

Bartunek, J.M., Rynes, S.L. and Ireland, R.D. (2006) 'What Makes Management Research Interesting and Why Does It Matter?,' *Academy of Management Journal*, 49: 9–15.

Befu, H. and Guichard-Anguis, S. (2001) *Globalizing Japan – Ethnography of the Japanese Presence in Asia, Europe, and America*, Routledge Curzon Japanese Studies Series (New York: Routledge Courzon).

Berg, B.L. (2009) *Qualitative Research Methods for the Social Sciences*, 7th ed. (Boston, MA: Allyn and Bacon).

Berköz, L. (1998) 'Locational Preferences of Producer Service Firms in Istanbul,' *European Planning Studies*, 6(3): 333–349.

Boston, T.D. and Ross, C.L. (1996) 'Location Preferences of Successful African American-owned Businesses in Atlanta,' *Review of Black Political Economy*, 24(2/3): 337–357.

Chen, G., Kirkman, B.K., Kanfer, R., Allen, D. and Rosen, B. (2007) 'A Multilevel Study of Leadership, Empowerment, and Performance,' *Journal of Applied Psychology*, 92: 331–346.

Cohen, D. and Prusak, L. (2001) *In Good Company: How Social Capital Makes Organizations Work* (Boston, MA: Harvard Business School Press).

Cox, K.R. (1972) *Man, Location and Behavior: An Introduction to Human Geography* (Hoboken, NJ: John Wiley & Sons).

Daily, C.M., Dalton, D.R. and Cannella, A.A. (2003) 'Corporate Governance: Decades of Dialogue and Data,' *Academy of Management Review*, 28(3): 371–382.

Denis, D.K. and McConnell, J.J. (2003) 'International Corporate Governance,' *The Journal of Financial and Quantitative Analysis*, 38(1): 1–38.

Dowling, P.J., Festing, M. and Engle, A.D. (2008) *International Human Resources Management: Managing People in a Multinational Context* (Cincinnati, OH: Cengage Learning).

Dunning, J.H. (2009) 'Location and the Multinational Enterprise: A Neglected Factor?,' *Journal of International Business Studies*, 40(1): 5–19.

Earley, P.C. and Gibson, C.B. (2002) *Multinational Teams: A New Perspective* (Hillsdale, NJ: Lawrence Erlbaum Associates).

Edgington, D.W. (1995) 'Locational Preferences of Japanese Real Estate Investors in North America,' *Urban Geography*, July (01): 373–396.

Eisenhardt, K.M. (1989) 'Building Theories from Case Study Research,' *Academy of Management Review*, 14(4): 532–550.

Eisenhardt, K.M. and Graebner, M.E. (2007) 'Theory Building from Cases: Opportunities and Challenges,' *Academy of Management Journal*, 50(1): 25–32.

Fernando, A.C. (2009) *Corporate Governance: Principles, Policies and Practices* (Englewood Cliffs, NJ: Prentice Hall).

Fey, C. and Furu, P. (2008) 'Top Management Incentive Compensation and Knowledge Sharing in Multinational Corporations,' *Strategic Management Journal*, 29: 1301–1323.

Flyvbjerg, B. (2006) 'Five Misunderstandings about Case-study Research,' *Qualitative Inquiry*, 12(2): 219–245.

Gertsen, M.C. (1990) 'Intercultural Competence and Expatriates,' *International Journal of Human Resource Management*, 1(3): 341–362.

Granovetter, M. (1985) 'Economic Action and Social Structure: The Problem of Embeddedness,' *American Journal of Sociology*, 91: 481–510.

Gummesson, E. (2007a) 'Case Study Research,' in B. Gustavsson (ed.), *The Principle of Knowledge Creation Methods* (Cheltenham: Edward Elgar).

Gummesson, E. (2007b) 'Case Study Research and Network Theory: Birds of a Feather,' *Qualitative Research in Organizations and Management: An International Journal*, 2(3): 226–248.

Harvey, M.G., Price, M.F., Speier, C. and Novicevic, M.M. (1999) 'The Role of Inpatriates in a Globalization Strategy and Challenges Associated with the Inpatriation Process,' *HR. Human Resource Planning*, 22(1): 38–50.

Heenan, D.A. and Bennis, W. (1999) *Co-leaders: The Power of Great Partnerships* (Hoboken, NJ: John Wiley & Sons).

Hodgetts, R. and Luthans, F. (2000) *International Management: Culture, Strategy, and Behavior* (New York: McGraw-Hill).

Hofstede, G. (1991) *Cultures and Organizations: Software of the Mind* (New York: McGraw-Hill).

House, R.J. (1977) 'A 1976 Theory of Charismatic Leadership,' in J.G. Hunt and L.L. Larson (eds), *Leadership: The Cutting Edge* (Carbondale, IL: Southern Illinois University Press): 189–207.

Johne, A. and Harbome, P. (2003) 'One Leader Is Not Enough for Major New Service Development: Results of a Consumer Banking Study,' *Service Industries*, 23(3): 22–39.

Kaeppeli, R.W. (2006) 'West-European Subsidiary Managers in Japan Identified and Weighted the Key Success Factors for their Organization,' *Japan Academy of International Business Studies*, 12: 237–251.

Kahn, J.A. (1992) 'Location Preferences of Family Firms: Strategic Decision Making or "Home Sweet Home,"' *Family Business Review*, 5(3): 271–282.

Khanna, T., Kogan, J. and Palepu, K. (2002) 'Globalization and Corporate Governance Convergence? A Cross-country Analysis,' *The Review of Economics and Statistics*, 88(1): 69–90.

Kronenwett, M. and Schönhuth, M. (2011) *Vennmaker 1.2. Manual*, http://www.vennmaker.com/en/dokumente/ [accessed August 4, 2013].

Lam, S.S.K. and Yeung, J.C.K. (2010) 'Staff Localization and Environmental Uncertainty on Firm Performance in China,' *Asia Pacific Journal of Management*, 27(4): 677–695.

Larcker, D.F., Richardson, S.A. and Tuna, I. (2007) 'Corporate Governance, Accounting Outcomes, and Organizational Performance,' *The Accounting Review*, 82(4): 963–1008.

Lewin, K. (1946) 'Action Research and Minority Problems,' *Journal of Social Issues*, 2(4): 34–46.

Mallin, C. (2010) *Corporate Governance* (Oxford: Oxford University Press).

Meester, W.J. (2004) *Locational Preferences of Entrepreneurs: Stated Preferences in the Netherlands and Germany* (Heidelberg: Physica-Verlag).

O'Sullivan, M. (2001) *Contests for Corporate Control: Corporate Governance and Economic Performance in the United States and Germany* (Oxford: Oxford University Press).

O'Toole, J., Galbraith, J. and Lawler, E.E. (2002) 'When Two (or more) Heads Are Better than One: The Promise and Pitfalls of Shared Leadership,' *California Management Review*, 44(4): 65–83.

Plattner, M. (2012a) 'Mobile Elite in the Global City: International Managers' Locational Preferences,' in R.D. Schlunze, N.O. Agola and W. Baber (eds), *Spaces of International Economy and Management* (Basingstoke: Palgrave Macmillan): 46–62.

Plattner, M. (2012b) 'Internationalization of Business Networks: How Do Managers with Divergent Cultural Norms Contribute?,' in R.D. Schlunze, N.O. Agola and W. Baber (eds), *Spaces of International Economy and Management* (Basingstoke: Palgrave Macmillan): 322–346.

Schein, E.H. (2004) *Organizational Culture and Leadership* (San Francisco, CA: Jossey-Bass).

Schlunze, R.D. (2012) '"Hybrid" Managers Creating Cross-cultural Synergy: A Systematic Interview Survey from Japan,' in R.D. Schlunze, N.O. Agola and W. Baber (eds), *Spaces of International Economy and Management* (Basingstoke: Palgrave Macmillan): 24–45.

Schlunze, R.D. and Ji, W. (2012) 'Co-leadership Success by Mutual Acculturation,' *Ritsumeikan Business Review*, 51(6): 1–16.

Schlunze, R.D. and Plattner, M. (2007) 'Evaluating International Managers' Practices and Locational Preferences in the Global City – An Analytical Framework,' *Ritsumeikan Business Review*, 46(1): 63–89.

Schlunze, R.D., Plattner, M. and Ji, W. (2013) 'Co-leadership Success by Sharing Local and Global Information Networks,' in M. Schonhuth, M. Gamper, M. Kronenwett and M. Stark (eds), *Visuelle Netzwerkforschung: Qualitative, quantitative und partizipative Zugänge* (Germany: Transcript Verlag): 181–198.

Schuler, R.S., Jackson, S.E. and Tarique, I. (2011) 'Framework for Global Talent Management: HR Actions for Dealing with Global Talent Challenges,' in H. Scullion and D. Collings (eds), *Global Talent Management* (London: Routledge): 17–36.

Scott, J. (1991) *Social Network Analysis: A Handbook* (Thousand Oaks, CA: Sage).

SIEM (n.d.) SIEM Workshop on Co-leadership at BKC, November 2012, http://www.siemrg.org/manager07.html [accessed November 1, 2012].

SIEM (n.d.) IHRM Workshop for International and R+students, http://www.siemrg.org/manager06.html [accessed November 1, 2012].

Tang, F. and Xi, Y. (2006) 'Exploring Dynamic Multi-Level Linkages in Inter-Organizational Networks,' *Asia Pacific Journal of Management*, 23(2): 187–208.

Tarique, I. and Schuler, R. (2009) 'Global Talent Management: Literature Review, Integrative Framework, and Suggestions for Further Research,' *Journal of World Business*, 45(2): 122–133.

Trompenaars, F. and Hampden-Turner, C. (1998) *Riding the Waves of Culture* (New York: McGraw-Hill).

Weick, K.E. (1989) 'Theory Construction as Disciplined Imagination,' *Academy of Management Review*, 14(4): 516–531.

Wenger, E., McDermott, R. and Snyder, W.M. (2002) *Cultivating Communities of Practice: A Guide to Managing Knowledge* (Boston, MA: Harvard Business School Press).

Wojcik, D. (2006) 'Convergence in Corporate Governance: Evidence from Europe and the Challenge for Economic Geography,' *Journal of Economic Geography*, 6(5): 639–660.

Yeung, H.W.C. (1997) 'Business Networks and Transnational Corporations: A Study of Hong Kong Firms in the ASEAN Region,' *Economic Geography*, 73(1): 1–25.

Yin, R.K. (2003) *Case Study Research: Design and Methods* (Thousand Oaks, CA: Sage).

Zander, L. and Butler, C.L. (2010) 'Leadership Modes: Success Strategies for Multicultural Teams,' *Scandinavian Journal of Management*, 26(3): 258–267.

7
Foreign Direct Investment and Economic Revitalization in Japan: The Role of the Foreign Firm in Niseko

Andrew Staples

7.1 Introduction

Foreign direct investment has traditionally played a marginal role in Japan's economy and business structure.[1] In recent years, however, official policy has become more liberal, and the government now actively promotes inward FDI and foreign participation in the economy (Dolles and Takahashi, 2011). The result has been an increase in annual flow and accumulated stock of FDI, although these remain modest in absolute and relative terms. An assumption underlying this policy trend has been that the tangible and, more importantly, intangible assets that such investments can bring would stimulate the domestic economy and promote structural reform. This chapter investigates these claims with reference to FDI in Niseko, a ski resort on the Northern island of Hokkaido where foreign investment and/or ownership has dramatically increased in recent years, leading to the so-called Niseko boom. Strikingly, this boom has been led largely by foreigners (as investors and tourists) and is notable for the relatively minor role played by domestic firms. Two questions thus guide this chapter: (1) to what extent is foreign direct investment contributing to the economic revitalization of the local and regional economy, and (2) what, if at all, are the implications of the Niseko experience for FDI-led economic revitalization elsewhere?

The following section surveys provides context for this study by examining the political economy of FDI in Japan in recent years, before considering the role of FDI in economic revitalization. Section three then documents the Niseko experience before presenting three firm-level cases of foreign players. A final section offers discussion of this analysis before drawing conclusions, identifying limitations. and detailing the future research direction.

7.2   The political economy of foreign direct investment in Japan

The Japanese multinational and the associated issue of outbound Japanese foreign direct investment has been a major topic of investigation within the sphere of international business since the 1980s (Trevor, 1983; Mason and Encarnation, 1994; Beamish et al., 1997; Encarnation, 1999; Basu, 2000; Hasegawa, 2001; Staples, 2008; Horn and Cross, 2010). Inward FDI, on the other hand, has been very much the poor relation and until relatively recently received only modest attention beyond attempts to explain why there was so little of it (Yoshitomi and Graham, 1996; Blomstrom et al., 2000; Fukao, 2003; Paprzyci, 2006; Paprzyci and Fukao, 2008). In terms of inbound and outbound FDI flows Japan consistently invests far more overseas than it receives from abroad, as shown in Figure 7.1.

Explanations for this imbalance have included the nature of Japanese business organization; ownership structures of Japanese firms; dominance in key industrial sectors including automobiles, electronics and consumer electrical goods; societal preferences for Japanese goods and employers; and a difficult and costly business environment (Francis, 2003; Nikkei, 2005; Paprzycki, 2007). Japan's postwar investment environment moved only slowly from outright prohibition in the 1950s and 1960s to gradual

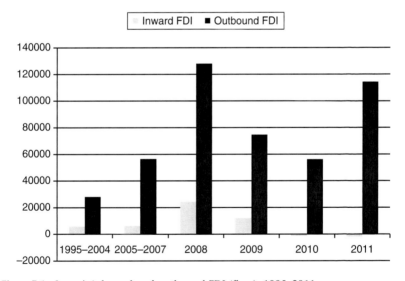

Figure 7.1   Japan's inbound and outbound FDI (flow), 1995–2011
Notes: Author's own compilation. Entries for 1990–2000 and 1995–2004 represent average annual inflows.
Unit: US$ million.
Source: UCTAD, *World Investment Report*, various years.

liberalization resulting from external requirements (IMF and OECD membership, for instance) into the 1970s and 1980s. Although these measures removed some restrictions (particularly around capital movements) and supposedly liberalized the investment regime, the impact was minimal until the bubble years of the 1980s, which witnessed a modest upswing in investment flows, although these were still far below those observed in other developed economies. In short, Japan's model of economic development consciously or otherwise largely excluded foreign investment and was matched by an ambivalence among policy-makers, executives and the general public.

Yet the anemic nature of the Japanese economy in the 1990s, characterized as it was by recession, low growth, intense global competition, bouts of high yen (*endaka*), financial crisis and corporate bankruptcies coupled with the demographic challenges of a falling birthrate and rapidly ageing society, compelled a significant change in attitudes toward inward FDI. Financial crisis in the mid to late 1990s led to an unravelling of cross-shareholding among financial and non-financial firms, which in turn presented opportunities for foreign investors. Indeed, foreign ownership on the Tokyo Stock Exchange increased from 5.3 per cent in 1987 to 26.7 per cent in 2005; instances of out–in mergers and acquisition activity (M&A), hostile takeovers and prevalence of activist investment funds also increased rapidly (Schade, 2006). Renault's rescue of Nissan in 1999 and subsequent dramatic turnaround led by Carlos Ghosn presented a positive case study of foreign involvement in the manufacturing sector. Similar investments in retailing (Costco, Ikea, Zara, Tesco), telecommunications (Vodafone) and financial services (Ripplewood Holdings, Citibank) heralded a new era for Japanese business and the broader economy in which foreign investment was both possible and welcomed.

While some efforts to promote rather than simply allow FDI were made earlier, including the establishment of the Japan Investment Council in 1994, Prime Minister Koizumi's term of office (2001–2006) exemplified the new policy of welcoming foreign involvement in the economy, and explicitly linked this with the notion of 'reform and revitalization.' This was enunciated most clearly by Koizumi himself who stated in 2003 that

> Foreign direct investment in Japan will bring new technology and innovative management methods, and will also lead to greater employment opportunities. Rather than seeing foreign investment as a threat, we will take measures to present Japan as an attractive destination for foreign firms in the aim of doubling the cumulative amount of investment in five years. (MOFA, 2003)

Other contributors to this emergent consensus included the Japan Investment Council's Expert Committee, staffed with politicians, bureaucrats, foreign and Japanese corporate executives, liberal-minded academics and the American Chamber of Commerce in Japan, who funded the 2003 Fukao report, which promoted inward FDI as a means for structural reform and the Keidanren among others.[2]

In essence this consensus promoted FDI as a means of stimulating Japanese business through increased competition, promoting structural reform through the deregulation of the investment environment, introducing innovative technology and management practices, and otherwise 'internationalizing' the economy. As such it is representative of the political agenda of Koizumi at this time, which stressed the need to reform the political, economic and societal structures of Japan.

By the early years of the twenty-first century Japan thus began to actively promote FDI through such measures as the reorientation of Japan's External Trade Organization (JETRO) toward investment promotion; adoption of revisions to legal, tax and accounting regulations; and the establishment of national and regional promotion initiatives. A concomitant improvement in the business environment in the early years of the twenty-first century[3] led to an increase in both stock and flow of FDI during this period, as shown in Figure 7.2.

Although inflows fell from 2009 onward, reflecting the general slowdown in the global economy in the wake of the (ongoing) financial crisis, Japan experienced a significant increase in FDI average annual inflows for the period 1995–2004, which reached just over US$ 5.7 billion, rising to US$ 6.2 billion between 2005 and 2007, and reaching US$ 24.4 billion in 2008 before falling back to US$ 11.9 billion in 2009 and a negative US$ 1 billion in 2010.

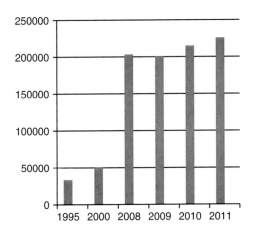

Figure 7.2 Japan's inbound FDI (stock), 1995–2011
Note: Author's own compilation. In US$ million.
Source: UCTAD, *World Investment Report*, various years.

In terms of accumulated stock, Japan's inbound FDI reached US$ 33.5 billion in 1995 and US$ 50.3 in 2000 before jumping to over US$ 200 billion in the three years to 2010. Although these figures represent a significant improvement in both annual flow and stock, comparison with other developed economies (Figure 7.3) demonstrates that Japan receives far less investment than its peers. Even though the government aimed in 2006 to double the cumulative amount of inward FDI to 5 per cent of GDP, even this modest target was missed, and the actual figure was 3.9 per cent.

Political drift after Koizumi gave way to the historic election win for the Democratic Party of Japan (DPJ) in 2009, but increased uncertainty for foreign investors given the party's position on key issues relevant to FDI. Prominent among these is the reform of the Post Office initiated under Prime Minister Koizumi. Indeed, Koizumi regarded this as a critical component of structural reform and forced an election on the issue in 2005. This process was first frozen and then apparently put into reverse soon after the DPJ's election, raising concerns about the government's commitment to reform.[4] Other contemporary issues include a downward revision to the

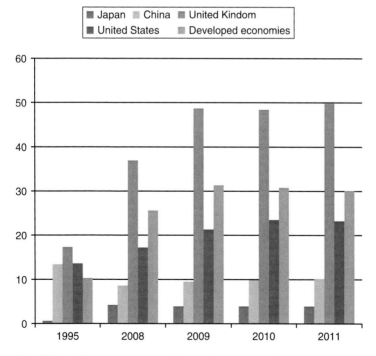

Figure 7.3 FDI stock as a per centage of gross domestic product, 1995–2011
Note: Author's own compilation. In per centage of GDP.
Source: UCTAD, *World Investment Report*, various years.

effective corporate tax rate (among the highest in the OECD at just under 40 per cent), which was mooted and then shelved in the wake of the Tohoku disaster; moves to repeal Koizumi-era labour market deregulation measures with reference to temporary and dispatched workers; and efforts to combat deflation through stimulating consumer demand.

7.3   Foreign direct investment and economic revitalization

As noted above, FDI has been promoted as a means of revitalizing the Japanese economy. The need for economic revitalization is perhaps most pressing in Japan's peripheral and rural 'shrinking'[5] economies. These regions are characterized by the decline of older and traditional industries, rapidly ageing and shrinking populations as the young migrate to major urban areas in search of economic opportunities, and growing financial concerns around unsustainable levels of public debt (Matsutani, 2012; Matanle, 2011). Seaton's (2010) examination of the financial collapse of Yubari, a former coalmining city in central Hokkaido, highlights this issue. In attempting to deal with the long-term economic decline of the city as the mining industry was wound up, local government, aided and abetted by central government, spent huge sums of public funds on developing a tourism industry. These efforts ended in failure, and the city was declared bankrupt in 2006, reflecting a new, more austere environment forced by regional devolution. This is not an isolated case as many rural regions have turned to tourism to maintain local economies. This has, in fact, been encouraged by central government through national campaigns to increase the number of foreign visitors to Japan. The Visit Japan campaign was initialled in 2003 by Koizumi, and the link between foreign visitors and economic revitalization is again made clear in a policy speech, which suggested that '… international visitors can result in regional revitalization and business expansion' (MILT, 2003). While the Yubari experience resulted in financial disaster a far more positive outcome is unfolding in Niseko, western Hokkaido, and it is to this which attention now turns.

7.4   Niseko

Niseko is located in the west of Hokkaido, approximately 90 minutes' drive from the regional capital, Sapporo. While Niseko town itself is a small administrative entity, Niseko Ski Area is taken to refer to the wider region, which includes ski fields located in the separate (and larger) administrative entity of Kutchan town, Grand Hirafu, Hirafu Onsen (hot spring) and Mt Niseko Annupuri. The region is a well-established vacation location for Japanese renowned for its natural splendour as a national park, which includes Mt Yotei, also known as Hokkaido's Mt Fuji given its distinctive conical form. Niseko gained prominence as a ski resort for its consistently heavy falls of high-quality powder snow, which is often ranked on a par with other premier resorts around the world. Apart from skiing the region is popular with holidaymakers in the summer who enjoy the natural scenery, pleasant temperatures, hot springs, adventure sports and other attractions. Peak seasons are thus winter (January to April) and summer (July and August). The regional economy is largely premised on agriculture and tourism, and Niseko/Kutchan has a combined population of approximately 20,000. Niseko Ski Area has a history stretching back over a century, but expanded as a resort during Japan's 'ski boom,' which lasted from the mid-1960s to the late 1980s/early 1990s. Economic recession in Japan in the wake of the bubble economy led to a lack of investment in infrastructure and facilities, and a rapid decline in tourist inflow. So far this represents a familiar story in Japan, which is dotted with disused amusement parks, bankrupted resorts and 'bubble buildings' that sprang up in the 1980s but which are no longer economically unsustainable, if indeed they ever were.

Yet Niseko's subsequent history stands in stark contrast to this bleak picture, and Niseko has become famous in Japan and throughout East Asia and beyond primarily for its growing stature as an Asian-based ski-resort to rival established resorts in North America and Europe. Indeed, Niseko is often promoted as the Aspen of the East.[6] The story of how this once domestically orientated resort with falling visitor numbers located in economically depressed Hokkaido[7] has revived itself through foreign participation has been promoted by regional and national government as an example of the unexpected ways in which FDI can revitalize the economy, with, in this case, particular reference to rural economies (JETRO, 2006).

A significant foreign presence in Niseko is traced back to the mid-1990s when individuals with an interest in skiing and other outdoor pursuits began to visit and stay in the area. A number of these individuals went on to establish small-scale operations including guiding and rafting. A second generation of investors, often tourists drawn to the area through word of mouth, began to establish supporting industries, including tour services and airport transfers in the following years, and the number of foreign visitors to the region began to increase. Established entrepreneurs and developers with backgrounds in tourism, the ski industry and hospitality characterize the third wave of investors, who brought both expertise and funding with them. As the resort developed in the first years of the new millennium investments began to focus more on land acquisition, property development and estate management services. More recently large-scale corporate investment has taken place from the likes of Citibank (2006), Pacific Century Premium Developments, a property arm of Hong Kong billionaire Richard Li's PCCW Ltd (2007), and YTL Corp., a major Malaysian conglomerate. Many of these foreign-owned businesses predominantly cater to the foreign tourist, the numbers of whom rapidly increased over the decade to 2010 (Figure 7.4).

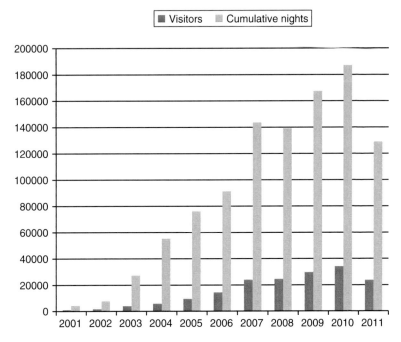

Figure 7.4   Niseko: number of foreign visitors and overnight stays, 2001–2010
Note: Author's own compilation.
Source: Kutchan Town Office.

As Figure 7.5 records, Australians represent the largest group by national-ity, although the national composition of visitors has changed over time. In 2005 Australians accounted for 80 per cent of all foreign tourists staying overnight, while the combined total for Asia reached 14 per cent. By 2010, however, both Australians and Asian visitors each accounted for 43 per cent of the total. Australians have been attracted to Niseko for a combination of factors, which include the reputation of Niseko's snow; the relative strength of the Australian dollar in recent years; the fact that even though Japan is a long-haul flight from Australia, it is more or less on the same time zone; travels concerns with regard to US destinations in the wake of the 2011 ter-rorist attacks; and the opportunity to combine a cultural experience of Japan with a skiing holiday.

While a straightforward comparison between the experiences of Niseko and Yubari is overly simplistic – Yubari is not a ski-resort, and Niseko did not have to deal with the collapse of a major employer – a number of points emerge. First, Niseko's revitalization has been led by foreign investors and foreign tourists. In contrast to the top-down investment of public funds by city officials in Yubari, private investment in Niseko has been bottom-up

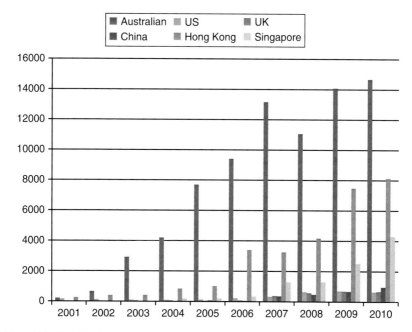

Figure 7.5 Niseko: foreign tourists by nationality
Note: Author's own compilation.
Source: Kutchan Town Office.

and foreign-led. Second, the development of Niseko has at times come in spite of rather than because of the involvement of local government. While many of the key developers are pushing to secure investment in infrastructure to raise the standard of the resort to international levels (see Niseko Masterplan below), local government harbours serious concerns about being dragged into a new cycle of boom and bust whereby they would be left to pick up the pieces (financially and socially) if and when foreign investors left. Third, the impact on the local economy has been dramatic in terms of land prices, employment and tax revenue.

As an example of FDI-led economic revitalization, the Niseko experience is unique within Japan and is thus a legitimate topic for investigation. The following section presents three mini-case studies of foreign-owned firms in Niseko to illustrate the diverse nature of actors and the impact that these investments have had on the local and regional economy.

7.5 Method

In this initial stage of research face-to-face interviews were arranged with key players through various channels, including personal contacts, introductions though JETRO and the Australian Consulate in Sapporo, and Hokkaido University. To date three rounds of interview have taken place (November 2010, March 2011 and May 2011) both in Niseko and Sapporo. The March 2011 round of interviews was prematurely curtailed as a result of the Tohoku earthquake and subsequent nuclear crisis (see below). In addition to the in situ fieldwork, two telephone interviews were conducted within the same period. The intention of conducting the interviews was first to gain a clearer understanding of the contemporary situation in Niseko; second, to see first-hand the nature of the developments; third, to learn from key individuals the issues that they face in conducting their business; and fourth, to help identify key research issues and lay the groundwork for a more in-depth study in the near future. As a consequence of these contacts this research topic has now been incorporated into a project based at Hokkaido University under the umbrella title of 'Sustainable Tourism in Hokkaido.' As such, the future research agenda will adopt a sustainable development framework for analysis.

7.6   Firms in Niseko

The following section seeks to illustrate the nature of foreign-owned firms in Niseko. Although the sample is small it covers firms in different sectors in an attempt to reflect the chronology and qualitative nature of FDI in the area. For these reasons the firms are presented as Company A: property development, sales and management; Company B: institutional investor; and Company C: the spillover effect.

Company A – Property development, sales and management.   Company A was established in 2003 by three Australian entrepreneurs, and was one of the pioneer investors of the fourth wave, as described above. Company A pioneered a model of real estate development relatively unknown in Japan but common in major ski resorts around the world, whereby land is purchased and condominiums built both for owner occupancy and as a source of rental income. Indeed, many owners invest in the properties as part of portfolio diversity in the same way that they might include equities, bonds and gold. Japanese, on the other hand, often purchase property as second homes that are used very infrequently, and therefore have regarded Company A's properties, which regularly exceed US$ 500,000, as too expensive for this use. As a result, approximately 95 per cent of all sales have been to foreigners. Company A's condominiums are strikingly designed and finished to a very high standard. Many offer 'ski-in/ski-out' access to the snow fields, and uninterrupted views across the valley to Mt Yotei or discrete rural locations. These high specifications were previously unknown in Niseko, where accommodation choices had traditionally ranged from large hotels to *ryokan* (guest houses) and log cabins. The construction of properties more commonly seen in the better ski resorts of North America or Europe significantly raised the standard of the resort and generated major revenue in the form of land tax for the local economy, yet also raised some concerns among local Japanese residents who regarded the developments as out of character. The first condominiums were completed in 2003, and were followed by individual resort homes in 2005 and penthouses in 2006. The company had completed the construction of 137 apartments and 44 houses by 2010.

In addition to the purchasing of land for the construction and sale of condominiums, Company A has evolved to offer a full set of management services for investors as well as operating as a traditional agent for accommodation and holiday packages. According to Company A, the market has changed somewhat in the wake of the 2008 'Lehman shock' in that demand is increasingly from high net value individuals from elsewhere in the region who are interested in individual houses for personal use in addition to the more market-driven condominium rental market. This mirrors the trend of increasing numbers of visitors from Singapore, Hong Kong, Malaysia and mainland China as surveyed above. Company A's rapid development is representative of the fast pace of change that Niseko has witnessed in the past decade. Moreover, the company's original vision of creating an international standard ski resort in Japan has underpinned the direction of the resort, which has recently been recognized by larger-scale institutional investors (see below). Company A regards the entry of such players as a win–win for all actors and further evidence of the viability of sustainable development in Niseko. Company A may therefore be seen as an innovative firm introducing global best practice and catering to predominantly wealthy individuals.

Company B – Institutional investor.   Company B is a major publicly listed conglomerate based in Malaysia, and active in the operation and maintenance of large-scale utilities and infrastructure projects, property development and resort operation. It was the first Asian non-Japanese company to list on the Tokyo Stock Exchange in 1996, and has investments in Tokyo commercial properties through a real estate investment trust (REIT). Company B entered the Niseko market in 2010 through the acquisition of Niseko Village, a resort complex consisting of two hotels, two golf courses, ski slopes and land for development. The previous ownership and control of this resort in itself offers a valuable insight into the changing nature of investments in Japan whereby the earlier sale of underperforming assets by Japanese firms to Western firms including investment funds has more recently been succeeded by the disposal of these assets to Asian investors.

Niseko Village was originally known as the Higashiyama Prince Hotel, which was owned and operated by Prince Hotels, a unit of Seibu Holdings, Inc., a major Japanese operator of railways, department stores, hotels and resorts, which traces its heritage back to 1894, although a major reorganization into a holding company was completed in 2005. Rather than invest in a major refurbishment itself, Prince Hotels sold the resort to a unit of Citigroup in 2007 for US$ 54 million. Attracted to the growth potential of Niseko, Citigroup made the acquisition with the intention of refocusing, renovating and rebranding the complex as a year-round global resort and, as part of this turnaround, appointed Hilton Hotels Corporation as the operator. Citigroup's tenure was cut short, however, as the company was forced to raise capital in the wake of the financial crisis that erupted in 2008 and subsequent bail-out by the US government.[8] Company B reportedly purchased the resort for JPY 6 billion (approximately US$ 64 million) in 2010 (Asterisk Reality, 2010).

Company B's investment represents the latest and most significant stage of East Asian-led investment. While the land and buildings were purchased outright, the resort complex itself continues to be operated by Hilton Hotels, which is common practice in this sector. In interviews with the resort's business development manager, the intention of the owners was stated as to balance the demands of both winter (ski) and summer markets. Of the winter market, approximately 50 per cent of guests tend to be from overseas, with Australians representing the largest group. From the spring onward, however, although the market remains roughly evenly split between foreign and domestic guests, East Asians represent the largest group among foreign guests. While Australians stay for the skiing, East Asian guests tend to come for golf, relaxation (spa) and cuisine. This qualitative difference in the guest segments is encouraged as a means to create and maintain a viable year-round resort, which echoes efforts being made elsewhere in the area by private operators and public agencies. In addition to representing the new trend of Asian-based investment, Company B also reflects the development of Niseko as a global resort. As well as the Niseko Village complex, Company B is also behind the development of a luxury residential complex and retail district that will emphasize shopping, dining and relaxation 'experiences,' and by doing so seeks to cater to the demands of wealthy East Asian visitor. This is clearly enunciated in press releases and other corporate material, which presents Niseko as 'the Aspen of the East' (press release, 2010).

Company C – the spillover effect.   Company C was established in Sapporo in 2007, and offers website management and digital marketing services such as search engine optimization (SEO). The founder initially worked in the English-language education sector and operated web-based services on a part-time basis until sufficient demand allowed for the switch to full-time operations. Company C's clients are predominantly foreign-owned firms in the tourism and hospitality sector, although clients have also included public sector organizations (mainly tourism-related) and Japanese firms in the food sector seeking overseas markets, particularly in China. The majority of the foreign-owned firms are clustered in the Niseko area, and clients include the range of firms surveyed above and others – property construction and development, real estate management services, adventure sports, restaurants and tour companies. Although relatively small (the company had six employees as of June 2011), Company C employs foreign (Canadian, American, German and Chinese) and Japanese staff, and is located in the regional capital, Sapporo. Company C's management was initially able to leverage personal connections within the Niseko foreign community to secure multilingual website design, construction and management business. The firm has subsequently evolved with a focus on digital marketing, and now outsources basic functions to programmers outside Japan. After three years of operation, the company successfully secured a commercial loan from a regional bank in 2011 to fund development and expansion. At the time of writing, however, expansion plans were on hold following the impact of the Tohoku earthquake on Japan's tourism industry.

Company C illustrates the 'spillover effect' that has spread from the initial investments in the Niseko area. Many of the Niseko-based enterprises target English-speaking foreign guests, predominantly from Australia and New Zealand, but increasingly from elsewhere in East Asia as documented above. These companies have spurred demand for both English and, increasingly, multilingual websites and supporting services. Company C has successfully identified a gap in the market between these needs of the foreign business community and the abilities of domestically orientated website management and marketing firms. This domestic orientation, mirrored in the practices and services of Japanese-owned hotels in Niseko (tatami rooms, futons, set meals, lack of English, cash orientation, etc.) is sometimes at odds with the demands of the global market. This has been a perennial issue in Japan where hoteliers have traditionally been able to depend on domestic demand leading to an ambiguous response to overseas guests (JETRO, 2007; The Guardian, 2008). Company C's key intangible asset that allows it to compete successfully with local firms is an understanding of both the foreign-owned firm in Japan and the target market coupled with a broader, and harder to define, empathy for global standards. Whether or not this has resulted in the so-called 'demonstration effect' that the foreign-affiliated firm may have on the domestic firm is a matter for future investigation.

7.7 Discussion

The Niseko experience of FDI would seem to support the claim that FDI has a role to play in the economic revitalization of Japan. This experience is all the more noteworthy for the relative lack of involvement by local, regional and national government, and Japanese firms. Further research is required to document impact of Niseko's FDI growth on the local economy in areas including employment and training, consumer spending, land tax revenue and demand for services, but Niseko's fortunes have revived on the basis of foreign investment and foreign tourism, and recent large-scale investments would appear to bode well for future development. The development of a world-class ski resort has also boosted the regional economy, and may serve as a basis for further development of the tourism sector in Hokkaido.

At the same time, it is highly questionable as to whether this experience can be replicated elsewhere in Japan. Understandably, Niseko has been promoted by JETRO and the regional government as a success story, and public officials from elsewhere in Japan have looked to Niseko as a role model for their own development. Niseko's development, however, may be attributable to a unique combination of physical features, timing, economic context and attractiveness to first movers (Australians) that other destinations will struggle to match.

It is also clear that foreign firms have had to struggle to communicate their vision of a leading international resort to the local community and governance structures. Most interviewees lamented a lack of coordination and expertise from local officials, who were reported as sometimes overwhelmed by the scale of demands placed on them by the resort's rapid development. It should not be forgotten that these are small, rural communities and that the emergence of foreign enterprises has taken place only recently and rapidly. As an example, the Niseko Masterplan proposed by the foreign business community, which seeks to put in place the infrastructure that guests expect at expensive resorts such as heated roads, landscaping of urban areas, etc., has only recently been approved and then only in part. Questions have been raised about the sustainability of the resort in the face of rapid land price inflation, land use and the shift in tourists from avid skiers from Australia to wealthy East Asians seeking relaxation, dining and shopping experiences. The impact of the Tohoku earthquake and subsequent nuclear disaster has already had an immediate and negative impact on tourism in Japan, and at the time of writing it remained to be seen whether foreign tourists and investors would return for the winter season in 2012.

This chapter has provided an initial survey of FDI in Niseko, and in doing has highlighted a number of areas for further investigation. At the macro level the Niseko experience holds relevance for policy-makers and the debate surrounding the role of FDI in the economy, with particular reference to economic revitalization through tourism. The issue of sustainable development has also recently gained attention, and is proposed here as a useful analytical framework to employ. Analysing the economic, social and environmental impact of FDI in Niseko will help to identify best practice and present policy recommendations at the local, regional and national level. In this way, our understanding of foreign direct investment in Japan can develop and deepen.

Notes

1. The focus here is on the post-war era, and foreign investments in earlier periods are acknowledged but remain outside the scope of this chapter.

2. See Staples (2007) for a fuller examination of this issue.
3. Japan enjoyed 69 consecutive months of economic growth from February 2002, 12 months longer than the famed *Izanagi* boom of the late 1960s.
4. Postal reform is regarded as a major issue for both domestic structural reform and foreign financial institutions given the size and role that the institution has in Japan. See Kaihara (2008) for a more detailed examination of this point.
5. See the Shrinking Regions project coordinated by Peter Matanle of Sheffield University.
6. Referring here to Aspen, Colorado, a ski resort famous for the patronage of the rich and famous.
7. Hokkaido is ranked 36th out of Japan's 47 prefectures in terms of prefectural income and has the eighth highest unemployment rate (Cabinet Office, National Economic Accounting).
8. Other examples of Asian investors acquiring Japanese assets from Western firms or investment funds include Morgan Stanley's purchase in 2004 of Crowne Plaza Kobe, subsequently sold to the Thai Chaereon Corporation (TCC) in 2009.

References

Asterisk Reality (2010) Hotel Transaction Record in Japan from 2002 (July) to 2010 (April) available at: http://www.asteriskrealty.jp [accessed June 17, 2011].
Beamish, P.W., Delios, A. and Lecraw, D.J. (1997) *Japanese Multinationals in the Global Economy*, New Horizons in International Business Series (Cheltenham: Edward Elgar).
Blomstrom, M., Konan, D. and Lipsey, R. (2000) *FDI in the Restructuring of the Japanese Economy*, National Bureau of Economic Research Working Paper No. 7693.
Cross, A. and Horn, S. (eds) (2010) *Japanese Multinationals in China* (Abingdon: Routledge).
Dolles, H. and Takahashi, Y. (2011) 'The "Lost Decade" and Changes in the Japanese Business Environment: Consequences for Foreign Direct Investment and Human Resource Management in Foreign Subsidiaries in Japan,' in S. Horn (ed.), *Emerging Perspectives in Japanese Human Resource Management* (Frankfurt: Peter Lang): 765–790.
Dipak, B. (2000) *Japanese Multinational Companies* (Bingley: Emerald Group).
Encarnation, D. (1997) *Japanese Multinationals in Asia: Regional Operations in Comparative Perspective* (Oxford: Oxford University Press).
Francis, S. (2003) *FDI Flows into Japan: Changing Trends and Patterns*, International Economic Development Associates, available at: http://www.networkideas.org/misc/statement.htm [accessed July 24, 2013].
Fukao, K. and Amano, T. (2003), *Inward FDI and the Japanese Economy*, available in English and Japanese at: http://www.accj.or.jp/document_library/The FukaoReport/1067587010.pdf [accessed July 24, 2013].
Fukao, K. and Paprzycki, R. (2008) *Foreign Direct Investment in Japan: Multinationals' Role in Growth and Globalization* (Cambridge: Cambridge University Press).
Guardian, The (2008) 'Japanese Hoteliers Turn Backs on Foreign Tourists,' Friday, October 10, 2008.
Hasegawa, H. (2001) 'Globalization and Japanization: Implications for Human Resource Management in Britain,' *Japan Forum*, 13(2), September 1: 159–175(17).
JETRO (2007) *Invest Japan*, 18, Autumn.
JETRO Hokkaido (2006) *Report on the Current Situation of Foreign Tourist Visits and Investment in Niseko Area*, available at: http://www.jetro.go.jp/jfile/report/05001141/05001141_001_BUP_10.pdf [accessed July 17, 2011].

Kaihara, H. (2008) 'Japan's Political Economy and Koizumi's Structural Reform: A Rise and Fall of Neoclassical Economic Reform in Japan,' *East Asia*, 25(4): 389–405.

Mason, M. and Encarnation, D. (eds) (1994) *Does Ownership Matter? Japanese Multinationals in Europe* (Oxford: Clarendon Press).

Matanle, P. and Sato, Y. (2010) 'Coming Soon to a City Near You! Learning to Live "Beyond Growth" in Japan's Shrinking Regions,' *Social Science Japan Journal*, 13(2): 187–210.

Matanle, P. and Rausch, A.S., with the Shrinking Regions Research Group (2011) *Japan's Shrinking Regions in the 21st Century: Contemporary Responses to Depopulation and Socioeconomic Decline* (Amherst, NY: Cambria Press).

Matsutani, A. (2006) *Shrinking Population Economics: Lessons from Japan* (Tokyo: International House of Japan).

Ministry of Foreign Affairs (2003) General Policy Speech by Prime Minister Junichiro Koizumi to the 156th Session of the Diet, January 31, 2003, available at: http://www.mofa.go.jp/announce/pm/koizumi/speech030131.html [accessed July 24, 2013].

Ministry of Land, Infrastructure, Transport and Tourism (2003) Visit Japan Campaign, available at: http://www.mlit.go.jp/kankocho/en/inbound/vjc.html [accessed July 17, 2011].

Nikkei, The (2005) *Japan's Experience with its Liberalization of Foreign Direct Investment and Insights Derived* (Tokyo: Nikkei Research Inc.).

Paprzycki, R. (2006) *The Impact of Foreign Direct Investment in Japan: Case Studies of the Automobile, Finance, and Health Care Industries* (Tokyo: Hitotsubashi University Research Unit for Statistical Analysis in the Social Sciences).

Paprzycki, R. (2007) *The Determinants of and Prospects for Foreign Direct Investment in Japan* (Tokyo: Hitotsubashi University Research Unit for Statistical Analysis in the Social Sciences).

Schaede, U. (2006) *Competition for Corporate Control: Institutional Investors, Investment Funds, and Hostile Takeovers in Japan*, Working Paper No. 248, Center on Japanese Economy and Business, Columbia Business School.

Seaton, P. (2010) 'Depopulation and Financial Collapse in Yūbari: Market Forces, Administrative Folly, or a Warning to Others?,' *Social Science Japan Journal*, 13(2): 227–240.

Staples, A. (2007) 'Inward FDI and Economic Revitalization in Japan: A Political Economy Approach,' in R. Bebenroth (ed.), *In the Wave of M&A: Europe and Japan* (Iudicium: Munich).

Staples, A. (2008) *Responses to Regionalism in East Asia: Japanese Production Networks in the Automotive Sector* (Basingstoke: Palgrave Macmillan).

Trevor, M. (1983) *Japan's Reluctant Multinationals: Japanese Management at Home and Abroad* (London: Pinter).

Yoshitomi, M. and Graham, E. (1996) *Foreign Direct Investment in Japan* (Cheltenham: Edward Elgar).

8
Exploring Thick Description in Business System Analysis: The South Korean Business System from a European Corporate Perception

Flora Bendt, Joakim Sanne, and Harald Dolles

8.1 Introduction

Being aware of the need to support economic growth for local companies the European Union (EU) has been intensifying its global efforts to enhance trade relations. As of July 2011 a free trade agreement (FTA) between the EU and the Republic of Korea (hereafter South Korea or Korea) commenced (EC, 2012). This agreement is considered as 'the most ambitious trade deal ever concluded by the EU' (EC, 2013) and its first with an Asian country, aiming incrementally to eliminate import duties as well as non-tariff barriers and provide an extensive liberalization of trade in services (EC, 2009). Additionally liberalization of investment, both in majority of the service and non-service sectors, is covered by this agreement, reflecting a more inclusive approach to recent trade negotiations by the EU with economic partners. In this way the EU aims to open newly industrialized economies, especially in Asia, and its attractive growth potential to European companies.

An initial evaluation marking the second anniversary of the EU/South Korea FTA reveals an EU trade surplus with South Korea for the first time in fifteen years (EC, 2013). In particular EU exports to South Korea went up by 16.2 percent, from €32.5 billion in 2011 to €37.8 billion in 2012. At the same time EU imports from South Korea grew less, from €36.2 billion in 2011 to €37.9 billion in 2012 (4.7 percent). In addition, the EU's share of total imports to South Korea had increased steadily, from 9.0 percent in 2011 to 9.7 percent in 2012, the largest increase when comparing with imports from China, Japan and the USA into South Korea. EU exports that have enjoyed the biggest boost from the FTA are North Sea oil, machinery, motor vehicles and automotive parts. Alternatively, the decline in South Korea's exports can also partly be explained by the fall in exports of electronics due to a large extent to production from Korea relocating to

South East Asia and those products, which are doing well worldwide and in the EU, are not being exported from South Korea under FTA preferences but rather from other Asian countries (ibid.).

Despite the political efforts to ease doing business in Asia by means of FTAs, the remaining differences in different political, economic and societal environments create a complex background when evaluating business and trade opportunities. Recent research in international business has attempted to address the complexity of the socioeconomic world in two ways. While scholars like Porter (2000) and Hall and Soskice (2001) focused on a rather normative approach on explaining comparative institutional advantage, other researchers followed a more descriptive line when elaborating on distinct societal market orders (Fligstein, 2001). At the same time studies to analyse complex international environments traditionally have examined fragmented analyses and decontextualized findings (Volberda, 2006; Redding, 2005). Reciprocal interactions between institutions and firm activities abroad have been recognized, for example, by Hall and Soskice (2001), Porter (1990) and Whitley (1999). However, neither the economic nor sociological streams of research have been able to converge in their understandings and effectively disentangle interactive effects between political, institutional and cultural traits that characterize historical economic growth and comparative national advantage. Redding (2005) also points on the necessity of analysing societal systems of capitalism including business systems and formal and informal institutions when identifying internationally differing firm-strategic characteristics and opportunities.

The international significance and economic importance of the free trade agreement between the EU and South Korea – actually the first signed free trade agreement between the EU and an Asian economy – and the assumed 'psychic distance' (Johanson and Vahlne, 1977) between both regions induced us to explore the research streams available to investigate the Korean business system by asking the following research questions: *(1) What are the characteristics of the South Korean business system? (2) How are the characteristics of the South Korean business system linked to each other from a foreign (European) corporate perception?* In the business system analysis itself we chose to focus on the perception by European firms on the South Korean market. This intercultural–interpretative approach (Dolles, 1997) builds upon adding non-economical explanations to management research in order to foster understanding of managerial actions and rationality within local contexts. Our assumption is that the intensive exchange with local business partners and institutions reflects comprehensive practical knowledge and experience with the South Korean business system on the one hand by still retaining a distant and comparative perspective on the other.

The chapter begins with the methodology section, reflecting on data collection characteristics. Then a literature review of influential societal aspects in business systems and the chosen research concept is presented.

The following part contains the illustration and analysis of empirical findings covering a novel model of key aspects and linkages of the South Korean business system from a European corporate perception. Managerial implications, limitations and suggestions for further research are addressed in the conclusion.

8.2 Methodology

8.2.1 Data collection

We conducted purposive, non-random sampling and created a sampling frame of managers and sales representatives from European companies holding responsibility for their companies' South Korean market activities. We targeted companies from Sweden and other European countries and from various industry sectors in order to provide eclectic and diversified insights of a European corporate perception of the South Korean business system (see Table 8.1 for details). Industry sectors selected include steel and iron, machinery, automotive, telecommunication and forestry products as well governmental and trade promotion agencies.

When starting the research process, an explorative interview with the South Korean-German Chamber of Commerce and Industry located in South Korea was conducted to identify prime factors of interest. In order to test the developed interview guide as well as to evaluate the chosen conceptual framework we first interviewed a corporate manager formerly responsible for establishing a European corporate sales organization in South Korea. The main investigation was executed afterwards during Spring 2010. Out of the eight interviews shown in Table 8.1, seven were conducted in the Swedish language and one in the German language. All interviews were recorded and transcribed to allow a full assessment. As we are of Swedish and German heritage, we translated the questionnaire from English into Swedish and German in order to meet the interviewees' linguistic diversity. Besides one face-to-face interview, all other interviews were conducted through phone calls. Addressing the disadvantages of phone interviews mentioned in the research methods literature, such as possible misunderstandings, interview summaries were sent to the interviewees for confirmation. All interview transcripts used for analysis have been confirmed.

8.2.2 Data analysis

Analysing the derived findings from the conducted interviews, we followed the logic of qualitative content analysis. Hsieh and Shannon (2009) describe this research technique as a method for subjectively interpreting the content of text data through a systematic process of coding and identifying patterns. In order to increase the validity of this research, a critical incident approach was considered to validate and specify responses with examples of the interviewees' experiences. Flanagan (1954) describes the essential nature of the

Table 8.1 Research sample: Main characteristics

Metrics/ Organization	Country of origin	Industry	Year of entry into Korea	Interviewee position
Company 1	Finland	Steel Manufacturing	1977	Market Development Manager
Company 2	Sweden	Global Hygiene and Paper	1994	Strategic Portfolio Director Developing and Emerging Markets
Company 3	Germany	Electronics	2009	Chief Executive Officer
Company 4	Sweden	Construction	1998	Global Account Manager
Company 5	Sweden	Automotive	1979	CEO for Korean daughter company
Company 6	Sweden	Telecommunication	1894	CEO for Korean daughter company
Organization 7	European	European Governmental Institution	–	Counselor for a European Ministry
Organization 8	Sweden	Trade Promoting Agency	1997	Chief for Korea and Japan

critical incident technique as a process through which specific decisive facts concerning behaviour in defined situations are gathered. The researcher is tasked to apply a set of probes in order to elicit critical information about specific incidents. Such probes involve descriptions of what led to a certain situation, what involved individuals did or did not do effectively, and results of an action.

The critical incidents technique was chosen in order to facilitate research based on understanding a complex context from the interviewees' point of view rather than proving a hypothesis of context details as requested by Redding (2005). Furthermore, the main interview transcript was sent to the participating interviewees in order to ensure both sides' understanding of the primary data collected. For this study information received from the interviewees was triangulated with secondary data from company (corporate reports, newsletters) or further secondary sources (trade reports, newspapers, magazines).

8.2.3 Delimitations

This research focuses on analysing the South Korean business system from an international point of view (secondary sources), accelerated by insights gained from the interviews with European corporate actors. As secondary data in the Korean language was not considered, limitations may result from the chosen distanced assessment by foreign academics and practitioners on the South Korean national business environments. Particular national insights into specific characteristics may have been neglected. At the same time, the linkages drawn between traits of the South Korean business system have a rather subjective character as they solely rely on the interviewees' perceptions. We must admit that the sample size is also relatively small, but still sufficient to draw linkages and to provide a solid ground for further investigation, thus comparing, for example, the Korean and the foreign perspective, or extending the sample with foreign companies from different regions.

8.3   Business system analysis: Theoretical considerations

8.3.1   Varieties of capitalism

As mentioned in the introduction, recent research in international business has attempted to address the complexity of the socioeconomic world in two ways. While scholars like Porter (2000) and Hall and Soskice (2001) focused on a rather normative approach on explaining comparative institutional advantage, other researchers followed a more descriptive line when elaborating on distinct societal market orders (Fligstein, 2001). However, as concluded by Redding (2005), neither the economic nor the sociological stream of research have been able to converge in their understandings and effectively disentangle interactive effects between political, institutional and cultural traits that characterize historical economic growth and comparative advantage in specific contexts.

Redding (2006) acknowledges Porter's (1990) attempt of explaining societal variation in industrial success within the diamond framework, but argues only for a 'weak' consideration of factor and demand conditions (Redding, 1994). Foss (1996) sees a lack of capturing relevant firm-specific features when isolating clusters using Porter's framework. Yetton (1992) further describes the adequateness of Porter's diamond for developed industrial regions rather than for developing countries. Van den Bosch and Van Prooijen (1992) point out the framework's weakness of incorporating national culture as an influencing factor on national comparative advantage.

In their reflection on comparative capitalism Hall and Soskice (2001) develop an approach to varieties of capitalism aiming at incorporating microeconomic perspectives into macroeconomic analyses. A distinct feature of this approach is the consideration of a range of institutions that condition strategic interactions between economic actors, thus enabling national and sub-national analyses of economic performance (ibid.). Whitley (2005b) reinforces the nation-state as a unit of systemic logic since it governs private property rights, regulates conditions for market entry and exit and competitive behaviour, and organizes labour markets. Additionally, Redding (2006) points out that the context of analysis of societal systems of capitalism may contain states, societies, industrial clusters or sectors. Nevertheless, Hall and

Soskice (2001) as well as Whitley (2005a, 2005b) attempt to centralize the role of firms and how institutions of the political economy influence their behaviour, thereby linking microeconomic and macroeconomic analyses. Standing at the center of Hall's and Soskice's (2001) analysis, the firm is seen from a relational point of view, meaning that the development and exploitation of dynamic capabilities and core competencies relies on the quality and coordination of their internal and external relationships. Generally, Whitley (2005b) addresses two key features of capitalism typologies. First, states can be distinguished by the extent to which they are involved in coordinating and steering economic development. This involvement shows strong relations to the state's extent of risk sharing in economic investments. The extent of active encouragement and structuring of independent intermediary associations that represent interest groups reflects the second key feature that helps to compare types of capitalism (ibid.).

The comparative capitalism literature offers several categorizations of market economies. While Amable (2003) distinguishes five types – comprising the market-based model, the social-democratic model, the Continental European model, the Mediterranean model and the Asian model – Hall and Soskice (2001) define two major forms of market economies, which Whitley (2005b) further separates into four state types. As we perceive the conceptualization of Hall and Soskice (2001) and Whitley (2005b) to be rather inclusive, the focus here will be on their categorizations.

Hall and Soskice (2001) categorize two distinct forms of capitalism found as ideal types at the poles of a continuum. One ideal category includes liberal market economies (thereafter LMEs), often exemplified by the political economy of the USA, which are characterized by their relatively strong degree of market coordination mechanisms through investment in transferable assets. The second ideal category of capitalism comprises coordinated market economies (thereafter CMEs), exemplified by the market economies of Germany and Japan, which are defined by their extent of market coordination mechanisms through investment in specific assets (ibid.). Non-market mechanisms governed by state institutions have a relatively large impact on firm behaviour (Jackson and Deeg, 2008). Such states are actively concerned with developing specific industries and actors. They provide financial assistance, sanction failure of specific firms, and have strong influence on entry into new industries. Interest group representation is supported to the extent to which it facilitates the state's coordinating role. Patient capital with a focus on long-term development, cooperative inter-firm relations, and extended vocational and firm-specific training, create a business environment enhancing competitive advantage through gradual innovation (ibid.). Hall and Soskice (2001) further highlight the importance of institutions for relationships that firms develop, especially in situations where markets and hierarchies alone do not lead to firms' coordination of their endeavours. They define institutions as a set of formal and informal rules that economic actors follow for normative, cognitive or material reasons. Such institutions comprise business or employer associations, trade unions, networks of cross-shareholding and collaborations.

Literature about comparative capitalisms focusing on distinct characteristics of institutional frameworks emphasizes the complementary of institutions as the characteristic feature of models of market economies (Deeg, 2005; Amable, 2003). The context of institutional frameworks is reflected by a particular systemic logic comprising rules leading to predictable patterns of behaviour by actors within the system, typical strategies and routine approaches (Jackson and Deeg, 2008). The approach of institutional complementarity suggests that states with a certain form of coordination in one area of an economy may also have evolved complementary practices in other spheres. Thus, institutional complementary would reinforce distinctions between particular forms of capitalism (Hall and Soskice, 2001).

Furthermore, Deeg (2005) describes how countries differ in their complementarity in reinforcing and discouraging certain forms of economic organization and firm behaviour. Whitley (2005b) states that the greater such contradictions between dominant institutional arrangements, the more opportunities companies' top managers have to develop idiosyncratic characteristics and individual firm strategies and capabilities. At the same time, the likelihood for an established cohesive national business system within a state may be low. This aspect reflects the complexity of national complementary institutions and their impact on associated business systems and firm characteristics (ibid.). Besides institutional reproduction of specific organizational capabilities, governance structures, inter-firm relations and employment relations, Redding amends Whitley's theory by addressing historical influences on the development of a nation's societal system of capitalism. Specific historical events, institutions, people or conditions may be found as influences on a nation's development. Redding (2005) highlights the significance of historical forces in their explanatory contribution for the analysis of international business. Furthermore, Hall and Soskice (2001) point out the relation between history and a nation's political economy in the form of actions leading to formal institutions and operating procedures on the one hand and repeated experience building up common expectations that guide actors to effectively coordinate their interactions on the other.

Emphasizing the role of culture, history and informal rules, Hall and Soskice state that formal institutions alone do not guarantee attaining a relevant equilibrium between economic actors. Shared understandings about likely behaviour of economic actors are based on common cultural comprehension. Thus, common understanding or available strategies for action that evolve from experience of acting in a certain environment reflect the concept of culture. A set of informal rules is a result guiding strategic interactions of a political economy. Informal rules based on culture complement situations of incomplete contracting between economic actors (ibid.).

8.3.2 Business system analysis

Amending Whitley's (1992, 1999) theory of business systems, Redding (2005, 2006, 2009) develops a comprehensive model of societal systems that attempts to include microeconomic and institutional features based on a cultural foundation in order to evaluate macroeconomic particularities and linkages across a specific national form of capitalism. Figure 8.1 displays Redding's business system analysis. In order to apprehend historical trajectories in a specific context, three layers need to be examined. The top layer or business system comprehends the main areas of business structures and processes that display a firm's coordination and control of economic activities, comprising ownership patterns, network activities and management styles (Whitley, 2005a). Business systems show specific adjustments and exploitations of the second layer, which reflects formal established orders of the institutional context. The basic layer comprises informal institutions collected under the general term culture (Redding, 2002). Cultural factors of authority, interests and ideology are seen as symbols strongly linked to activities of actors in a system (Weeks and Galunic, 2003; Geertz, 1973).

Starting from the bottom, the culture layer reflects contextual values, norms and socially constructed realities, which have a profound impact on the behaviour of individuals and groups in a society. The *rationale* component of culture represents a society's understanding of the reasons for companies' existence, why economic activities are conducted, and how to conduct such activities. A society's interpretation of horizontal order determines the way individuals are related to each other and reflects the cultural dimension of *identity*. Vertical order, on the other hand, complements a society's culture with the extent to which power based on *authority* is morally legitimized, defined and conducted (Redding, 2005). The cultural concept of authority has also been addressed in Whitley's (2005b) categorization of state types as prevalent norms governing subordination. However, cultural influences on the shape of market economies have often been disregarded or poorly considered (Hall and Soskice, 2001; Gourevitch, 1996).

In Redding's (2005, 2006, 2009) framework, culture underlies the institutional layer, which represents formal forms of order and reflects a standardized and predictable environment for corporations and exchange. Analysing institutions of *capital* includes the accessibility of money and which key actors and tensions are typical in a certain society. Whitley (2005b) refers to financial regulations as the extent of state involvement in economic development involving financial assistance and sanctioning of specific firms, groups and industries. Gourevitch (1996) mentions the influence of financial systems to shape firm structures and relationships among financial institutions, between finance and borrowers as well as each of them and governmental regulators. Furthermore, *human capital* reflects how people are educated in order to contribute to a business system and how the interest group of employees is organized in a labour market with a specific degree of regulation, bargaining and welfare (Redding, 2005). Having a major

BUSINESS SYSTEM		
OWNERSHIP	NETWORKS	MANAGEMENT
Nature of control via ownership (direct, market, alliance) Integration of productions chains under ownership Integration of units in different sectors under ownership	Alliance coordination of production chains Collaboration between competitors Alliance coordination across sector	Employer-empoyee interdependence Delegation to employees

INSTITUTIONS		
CAPITAL	HUMAN CAPITAL	SOCIAL CAPITAL
Sources of funding Conditions of access How is capital mkt. behavior monitored Forces affecting use of capital Key actors Key tensions	Education and training Interest groups: work-related social groupings Labor markets/structures • Active labor market policy programs • Employment protection legislation • Welfare benefits system • Centralization of wage bargaining	Institutionalized trust • Law • Established societal fabric Interpersonal trust • Moral base • Pattern (who is trusted)

ROLE OF THE STATE	ROLE OF CIVIL SOCIETY
• Extent of state dominance and risk sharing • State antagonism to intermediaries • Degree of formal regulation of markets	• Responsibility for order (e.g. professions) • Ethics of trustworthiness to foster exchange • Empowerment decentralization bourgeoisie

CULTURE		
RATIONALE	IDENTITY	AUTHORITY
Formal – instinctive use of maths, scientific, method, economic, logic, accounting Substantive (ends) • What is the firm for? • What is wealth for? • Who is the economy serving? Substantive (means) • Primary carriers • Secondary carriers	To whom does the person instinctively owe allegiance Patterns of support and dependence (looking sideways, not up and down) Options: self, family, working-group clan, professions, community, society at large	On the what basis is authority seen as legitimate How sensitive is the society to hierarchy Related moral norms The conception of control: how do bosses justify their power in the economy

Figure 8.1   A framework for business system analysis
Source: Excerpt from the questions to be asked to construct the analysis of a business system by Redding, 2005: 134.

academic impact on Redding's framework, Whitley (2005b) relates the component of human capital to standardization of skill formation systems and labour relations as well as of interest group representation. Gourevitch (1996) highlights labour relations, national research systems and human resources training as influential policies shaping firm behaviour and organization as well as macroeconomic national distinctions. *Social capital* then defines a society's perceived trust in institutions and a state's legal system as well as perceived trust between individuals. This form of capital is a major reflection of stability patterns of economic exchange (Redding, 2005). Whitley (2005b) in turn addresses the importance of the reliability of legal systems and formal institutions for encouraging economic opportunism or commitment and cooperation among economic actors.

In addition, Redding (2005) includes the *role of the state* as a domain of the institutional layer in order to capture the extent to which a government dominates economic development, the extent of antagonism toward professions, independent banks or parts of civil society, and the degree of formal regulations of markets. This feature can be found in Whitley's (2005b) framework in the form of market segmentation and entry constraints organized by governments. Furthermore, Redding (2005) includes the role of civil society, if developed, to supplement or replace forms of state order. In order to understand how particular cultural traits and institutions have shaped South Korea's business environment, a historical perspective on the country's development is inevitable (Whitley, 1999). Redding (2006) proposes to incorporate *historical trajectories* in his analysis of business systems. Considering that his attempt to capture comprehensive outlines of capitalisms has a rather snapshot character, Redding points out that internal dynamics might be existent yet usually inhibited by constraints of certain ideologies or distinct forms of state planning (ibid.). A historical perspective on the development of national forms of capitalism thus contributes to understanding specific features (Whitley, 1999).

The third layer of a specific business system is strongly shaped by its institutional environment and its underlying culture. It reflects firms, inter-firm relations, and typical management styles. The component *ownership* includes ownership structures as well as boundaries of controlling ownership (Redding, 2005). Market economies show different extents of vertical and horizontal integration of production activities under single corporations. Such structures are strongly influenced by national legal systems (Gourevitch, 1996). However, national industries are too complex to allow a general statement about just one typical structure of a national business system (Redding, 2005). *Networks* reflect links across the economy and between firms, including alliances of production chains and sectors, sourcing or subcontracting relationships and collaboration agreements (Redding, 2005). Gourevitch refers to antitrust policies and linkages to suppliers and distributors for evaluating production systems. The legal system related to cooperation and alliance opportunities considerably shapes a nation's innovation capability and power relations between small and medium-sized enterprises (hereafter SMEs) and major corporations (Gourevitch, 1996). The third domain of business systems comprises the *management* of human, technical and financial resources. There is a specific focus on employee–employer management, interdependent delegation to employees and interaction with labour markets (Redding, 2005).

8.4   Business system analysis: Filling the research framework with data

The results of the analysis are visualized in Figure 8.2. This is built upon the research framework developed in Figure 8.1, filled with the specific characteristics of the South Korean business system as described in the literature and confirmed in the interviews. The factors accentuated by the interviewees will be the prime focus in the following analysis (marked in italic type). Additional attributes of the South Korean business system emphasized during our interviews are marked in bold type. In order to enhance visual clarity, perceived linkages between factors highlighted by our interview partners are displayed in different line layouts. It needs to be noted that the following analysis presents the research results in a very condensed form. A more detailed characterization of the South Korean business system supported with interview statements can be retrieved in Bendt and Sanne (2010). A detailed case analysis showing how radical the transformation of the Korean industry has been during recent years is to be found in the chapter by Park et al. (2013) in this volume.

8.4.1   The South Korean business system – ownership

Policy restructurings after the Asian financial crisis in 1997/98 have resulted in the growing importance of privately owned companies in South Korea (Yanagimachi, 2004). At the same time the public sector still holds a prominent role in the country's economy (Jung, 2001). Previously dominant governmental ownership in banks and large companies was reduced and accompanied by a rising share of foreign ownership in firms. The South Korean economy has been dominated by business groups called *chaebols*, which can be characterized by their diversified business portfolio (Whitley, 1998). Among the largest Korean chaebols production chains are both vertically and horizontally diversified. This implies that upstream and downstream activities are coordinated under one company, which at the same time offers a variety of products and services within different industry sectors (Chung, Lee and Jung, 1997; Hemmert, 2012).

Analysing the development of their Korean subsidiary's ownership structure, all interviewed corporate managers mentioned an increasing gradual commitment to the market. A previously typical market entry was marked by unsolicited customer orders that led to a representation through local distributors and agents. An explanation for the preferred set-up of wholly

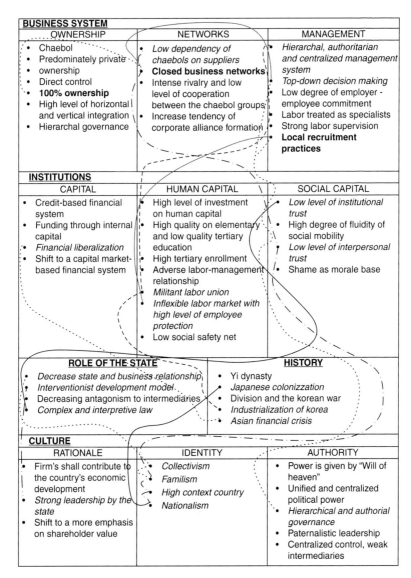

Figure 8.2 Characteristics and linkages of the South Korean business environment

owned subsidiaries may be found in previously stringent FDI regulations, which restricted foreign ownership of Korean companies, as well as a reluctant attitude among Korean companies to cooperate with outsiders. The CEO of a Korean subsidiary concluded: *Some of our competitors that entered the market in recent years have experienced much more difficulties to find good business partners as those are already tied up and Korea is a very closed society* (Interview 5). Therefore we added the characteristic of '**100 per cent ownership**' to the domain ownership. Also, there is a palpable linkage between *ownership* and *networks*, whereas an important foundation for closed networks can be found in the country's cultural domain *identity*.

8.4.2   The South Korean business system – networks

Being of large size, Korean chaebols are quite self-sufficient and exhibit low dependency on suppliers and distributors. Their dominant bargaining power enables chaebols to dominate business partners, which are mostly SMEs that have adjusted their business activities to single corporate customers. When building alliances with firms outside their business group, personal trust is crucial for South Korean companies. Once local distributors and suppliers have entered economic relationships they tend to be strongly bonded to their partners. Committing exclusively to one customer is described by one interviewee as a matter of honour (Interview 5). Thus, the newly identified characteristic '**closed business networks**' can be added to the business system domain of networks. Rather closed business networks reflect a considerable barrier to doing business as trust historically is predominantly acquired through social ties such as the family or the group, and is considered to take time and patience (Bstieler and Hemmert, 2008). According to the CEO of an automotive daughter company in South Korea, fruitful business relations are perceived to depend first and foremost on the ability to build mutual trust between partners, which was supported by the CEO of a telecommunication subsidiary who mentioned: *You need to know that you can rely on people. You need to feel some trust. Then, the contract does not matter that much* (Interview 6). A strong linkage between business *networks* and *social capital* can be drawn. At the same time that the building of mutual trust has been perceived to be strongly connected to familism and nationalism, the linkage between *networks* and *social capital* can be extended to the cultural characteristic of *identity*.

8.4.3   The South Korean business system – management

The organizational system of South Korean corporations can be characterized as hierarchical and disciplined as it reflects the prevailing social pattern. Respect for authority, seniority and job status is a traditional norm. Employees are expected to show a high degree of loyalty toward their employer. At the same time, employees are perceived to be a highly valued asset (Morden and Bowles, 1998). However, Whitley (1999) describes the level of employee–employer commitment for manual workers in most chaebols as limited. While labour mobility has contributed to facilitating structural changes in a dynamic economy, it has also created difficulties for South Korean companies in retaining skilled labour and training staff (Coyner and Jang, 2007). The seniority-based compensation and promotion system during the process of globalization has been gradually adapted to a more competitive environment (Hemmert, 2012). It is also noted by the same author that Korean companies have made these changes at a much faster pace than has been the case in Japan, which was the traditional model for Korean human resource management (Hemmert 2008, 2012).

In our sample several interviewees described Korean employees to be diligent yet reluctant to take decisions within their responsibility without guidance of their managers (Interviews 3 to 6). Hence, European companies attempt to recruit Korean employees who value a European management style marked by appreciation for employee initiative (Interviews 1, 5, 6). A new characteristic of '**local recruitment practices**' thus can be added to the domain of management. In that sense, the domain *management* can be linked to *authority* norms. Four interviewees (1, 2, 6 and 7) highlighted the importance of establishing contacts with managers who have critical power in decision-making. Those contacts in turn imply great potential for building a network leading to successful local business activities. Thus, the relation between *management* and *authority* can be extended to a linkage between *management* and *networks*.

8.4.4 South Korean institutions – capital

Until recently, the South Korean economy was strongly influenced by the governmental Economic Planning Board, which played a central role in mapping industrial development. Through its institutions, the government exercised its role as resource allocator and regulator, including strict control over the financial system and economic decision-making. The Bank of South Korea was directly controlled by the Ministry of Finance (Dicken, 2007). A nationalized banking system along with the government's exclusive right to borrow capital abroad created an underdeveloped domestic capital market, which made it rather difficult for companies in South Korea to raise large amounts of funds (Kim et al., 2004). Governmental control of essential resources, including credits, preferential tax treatment, foreign exchange and licenses for new businesses, led to a strong necessity for private companies to nurture relations with the government and bureaucrats (Jung, 2001). In 2005 South Korea's capitalization rate over its GDP had only reached 88 per cent. Furthermore, corporate financing through capital market remains a sparsely utilized option (Kim, 2008). Recently, however, a younger generation of managers and owners has supported a financial system of indirect and direct financing similar to the US system (Redding and Witt, 2004). Financial liberalization is also reflected by significantly growing inward FDI figures during the financial crisis (Alexander, 2008). One of our interview partners (5) mentioned the acquisition of a former Korean distributor as an opportunity resulting from the business partner's bankruptcy during the financial crisis. Hence, a linkage between *history* and *capital* can be identified.

8.4.5 South Korean institutions – human capital

One of the main national priorities has been to invest in human capital (Lee, 2002). In 2005, the total educational investment from both public and private side was around 7 percent of total GDP, which is well above the average expenditure of around 6 percent among the member states of the Organization for Economic Co-operation and Development (hereafter OECD). In the Global Competitiveness Reports issued by World Economic Forum (hereafter WEF), South Korean primary education was ranked 29th of 133 countries in terms of quality in 2009 and had advanced to 14th place in 2012 (out of 144 countries) (Schwab and Sala-i-Martín, 2009, 2012). South Korea has also significantly expanded its tertiary education over the last twenty years, which has resulted in the highest enrolment rate among OECD countries (ibid.). The WEF ranked South Korea as 49th of 133 countries (2009) and as 44th of 144 countries in terms of the quality of its higher educational system (ibid.).

South Korea has adopted a modern labour institution similar to that of Japan (Yoon, 2005). However, the labour–management relationship in South Korea is of a rather adversarial nature and has become a conflict model that is more similar to Western models (Morden and Bowles, 1998). The labour–management relationship is characterized by the militant attitudes of labour unions towards the management (Yoon, 2005). At the same time, there is tendency among South Korean companies of not hiring members of unions and of actively discouraging employees to join labour unions. The conflictual labour–management relationship is reflected by South Korea's rank in the Global Competitiveness Report of 2012–2013 as 129th out of 144 countries in terms of cooperation in labour–management relations (Schwab and Sala-i-Martín, 2012).

The local CEO of a trade-promoting agency's activities in South Korea and Japan mentioned a strong historical influence on the structure and attitude of labour unions. As labour unions were kept from corporate management decisions during the country's period of industrialization, they developed a rather adversarial attitude towards companies; the CEO added: *Labor union strikes have evolved as an issue for international companies*. A strong linkage between *human capital* and the country's *history* thus needs to be taken into consideration. Thus, a further linkage between *human capital* and *management* can be outlined.

The South Korean labour market is characterized by its relative inflexibility (Hwang, 2006; Kim and Cheon, 2004). This feature is illustrated in the Global Competitiveness Report of 2009–2010, which ranked South Korea as 92nd out of 133 countries in terms of employment rigidity (Schwab and Sala-i-Martín, 2009); largely impeded by regulations in terms of hiring and firing practices, it ranked 109th out of 144 countries (Schwab and Sala-i-Martín, 2012). Furthermore, in a survey conducted by the WEF in 2009, business executives perceived restrictive labour regulations as most problematic for doing business in their countries and ranked it as 4th among 15 other issues (Schwab and Sala-i-Martín, 2009). Highly restrictive lay-off regulations only allow labour downsizing if the company's survival is directly related to this measure. Interviewees 5 and 6 were aware that Korean lay-off regulations are restrictive even in cases of personal misbehaviour shown by employees. In order to prevent such situations the CEO of a telecommunication daughter company in Korea gave special attention to recruitment and selection of employees who will fit into the European corporate culture and are eager to work in such an environment. Hence, a distinct linkage can be found between *human capital* and the business system domain of *management*.

8.4.6   South Korean institutions – social capital

In their studies, Fukuyama (1995) and Peng (2009) categorize South Korea as a low-trust society. Hahm (2003) argues that the high level of distrust can be explained by Korea's cultural heritage, which has assessed law as unnecessary to enable a functioning society as well as a poor substitute for virtue and ethics mentioned by Whitley (1992). Recent studies have identified considerable distrust in social, political and economic institutions, embodied by the legal system, law enforcement or large companies in contemporary Korea (Bstieler and Hemmert, 2008). Interviewee 6 perceived legal enforcement to bear some difficulties for foreign companies as a lack of transparency and an international legal approach has been a hampering factor for committing investments into the South Korean market. The CEO of an automotive company pointed out that despite its non-corrupt character law courts tended to favour South Korean companies in legal disputes. The Counselor for a European Ministry concluded: *Within the frame of laws bureaucrats are given considerable space for finding issues to close contacts' advantage*. Hence, a linkage can be identified between the *role of the state* and *social capital*.

As a result of the rapid economic growth contemporary South Korea displays a strong resemblance to other industrial and post-industrial societies in which wealth, occupation and education determine a person's social status to a large extent (Hwang, 2007). Park (2003) argues that South Korea has displayed a distinctive feature in class distribution and upward social mobility, reflecting the rapid and compressed process of industrialization. South Korea's society is marked by strong familism and an inclination to work with the people within a personal network. Park describes how individuals tend to group in networks based on close interpersonal ties such as blood ties, place of origin and schooling. Individuals outside such networks are not perceived as trustful (ibid.).

8.4.7   The role of the South Korean state

Prior to the Asian financial crisis the government closely interacted with corporations and banks in order to mobilize and channel capital to strategic industries and favoured projects. In line with the Confucian ideology, the government has been applying a patriarchal role toward chaebol companies and established forms of direct control (Tsui-Auch and Lee, 2003). Close relationships between government and business helped to accelerate the country's development while the success of any company became dependent on such relations with the state (Coyner and Jang, 2007). Being identified as one cause for the Asian financial crisis (Sharma, 2004), financial reforms were implemented to transform the relationship between the government and industry (Lee et al., 2002). Still, the Global Competitiveness Report ranked South Korea as 114th out of 144 countries in terms of burden of government regulation and 133th of 144 countries in transparency of policy-making (Schwab and Sala-i-Martín, 2012). In addition, the WEF's survey of business executives in 2009 ranked inefficient government bureaucracy as the main obstacle to doing business in South Korea (Schwab and Sala-i-Martín, 2009). South Korean politicians holding high positions partly have their origin in the country's economic environment, thus ensuring intense interactions between both parties. Successful market entry and penetration still depends on contacts with state representatives (Interviews 2, 5, 7). Until some decades ago, South Korea was a developing economy, in which bonding with the family was a safe investment for a decent living as a state. This cultural behaviour led to a degree of corruption among people with decision-making power (Interview 5). Interview partner 6 experienced that the relation between collectivism, cultural familism and governmental relations in the South Korean economy thus seems to facilitate nepotism. Hence, a linkage between the *role of the state* and *identity* can be proposed.

Apart from tariff duties, non-tariff barriers are perceived to have considerable impact on European companies' local business. In some industries, South Korean regulations and technical standards consist of a collection of US, European and Korean restrictions. Two interview partners assessed the resulting complexity of regulations as raising difficulties for European companies in meeting these demands. The CEO of an electronics company complained: *Getting approvals can easily take up to half a year, a long time during which you cannot realize earnings from a product.* Considering tariff and non-tariff barriers, the distinct interventionist role of the South Korean government reflects the cultural perception of expected strong leadership by the state. Hence, a linkage can be assumed between the *role of the state* and cultural *rationale*. In their survey of the perception of the international business climate in South Korea, Kim and Lee (2007) concluded that one of the major frustrations for foreign investors was the inconsistent interpretation and application of regulations among government agencies. The framing of laws and regulations is usually done rather generally, which makes the application of the law dependent on the discretionary interpretation of working-level officials. These practices have facilitated discrimination and corruption. As a consequence, personal relationships are of more importance (Lee and Hobday, 2003).

8.4.8   South Korean historical influences

Whitley suggests that countries like South Korea that underwent industrialization recently and over a short period of time, did not face the impact of individual detachment from families, pre-industrial structures and values as a result of the gradual alteration of the state. South Korean society could maintain a high degree of homogeneity and isolation from external influences over the centuries, which led to an undiminished leading influence of Confucian values and norms on Korean culture (Whitley, 1991). Hemmert (2012: 21) has labelled the Korean business system 'tiger management,' which he summarizes as a product of a combination of four strong forces – Confucianism, the Japanese influence, the American influence and the military-led industrialization. Interviewee 8 mentioned a distinct nationalist attitude among the South Korean people. When establishing in and penetrating the local market, European companies have experienced a strong nationalistic pride affecting consuming behaviour toward international products, as confirmed by 50 percent of our interviewees. Manufacturing components in South Korea has had a positive side effect of being associated with Korean origin, as stated by the CEO of an automotive company. The counsellor for a European Ministry identified the inward focus of Koreans as a result of historical political threats by colonial powers like Japan. Thus, a linkage between *history* and *identity* can be proposed.

In 1980, the South Korean economic policy started to shift toward a greater degree of liberalization (Dicken, 2007) as the government reduced its role as credit allocator (Kim et al., 2004). Loans, associated with preferential interest rates from the government, were gradually removed while commercial banks were privatized. Nevertheless, there were still factors that imposed barriers on the development of a domestic capital market in South Korea, such as lack of transparency and weak corporate governance (Kim et al., 2004). The financial crisis in the 1990s highlighted structural weaknesses in the South Korean financial system, such as an inefficient credit system (Demetriades and Fattouh, 1999). As a result of South Korea's critical situation, the IMF proposed a rescue package consisting of macroeconomic policies addressing flexible exchange rates, financial sector restructuring, and other structural reforms. On a macroeconomic level, South Korea's market was opened to international trade and capital account liberalization. Further structural reforms addressed the structure and corporate government of chaebols. Although having committed to the IMF rescue package and witnessed a rapid economic recovery, the reform of the South Korean economy remains unfinished. Continued possibilities of state interference in a not fully privatized banking sector, chaebol ownership of non-banking institutions and strong family control over the company, discouragement of labour dismissals, and a remaining protection of the domestic market from the global economy reflect the difficulty of significantly changing the South Korean national economy within a few years (Kwon, 2007).

8.4.9 South Korean culture – rationale, identity and authority

An underlying business rationale in South Korean society puts emphasis on the responsibility of firms to contribute to the country's economic development (Redding and Witt, 2007). This rationale is closely linked to national pride and a shared feeling of vulnerability, which originates from a history marked by perceived aggressions from China and Japan as well as a potential war with North Korea (Redding, 2005). Instead of selfishly pursuing individual economic interests, emphasis is put on common needs (Lee-Peuker, 2007). However, this rationale of business is starting to change among a younger generation of managers and owners. A study conducted by Redding and Witt (2007) concluded that this younger generation had a higher propensity to emphasize shareholder values. The Asian financial crisis as well as study visits in the USA have had particular influence on the increasingly Western perception of shareholder value in South Korea (ibid.).

Contemporary South Korean society's strong consideration of the Confucian ideology is reflected in its distinct collective thinking. Among Koreans it is commonly accepted that loyalty is shown by fulfilling expected obligations toward both family and society at the expense of individualism (Hyun, 2001). Interviewee 5 summarized: *Korea is a country which strongly builds on relations. Earlier, the country did not have a social welfare system, which made it necessary to provide and receive help among families and friends. Thus, it is highly important to maintain good relations to authorities.* The strong importance of familism has contributed to a distinct extent of social issues such as nepotism, regionalism and corruption, which in turn is undermining interpersonal trust among the Korean people.

The concept of high- and low-context cultures was introduced by Edward T. Hall in 1960. A high-context culture is marked by characteristics such as eating perceived as a social event, where communication is rather indirect and implicit, and business and work habits tend to be relationship-oriented, with an understanding of building friendships before making business. Also, rewards are based on seniority, work is perceived as a necessity, and respect is associated with hierarchical status and authority. At the same time, individuals in a high-context country show a high degree of acceptance of one's perceived destiny. Kim, Pan and Park (1998) identified South Korea to be a high-context culture as people would tend to be rather socially oriented, satisfied with their existing life, and less confrontational.

Although a majority of countries with Confucian heritage have adopted government institutions similar to Western institutions, the division of governmental power into executive, legislative and judicial bodies rather follows the understanding of imperative unity, which is reflected in a concentration of power in bureaucracy (Ramirez, 2010). Hence, separation of powers was not acknowledged as a necessary means in Korea. The structure of a Confucian government can be characterized as hierarchal, with officials being subordinated to a central political power. While Confucianism supports the notion that governments require acceptance by their subordinates, citizens are not supposed to participate in governmental matters (ibid.). Thus, Ramirez (2010) argues that a Confucian governmental system is not built upon democratic principles. Family types of relationships within a bureaucracy mark the Confucian relationship system. Regulation of mechanisms in a Confucian government is rather conducted by paternalistic leaders than by impersonal authorities. Hence, Confucian bureaucracy is of paternalistic nature (ibid.).

8.5 Conclusion

The description of the South Korean business environment developed in our research (see the summary in Figure 8.2) adds empirical insights of key business system aspects while enlarging earlier work in the field. Summarizing the empirical results, governmental dominance in business structures, network relations among business partners, and institutional trust remain as prominent factors in describing the South Korean business system. At the same time, the strong impact of historical circumstances on the current situation and behaviour has to be confirmed. European companies and organizations highlighted in the interviews the urgent need to consider cultural traits of identity when evaluating the environment for business purposes. At the same time, when doing business in international markets specific characteristics of a business system are perceived by the interview partner as less decisive when compared to local product demand and a stable institutional environment. Increasing local embeddedness in national business systems was assessed to be a rather logical form of business behaviour. Nevertheless, and also mentioned by our interview partners, European companies are able to gain competitive advantage in the South Korean market by applying non-Korean management styles.

This dual nature of adaptation to local conditions might be explained by using the 'adaptation spectrum' developed in research (Dolles and Takahashi, 2011; Kumar and Steinmann, 1989, 1990; Kumar, Steinmann and Dolles, 1993). An adaptation mode of 'social obligation' is followed,

> when the degree of adaptation practised tallies with the perceived differences between home and host country cultural influences. This is the case when the subsidiary responds to market and cultural forces in a manner that meets the imposed constraints or what is almost totally required by economic and legal necessity in the host country. In this case firms hardly have a choice other than to abide by legal and economic rules and institutions. Not adapting to these norms would mean dysfunctionality. (Dolles and Takahashi, 2011: 167)

At the other end of the adaptation spectrum the 'mode of social responsiveness' is proposed, when the degree of adaptation practiced is smaller than the perceived difference between home and host country cultural influences:

> In this case, foreign subsidiaries deliberately behave differently (standardize more) than what present (and changing) host country norms and management practices are perceived to dictate. By reacting differently, foreign subsidiaries strive to compensate for the handicap of foreignness or even get an edge over local enterprises. The assumption is that local stakeholders often will be accommodating towards a foreign subsidiary and its non-conforming management, which in the end may even turn out to be more efficient than prevailing practice. Foreign subsidiaries thus have a change agent function in the host market. (ibid.: 167)

The hypothesized linkages identified by European companies and organizations supported the business system research framework's vertical order of its layers. It can be concluded that business systems depend on formal categories, which in turn are strongly affected by cultural distinctions. At the same time, such linkages need to be confined in their significance as more or less strong interrelations can be identified among any traits of business environments. It can be concluded from the interviews that aligned technical standards, increasing transparency, improving dispute settlement systems, and a more friendly business atmosphere are likely to contribute to increased international competition in the South Korean market. By enhancing Korean companies' competitiveness through local business activities, European companies may in turn have a considerable effect on the shape of the South Korean business system in the future – which is one of the proposed impacts of the EU/Korea Free Trade Agreement.

The political and economic importance of the free trade agreement between the EU and South Korea was as a catalyst to investigate the South Korean business system, which gains added relevance in the EU's international business relations. Choosing an outside perspective for analysing a business system proved to deliver comprehensive insights and assumed linkages between factors that might need a reflective distance to be recognized. The interviewees also confirmed and enhanced by thick description of valuable short stories the main characteristics of our review of the literature on the South Korean business system. The developed framework provides a comprehensive graph of the South Korean business system and implies opportunities for further research. As the South Korean business system is likely to continue undergoing incremental changes, there is a need for follow-up longitudinal studies. Additional insights might also be gained by adding the Korean insiders' perception in research. The main focus of this study was to explore and apply thick description, thereby supporting its relevance as a suitable research method in international business.

Institutional environments need to be analysed in an eclectic context as an isolated assessment will barely meet the variety of environmental influences. Whether filled with primary or secondary data, Redding's model of societal systems and its simple yet comprehensive logic is still one of the most advanced methods in this stream of research.

By considering the elaborated findings of corporate experience and acknowledging cultural implications for business relationship-building, European companies planning to start business activities in South Korea can surpass early irritations and drawbacks resulting from unfamiliarity with the local business environment. Hence, this study provides managers with insights into interrelations between particular characteristics of the South Korean business system that contribute to identifying potential challenges and assessing business opportunities.

References

Alexander, A. (2008) 'Mergers and Acquisitions in Korea: The Leading Edge of Foreign Direct Investment,' US-Korean Institution at SAIS, http://uskoreainstitute.org/bin/g/o/KES08-02.pdf [accessed May 14, 2010].

Amable, B. (2003) *The Diversity of Modern Capitalism* (Oxford: Oxford University Press).

Bendt, F. and Sanne, J. (2010) *The Korean Business System: National Characteristics and the Impact of the FTA between Korea and the EU from a European Corporate Perception*, Centre of International Business Studies, School of Business, Economics and Law at the University of Gothenburg.

Bstieler, L. and Hemmert, M. (2008) 'Trust Formation in Korean New Product Alliances: How Important are Pre-existing Social Ties?,' *Asia Pacific Journal of Management*, 27(2): 299–319.Chung, K., Lee, H. and Jung, K. (1997) *Korean Management: Global Strategy and Cultural Transformation* (Berlin: Walter de Gruyter).

Coyner, T. and Jang, S. (2007) *Mastering Business in Korea: A Practical Guide* (Seoul: Seoul Selection).

Deeg, R. (2005) 'Path Dependency, Institutional Complementarily, and Change in National Business Systems,' in G. Morgan, R. Whitley and E. Moen (eds), *Changing Capitalisms? Internationalization, Institutional Change, and Systems of Economic Organization* (Oxford: Oxford University Press): 21–52.

Demetriades, P. and Fattouh, B. (1999) 'The South Korean Financial Crisis: Competing Explanations and Policy Lessons for Financial Liberalization,' *International Affairs*, 75(4): 779–792.

Dicken, P. (2007) *Global Shift: Mapping the Changing Contours of the World Economy*, 5th ed. (London: SAGE).

Dolles, H. (1997) *Keiretsu: Emergenz, Struktur, Wettbewerbsstärke und Dynamik japanischer Verbundgruppen* [Keiretsu: Emergence, Structure, Competitive Strengths and Organizational Dynamics of Corporate Groupings in Japan] (Frankfurt am Main: Peter Lang).

Dolles, H. and Takahashi, Y. (2011) 'The "Lost Decade" and Changes in the Japanese Business Environment: Consequences for Foreign Direct Investment and Human Resource Management in Foreign Subsidiaries in Japan,' in S. Horn (ed.), *Emerging Perspectives in Japanese Human Resource Management* (Frankfurt am Main: Peter Lang): 165–190.

European Commission (EC) (2009) 'EU-Korea FTA: A Quick Reading Guide,' European Commission, http://trade.ec.europa.eu/doclib/docs/2009/october/tradoc_145203. pdf [accessed February 10, 2010].

European Commission (EC) (2012) 'Countries and Regions: South Korea,' European Commission, http://ec.europa.eu/trade/creating-opportunities/bilateral-relations/ countries/korea/ [accessed January 29, 2013].

European Commission (EC) (2013) 'EU-Korea FTA Sees Strong Rise in EU Exports,' http://trade.ec.europa.eu/doclib/press/index.cfm?id=931 [accessed July 30, 2013].

Flanagan, J. (1954) 'The Critical Incident Technique,' *Psychological Bulletin*, 51(4): 327–358.

Fligstein, N. (2001) *The Architecture of Markets* (Princeton, NJ: Princeton University Press).

Foss, N. (1996) 'Research in Strategy, Economics and Michael Porter,' *Journal of Management Studies*, 33(1): 1–24.

Geertz, C. (1973) *The Interpretation of Cultures: Selected Essays* (New York: Basic Books).

Gourevitch, P. (1996) 'The Macropolitics of Microinstitutional Differences in the Analysis of Comparative Capitalism,' in S. Berger and R. Dore (eds), *National Diversity and Global Capitalism* (Ithaca, NY: Cornell University Press): 239–259.

Hahm, C. (2003) 'Law, Culture, and the Politics of Confucianism,' *Columbia Journal of Asian Law*, 16(2): 254–301.

Hall, P. and Soskice, D. (2001) *Varieties of Capitalism: The Foundations of Comparative Advantage* (Oxford: Oxford University Press).

Hemmert, M. (2008) 'Innovation Management of Japanese and Korean Firms: A Comparative Analysis,' *Asia Pacific Business Review*, 14(3): 293–314.

Hemmert, M. (2012) *Tiger Management: Korean Companies on World Markets* (Abingdon: Routledge).

Hwang, S. (2006) 'Wage Structure and Skilled Development in Korea and Japan,' Korean Labor Institute, http://www.jil.go.jp/profile/documents/Hwang.pdf [accessed February 21, 2010].

Hwang, K. (2007) 'Nation, State and the Modern Transformation of Korean Social Structure in the Early Twentieth Century,' *History Compass*, 5(2): 330–346.

Hyun, K. (2001) 'Sociocultural Change and Traditional Values: Confucian Values among Koreans and Korean Americans,' *International Journal of Intercultural Relations*, 25(2): 203–229.

Jackson, G. and Deeg, R. (2008) 'Comparing Capitalisms: Understanding Institutional Diversity and its Implications for International Business,' *Journal of International Business Studies*, 39(4): 540–561.

Johanson, J. and Vahlne, J.-E. (1977) 'The Internationalization Process of the Firm: A Model of Knowledge Development and Increasing Foreign Market Commitments,' *Journal of International Business Studies*, 8(1): 23–32.

Jung, K. (2001) 'Ownership and Governance Structure of Korean Business Groups,' *International Journal of Asian Management*, 1(1): 69–83.

Kim, D. (2008) 'The Capital Market Consolidation Act and the Korean Financial Market,' in Korean Economy Institute and Korean Institute for International Economic Policy (ed.), *Korea's Economy*, http://www.keia.org/Publications/ KoreasEconomy/2008/Dong-hwan1.pdf [accessed March 6, 2010].

Kim, D., Pan, Y. and Park, H. (1998) 'High- Versus Low-Context Culture: A Comparison of Chinese, Korean, and American Cultures,' *Psychology & Marketing*, 15(6): 507–521.

Kim, H., Hoskisson, R., Tihanyi, L. and Hong, J. (2004) 'The Evolution and Restructuring of Diversified Business Groups in Emerging Markets: The Lessons from Chaebols in Korea,' *Asia Pacific Journal of Management*, 21(1–2): 25–48.

Kim, S. and Cheon, B. (2004) 'Labor Market Flexibility and Social Safety Net in Korea,' Presentation, Korea Labor Institute ADB-Korea Conference on Dynamic and Sustainable Growth in Korea and Asia, Seoul, May 14, 2004.

Kim, W. and Lee, Y. (2007) *The Korean Economy: The Challenges of FDI-led Globalization* (Cheltenham: Edward Elgar).

Kumar, B.N. and Steinmann, H. (1989) 'Managing Subsidiaries of German Companies in Japan: Some Findings of Adaptation Strategies,' in K. Shibagaki, M. Trevor and T. Abo (eds), *Japanese and European Management: Their International Adaptability* (Tokyo: University of Tokyo Press): 244–260.

Kumar, B.N. and Steinmann, H. (1990) 'Managing Japanese Subsidiaries of German Companies: Some Findings for Theory-building on Foreign Subsidiary Management in Japan,' in J. Stam (ed.), *Industrial Cooperation between Europe and Japan* (Rotterdam: Erasmus University Press): 99–114.

Kumar, B.N., Steinmann, H. and Dolles, H. (1993) 'Das Management in Niederlassungen deutscher Unternehmen in Japan – eine empirische Untersuchung unter besonderer Berücksichtigung von Klein- und Mittelbetrieben [Subsidiary Management of German Companies in Japan. An Empirical Investigation with a Focus on Small and Medium-sized Companies],' *Diskussionsbeitrag des Lehrstuhls für Betriebswirtschaftslehre insbesondere Internationales Management (Prof. Dr. Brij N. Kumar)*, no. 2, Friedrich-Alexander-University Erlangen-Nuernberg.

Kwon, O. (2007) 'South Korea,' in A. Chowdhury and I. Islam (eds), *Handbook on the Northeast and Southeast Asian Economies* (Cheltenham: Edward Elgar): 42–60.Lee, C., Lee, K. and Lee, K. (2002) 'Chaebols, Financial Liberalization and Economic Crisis: Transformation of Quasi-Internal Organization in Korea,' *Asian Economic Journal*, 16(1): 17–35.

Lee, J. (2002) *Education Policy in the Republic of Korea: Building Block or Stumbling Block?*, The International Bank for Reconstruction and Development and The World Bank, http://siteresources.worldbank.org/WBI/Resources/wbi37164.pdf [accessed February 15, 2010].

Lee, Y. and Hobday, M. (2003) 'Korea's New Globalization Strategy: Can Korea Become a Business in Northeast Asia?,' *Management Decision*, 41(5): 498–510.

Lee-Peuker, M. (2007) 'A Heuristic Attempt at Understanding Economic Action in South Korea,' *International Journal of Cross Cultural Management*, 7(3): 333–358.

Morden, T. and Bowles, D. (1998) 'Management in South Korea: A Review,' *Management Decision*, 36(5): 316–330.

Park, H. (2003) 'Intergenerational Social Mobility among Korean Men in Comparative Perspective,' *Research in Social Stratification and Mobility*, 20: 227–253.

Park, S.C., Alvstam, C.G., Dolles, H. and Ström, P. (2013) 'Samsung Electronics: From "National Champion" to "Global Leader,"' in C.G. Alvstam, H. Dolles and P. Ström (eds), *Asian Inward and Outward FDI: New Challenges in the Global Economy* (Basingstoke: Palgrave Macmillan): 179–200.

Peng, I. (2009) 'The Political and Social Economy of Care in the Republic of Korea: Gender and Development Programme Paper,' United Nations Research Institute for Social Development, http://www.unrisd.org/unrisd/website/document.nsf [accessed February 22, 2010].

Porter, M. (1990) *The Competitive Advantage of Nations* (London: Macmillan).

Porter, M. (2000) 'Attitudes, Values and Beliefs and the Microeconomics of Prosperity,' in L. Harrison and S. Huntington (eds), *Culture Matters* (New York: Basic Books): 14–28.

Ramirez, L. (2010) 'Culture, Government and Development in South Korea,' *Asian Culture and History*, 2(1): 71–81.

Redding, G. (2002) 'Incorporating Culture Into the Explanatory Framework for Divergent Capitalisms,' in D. Sachsenmaier, J. Riedel and S. Eisenstadt (eds), *Reflections on Multiple Modernities* (Leiden: Brill): 241–268.

Redding, G. (2005) 'The Thick Description and Comparison of Societal Systems of Capitalism,' *Journal of International Business Studies*, 36(2): 123–155.

Redding, G. (2006) 'Asia and its Actors, their Logic and the Challenges,' in S. Söderman (ed.), *Emerging Multiplicity: Integration and Responsiveness in Asian Business Development* (Basingstoke: Palgrave Macmillan): 15–32.

Redding, G. (2009) 'The Business Systems of Asia,' in H. Hasegawa and C. Noronha (eds), *Asian Business and Management: Theory, Practice and Perspectives* (Basingstoke: Palgrave Macmillan): 7–30.Redding, G. and Witt, M. (2004) *The Role of Executive Rationale in the Comparison of Capitalisms: Some Preliminary Findings*, Working Paper of the Euro Asia and Comparative Research Centre, INSEAD, Fontainebleau.

Redding, G. and Witt, M. (2007) *The Future of Chinese Capitalism: Choices and Chances* (Oxford: Oxford University Press).

Schwab, K. and Sala-i-Martín, X. (2009) *The Global Competitiveness Report 2009–2010* (Geneva: World Economic Forum), http://www3.weforum.org/docs/WEF_GlobalCompetitivenessReport_2009-10.pdf [accessed July 28, 2013].

Schwab, K. and Sala-i-Martín, X. (2012) *The Global Competitiveness Report 2012–2013* (Geneva: World Economic Forum), http://www3.weforum.org/docs/WEF_GlobalCompetitivenessReport_2012-13.pdf [accessed July 28, 2013].

Sharma, S. (2004) 'Government Intervention or Market Liberalization: The Korean Financial Crisis as a Case of Market Failure,' *Progress in Development Studies*, 4(1): 47–57.

Tsui-Auch, L. and Lee, Y. (2003) 'The State Matters: Management Models of Singaporean Chinese and Korean Business Groups,' *Organization Studies*, 24(4): 507–534.

Van den Bosch, F. and Van Prooijen, A. (1992) 'The Competitive Advantage of European Nations: The Impact of National Culture – A Missing Element in Porter's Analysis?,' *European Management Journal*, 10(2): 173–177.

Volberda, H. (2006) 'Bridging IB Theories, Constructs and Methods across Cultures and Social Sciences,' *Journal of International Business Studies*, 37(2): 280–284.

Weeks, J. and Galunic, C. (2003) 'A Theory of the Cultural Evolution of the Firm: The Intra-Organizational Ecology of Memes,' *Organization Studies*, 24(8): 1309–1352.

Whitley, R. (1991) 'The Social Construction of Business Systems in East Asia,' *Organization Studies*, 12(1): 1–28.

Whitley, R. (1992) *Business System in East Asia: Firms, Markets and Societies* (London: SAGE).

Whitley, R. (1998) 'Internationalization and Varieties of Capitalism: The Limited Effects of Cross-national Coordination of Economic Activities on the Nature of Business Systems,' *Review of International Political Economy*, 5(3): 445–481.

Whitley, R. (1999) *Divergent Capitalism: The Social Structuring and Change of Business System* (Oxford: Oxford University Press).

Whitley, R. (2005a) 'Developing Transnational Organizational Capabilities in Multinational Companies: Institutional Constraints on Authority Sharing and Careers in Six Types of MNC,' in G. Morgan, R. Whitley and E. Moen (eds), *Changing Capitalisms? Internationalization, Institutional Change, and Systems of Economic Organization* (Oxford: Oxford University Press): 235–276.

Whitley, R. (2005b) 'How National are Business Systems? The Role of States and Complementary Institutions in Standardizing Systems of Economic Coordination and Control at the National Level,' in G. Morgan, R. Whitley and E. Moen (eds), *Changing Capitalisms? Internationalization, Institutional Change, and Systems of Economic Organization* (Oxford: Oxford University Press): 190–231.

Yanagimachi, I. (2004) 'Chaebol Reform and Corporate Governance in Korea,' Presentation at 1st Keio-UNU-JFIR Panel Meeting 'Economic Development and Human Security: How to Improve Governance at the Inter-Governmental, Governmental and Private Sector Levels in Japan and Asia,' Keio University, Tokyo, February 13–14,, 2004.

Yetton, P. (1992) 'Are Diamonds a Country's Best Friend? A Critique of Porter's Theory of National Competition as Applied to Canada, New Zealand and Australia,' *Australian Journal of Management*, 17(1): 89–119.

Yoon, B. (2005) 'Labor Militancy in South Korea,' *Asian Economic Journal*, 19(2): 205–230.

9
Samsung Electronics: From 'National Champion' to 'Global Leader'

Sang-Chul Park, Claes G. Alvstam, Harald Dolles, and Patrik Ström

9.1 Introduction

Samsung Electronics, headquartered in Samsung Town, Seoul, is the flag-ship company of the largest and oldest of the Korean *chaebol*, the Samsung Group. It is one of the world's leading conglomerates, with revenues in 2012 of US$ 248 billion and 369,000 employees (Samsung Electronics, 2012a). Samsung Electronics alone is ranked 20th in the Fortune Global 500 list, with revenues of US$ 184 billion and 222,000 employees (Fortune, 2013). The group started with the founding of Samsung Corporation, a trading company, established by Lee Byung-Chull in 1938, selling fish, vegetables and fruit to China. Within a decade Samsung had flour mills and confectionery machines. The trading function continued to be important, but from what was, according to Chang (2008), a humble beginning, soon embarked on a strategy of rapid diversification into sugar, textiles, various financial services, petrochemicals, shipbuilding, heavy machinery equip-ment and aerospace. By 1950 Samsung had become one of Korea's top ten firms.

Samsung has recorded remarkable achievements in product development, market penetration, strategic acquisitions and sales. As late as in the 1990s, most of its products were categorized as low-cost or medium-cost consumer goods in the advanced economies, although it had been the 'national cham-pion' in its home market for several decades. When the company was hit by the Asian financial crisis in 1997, its chairman, Lee Kun-Hee, was severely criticized for the general management strategy, in particular for the newly started automobile business, Samsung Automobile Co. Ltd. As a result, the owner commenced a major restructuring of the entire group by divesting this part of the conglomerate to the French carmaker Renault, also meeting the requirements of the government to reduce excessive industrial produc-tion capacity as well as to compensate for large losses. Another measure was to sell Samsung Heavy Equipment Co. Ltd to the Swedish Volvo Group in

1998. This deal accounted for US$ 700 million, and was at that time the single largest inward FDI in South Korea.

In the mid-1990s Samsung Electronics chose the Swedish company Ericsson to be one of its benchmarking companies along with General Electric and Sony, in order to strengthen its image as a state-of-the-art technology-based company. It adopted Ericsson's business strategy of aspiring to be the leader in its own field, mobile communication technology equipment. By importing bluetooth technology from Ericsson at the end of the 1990s, the company managed to launch its own mobile telephone business and had become the second largest mobile phone producer in the world by 2005. Finally, in 2012 it overtook Nokia's fourteen-year-long tenure as the world's biggest seller of mobile handsets (Milne, 2013). Samsung Electronics had set its target in the field of home appliances as taking over Sony's position in the global market. Sony produced luxury TV sets and held its largest market share in the 1990s and 2000s. Samsung's TV sets, compared with Sony's, were regarded as medium-range price products in the advanced nations, although it was the world's largest producer in the 1990s. Entry into the luxury TV market at the beginning of the 2000s seemed therefore to involve a high risk, given the high technological barriers and Sony's strong market position. The majority of the Board of Directors were sceptical about the adoption of this strategic target, but were persuaded by Chairman Lee Kun-Hee, who pointed to the opportunities to increase the brand's power in private households. Since Samsung supplied more than 20 per cent of total IC chips and had become the largest producer in the world, it was more known as a business-to-business-actor. The move to become a global player within the high-end consumers' market was in addition a measure to strengthen the brand image. This strategy proved to be successful as Samsung Electronics took over Sony's place in 2005.

Since then, the company's vision for worldwide activities has been to be the leader in the global digital convergence movement. In order to continuously strengthen its position, it aims to develop efficient and innovative technologies in its products portfolio. The present mission to become the best 'Digital eCompany' affects its overall corporate strategies and operations. Indeed, the success of Samsung Electronics to first become a 'national champion' in South Korea, and later to reach global leadership, is closely linked to the industrial policy of the domestic government as well as an aggressive investment strategy based on the strong entrepreneurship of its founder within a conglomerate, family-dominated structure. This is a pattern that is typical for Asian business in general, but may be particularly apparent in the Korean corporate culture. In this context we refer for broad surveys of the fundaments of the Korean business culture and its underlying institutional structure, including Amsden (1989), Chen (2004), Chung, Lee and Jung (1997), Ungson et al. (1997) and, more recently, Hemmert (2008, 2012).

In this chapter we focus on how a company in an emerging economy can succeed in becoming a 'global leader' in the industry, where the main aim is to trace hitherto less observed factors behind international success. It is assumed that Korea with its tradition of creating strong national conglomerates provides a good example in the current process of rapid internationalization in other emerging Asian economies, and that Samsung Electronics in its turn can be seen as a 'role model' for such an expansion strategy. It is described in the chapter how Samsung Electronics was able to take the step from national to global leadership in such a short time, and what lessons that can be drawn from the successful, though not uncontroversial, corporate strategy carried out at group level. It is furthermore based in the methodological tradition of management geography, that is, the identification of the changed economic-geographical patterns as seen from the firm level – a dimension that, in our opinion, has been neglected in economic research (see also Pellenbarg and Wever, 2008; Schlunze, Agola and Baber, 2012; Yeung, 2012). Empirically, the study is mainly based on publicly available secondary data, complemented by qualitative interpretations of strategic changes throughout the studied time period, as suggested by Marschan-Piekkari and Welch (2004), and Yin (2013). In addition, relevant information concerning strategies and competitors in the electronics and telecommunication sector as a whole was used for comparison.

9.2   Theoretical framework

The internationalization process and its geographical expansion of economic activities of a firm can be analysed from two different perspectives (Benito, Petersen and Welch, 2007): the *'economic–strategic'* view, and the *'behavioural, or process-oriented'* view. The economic approach indicates that companies aim to achieve a balance between economic benefits and the appropriate degree of control that enables the company to control risk exposure and have strategic flexibility when it comes to location and entry mode choices (Anderson and Gatignon, 1986). This stream of literature consists of different approaches (Benito, Petersen and Welch, 2007), but for the purpose of this case, we will focus only on two of them. First is the resources-based view, suggesting that the choice of foreign entry mode is driven by the specific resources a particular firm attains; and second is the eclectic paradigm of Dunning (1980, 1993).

The resources-based view is built upon the view that a firm's competitive advantage relates to firm-specific resources, which create unique value and reside in an effective organization. Resources are defined by Barney (1991) as simultaneously valuable, rare, imperfectly imitable, and imperfectly substitutable. When firms go international, we might conclude that firms need to utilize those resources and develop new resources to overcome inherent disadvantages in the new environment. In other words, a firm's successful international development experience presents firm-specific tacit knowledge that is hard to copy (Barney, Wright and Ketchen, 2001). The resources-based view encourages also the involvement of resources in foreign markets as argued by Peng (2001), and therefore expands firms' views toward internationalization and growth strategies. Hoskisson et al. (2000) emphasize the importance of using the resources-based view framework in the context of explaining FDI streams between Western and emerging economies. The traditional approach notes that multinational enterprises from Western economies build their overseas investments with administrative heritage (Bartlett and Ghoshal, 1991), seek competitive advantages through global learning (Bartlett and Ghoshal, 1989), and then reap the benefits as first movers in markets (Hoskisson et al., 2000). The reverse stream argues that multinational enterprises from emerging economies seek market technologies in Western economies and build subsidiaries there in order to access technologies and to compete in the global market (Yeung, 1999).

In contrast to the economic approach, which puts strong emphasis on rational decision-making, the behavioural or process-oriented approach explains firms' international expansion activities from the decision-making process of the entrepreneur, initially suggested by Johanson and Vahlne (1977), and labelled 'The Uppsala model' of internationalization. This internationalization process is not solely based on economic criteria and might include other arguments, such as personal preferences or experiences of the decision-makers in the firm, and was initially developed as a 'stage model,' or 'process theory of internationalization' (Autio, 2005). Johanson and Vahlne later revised their model by strengthening the importance of networks in the internationalization process of firms and by considering trust-building and knowledge creation as important factors (Johanson and Vahlne, 2009). They emphasize now that firms are embedded in business networks that include different actors involved in interdependent relationships, both externally and internally. Internationalization might therefore be analysed as an activity to strengthen or improve a firm's position in its network.

Existing business relationships of a firm influence the selection of foreign markets the firm would like to enter, as well as the selection of the entry mode. The importance of the existing business relationships is led by their ability to provide access to recognize and exploit new opportunities. Johanson and Vahlne point out that learning and commitment building, which take place in the development of business networks, have positive relationships with the identification of opportunities (ibid.). Because some types of knowledge are difficult to access or are limited to network insiders, a strong commitment to partners provides opportunities to firms to access such knowledge. As in the 1977 framework, Johanson and Vahlne's revised model consists of two sets of variables: state variables and change variables, which impact each other. The framework describes processes that are dynamic and cumulative – processes of learning, trust and commitment building. Thus, an increased level of knowledge impacts both trust building and commitment. The authors also added the 'recognition of opportunities' to their conceptualization of 'knowledge.' The identification of opportunities is the most significant element of the body of knowledge that drives the internationalization process. In addition, there are other components, such as needs, capabilities, strategies and networks that are directly or indirectly related to the firms' institutional contexts. The *'learning, creating, and trust-building'* box emphasizes the importance of *'experiential learning,'* thus focusing on the subjective, direct experience in the learning process. In this sense knowledge results from the combination of grasping and transforming individual experience (Kolb, 1984). The *relationship commitment decisions* variable implies the decisions of the firm to increase or decrease the level of commitment to one or several relationships in its network. These decisions would be presented by changes in entry modes, the size of investments, organizational changes, and definitely in the level of dependence. However, a change in commitment would lead to the possibility of both strengthening and weakening the relationship. Generally, there are two types of decisions in terms of commitment to the relationship. The first is to create new relationships, and the second is to build a bridge to new networks and fill structural holes.

It was early observed that FDI from emerging economies followed different patterns when compared to the traditional FDI home countries, and the Western-based theory has gradually been adjusted and amended in order to offer new explanations, with contributions by scholars such as Cantwell and Tolentino, 1990; Chen, 2004; Dunning, 1998; Lall and Chen, 1983; Mathews, 2002; Wells, 1983; and Yeung, 1999. The major differences are to be found, first, in the exogenously, rather than endogenously, based growth of multinationals from emerging economies, which had developed from importing capital, technology and knowledge from abroad, and from foreign-invested enterprises in their own countries; second, when it comes to the active and supporting role of the state in the home country in the creation of national champions. In the 2000s, the theory of outward FDI from emerging economies has further developed, particularly to explain China's growing role as a home country for outward FDI (see e.g. Alon, Fetscherin and Gugler, 2012; Liu, 2007).

9.3   Samsung Electronics

9.3.1   The strategy of Samsung Electronics to become a 'national champion'

After Samsung Electronics was founded in January 1969 as a further step in the diversification strategy of the Samsung Group with an investment of Korean Won 330 million (about US$ 1 million) and given its lack of previous experiences in electronics, a joint venture (Samsung-Sanyo Electronics) was set up in December 1969, with Japan's Sanyo Electric (holding 40 per cent) and Japan's Sumitomo Trading (10 per cent).[1] Manufacturing began in 1970 by producing black and white TV sets, but it was not until 1972 when the venture was able to start selling in large quantities. By 1976 the first million black and white TV sets had been sold from the joint production site in Korea. The first collaboration agreement was followed by another joint venture with NEC in January 1970, with NEC holding 40 per cent and Sumitomo Trading holding 10 per cent, to manufacture home appliances and audio-visual devices.[2] In March 1973 another joint venture, Samsung-Sanyo Parts, was established. Its shareholders were Samsung-Sanyo Electronics, Samsung Electronics and Sanyo Electric. This joint venture was founded to produce parts for televisions, including tuners, deflection yokes, transformers and condensers.[3] In December 1973 Samsung Electronics formed a 50:50 joint venture company with the American Corning Glass Works to produce glass bulbs for the production of cathode ray tubes (Kim, 1997).[4]

It its initial years Samsung Electronics was simultaneously involved in learning a number of different technologies. To accomplish this, it needed foreign partners and expertise. The newly established Samsung Electronics recruited 137 trainees in 1969. They were sent to Sanyo Electric and NEC in 1970 to learn about producing radio condenser speakers, deflecting coils (DY) and transformers (FBT) at Sanyo Electric and about Braun tubes, vacuum tubes, discharge tubes and others at NEC (Samsung Tomorrow, 2012). However, in both joint venture agreements, Samsung only had local market sales rights whereas Sanyo Electric and NEC kept the rights for exports. The electronics business represented at this time a promising, but high-risk opportunity for Samsung. The manufacturing operations began in 1970 by producing black and white TV sets, which were an outdated product even at the time, but more importantly it lacked the necessary technology capability for colour TVs (Kang, 1996). In order to overcome this technological barrier, it managed to persuade Matsushita Denki to supply colour picture tubes for TVs in 1974. One might assume that Matsushita Denki and other Japanese producers judged at this time that Samsung Electronics was far behind in managing the picture tube technology although they offered it.

Despite its late entry and the technological barrier, the company was enabled to produce refrigerators, washing machines, colour TVs, computer monitors and microwaves within a short period of time. But in fact, Samsung Electronics was only able to assemble its parts and key components imported from Japanese suppliers until the late 1970s. As it began producing its own products, many of them were of extremely poor quality. A concept of total quality control did not exist, and the company was not able to improve the quality of its products by itself. One strategy used by Samsung to overcome the technology gap was through 'reverse engineering'. Kim (1997) explains that a product development team was formed in 1976, which began to dismantle a Panasonic microwave oven. The project was successfully completed in 1978. In 1979, Samsung succeeded in developing its own VCR through reverse engineering. According to Jun and Han (1994: 317), Samsung Electronics at that time showed no improvement in creative development unless a similar sample or manual was available as the basis for it to replicate.

In order to increase its production capability and also to secure production of key electronic components the company continued its collaborative or acquisition strategy. In fact, Samsung Electronics secured technology and production facilities for microwave articles by acquiring a US company, Ampherex, which manufactured the key component named as magnetron. As a result, microwave products became a flagship export item for Samsung Electronics for a long time. The company also used to secure production technologies by acquiring private exchanges, jointly developed by the General Telephone and Electronics Corporation (GTE) in the US, and KIST, the Korean Institute of Science and Technology (Chang, 2008). This strategy enabled the company to grow rapidly and systematically, which is one of the major advantages for a conglomerate, and the revenues grew significantly.

The decision by Lee Kun-Hee to enter the semiconductor business became a turning point for the company. The initial reason was to secure a stable supply of components. As a result of the first oil crisis in 1973, Japanese companies could not supply semiconductors properly, which caused vast scheduling problems and led to hold-ups in the TV and refrigerator production facilities. American and Japanese companies owned the necessary technology while the Koreans were only capable of assembling OEM products. The barriers to entry were immensely high, due to the vast capital investment needed in research and product development. Moreover, several US companies, such as Motorola and Fairchild, were already present in the Korean market and refused to carry out any technology transfer to its local competitors. Despite these obstacles, Samsung Group in 1974 took the decision to acquire Korea Semiconductor, at the time an almost bankrupt company, and renamed it Samsung Semiconductor. The first years were difficult, with a lack of technical know-how, and bad timing for the expansion. The company was almost out of business by the late 1970s, but was rescued through bringing in technical expertise from Japan, and a thorough reorganization of production (Lee, 1997).

After the semiconductor industry was stabilized in the early 1980s, Lee Kun-Hee decided to take an even more risky step by entering the 'Very Large Scale Integration' segment with the use of general purpose technologies such as DRAMs. This decision was based on his personal strong belief in the future development of memory chips and the growth of the information technology industry in general. Economies of scale played the most important role in achieving success, and the investment had to be huge. At this point the timing and the size of investment were perfect. Samsung Electronics had become the 'national champion' in its business, and moved continuously to build an Asia-wide company at the beginning of the 1990s. The plant in Giheung, near Seoul, grew to become the world's largest semiconductor production site in 1993 (Ballhaus, Pagella and Vogel, 2009).

In summary, the elements of the corporate strategy of Samsung Electronics to become a national champion were: first, to acquire or to close strategic alliances with foreign firms in order to overcome technology barriers as quickly as possible; second, to take advantage of government industrial policy, which provided various benefits such as R&D funding, financial subsidies, establishing favourable technological standards etc., in order to foster strong domestic companies in strategic sectors; and last, but not least, the fierce entrepreneurship of the owners, being able to take unusually high risks and make vast capital investments. It had not been a big step for Samsung Electronics to become one of the dominant actors in the domestic market. The Korean government had in 1985 introduced a new policy, which included the picking up of 'national champions' and it regarded the electronics sector as a strategic industrial area. Samsung Electronics and its main domestic competitor, LG Electronics (former Lucky Goldstar), were the only candidates for this position. Another example of the close connection between government policy and commercial success in the private sector was when the CDMA (Code Division Multiple Access) was chosen as a standard technology for the mobile communication system in the early 1990s. This decision enabled Samsung Electronics to become the first mover in CDMA technology. The mix of a corporate culture to bring up strong family-based conglomerates in the *chaebol* tradition with a propensity for high-risk ventures, taking advantage of the strong government support, and the close technical and commercial relations with Japanese and American model corporations, paved the way for taking the step from the national to the global arena in a strikingly short time.

9.3.2   Next step: To become a 'global leader'

In June 1993, Chairman Lee Kun-Hee gathered all CEOs in the Samsung *chaebol* at a conference in Frankfurt (Germany), in which he announced a new management strategy, known as 'changing everything but their wives and children' (Grobart, 2013). At that time Samsung Group was the largest *chaebol* in Korea and had attained national championship in most of its business areas. However, Chairman Lee was shocked when he saw how Samsung's products were displayed in remote corners by the major retailers in the advanced nations. After realizing that despite being a champion at home, the company was regarded as a second-class brand in the global market, the Board of Directors set a target for the entire group to become global leader in its various business areas with Samsung Electronics as its main flagship (ibid.).

The first global success had already been secured in the same year by Samsung Semiconductor. When Japanese producers had introduced the 4M DRAM, Samsung Semiconductor was just slightly behind. However, it managed to catch up when it introduced the 16M DRAM, and finally surpassed its competitors with the introduction of the 64M DRAM. Thereafter it maintained its lead through the introduction of the world's first Giga DRAM chip in 1999 (Chang, 2008).

One secret behind its success was to be faster than its competitors from innovation to market, due to a combination of its ability to initiate the development for next-generation products through rapidly growing R&D investments (see Figure 9.1) and to manage the mass production of the current generation (Chang, 2004, 2008; Shin and Jang, 2006). As a result, it contributed to accelerated new product development and was able to generate new technologies, which could be directly applied to next-generation products. Furthermore, it adopted the parallel development method to other related memory products such as the flash memory, which could accelerate the development speed of all products. The company also developed a combined production process technology, which improved production yields (Shin and Jang, 2006). The basic function of the production process technology is that the R&D and production departments interact closely in order to avoid the traditional sequential approach from the process engineers after completing design to the test engineers after taking over the production process. This system forces engineers from design and manufacturing to cooperate with each other, and solves simultaneously many

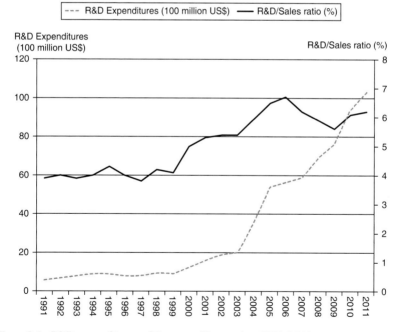

Figure 9.1　R&D expenditures of Samsung Electronics, 1991–2011

Source: Authors' own compilation based on Korea Investors Service (2011); Samsung Electronics (2012a).

technical problems related to the transformation from product development to mass production.

Its huge R&D investment portfolio has resulted in a continuously growing number of patents worldwide. It was ranked no. 2 among global companies, second only to IBM, with almost 5,000 patents granted by the US Patent and Trademark Office in 2011, from a modest level of about 200 patents annually twenty years earlier (see Figure 9.2). Furthermore, the company has also developed a yield estimating system while developing new products or technologies. It is able to estimate how much these can generate market volume or profit from the pilot development stage by integrating the development and production processes. It has furthermore built an internal knowledge sharing system, in which detailed information collected during the development and production processes is stored, and it assigns more than half of the engineers having worked on existing lines in order to build new ones, and enable knowledge sharing between existing and new lines (Chang, 2008).

Another strategy has been to focus on technologies with clear trajectories. After becoming the global leader for DRAMs, the company expanded into flash memory and LCDs. These are high-value-added products, and their production processes are rather similar to those of DRAMs. Therefore, their production lines can be easily shared. Additionally, these products have industrial standards like DRAMs that can be produced with general purpose technologies. It is one of the major competitive assets in Samsung Electronics, because the company can produce commodities with cost

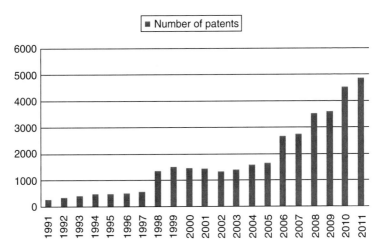

Figure 9.2 Patents assigned to Samsung Electronics by US Patent and Trademark Office, 1991–2011

Source: Authors' own compilation based on US Patent and Trademark Office, Patent Technology Monitoring Team (2012).

advantages compared with competitors. Accordingly, it usually invests in technologies strategically, which have clear trajectories with clear evolutionary progress and industrial standards. This resulted, as was demonstrated in Figure 9.2, in a rapid growth of US patents. Furthermore, the company has had a high patent to investment ratio compared to its competitors, although its R&D investment ratio has not been extremely high. The focus on general purpose technologies has made it possible to rapidly shift to new product development and production efficiency despite its initial weakness regarding technological know-how (Chang, 2004, 2008).

Yet another important strategy of Samsung Electronics was to set a target of aggressive investment and high speed for the TFT-LCD business in the mid-1990s. At that time the company had defect rates as high as 40 to 50 per cent on its 11-inch line for PCs owing to technological weakness (Chang, 2008). Japanese competitors aggressively lowered their product prices in order to cut out Samsung Electronics in the global LCD market. The company responded with aggressive investment in LCDs and outflanked the Japanese by starting a 12-inch line (Asakawa, 2007; Kim, Shi and Gregory, 2004). This was a turning point, and since then, the company has continued its technological upgrading to produce up to 46-inch panels by using the same aggressive investment strategy as it had done previously in semiconductors (Chang, 2008).

There are many other examples as well. In the development of new mobile phone Samsung's design engineers are able to complete the work within three to six months, and to develop eight to ten new platforms per quarter. This is the world's highest speed as well as the broadest platform compared to other global competitors such as Nokia and Motorola, which can release only four to five new products per year with a design cycle of 12 to 18 months. This trend continued until smart phones came to the market in 2009. The reason for the highest speed of new products is mainly based on strong competition between development teams. It means that the competition among models speeds up new product development in Samsung's Mobile Telecommunication division.

Finally, the vertically integrated production processes for key parts such as IC chips or LCDs to end products was another cornerstone in the compound strategy of Samsung Electronics to gain global leadership. The company set its strategic targets to control four central areas: semiconductors or LCDs, computers, communication and consumer electronics in a more tightly connected integration than its competitors. For instance, DRAMs, flash memory, mobile phone chips produced by the Semiconductor division were supplied to the firm's white goods appliances, computers, digital home appliances, communication etc. In order to strengthen its strategy for vertically integrated production systems, it has rearranged its major business areas such as digital media, mobile communications, semiconductor and LCD since 2009 (Jin, 2006; Lee and Slater, 2007; Samsung Electronics, 2012b; Shin and Jang, 2006).

The largest challenge in a vertically integrated business structure is to minimize procurement costs and to enhance the speed of design, development and production. The company was early to introduce advanced supply chain management (SCM) in order to create fast delivery and low inventory costs. As a result, the company can supply products within two to four weeks after receiving an order from foreign dealers. Thanks to its advanced SCM system, it can forecast demand in detail and optimize the results in connection with enterprise resource planning (ERP) by considering various variations such as market demand, trends, past experience and target market share. These systems are valid for all major business areas covering the majority of all products. Additionally, it continuously seeks global suppliers in order to maintain the world's best, based on values such as openness, fairness, win–win (Chang, 2008; Samsung Electronics, 2012b).

9.3.3   The creation of an appropriate organizational structure for a global company

As described previously, the level of globalization in Samsung Electronics was very limited until the early 1990s, with a strong emphasis on local OEM production for exports. Even though the company operated its own local sales subsidiaries in the major markets such as North America and Western Europe, it relied on indirect sales in Southeast Asia, South America and Africa, mainly through the general trading company within the group, Samsung Corporation. When its aggressive globalization strategy started with the 'New Management Movement' initiated by the Chairman Lee Kun-Hee in 1993, the building up of manufacturing abroad was a key issue. As a result, Samsung Electronics had built six production units in North, Central and South America, Malaysia, UK and China by 2006. These plants were completely integrated to cover the entire value chain from parts to components manufacturing to the sales of assembled consumer products. By doing this, the company created various synergies, such as sharing local knowledge, saving labour costs, joint purchase for components and quickly diagnosing management problems (Chang, 2008).

In addition, the entire Samsung Group implemented a regional headquarter system in 1996 in order to strengthen the efficiency of its production and sales units, and to transfer decision-making to the overseas subsidiaries. It was planned that the regional headquarters should operate as the group headquarters in their respective regions. However, the initial results were not as positive as expected. Some of the overseas operations within the group were not profitable because each separate subsidiary in a complex paid the same wages, and production costs for some subsidiaries were higher than elsewhere. Accordingly, actual synergies were limited because the characteristics of the respective business unit were different. Eventually, the regional headquarter system was discontinued (Chang, Yoon and Sohn, 2004). After the dissolution of the regional headquarter system at the group level, Samsung Electronics created a Global Product Manager (GPM) organization in 1998. The organization consisted of 17 business divisions, and each division was responsible for global production and sales organization. The GPM head, located in Korea, had the authority to decide on all crucial issues on strategies, technical support, pricing, production scheduling, etc. The most important goal of GPMs was to increase the productivity and save more on material costs. Local organizations had to follow a GPM's decisions subject to local conditions. Although the GPM system was a clear centralization measure and insensitive to local needs, it worked successfully because the products were mostly global (Lee and He, 2006).

Despite its success, the GPM system had its limitations when it came to further refinement. The GPM heads used to be engineers who had built their careers in production and design centres. Their priorities were often too much focused on increasing production efficiency, and less on understanding how to run overseas businesses. In order to overcome this imbalance, the company carried out a restructuring from GPM to a Global Business Manager (GBM) system in 2001. The GBM functioned in a similar way to GPM, but aimed at widening the perspectives to a focus on the whole business (see Table 9.1).

9.3.4 How to maintain global leadership

As Samsung Electronics has established itself as a leading company on the world market, a number of challenges lie ahead. The company's strategic aim is to be a recognized leader within the global digital convergence movement, bringing together four industries: Information Technologies, Telecommunication, Consumer Electronics and Entertainment (ITTCE) (Samsung Electronics, 2012b). Samsung Electronics perceives itself as well

Table 9.1 Globalization strategies of Samsung Electronics

Period	Strategy	Character	Remark
Early 1990s	Regional Headquarter System	Five Regional HQs and three smaller Regional HQs Decentralized structure and synergy effects	Limited synergy effects
Late 1990s	Global Product Manager (GPM)	Centralized structure and high responsibility Product efficiency and saving material costs	Engineering oriented Limited further refinement
2000s	Global Business Manager (GBM)	Focus on business rather than product Maximizing profits and optimizing global management system	Holistic approach to engineering, design and business

Source: Authors' elaboration.

positioned for this goal through using its different technologies and electronic platforms within telecom, media and audio equipment. The global growth rate in the electronics industry has been sustained despite the 2008–09 recession in advanced economies and the poor forecasts in the old industrial core countries in Europe during the following years. Samsung Electronics is particularly well positioned in emerging markets in Asia, and has a pole position to take advantage of growing consumer demand for electronic products in Africa. The main future competitors will undoubtedly be from China, including, for example, various Chinese '*shanzhai*' brands (imitation and pirated brands and goods) in the mobile phone segment, Skyworth and Hisense producing LCDs, Huawei and ZTE in telecommunications, and Lenovo and Haier within digital media.

The innovative capability of Samsung Electronics together with the commitment of building a strong brand name is important for its development. This creates trust in the market. In order to become a leader within the digital economy the company also recognized the need for building organization capability and to constantly improve production processes to deliver products ahead of competition. Below we summarize a number of crucial factors in terms of strengths, weaknesses, opportunities and threats:

- *Continuous focus on R&D*. The share of R&D investment to sales has continuously increased and amounted in 2011 to 6.2 per cent (see Figure 9.1). As of 2012 Samsung Electronics has expanded to a global network of 24 R&D centres in more than ten different countries, and 42 research facilities around the world (Samsung Electronics, 2012a).
- *Economies of scale*. Compared to its competitors Samsung Electronics is today much larger, and continues to grow. Its revenues in 2011 surpassed the combined revenues of its main global challengers, Sony, Panasonic, LG Electronics and Philips Electronics. The advantages of scale are consistent through the entire value chain, reaching from procurement of raw materials and input components and semi-manufactures, production in its horizontal and vertical segments, to distribution and sales. Samsung offers a wider product range than its competitors within the smart phone area, with a complete portfolio from premium to low-end, which push the unit costs downwards. It is estimated that the smart phone Galaxy S3 sold about 15 million units and about 8 million of its Galaxy Note 2 miniature tablets in 2012 (Mundy, 2013a).
- *Continuous expansion of market position and acquisition of new technology*. Samsung Electronics today is world-leading in most of its production segments, and among the top three in the remaining areas. It has gradually changed from greenfield investments in advanced economies to making aggressive acquisitions in North America and Europe in order to control new technology. The timing has been right. The Korean Won has appreciated against the US dollar as well as the Euro during recent years. In 2012 alone

Samsung Electronics acquired the mobile connectivity and location technology of the British chipmaker CSR, achieved a minority position in the Dutch semiconductor maker ASML, and took over the Swedish semiconductor maker Nanoradio (Song, 2013; Stevenson, 2012; Wallström, 2012).

- *Increasing focus on quality control.* The large scale of operations is also a challenge to quality. Samsung Electronics had to deal with an increasing number of product recalls, due to production errors, and needs to put more emphasis on quality control, in order to avoid negative effects on consumer confidence. Samsung Electronics had adopted the six sigma quality control system implemented by the US company General Electric from the late 1990s, and improved its quality control dramatically. It continues to invest and research on its own quality control system, particularly in the smart phone area (Korea Times, 2011).

- *Diversified business portfolio.* With its extremely diversified production within digital media, telecommunications, semiconductors and LCD technology Samsung Electronics has generated synergies in terms of improvement of market share across the different segments, and has been able to leverage its strength in one segment to others. The diversification has also limited its exposure to risks associated with a particular segment. For example, when the Memory Division accumulated heavy losses, it was supported by the Home Appliance and Telecommunication Divisions; without this support, it was speculated, the Memory Division would not have survived (Chang, 2008). On the other hand, the extreme success in the business area of handsets, whose profits were estimated to account for about two-thirds of total revenue during the final part of 2012, may leave the company too dependent on a single profit source, and it should therefore diversify its earning base into tablets and PCs, according to independent analysts (Mundy, 2013a).

- *Strategic alliances.* The company has been intensely active in forming various types of strategic alliances with other companies – also potential competitors – in different countries for different purposes. Usually these measures have created synergies and reduced development costs through technical collaboration between leading technology companies with different specializations.

- *The monocultural challenge to creativity.* The transition from being a follower to becoming the leader and the benchmark is a main challenge when it comes to giving room to creativity. The corporate culture has hitherto been emphasizing hierarchies, obedience, and execution with a strong orientation on financial targets. Even though this culture has served the company well it can also encumber new ideas and unconventional technical solutions. The preference to hire Koreans or Korean-Americans should also be challenged in a company that will seek to maintain and consolidate global leadership (Chang, 2008; Hemmert, 2012; Lee, 2010; Michell, 2010).

- *Patent litigation lawsuits.* With increasing global presence and market leadership, the number of patent conflicts with main rivals has soared. There are numerous legal suits with Apple in different parts of the world, such as its smart phone innovations. The company has recently stopped seeking a sales ban on Apple's devices, but risks facing charges from EU competition authorities for the breaching of antitrust rules (Song, 2012, 2013). Furthermore, there is a growing conflict with Sweden's Ericsson for alleged infringement of patents in telecommunication network equipment. There is also a growing patent conflict with LG Display in the Korean home market. These different conflicts symbolize an emerging importance of intellectual property rights in a rapidly changing technological environment, and may hamper further development and dramatically raise costs for protecting patents in different parts of the world.
- *Government regulations.* Despite decades of accelerating globalization, national governments still keep the control of regulation and the interpretation of laws within their respective territories. Samsung Electronics has its roots in a country with an unusually high level of active government policy aiming at supporting and protecting its national champions, and has historically taken advantage of less protective measures against foreign companies in countries whose markets they have penetrated. It operates furthermore within areas that traditionally are imposed with formal regulations regarding environmental protection, human health, product safety, consumers' rights, etc. Such regulations are technically equally binding for all companies, domestic and foreign, but can create a competitive advantage for those who have implemented strategies to not only fulfil, but also exceed these requirements, and continuously secure that they are ahead of legislation. It should not be ruled out, however, that in the absence of a powerful multilateral framework, such as the World Trade Organization, the legislative tool may become a more active measure for national governments to push for favouring of local companies as an element in their enterprise policy. In such a case, a company like Samsung Electronics may be particularly vulnerable in the absence of a strong home base, and in the global public eye representing a country with a history of distorting competition for foreign rivals. There is also an increasing awareness of the need to follow its official code of conduct and alleged ethical standards, which in Samsung's case has been questioned in a recent French legal issue (Mundy, 2013b).

9.4   Lessons and conclusions

The case of Samsung Electronics illustrates the speed of globalization and economic transformation in Asia. During a time span of about a decade – from the early 1990s to the early 2000s – the company managed to challenge the traditional industry leaders on the global market within a large number of manufacturing sectors at the same time and with the same success, and it has thereafter managed to consolidate and further strengthen its global position. The combination of several underlying factors can explain this development. It is obvious that the company was able to combine intrinsic entrepreneurial capabilities with Korean government incentives to become a national champion. The commitment to further internationalization through a massive effort to establish production overseas through outward FDI became powerful, and these investments were continuously made to overcome the liability of outsidership in regional markets through production and market establishments as well as a parallel effort to establish a global R&D platform through a superior ability to gain new patents within broad areas. The strong foothold in Asia acted as an incremental process for venturing on the global market. Combined with heavy investments in the brand, it helped to create awareness. Through this process the capability of the company to evaluate and alter the organization, and use the business rather than the product as a guiding platform, has proven to be a successful learning development. This continuous positive attitude to learn and change as well as toward knowledge creation could be recognized in line with Johanson and Vahne's (2009) perspective that learning has a positive relationship with the identification of new opportunities. The role of business networks, as emphasized by Johanson and Vahne (2009), is easy to support in the case of Samsung Electronics. This refers back to the initial set-up of Samsung Electronics, its relation with the Samsung *chaebol*, and the strong government support.

Samsung was founded in 1938 by Lee Byung-Chull, who was educated at Waseda University in Japan (however he did not complete his degree). He was also involved when the treaty-normalizing relation with Japan was signed in 1965, which included payment of reparations and the making of soft loans from Japan and led to increased trade and investment between South Korea and Japan. Thus Lee Byung-Chull had his own informal network with the Japanese to build upon. However Kim (1997) claims that Samsung had initially considered collaborating with American firms, but Sanyo Electric and NEC as joint venture partners were chosen because of the language difficulties inherent in learning about American technology. This confirms the initial finding of Johanson and Vahlne (1977) that the internationalization process is not solely based on economic criteria and includes other arguments, such as personal preferences or experiences of the decision-makers in the firm.

When investigating the initial joint venture partners further the Japanese industrial network structure (*keiretsu* structure) becomes an important feature to explain the selection. NEC and Sanyo Electric were both members of the Sumitomo conglomerate, and thus the involvement of Sumitomo Trading with a minority share in the joint ventures was a 'necessary requirement.' This was based on the way that business relationships were organized in Japan until the end of the 1980s, with major industrial conglomerates and implicit as well as explicit relationships within (Dolles, 1997; Hemmert, 1993). The collaboration with Matsushita Denki later followed the same logic, as Sanyo Electric was founded as a spin-off by Matsushita Denki, but still with close ties.

Samsung Electronics' pace toward globalization might further be explained with comments by Hemmert (2012: 48), who notes that Samsung, in contrast with other *chaebols*, was a 'born global' business in the sense that it started as a trading company. Born global firms are recognized in the literature as early adopters of internationalization, who expand into foreign markets and exhibit international business prowess and superior performance from or near their founding (Knight and Cavusgil, 1996, 2004). The Samsung case highlights the driving forces leading to the rise of born global firms (such as an entrepreneurial spirit and a learning attitude) and the factors that influence their performance (for example, the Korean government's supportive industrial policy).

Samsung Electronic's initial strategy could also be explained as nothing more (or less) than the mimicking of its Japanese rivals at that time: 'Its aim was to become a vertically integrated electronics firm from materials to components to end-products, including consumer and industrial electronics' (Kim 1997: 5). In later stages of its development Samsung Electronics has considered itself as the center of a business network, thus its activities solely aim to support its focal position and advanced technology status in the global network. Realizing that Samsung started to construct its first microwave in 1978 through the help of 'reverse engineering,' it now sets technologically advanced standards, for example, by being the first company in the world to receive a microwave certification mark for anti-bacterial technology, thus recognizing the company's ceramic enamel cavity (Korea Newswire, 2011).

One of the more challenging tasks for Samsung Electronics in the future will be the ability to attract high-potential employees on the global market, and in this sense to become a truly global actor. This has been a problem for many Japanese firms on the global market. To sustain the creative edge a continuous supply of skilled talent, particularly in filling international leadership positions, will be vital.

We might conclude this longitudinal case analysis by suggesting that the dominant Western-based theoretical approaches to understanding the internationalization of the firm have to be amended to better cope with the experiences of companies from emerging economies. Their development is characterized by being laggards in technology, knowledge, and management, as well as initial phases marked by the lack of strong and affluent home markets in which to test new products and new ideas. The Samsung case also demonstrates that a strong coordinated and enduring effort can contribute to overcome these liabilities of double outsidership.

Notes

1. Sanyo Electric's interest was withdrawn during the 1980s, and the company merged with Samsung Electronics.
2. This became the foundation for Samsung SDI, expanding the business from vacuum/picture cathode ray tubes to today's leading LCD, PDP and AMOLED TVs.
3. Sanyo Electric's interest was withdrawn in 1987. The company was renamed Samsung Electro-Mechanics, and is now known a manufacturer of key electronic components, the leading electronic parts maker in Korea and a major global player, with US$ 6.12 billion in revenue (2011). It is the flagship subsidiary of the Samsung Group (Samsung Electro-Mechanics, 2013).
4. Corning Inc. is still collaborating with Samsung, and the Samsung Corning Precision Glass Joint Venture, established in 1995, produces optimizing materials for the electronics industry and glass substrates that are a critical part of TFT-LCDs in Korea.

References

Alon, I., Fetscherin, M. and Gugler, P. (eds) (2012) *Chinese International Investments* (Basingstoke: Palgrave Macmillan).

Amsden, A. (1989) *Asia's Next Giant: South Korea and Late Industrialization* (New York: Oxford University Press).

Anderson, E. and Gatignon, H. (1986) 'Modes of Entry: A Transaction Cost Analysis and Propositions,' *Journal of International Business Studies*, 17(3): 1–26.

Asakawa, K. (2007) *Metanational Learning in TFT-LCD Industry: An Organizing Framework*, RIETI Discussion Paper Series, No. 07-E-029 (Tokyo: Research Institute of Economy, Trade and Industry).

Autio, E. (2005) 'Creative Tension: The Significance of Ben Oviatt's and Patricia McDougall's Article: Toward a Theory of International New Ventures,' *Journal of International Business Studies*, 36(1): 9–19.

Ballhaus, W., Pagella, A. and Vogel, C. (2009) *A Change of Pace for the Semiconductor Industry?* (Hechingen: Kohlhammer und Wallishauser).

Barney, J. (1991) 'Firm Resources and Sustained Competitive Advantage,' *Journal of Management*, 17(1): 99–120.

Barney, J., Wright, M. and Ketchen, D.J. (2001) 'The Resource-based View of the Firm: Ten Years after 1991,' *Journal of Management*, 27(6): 625–641.

Bartlett, C. and Ghoshal, S. (1989) *Managing Across Borders* (Boston, MA: Harvard Business School Press).

Bartlett, C. and Ghoshal, S. (1991) 'Global Strategic Management: Impact on the New Frontiers of Strategy Research,' *Strategic Management Journal*, 12 (Summer): 5–16.

Benito, G.R.G., Petersen, B. and Welch, L.S. (2007) *Foreign Operation Methods: Theory, Analysis, Strategy* (Cheltenham: Edward Elgar).

Cantwell, J. and Tolentino, P. (1990) *Technological Accumulation and Third World Multinationals* (London: Routledge).

Chang, S.-J. (ed.) (2004) 한국기업의 글로벌 경영 사례집 *[Cases of Korean Companies' Global Management]* (Seoul: Parkyoungsa).

Chang, S.-J. (2008) *Sony vs. Samsung: The Inside Story of the Electronics Giants' Battle for Global Supremacy* (Singapore: John Wiley and Sons (Asia)).

Chang, S.-J., Yoon, C. and Sohn, K. (2004) '삼성전자의 해외사업조직 2003년 [Samsung Electronics' Overseas Business Organization 2003],' in S.-J. Chang (ed.), 한국기

업의 글로벌 경영 사례집 *[Cases of Korean Companies' Global Management]* (Seoul: Parkyoungsa): 250–265.

Chen, M. (2004) *Asian Management Systems: Chinese, Japanese and Korean Styles of Business*, 2nd ed. (London: Thomson Business Press).

Chung, K.-H., Lee, H.-C. and Jung, J.-H. (1997) *Korean Management: Global Strategy and Cultural Transformation* (Berlin: Walter de Gruyter).

Dolles, H. (1997) *Keiretsu: Emergenz, Struktur, Wettbewerbsstärke und Dynamik japanischer Verbundgruppen [Keiretsu: Emergence, Structure, Competitive Strengths and Organizational Dynamics of Corporate Groupings in Japan]* (Frankfurt am Main: Peter Lang).

Dunning, J.H. (1980) 'Toward an Eclectic Theory of International Production: Some Empirical Tests,' *Journal of International Business Studies*, 11(1): 9–31.

Dunning, J.H. (1988) 'The Eclectic Paradigm of International Production – A Restatement and Some Possible Extensions,' *Journal of International Business Studies*, 19(1): 1–31.

Dunning, J.H. (1993) *Multinational Enterprises and the Global Economy* (New York: Addison Wesley).

Dunning, J.H. (1998) 'Location and the Multinational Enterprise: A Neglected Factor,' *Journal of International Business Studies*, 29(1): 45–86.

Electronic News (2006) 'Samsung, Siltronic Team Up for $1B Fab,' *Electronic News*, 52(30): 6.

Fortune (2013) 'The 500 Largest Corporations in the World,' available online: http://money.cnn.com/magazines/fortune/global500/index.html [accessed July 19, 2013].

Grobart, S. (2013) 'How Samsung Became the World's No. 1 Smartphone Maker,' *Bloomberg Businessweek*, March 28.

Hemmert, M. (1993) *Vertikale Kooperation zwischen japanischen Industrieunternehmen [Vertical Cooperation between Japanese Industrial Firms]* (Wiesbaden: Deutscher Universitätsverlag).

Hemmert, M. (2008) 'Innovation Management of Japanese and Korean Firms: A Comparative Analysis,' *Asia Pacific Business Review*, 14(3): 293–314.

Hemmert, M. (2012) *Tiger Management: Korean Companies on World Markets* (Abingdon: Routledge).

Hoskisson, R.E., Eden, L., Lau, C.M. and Wright, M. (2000) 'Strategizing in Emerging Economies,' *Academy of Management Journal*, 43(3): 249–267.

Jin, D. (2006) 감성 경영 *[Manage Passion]* (Seoul: Kimyoungsa).

Johanson, J. and Vahlne, J.-E. (1977) 'The Internationalization Process of the Firm: A Model of Knowledge Development and Increasing Foreign Market Commitments,' *Journal of International Business Studies*, 8(1): 23–32.

Johanson, J. and Vahlne, J.-E. (2009) 'The Uppsala Internationalization Process Model Revisited: From Liability of Foreignness to Liability of Outsidership,' *Journal of International Business Studies*, 40(1): 1412–1425.

Jun, Y. and Han, J.W. (1994) 초일류기업으로 가는 길, 서울: 김영사 *[A Way Toward a Best Firm: The Growth and Change of Samsung]* (Seoul: Kimyoungsa).

Kang, J. (1996) 삼성전자 신화의 그 비결 *[The Myth of Samsung Electronics and Its Secrets]* (Seoul: Kyryoone Publishing).

Kim, Y. (1997) *Technological Capabilities and Samsung Electronics' International Production Network in Asia*, BRIE Working Paper No. 106 (Berkeley, CA: University of California, Berkeley Roundtable on the International Economy).

Kim, W., Shi, Y. and Gregory, M. (2004) 'Transition from Limitation to Innovation: Lessons from a Korean Multinational Corporation,' *International Journal of Business*, 9(4): 329–346.

Knight, G.A. and Cavusgil, S.T. (1996) 'The Born Global Firm: A Challenge to Traditional Internationalization Theory,' in S.T. Cavusgil and G.A. Madsen (eds), *Advances in International Marketing*, 8 (Greenwich, CT: JAI Press): 11–26.

Knight, G.A. and Cavusgil, S.T. (2004) 'Organizational Capabilities and the Born Global Firm,' *Journal of International Business* Studies, 35(2): 124–141.

Kolb, D.A. (1984) *Experiential Learning: Experience as the Source of Learning and Development* (Englewood Cliffs, NJ: Prentice Hall).

Korea Newswire (2011) 'Samsung's Microwave Oven is World's First to Win Anti-bacterial Certification,' available online: http://m.newswire.co.kr/newsRead.php?no=542900 [accessed 2 August 2, 2013].

Korea Times (2011) 'Samsung Chairman Stresses Quality Control,' July 20.

Lall, S. and Chen, E. (1983) *The New Multinationals: The Spread of Third World Enterprises* (New York: John Wiley and Sons).

Lee, J. and Slater, J. (2007) 'Dynamic Capabilities, Entrepreneurial Rent-seeking and the Investment Development Path: The Case of Samsung,' *Journal of International Management*, 13(3): 241–257.

Lee, K. (1997) 이 건 희 에세이: 생각 좀 하며 세상을 보자 *[Kun-Hee Lee Essay: Let's Think Before We Look at the World]* (Seoul: Donga Ilbo).

Lee, K. and He, X. (2006) 'Capability of the Samsung Group in Project Execution and Vertical Integration: Creating in Korea and Replicating in China,' *Asian Business & Management*, 8(3): 277–299.

Lee, Y. (2010) 'Samsung's Lee Shifts Strategy in Challenge to Apple,' August 30, available online: http://www.bloomberg.com/news/2010-08-30/samsung-s-rebounding-lee-sees-product-crisis-as-choi-tries-to-triple-sales.html [accessed July 31, 2013].

Liu, C.Z. (2007) 'Lenovo: An Example of Globalization of Chinese Enterprises,' *Journal of International Business Studies*, 38(4): 573–577.

Marschan-Piekkari, R. and Welch, C. (2004) 'Qualitative Research Methods in International Business: The State of the Art,' in R. Marschan-Piekkari and C. Welch (eds), *Handbook of Qualitative Research Methods for International Business* (Cheltenham: Edward Elgar): 5–24.

Mathews, J.A. (2002) *Dragon Multinationals: A New Model for Global Growth* (Oxford: Oxford University Press).

Michell, A. (2010) *Samsung Electronics and the Struggle for Leadership in the Electronics Industry* (Singapore: John Wiley and Sons (Asia)).

Milne, R. (2013) 'Nokia Sends Out Stronger Signal,' *Financial Times*, January 11: 13.

Mundy, S. (2013a) 'Galaxy Helps Samsung Hit Record,' *Financial Times*, January 9, available online: http://www.ft.com/cms/s/0/ccfbf8e2-5932-11e2-b59d-00144feab49a.html#axzz2ZrezznfE [accessed July 19, 2013].

Mundy, S. (2013b) 'Samsung Code of Conduct Put to Test,' *Financial Times*, March 3, available online: http://www.ft.com/cms/s/0/2b6d8012-83e0-11e2-b700-00144feabdc0.html#axzz2ZrbO1PPX [accessed July 19, 2013].

Pellenbarg, P. and Wever, E. (eds) (2012) *International Business Geography: Case Studies of Corporate Firms* (Abingdon: Routledge).

Peng, M. (2001) 'The Resource-based View and International Business,' *Journal of Management*, 27(6): 803–829.

Samsung Electronics (2012a) *Annual Report 2012*, available online: http://www.samsung.com/us/aboutsamsung/ir/financialinformation/earningsrelease/IR_Earnings2007.html [accessed July 19, 2013].

Samsung Electronics (2012b) *Global Harmony with People, Society and Environment*, Sustainability Report 2012, available online: http://www.samsung.com/us/about

samsung/sustainability/sustainabilityreports/download/2012/2012_sustainability_
rpt.pdf [accessed July 19, 2013].

Samsung Electro-Mechanics (2013) 'Samsung Electro-Mechanics – The Future-making
World Class Electromechanical Company in the World,' available online: http://
www.samsungsem.com/introduce/biz_about.jsp?lang=en [accessed August 2, 2013].

Samsung Tomorrow (2012) *The History of Samsung Electronics (1): Paving a New Path (1968–
1970)*, available online: http://global.samsungtomorrow.com/?p=13544#sthash.
wm1xdijO.dpuf [accessed August 2, 2013].

Shin, J. and Jang, S. (2006) 삼성반도체 세계일등 비결의 해부 *[Dissecting the Secrets of
How Samsung Semiconductors became No. 1 in the World]* (Seoul: Samsung Economic
Research Institute).

Schlunze, R.D., Agola, N.O. and Baber, W.W. (eds) (2012) *Spaces of International
Economy and Management: Launching New Perspectives on Management and Geography*
(Basingstoke: Palgrave Macmillan).

Song, J.A. (2012) 'Samsung Seeks US Ericsson Sales Ban,' *Financial Times*, December
26, available online: http://www.ft.com/intl/cms/s/0/137aacec-4f3c-11e2-856f-
00144feab49a.html#axzz2Zrezznf [accessed July 19, 2013].

Song, J.A. (2013) 'Korean Focus on European Deals,' *Financial Times*, January 2: 14.

Stevenson, A. (2012) 'Samsung Buys Handset Operations from UK Firm CSR for
$310m,' *V3.co.uk News*, July 17, available online: http://www.v3.co.uk/v3-uk/
news/2192124/samsung-buys-handset-operations-from-uk-firm-csr-for-usd310m
[accessed July 23, 2013].

Ungson, G.R., Steers, R.M. and Park, S.-H. (1997) *Korean Enterprise: The Quest for
Globalization* (Boston, MA: Harvard Business School Press).

U.S. Patent and Trademark Office, Patent Technology Monitoring Team (2012) *All
Technologies (Utility Patents) Report*, available online: http://www.uspto.gov/web/
offices/ac/ido/oeip/taf/all_tech.htm [accessed December 26, 2012].

Wallström, M. (2012) 'Samsung köper svensk it-bolag' [Samsung buys Swedish IT
company], IDG.se, June 1, available online: http://www.idg.se/2.1085/1.451974/
samsung-koper-svenskt-it-bolag [accessed January 2, 2013].

Wells, L. (1983) *Third World Multinationals: The Rise of Foreign Investments from
Developing Countries* (Cambridge, MA: MIT Press).

Yeung, H.W.C. (1999) *The Globalization of Business Firms from Emerging Economies*
(Cheltenham: Edward Elgar).

Yeung, H.W.C. (2012) 'Foreword: Challenges for Management Geography:
Transnational Management and Global Production Networks,' in R.D. Schlunze,
N.O. Agola and W.W. Baber (eds), *Spaces of International Economy and Management:
Launching New Perspectives on Management and Geography* (Basingstoke: Palgrave
Macmillan): xiii–xix.

Yin, R.K. (2013) *Case Study Research, Design and Methods*, 5th ed. (Thousand Oaks, CA:
Sage).

10
A Business Tale on Marriage, Divorce and Remarriage in the Corporate World: A Conceptual Framework of Firms' Disintegration Process

Roger Schweizer and Katarina Lagerström

10.1 Introduction

Whereas outward foreign direct investment (FDI) by firms from emerging countries is not a new phenomenon, in the current decade emerging multinational companies (MNCs) have entered into a new phase of overseas expansion (Gammeltoft et al., 2010). In 2010, FDI from emerging markets represented 28 per cent (compared to 16 per cent in 2008) of global total FDI (UNCTAD, 2011). Not least, FDI in the form of overseas acquisitions has risen considerably faster than that from developed countries (Cantwell and Barnard, 2008; Duysters et al., 2009; Sauvant, 2008). Cross-border mergers and acquisitions (M&As) accounted for 30.7 per cent of the outward FDI flow from emerging economies compared to 25.2 per cent from developed economies in 2010 (UNCTAD, 2011). Gammeltoft et al. (2010) argue that it seems as though MNCs from emerging markets can turn the crisis in many developed markets into an opportunity to accelerate their international expansion through acquisitions. Indeed, by acquiring firms in developed countries, firms from emerging markets gain not only tangible, but also intangible resources instantaneously – resources and capabilities that otherwise would take time to build internally (cf. Thomas et al., 2007; Wright et al., 2005). Thereby, these firms not only actively consolidate various global industries, and establish themselves as important global players, but also acquire hard-to-develop resources such as brands and technologies. The acquisition of well-known brands is also means for the emerging firms to attain legitimacy in the global marketplace for their own products – Lenovo Group's acquisition of IBM's personal computer business is a well-known example. A study by Athreye and Godley (2009) also accentuates that MNCs from emerging markets prefer acquisitions rather than alliances when expanding internationally since the former allow these firms – often with still relatively weak bargaining power – to attain better control over the acquired asset.

The rise of acquisitions used by MNCs from emerging markets as a means to gain legitimacy and access to essential resources and thereby further expand internationally, results in an additional challenge related to the transaction – a challenge that hitherto has been neglected in the M&A literature. Since many of these firms – for example, Huawei, Tata Motors and Zhejiang Geely Holding Group (Geely) – are latecomers on the international arena (e.g. Luo and Tung, 2007), increasingly, the acquired firms are firms that have already been acquired previously and that first have to be demerged, in order to allow an acquisition by the MNCs from emerging markets. A demerger is essentially the exact opposite of an acquisition, that is, corporate restructurings in which business operations are segregated into two or more entities (cf. Bryer, 2002), with the future intention to operate as completely separate entities. The demerger process is thus of course often a lengthy process where the two firms have to find solutions to divide previously often tightly integrated activities. Nevertheless, what often further complicates many of the demerger processes is that there may be a new partner waiting for the separation to pull through, as in many of the contemporary demergers in the vehicle industry. To name a few: Tata Motors' acquisition of Jaguar and Land Rover, and Geely's acquisition of Volvo Car Corporations (VCC) were only possible after these units were disintegrated from Ford Motor Cooperation (FMC). Further, the planned acquisition of Hummer by Sichuan Tengzhong Heavy Industrial Machinery Company will require that Hummer is disintegrated from General Motors first.

A very common metaphor used when discussing M&As among academics as well as practitioners is to portray such a deal as a marriage (e.g. Cartwright and Cooper, 1993; Dooley and Zimmerman, 2003; Schweizer, 2005). In this analogy, we mean that MNCs from emerging markets often decide to marry late, so that many potential partners that are attractive to MNCs from emerging markets are already married, although not necessarily happily married. Hence, various potential partners still are or have been married before, and therefore are colored by their previous relationships. As implied with the Tata and Geely examples above, MNCs from emerging markets seem frequently acquire firms that have been part of a deal where the objectives of the acquisition were not reached or could not be reached due to changes in industry dynamics or global market trends. This, in turn, implies – as is discussed later in more detail – that the already challenging integration process that follows an M&A is preceded by an equally demanding demerger and disintegration process in which 'the new acquired partner has to go through a divorce and a distribution of marital property in order to be able to re-marry.' Important to note is that, whereas the MNC from the emerging market—as the acquirer – is the governing partner during the integration process and thereby is able to ensure that the purpose of the acquisition is reachable, this is not true for the disintegration process. The latter is a process between the seller and the demerging unit in which the new acquirer has little insight in or control.

The prevailing M&A literature has hitherto neglected the disintegration process following a demerger. Hence, the purpose of this chapter is twofold. First, we contribute to the M&A research by providing a process perspective of a demerger process with a specific focus on the disintegration process. Second, we contribute to the literature on MNCs from emerging markets by discussing the potential additional challenges when integrating an acquired firm that simultaneously is going through a disintegration process.

The chapter draws on empirical evidence from the disintegration process of VCC from FMC in order to conceptualize a process description of a demerger process, with a specific focus on the disintegration process within the Product Development Unit. The empirical evidence depicted in this chapter originates from the study carried out by Thorén and Grahn (2011) as part of a larger ongoing research project related to Greely's acquisition of VCC from FMC, where a wide spread of aspects are captured. However, collection of empirical data on the disintegration process is still continuing. To date more than 20 interviews with persons directly involved in the disintegration process both from VCC and FMC have been conducted. Moreover, the interview data is complemented with documents, company notes, and memos directly connected to the firms' disintegration process.

The chapter begins with a discussion of the hitherto neglected phenomenon of firms' disintegration processes. Thereafter, we draw on the M&A integration process literature and the above mentioned empirical data in order to conceptualize a process description of a demerger process, again with a specific focus on the disintegration process. Finally, we discuss the implication of the disintegration process on MNCs from emerging markets when internationalizing through cross-border M&As.

10.2   The demerger and disintegration process – A neglected phenomenon

M&As have fascinated researchers and practitioners for decades, not least since many firms that acquire or merge with other firms experience their acquisition as disappointing (Risberg, 1999). Indeed, as reported by Gugler et al. (2003), over the last two decades, 43 percent of all merged firms worldwide had lower profits than comparable non-merged firms. Also, earlier studies (e.g. Buono and Bowditch, 1989; Cartwright and Cooper, 1996; Hunt, 1990) suggest that managers of firms involved in M&As rate nearly half of them as unsatisfactory. Two of the commonly used notions for explaining M&A failures are lack of strategic and organizational fit (e.g. Salter and Weinhold, 1981; Shelton, 1988), resulting in cultural clashes (e.g. Buono and Bowditch, 1989; Walter, 1985). Since the seminal paper by Jemison and Sitkin (1986) most scholars agree that the M&A process itself is an important determinant for M&A activities and outcomes. Advocates of such a process perspective see implementation as the key factor for success or failure of M&As, as potential synergies result in superior performance only if these eventually can be realized through effective post-M&A implementation (Olie, 1994). Whereas all the different phases of the process (i.e. from the initial idea to the final integration) are important for the potential success or failure of a deal (Haspeslagh and Jemison, 1991), the most important phase is the actual integration process (Pablo, 1994). As mentioned by Haspeslagh and Jemison (1991: 105), 'integration is the key to making acquisitions work. Not until the two firms come together and begin to work toward the acquisition's purpose can value be created.' Not surprisingly, an abundance of studies discuss challenges faced and management approaches employed during the process, which involves actions taken to secure the efficient as well as effective direction of organizational activities and resources toward the accomplishment of a particular set of common organizational goals (for a review, see Schweizer, 2005).

A hitherto neglected consequence of the many M&A failures is that also many demergers can be observed. For example, previously merging firms might separate again completely due to low or negative profits (as in the case of DaimlerChrysler demerger after nine years of struggle) or might divest parts of the previously merged activities due to a change in the strategic agenda (as in the case of Novartis, which divested its merged Agribusiness division in 1999, three years after its creation). Also, as argued in the introduction, the late emergence of MNCs from emerging markets on the global stage functions as a catalyst for 'divorces.'

Whereas, as we sketched above, research in the past has heavily focused on the integration process of combining firms, the disintegration process of demerging firms has been neglected. We argue that by analogy to the importance of a well-implemented integration process for the success for an M&A, disintegration is the key to make a demerger work. A paradox is that there are indications that the more time and effort are spent on the critical integration process, the more time and effort are required to handle the disintegration (cf. Andrews, 2000).

10.3   The demerger process – A conceptual framework

In the following section, inspired by a process perspective on M&As (e.g. Haspeslagh and Jemison, 1991) and empirical evidence from the demerger/disintegration process of VCC from FMC, with special focus on the Product Development Unit within VCC (Thorén and Grahn, 2011), we propose that also a demerger process can be described as consisting of various phases.

The process perspective on M&As has since the early 1990s been the predominant perspective used in order to understand how an M&A unfolds (e.g. Garbuio et al., 2010; Haspeslagh and Jemison, 1991). A common distinction is to divide the process into three main phases, namely (1) pre-M&A phase, including the formation of the strategic objective to merge or acquire another firm and the initial search and screening of a potential partner; (2) evaluation phase, including financial, cultural and strategic evaluation (various forms of due diligence), negotiations and the final agreement; and (3) the post-M&A phase, consisting of activities related to the physical, procedural and cultural integration of the two firms (e.g. Jemison and Haspeslagh, 1991; Pablo, 1994; Schweizer, 2005; Shrivastava, 1986).

In a similar vein and based on evidence from the demerger between FMC and VCC that enabled the acquisition of the latter firm by Geely, we propose that a demerger can divided into three interrelated phases, namely (1) pre-demerger phase; (2) demerger negotiation; and (3) disintegration process. However, our main focus is on one of these phases, the disintegration process. The disintegration process is conceptualized as the opposite of firm integration and, based on Pablo's (1994: 806) definition of an integration process, we define a disintegration process as the making of changes in the functional activity arrangements, organizational structures and systems and cultures of demerging organizations to facilitate their separation into two (or more) functioning wholes. Moreover, we offer a discussion on various challenges that expectedly occur during such a disintegration process and offer potential measures to be taken in order to reduce these challenges.

10.3.1 The pre-demerger phase

During the pre-demerger phase, the actual decision to demerge a previously acquired firm is made. As in the case of M&As where there are myriad potential motives (e.g. to create and exploit synergies; to increase market shares; to protect markets by weakening or eliminating rivals; to acquire products/techniques; to gain footholds in new (foreign) markets, or to achieve critical mass or competitive size), the demerger decision can also be based on a multitude of different motives. For example, two previously merged firms might decide to go their separate ways again since the merger never really resulted in the expected synergies or cost reductions, or even had a negative impact on business results. Furthermore, a 'divorce' might occur since the owners of two merged firms cannot agree upon future common strategic directions. Another reason for a demerger, and perhaps the most common publicly communicated one, is that the industry and the market and its dynamics might have changed since the M&A took part. Hence, whereas the M&A decision at the time made perfect sense, due to subsequent changes, this might not be the case later. Also, a demerger idea might be born when new top management arrives that sees a different strategic horizon than the previous management. Drawing on the M&A literature (e.g. Jemison and Sitkin, 1986; Larsson, 1990; Napier, 1989), we distinguish between three different main categories of demerger motives, namely (1) economic motives – the expected synergies with the M&A have not been reached and the value of demerged firms is higher than the merged; (2) organizational motives – the demerger is made in order to reduce risk, for example, by focusing on core competences due to changes in the environment; and (3) managerial motives, – demerger due to management's prestige and personal incentives.

In reality, however, the motives for demergers are most likely to be a mixture of the above suggested categories. For example, whereas FMC acquired VVC in 1998 in an attempt to create a Premier Automotive Group (PAG) with several high-end brands besides VCC, such as Aston Martin, Land Rover, Jaguar and Lincoln, made perfect sense strategically, FMC never really succeeded in capturing those synergies due to integration challenges as well as the changes in the industry dynamics. Furthermore, the previous multibrand strategy had become outdated due to industry changes, and in 2007 a new CEO and a global management team was appointed at FMC, which introduced a new strategic agenda, the so-called 'One Ford' with a focus on integrating FMC operation globally, making the old agenda with different separate brands obsolete. To generalize, the two major interlinked explicatory forces eventually leading to the demerger of the high-end brands from FMC can be summarized as first, the external restructuring of the vehicle industry as a result of the economic downturn, and second, the internal new strategic agenda of the Ford management team.

It is interesting to note is that whereas many M&A studies have accentuated the strategic intent (i.e. the objectives, motives or rationales) behind an M&A as an important determinant for the type of integration approach used in regard to, for example, the level of integration and the means used in order to achieve the intended integration (e.g. Buono and Bowditch, 1989; Haspeslagh and Jemison, 1991; Nahavandi and Malekzadeh, 1988; Napier, 1989; Pablo, 1994; Shrivastava, 1986), we argue that the underlying motive that eventually results in a demerger has no direct impact on the subsequent disintegration process. Rather, as is discussed in detail below, it is the negotiation phase and the degree of pre-demerger integration that determine the subsequent disintegration process. Indeed, whereas the same strategic change at FMC eventually resulted in a FMC demerger and the sale of Land Rover and Jaguar in 2008 and VCC in 2010, the disintegration processes of these units proceeded quite differently. In contrast to the VCC process described below, the demerger of Land Rover and Jaguar and the subsequent sale to Tata Motors were fast and straightforward, and subsequently the negotiation less complicated. The main explanation to this difference is that none of these units were as heavily integrated in the FMC organization as the VCC organization was, but there are also indications that both FMC and VCC had realized the importance of taking an active part in the demerger process. Furthermore, FMC's experiences of how to handle a disintegration process as well the firm's realizations of the decisions made during the process became an important knowledge base when later implementing the demerger with VCC.

Moreover, we argue that, similar to M&As, the sensitive nature of demergers results in the fact that very few individuals are involved in the decision-making process (cf. Jemison and Sitkin, 1986). The non-involvement of those who later need to work with the demerger has essential implications on the disintegration process (cf. Schweizer, 2005). The decision to disintegrate the various units was of course taken by the top management team, Ford's headquarters in US, but the process of handling the disintegration processes was delegated to the top management team of Ford Europe, and FMC US were basically only informed about the overall progress.

Remarkably, in the VCC case the VCC top management team was kept uninformed about the demerger, and only the top management of FMC Europe was aware of the implications of the new 'One Ford' strategy in January 2008, the time of the demerger and the subsequent sale of VCC. The VCC top management was only 'informed' in the late spring. Moreover, the information given was ambiguous: on one hand, VCC was asked to engage in a common development project that would increase the integration between the two firms, while on the other, VCC management was asked to form a project – the Delta 1 project – with the objective to evaluate if it was possible to develop an independent company with a business plan that would ensure sustainable profitability. The VCC management most likely, of course, realized at that moment of time what the strategic agenda of FMC was and thereby a negotiation process started in the late spring of 2008. During this process, in which both the eventually demerged firms were involved, the timeline and characteristics of the forthcoming demerger were evaluated and decided. This plan was of course heavily based on the degree of integration between the two units in all parts of the value chain. It is in this phase that the real political game begins – with give and take—that later on turns out to have a huge impact on the nature of the subsequent disintegration process and the challenges arising. In the VCC/FMC Product Development Unit case studied, the process is complicated as many of product development activities were highly integrated, and prior development projects had resulted in commonly owned automobile parts, as well as production tools and production capacity at suppliers.

10.3.2   The negotiation phase

In the negotiation phase, the first actual actions are taken to separate the two previously merged firms. The official initiative to start this phase often comes from the previous acquirer, even if a previously acquired firm in some instances might have sensed what is coming and therefore have started a process of its own to prepare for an eventual termination of the relationship. In the FMC/VCC case, the starting point of the negotiation phase was when the assignment was given to VCC to evaluate their potential of survival in case of autonomy within the VCC-run Delta 1 project in spring 2008. Based on the new 'One Ford' strategy, the question asked was: Is it possible to develop an independent company with a business plan that ensures sustainable profitability? In other words: Can the previous integration between

FMC and VCC be reversed, and if so, how? What resources are required to create an independent company of VCC? The Delta 1 project team worked with the project for two months and came back with a simple answer to the above questions, namely that it would be impossible for VCC to survive without synergies from being part of the FMC group. FMC stopped the Delta 1 project and put the VCC demerger on hold. Also, the FMC's managerial capacity was at that time occupied with the ongoing demergers of Land Rover and Jaguar, which were completed in August of 2007.

The result of the Delta 1 project and the realization that VCC most likely would suffer the same fate as the other two high-end brands, led VCC management to start focusing on the task of developing a new corporate business strategy of its own – a task that had begun after the announcement of the new 'One Ford' strategic agenda. After the initial announcement of 'One Ford' and the expected subsequent changes, many VCC employees were shocked and could not see a future for VCC without being a well-integrated part of FMC, something that many had worked diligently to achieve for almost six years. However, there seemed to be a general shift toward a more optimistic attitude during the process of identifying a new 'strategy' for VCC. Employees started to experience more positive emotions and felt more involved. Management perceived that it was relatively easy to get the organization motivated to start developing the new VCC strategy, which was to target becoming a real premium brand, instead of the previous targeting of a 'near premium brand'. Many employees also experienced the relief of making their own decisions again – not least since a shared understanding was that when being an integrated part of FMC VCC's interests were not prioritized. Hence, very similar phenomena on an individual level that were observed during M&A processes were seen in the demerger case (cf. Schweizer, 2005). When realizing – though still not spoken aloud – that their firm was to be demerged, VCC employees first reacted with shock (cf. Marks and Mirvis, 1998). Also, we note that employees at least initially experienced a high degree of uncertainty (cf. Schweiger and DeNisi, 1991), stress (cf. Jemison and Sitkin, 1986), and loss of identity (cf. Zaheer et al., 2003), as well as being focused on themselves and their own future (cf. Marks and Mirvis, 1998). Then again, we argue that these reactions differed from individual to individual, but two major groups could be distinguished when it came to their attitude toward the forthcoming demerger. A first group, mainly consisting of those who had made a career as a result of the previous acquisition of VCC by FMC and/or those who were heavily involved in the integration between FMC and VCC, expressed feelings of disappointment, while a second group, consisting of individuals who perceived that the VCC/FMC deal was not a good idea in the first place, felt relieved.

Eventually, VCC not only succeeded in developing a future product plan, but also mapped the necessary technology development required to become a premium brand. FMC top management approved the new strategy on June

27, 2008. Important to note is that the product plan was a necessary tool in order to realize the separation from FMC. Both firms also understood that the disintegration process would be protracted, not least due to the fact that the two firms would need to share their commonly developed small platform until 2017.

The above-described work of VCC in trying to identify a new strategic roadmap as an independent firm can be described as a reversed form of a strategic evaluation phase in M&As, in which the acquiring firm tries to map the prevailing resources and capabilities of the to-be-acquired firm more in detail in order to reveal if there indeed is a strategic fit between the two (cf. Haspeslagh and Jemison, 1991). In the demerger case, in contrast, it is the to-be-demerged firm that tries to evaluate what resources and capabilities it would need as an independent firm.

Whereas it was not openly communicated, most of those involved under-stood and expected that VCC eventually would be sold to a third party rather than continue as a standalone independent company. With the benefit of hindsight, we can argue that what FMC did was trying to dress the partner, that is, to make VCC more attractive, and thereby also more expensive, in a future sales process. Based on VCC's new strategic agenda, a new plan was developed for the technologies, systems and components that the firm needed access to in the future in order to execute the strategy. These requirements were thereafter used in negotiations with FMC when discuss-ing and later signing contracts related to the common technologies VCC would be allowed to have access to in the future. Important to highlight is that since FMC previously had acquired VCC, all patents, IP rights and technologies – even those developed before the acquisition – were owned by FMC. Again, drawing on insights from the M&A literature, the above can be described as a form of due diligence where VCC and FMC tried to evaluate and negotiate about future responsibilities and obligations.

10.3.3 The disintegration phase

The disintegration phase is the phase during which the two previously integrated firms are separated from each other. The demerger in this phase is made official, most likely internally to begin with, but soon also becomes publicly known. Just as in the case of an M&A both firms, but perhaps to a higher extent the demerged unit, experience extensive changes in own-ership, management, organizational structure, personnel structure and of course in culture and identity (cf. Schweizer, 2005).

In the VCC/FMC case the disintegration phase began in the autumn 2008 when VCC top management, this time officially, was informed that FMC had plans to sell the unit. As a result, at the beginning of 2009, a new project group, the Delta 2 project, was created with the aim of leading and managing the separation from FMC. The disintegration was to be handled in such a way that VCC after the separation would be able to function as an independent unit. The original expectation from FMC was that the separation should be completed by 2013, while VCC realized that the firm would have substantial problems to be independent as soon as this since FMC/VCC processes, especially within Product Development, were quite integrated. For example, did the two firms share a commonly developed platform used for their respective smaller car models? Then again, VCC had kept its own system for production and product management. Eventually, the final agreement for completion of the separation was the year 2017. VCC was much more heavily integrated with FMC than Jaguar or Land Rover were. The latter firms basically only shared logistic systems with FMC. Hence, not surprisingly, the disintegration process between FMV and Jaguar as well as Land Rover took less time than VCC's disintegration from FMC.

Irrespective of the final end-date of the separation, the plan was that VCC's disintegration should not be dependent on the cost and motivation of a potential new owner – that is, new potential acquirer – buying them from FMC. Hence, all necessary business functions for enabling the creation of an independent unit were to be pursued; then again VCC was not expected to have all functions in-house (e.g. legal and tax services could be bought). Whereas the project at operational level initially was led by one VCC and one FMC manager, as time passed VCC took over the process completely. Consistent with an integration process in an M&A, external consultants were hired in the spring of 2009 to provide support in the demerger, and FMC choose to engage the same consultancy firm that was previously involved in the Land Rover and Jaguar disintegration (cf. Schweizer, 2005). Likewise, the project group was divided into various sub-groups of functional committees, such as for manufacturing, purchasing and product development (cf. Schweizer, 2005). These functional committees were further divided into various forums during the disintegration processes, the so-called task forces, in order to handle the disintegration smoothly.

The project structure was rigorous. Each functional committee was asked to establish milestones, which when approved were followed up to ensure completion. When an activity was delayed, this had to be reported to VCC's top management team directly. In addition, an executive steering committee consisting of both FMC and VCC top managers chaired the whole process. Once more, this way of trying to structure the complex implementation of the demerger is reminiscent of what has been seen in studies of M&A integration processes. A study by Schweizer (2005) of a local integration process between two globally merging MNCs' subsidiaries shows how difficult, if not impossible, it is for management to clearly decide how the integration is to be implemented. One way to overcome this challenge is to set out a broad framework for the processes and then leave it to those who actually work with implementation to come up with more practical plans and to set goals. FMC management seemed to have this broad approach as a 'vision' for the demerger, and the goal of establishing an independent

VCC was communicated. However, once the functional committees and forums had proposed suggestions and clear goals to achieve, and those were approved, control was tight to make sure that the necessary speed of the demerger would be maintained. In contrast to an integration process, however, where the implementing units start by identifying the synergies to be gained (Schweizer, 2005), in the demerger case, the focus per definition is on trying to identify ways to reverse the previously achieved synergies.

An important aspect to consider is the degree of integration between the two demerging firms. It is reasonable to assume that the more integrated the firms are the more time and effort are needed to reverse the process – that is, to disintegrate the firms. The high level of integration sought in order to achieve planned synergies was the result of much hard work that would take time to reverse (cf. Andrews, 2000). Another aspect to consider is that of course not all functions of the two firms are equally integrated, that is, the degree of integration differs between units. Hence, we cannot expect a homogeneous disintegration process throughout the entire organization, just as the degree of integration is seldom the same in various functions in an M&A.

Whereas the VCC organization clearly was committed to the Delta 2 project, this was not the case within FMC Europe. Given a lack of dedicated disintegration resources and poor communication from FMC top management on what was expected by FMC Europe employees during the separation, VCC often had difficulties in 'finding' a counterpart at FMC Europe with whom to discuss disintegration-related challenges. Important to remember here is that VCC's activities were most of all integrated with the activities of FMC Europe, whereas the demerger decision came from FMC headquarters in the US. Not until the spring of 2009 did FMC top management realize that they had to put more focus on the disintegration process, that is, to allocate resources and to communicate the importance of the disintegration process internally in the FMC organization. At that time even the FMC top management became actively involved in the process, starting to follow up the processes. A potential explanation for why it took time for FMC to realize that it needed to be more engaged in the disintegration process is that FMC, based on the previous experience of separating Land Rover and Jaguar, which were not as integrated as VCC, underestimated the magnitude of the VCC disintegration process.

Drawing heavily on the Delta 1 project findings, the Delta 2 project group succeeded in mapping all shared operations between the two firms in a so-called Shared Delivery Model, which described all business processes within the various functions in one month. The project team detected two types of processes, which demanded totally different degrees of effort to map and then develop a plan for disintegrating. The first type was the processes that previously had been mapped and described in a business mapping format, and therefore could be planned quite straightforwardly. For the second type, which turned out to be numerous operations, there were few records and therefore processes had to be traced and then described through interviews conducted by consultants with previously involved employees from both firms – a task that was described as detective work. All the identified shared operations, how these should be disintegrated, and how the future cooperation between VCC and FMC should be managed under new ownership were described in detail in books. Already at this stage it seemed relatively clear to everyone that Geely was to acquire VCC.

The nitty-gritty work behind the mapping was highly resource-consuming. For example, a challenge faced by the product development function, one of the most central functions in the vehicle industry, was to identify all common parts in VCC and FMC cars. The two firms had never completely integrated their production and product management systems as mentioned above, and they worked with different systems that only to some extent overlapped. In this particular case the lack of integration actually made the identification of common parts very difficult, and in the end it was necessary to map all parts manually. Also, no clear documentation of ownership of the production tools, both in-house and located at suppliers, existed. Interestingly, thus, is that the upholding of a system of their own later became important when VCC started to act as a standalone firm. Again, the above-described activities are the reverse of actions undertaken during an integration process when trying to identify potential synergies (cf. Schweizer, 2005).

Three types of disintegration agreements were signed between FMC and VCC, namely (1) delivery agreements of, for example, engines and component supply; (2) transitional service agreements, for example IT, treasury, marketing, but also powertrain, platform and R&D projects; and finally (3) cooperation agreements concerning, for example, IP rights and tooling. All in all it was very time-consuming – altogether it took two years – and complex process (the supporting paperwork was 3,500 pages, containing details on delivery agreements, quality, warranties, etc.). All contracts, furthermore, contained a clause that described what would happen if one of the parties wanted to end the contract prior to expiry date. On its own initiative, VCC developed working routines (added as appendices to the contracts) that were meant to facilitate the future daily work between FMC and VCC. An example is that it was described in detail how requests for changes on common tools should be handled. During the spring of 2009, mandated by FMC, the focus was on establishing Transnational Service Agreements (TSAs). TSAs were needed to establish rules for how the cooperation between the two firms was to be governed in the areas where VCC and FMC would need to cooperate after the demerger. The transfer of competence – an area that was restricted due to competition laws – was handled in a separate TSA in which it among others was defined for how long VCC could get support from FMC if needed. Of course, there are reasons to expect that the amount of details and the degree of security surrounding a demerger agreement are influenced by the identity of a potential new acquirer.

VCC's ability to share information or even engage in a dialogue with their new forthcoming owner Geely was of course very restricted; VCC employees were not really allowed to talk with Geely at all. FMC had indeed learned its lesson from the demerger of Land Rover and Jaguar, where secrets were leaked to the buyer quite freely during the negotiations as Tata Motors early on moved their employees to Land Rover and Jaguar. This undeniably gave Tata Motors a strong position during the negotiations. In reality, the restriction to inform the future owner Geely of important input during negotiations meant that it was the members of the Delta 2 project that at least indirectly negotiated with FMC in order to be able to guarantee a good start after the demerger. Negotiations regarding IP rights were conducted directly between Geely and FMC without the direct involvement of VCC, which, however, provided the information to Geely on what IP rights were needed in the future. This was a time-consuming process, and was not finished when the deal was officially closed on August 2, 2010, but continued until the end of 2010.

The actual implementation of the disintegration of VCC and FMC started in the summer of 2009 and lasted until the beginning of 2010, even if the time frame differed somewhat between different functions. One practical problem was to locate the machine tools and to transfer those to either VCC or FMC. It became obvious that neither FMC nor VCC had a clear knowledge where the tools were located at their many and geographically dispersed suppliers.

For VCC employees who all were affected by the disintegration, even if they were not directly involved in the process, it became a familiar part of their daily working life. This meant that on an overall level they were well updated and knowledgeable of at least the big picture, while that was not the case within FMC Europe. Nevertheless, the implementation of the cooperation agreements explaining the guidelines for working with VCC as a stand-alone firm within FMC had already started in 2010, and the process began with information meetings for all employees in which the new working routines, for example, were explained. The Delta 2 project also met once a week in order to make sure that all the concerns raised and challenges occurring were handled accordingly. Also, new communication systems were established with external share points between the firms. Still, for the FMC employees it was difficult to understand that on one hand they were separated from VCC and on the other hand had to support them. With time, a governance structure was built, with various forums consisting of both FMC and VCC managers to support both actors in this process. If any difficulties cropped up in daily work, these were brought up in these forums and most often solved. If a solution could not be reached, there was always a risk of escalation, but both firms did their uttermost to work out the difficulties without involving external parties.

10.4   Conclusions

We started this chapter by highlighting that MNCs from emerging markets increasingly make use of cross-border acquisitions in order to access hard-to-develop resources and competencies, and to gain legitimacy in the global market. In many recent observed cases, such acquisitions were preceded by demergers where the eventually acquired firm had to be disintegrated first. We noted that demerger and disintegration processes have been neglected in the prevailing M&A literature. Therefore, using empirical illustrations from the demerger of VCC from FMC – which was a prerequisite for Geely's subsequent acquisition of VCC – we pioneer the field of research by offering a process description of a demerger process. We distinguish between three interrelated phases, namely (1) the pre-demerger phase; (2) the negotiation phase; and (3) the disintegration phase, and give examples of experienced challenges and chosen solutions. When offering such a process description of a demerger, we see many parallels with an M&A and the integration process. More specifically, we argue that a demerger process indeed to a large extent is a mirror image of an M&A process.

Finally, we ask the question: How does the demerger and disintegration process, which at least partially is implemented in parallel with the subsequent acquisition/integration process of the demerged firm by MNCs from emerging markets, influence the latter? We can conclude from the VCC/FMC case that the new owner – Zhejiang Geely Holding Group – was clearly held outside the ongoing disintegration process. It was the members of the Delta 2 project, responsible for the disintegration, who had to think and act in the interest of the new owner without knowing the interests of the buyer. Moreover, the Delta 2 project members could also only speculate on what the new owners were interested in, since they were not allowed to engage in a dialogue with Geely. Moreover, the opposite was true when Geely and FMC negotiated about the IP rights, for here VCC were not part of the discussion but could only provide overall information on what type of access it needed after the disintegration to be able to continue to produce and support the existing car models. The strict separation of course complicated the demerger of VCC. In this particular case, is it is reasonable to assume that the strict separation of Geely and VCC from each other partially is explainable by the country of origin of the new acquirer. However, since the number of acquisitions of firms from developed markets by firms from emerging market is increasing, it is reasonable to expect that this case is not unique as the laws and regulations in many emerging countries are still under development.

A second implication of this is that in contrast to a case where the to-be-acquired firm is already independent and it is rather clear to the acquirer what it gets, in a case where a demerger precedes a merger it is not until the deal is closed that the new owner definitely knows for sure what it has really bought. Hence, there is a higher degree of uncertainty involved compared to a case where a proper due diligence can be performed beforehand. Finally, a realization that the demerged unit will often for many years to come be tied to the first acquirer is also of relevance to acknowledge since there is always a risk of differences in opinion when it comes to ownership and IP rights, which might lead to open disagreements.

Indeed, to go back to the metaphor in the introduction, the new partner has to accept that the previously married partner first has to go through a divorce before being able to get involved for real in a new marriage, and the new partner cannot possibly in advance know how this divorce will influence the future partner.

Note

The authors have equally contributed to the paper.

References

Athreye, S. and Godley, A. (2009) 'Internationalization and Technological Leapfrogging in the Pharmaceutical Industry,' *Industrial and Corporate Change*, 18(2): 295–323.

Buono, A.F. and Bowditch, J.L. (1989) *The Human Side of Mergers and Acquisitions* (San Francisco, CA: Jossey-Bass Publishers).

Cantwell, J.A. and Barnard, H. (2008) 'Do Firms from Emerging markets Have to Invest Abroad? Outward FDI and the Competiveness of Firms,' in K.P. Sauvant (ed.), *The Rise of Transnational Corporations from Emerging Markets: Threat or Opportunity?* (Cheltenham: Edward Elgar): 55–85.

Cartwright, S. and Cooper, C.L. (1993) 'Of Mergers, Marriage and Divorce – The Issues of Staff Retention,' *Journal of Managerial Psychology*, 8(6): 7–10.

Cartwright, S. and Cooper, C.L. (1996) *Managing Mergers, Acquisitions and Strategic Alliances: Integrating People and Cultures* (Oxford: Butterworth-Heinemann).

Dooley, K.J. and Zimmerman, B.J. (2003) 'Merger as Marriage: Communication Issues in Postmerger Integration,' *Health Care Management Review*, 28(1): 56–67.

Duysters, G., Jacob, J., Lemmens, C. and Jintian, Y. (2009) 'Internationalization and Technological Catching Up of Emerging Multinationals: A Comparative Case Study of China's Haier Group,' *Industrial and Corporate Change*, 18(2): 325–349.

Gammeltoft, P., Pradhan, J.P. and Goldstein, A. (2010) 'Emerging Multinationals: Home and Host Country Determinants and Outcomes,' *International Journal of Emerging Markets*, 5(3/4): 254–265.

Garbuio, M., Lovallo, D. and Horn, J. (2010) 'Overcoming Biases in M&A: A Process Perspective,' in L. Cary, C.L. Cooper and S. Finkelstein (eds), *Advances in Mergers and Acquisitions*, 9 (Bingley: Emerald): 83–104.

Gugler, K., Mueller, D.C., Yurtoglu, B.B. and Zulehner, C. (2003) 'The Effects of Mergers: An International Comparison,' *International Journal of Industrial Organization*, 21(5): 625–653.

Haspeslagh, C.P. and Jemison, D.B. (1991) *Managing Acquisitions – Creating Value through Corporate Renewal* (New York: The Free Press).

Hunt, J.W. (1990) 'Changing Pattern of Acquisition Behaviour in Takeovers and the Consequences for Acquisition Processes,' *Strategic Management Journal*, 11(1): 69–77.

Jemison, D.B. and Sitkin, S.B. (1986) 'Corporate Acquisitions: A Process Perspective,' *Academy of Management Review*, 11(1): 145–163.

Luo, Y. and Tung, R.L. (2007) 'International Expansion of Emerging Market Enterprises: A Springboard Perspective,' *Journal of International Business Studies*, 38(4): 481–498.

Napier, N.K. (1989) 'Mergers and Acquisitions – Human Resource Issues and Outcomes: A Review and Suggested Typology,' *Journal of Management Studies*, 26(3): 271–289.

Nahavandi, A. and Malekzadeh, A. (1988) 'Acculturation in Mergers and Acquisitions,' *Academy of Management Review*, 13(1): 79–90.

Olie, R. (1994) 'Shades of Culture and Institutions in International Mergers,' *Organization Studies*, 15(3): 381–405.

Pablo, A.L. (1994) 'Determinants of Acquisition Integration Level: A Decision-making Perspective,' *Academy of Management Journal*, 37(4): 803–836.

Rabbiosi, L., Elia, S. and Bertoni, F. (2012) 'Acquisitions by EMNCs in Developed Markets – An Organizational Learning Perspective,' *Management International Review*, 52(2): 193–212.

Risberg, A. (1999) 'Ambiguities Thereafter – An Interpretive Approach to Acquisitions,' Doctoral Dissertation (Lund: Institute of Economic Research, Lund University).

Salter, M.S. and Weinhold, W.A. (1981) 'Choosing Compatible Acquisitions,' *Harvard Business Review*, 59(1): 117–127.

Sauvant, K.P. (ed.) (2008) *The Rise of Transnational Corporations from Emerging Markets: Threat or Opportunity?* (Cheltenham: Edward Elgar).

Schweizer, R. (2005) *An Arranged Marriage under Institutional Duality – The Local Integration Process between Two Globally Merging MNCs' Subsidiaries* (Kungälv: BAS Publishing).

Shelton, L.M. (1988) 'Strategic Business Fits and Corporate Acquisitions: Empirical Evidence,' *Strategic Management Journal*, 9(3): 279–287.

Shrivastava, P. (1986) 'Postmerger Integration,' *Journal of Business Strategy*, 7(1): 65–76.

Thomas, D.E., Eden, L., Hitt, M.A. and Miller, S.R. (2007) 'Experience of Emerging Market Firms: The Role of Cognitive Bias in Developed Market Entry and Survival,' *Management International Review*, 47(6): 845–867.

Thorén, L. and Grahn, F. (2011) 'Disintegration of a Business within a Multinational Company,' Master's Thesis for the Executive MBA Program at the School of Business, Economics and Law, University of Gothenburg.

United Nations Conference on Trade and Development (UNCTAD) (2011) *Global Investment Trends Monitor* (New York and Geneva: UNCTAD).

Walter, G.A. (1985) 'Culture Collisions in Merger and Acquisitions,' in P.J. Frost, L.F. Moore, M.R. Louis, C.C. Lundberg and J. Martin (eds), *Organizational Culture* (Thousand Oaks, CA: Sage): 301–314.

Wright, M., Filatotchev, I., Hoskisson, R.E. and Peng, M.W. (2005) 'Strategy Research in Emerging Economies: Challenging the Conventional Wisdom,' *Journal of Management Studies*, 42(1): 1–33.

11
The 'Hybrid' Emerging Market Multinational Enterprise – The Ownership Transfer of Volvo Cars to China

Claes G. Alvstam and Inge Ivarsson

11.1 Introduction

11.1.1 New patterns of FDI flows – New categories of emerging market MNCs

This chapter deals with the issue of how the systematic process of comprehensive strategic asset-seeking FDI by emerging market firms through acquisitions of well-established developed market companies, possessing globally recognized brands and the latest technological capabilities, creates new categories of internationalized companies. It is argued that the catching-up process in order to reach ownership-specific advantages in the global marketplace, following the argument of Mathews (2002, 2006), as well as adopting the 'springboard' perspective – the ambition to use the foreign acquisition to strengthen its position at the domestic market (Luo and Tung, 2007; Ramamurti and Singh, 2009; Ramamurti, 2012; Williamson et al., 2013) – have together given rise to a new dimension of both the concept of 'liability of foreignness' (Miller and Eden, 2006: Miller et al., 2008; Zaheer, 1995, 2002; Zaheer and Mosakowski, 1997), and the 'liability of outsidership' (Johanson and Vahlne, 2009; Petersen and Seifert, 2013; Vahlne and Johanson, 2013; Yildiz and Fei, 2012). There is an increasing number of cases where a developed market firm becomes politically and commercially controlled by new domestic interests in an emerging market after a transfer of ownership, but, for historical and other reasons, is still considered as a foreign corporation, both by the domestic authorities in the new country, and in the eyes of the general public at the global level. It can also be seen as a new aspect of the liability of origin (Ramachandran and Pant, 2010), in that the national origin of the acquired company becomes blurred.

Such an 'in-between' position creates a number of confusions regarding the international strategic management of the company, and contributes to general uncertainty when it comes to the long-term development of the geographical balance of production capacity and customers in the global context in which such companies operate. It is suggested in this chapter that this category of firms should be labelled *'emerging market hybrid firms.'* After the acquisition these firms are positioned in a grey zone between being on the one hand still a global company but with only marginal activity in the new home country, and on the other hand have been acquired in order to strengthen the competitive advantage of the acquiring firm in its domestic market. They are furthermore legally foreign-owned and private, but in reality indirectly controlled by public interests in the home country.

This 'in-between' position is complex enough when the acquiring firm is a state-owned enterprise in its home country, or privately owned with close links to domestic business groups, and has its legal domicile in the same country. The situation becomes increasingly 'blurred' when the acquired foreign firm has been transferred to a new abode, and at the same time is still foreign in a strict legal sense, since the new majority-owners control it from a holding group incorporated in a third-country tax haven, and it is registered and floated on a stock market, also located abroad. The emergence of such 'hybrid' emerging market firms is a natural consequence of an ongoing globalization process in newly emerging economies, where cross-border direct investments become an integrated part of firm growth in all sectors of industry, according to the 'springboard' approach, and where increasing ownership and control over multinational firms with roots elsewhere and foreign identities becomes normality rather than exceptional. With growing financial assets outside the domestic market in emerging economies, the share of 'foreign' ownership and control of business activities at home ground will subsequently increase.

This development may become particularly common in China, compared to other emerging economies, considering the transition from a traditional dominance of state-owned enterprises to increased privatization, combined with the rapid growth of outward foreign direct investment (OFDI) in recent years, and the expected accelerating development of internationalization in coming years.

11.1.2   The need for adaptation to new realities

In the classic theories of international business it is normally held that the foreign companies have gone through an internationalization process from a strong home base, and that their image in the host markets is to be 'foreign'; accordingly, they are treated as such by official authorities as well as by customers. Until recently, the large majority of these firms featured their provenance in advanced economies among the 'old industrial core' countries. Now, when strong domestic firms also expand abroad from emerging economies, they are henceforth seen as domestic in their home market, and the main reason for growing internationally may likewise be through 'resource-seeking,' 'market-seeking,' 'efficiency-seeking,' 'strategic asset-seeking,' and particularly 'technology- and knowledge-seeking,' etc. in accordance with the established theories (Dunning and Lundan, 2008: 67ff). Furthermore, it is generally assumed that there exists initially a technology-deficit of domestic companies vs foreign TNCs in the emerging economies, and that this gap is gradually shrinking through technology and knowledge transfers until the day when the first domestic company is ready for take-off in an international expansion process. In the cases of the internationalization of emerging market corporations, these firms usually also bring their own brand and corporate culture – the best historical examples being firms from Japan, South Korea and Taiwan.

The expansion is initially through greenfield investment rather than via mergers and acquisitions, and in those cases where a foreign firm is acquired in order to establish manufacturing production in the host market, the acquired company is normally smaller and less powerful than the acquirer. It has so far been much more unusual to watch a domestic emerging market company expand abroad through an acquisition, where the main (spring-board) objective is to gain the latest technology and to take advantage of a global brand image in order to build up a strong production and sales base at home, and where the acquired company is far larger and historically more powerful. The acquired company maintains its global operations, but it commences a process of casting its skin, beginning with the new home base, and, thus, it could be viewed as a 'foreign' or a 'domestic' company depending on the specific circumstances. This phenomenon of an acquired company under nationality-sloughing should be distinguished from the traditional joint venture in equity or non-equity modes, or majority- and minority-owned ventures, since these have normally been subject to special regulations, although not always to transparent interpretation when it comes to government–firm relationships.

While there are many cases described in the literature on transnational corporations where a foreign acquisition of a national brand also changes the general image of the company, as well as how it is treated by national public authorities, there are fewer cases of the reverse situation, that is, where a foreign company is 'domesticized' in formal/legal terms, but still remains 'foreign' in a number of important aspects. The reason for this asymmetry might be that the main part of existing and successful trans-national corporations is rooted in countries with a historical tradition of a dominance of OFDI, that is, where the main domestic companies have 'gone abroad,' while there are much fewer examples of acquisitions of globally successful firms by companies from countries with an imbalance in favour of inward FDI (IFDI). Since the early 1980s there have accordingly been many relevant calls for a new theoretical framework of the internationaliza-tion process with origins in emerging markets in which these aspects are taken into consideration. Since the majority of examples are rooted in the Asian context, it is natural that most contributions that have criticized the

Western-based theoretical assumptions have called for a theoretical development that better fits the Asian realities (Agrawal and Agmon, 1990; Alon and
McIntyre, 2008; Alon et al., 2008, 2009, 2012; Buckley et al., 2007; Cantwell
and Tolentino, 1990; Cuervo-Cazurra, 2012; Dunning, 1998; Gammeltoft
et al., 2010; Lall and Chen, 1983; Luo and Rui, 2009; Narula, 2012; Rugman,
2009; Wells, 1983; Williamson et al., 2013; Yeung, 1999, 2012).

11.1.3   Choice of empirical example and aim of the chapter

The specific example taken in this chapter to illustrate the phenomenon of
Asian-rooted emerging market firms is the acquisition in 2010 of the originally Swedish company Volvo Car Corp. (VCC) by the Chinese Zhejiang
Geely Holding Group (Geely) from the American giant Ford Motor Corp.
The explicit objective of the acquisition was to build up a large production
capacity in China for the domestic market, taking advantage of the prestigious Volvo brand, and at the same time to learn from VCC's technological
achievements in safety, product design, environmental consciousness, func-
tionality and general quality control, in order to upgrade its existing Geely
models. The move can be said to have used the springboard approach to
acquire strategic assets abroad with the aim of strengthening their positions
at home, and at the same time creating a new 'in-between,' or hybrid, category of 'foreign vs non-foreign' and 'insider vs outsider' firms.

  This case is up to the present probably the best example of an acquisition
by a Chinese company to gain worldwide control of a premium branded
consumer product within the automotive industry, and, indirectly, to attain
technology and knowledge transfer to its own products by building up
substantial production capacity under the foreign brand in the domestic
market. What makes this case different from similar acquisitions, such
as Nanjing Automobile Group's purchase of British MG Rover in 2005 or
Beijing Automotive Industry Corporation (BAIC) acquiring the technical
rights to assemble models of Swedish Saab in 2009, is the fact that in the latter cases, the acquirers were well-established state-owned enterprises, while
in the case of Geely–Volvo, the acquisition was made by a relatively small
private company listed and incorporated outside China, but financed by a
mix of private and local public interests. We argue that this new feature of
internationalization of Chinese enterprise has come to stay and will grow
rapidly in the future. Therefore, there is a need to clear up the confusion
around the grey zone situation between the 'domestic' and the 'foreign,'
between being 'outsider' and 'insider,, and being neither a wholly owned
foreign enterprise, nor a domestic–foreign joint-venture company, in order
to reduce the uncertainty of which political/legal rules and regulations that
should be adapted to such 'hybrids.' *The specific research question is to investigate whether this is really a new category of the liability of foreignness and the
liability of outsidership or not, and, if this is the case, to identify criteria for delimi-
nating the 'hybrid' emerging market firm from other varieties of internationalizing*

emerging market companies. The method adopted has been to make a longitudinal study by systematically tracing the subsequent events – more or less 'online' – after the acquisition in close interaction with the companies involved through frequent interviews with key personnel in the Swedish headquarters, and through several field studies and interviews at VCC's locations in China, as well as in Geely's headquarters, during 2010–2013.

11.2   China's internationalization process in the perspective of Asian emerging markets

The typical recent feature of emergent economies, particularly in Asia, has been the slow, though clearly apparent transformation from being predominantly host markets for IFDI, to at a rising degree also becoming home markets for indigenous firms that expand internationally through OFDI, thus tilting the balance between inward and outward FDI stock. In most Asian newly emerging economies, there is still a clear imbalance in favour of IFDI cumulated stock, but the gap is continuously shrinking, or, in some cases, the OFDI stock has surpassed the IFDI stock. Singapore (Ellingsen et al., 2006), South Korea (Hemmert, 2012), Taiwan (Chen, 2006; Chen et al., 2013), Malaysia (Goh and Wong, 2011), and recently also Thailand (Pananond, 2013), can all be seen as examples of economies that have undergone such a gradual transformation during recent decades, while Mainland China is a new case with a much higher long-term potential. Thus, China differs from its forerunners in terms of the sheer size of its home base and its recent rise to become a new global power. The IFDI to China commenced at a modest scale in the early 1980s in the wake of the opening up of the country through a 'coming-in' (*yin jin lai*) strategy (Tang et al., 2008: 37) after the relaunch of the 'Four Modernizations' in 1978, and increased steadily from an average level of about US\$ 12 billion per year in 1986/90, via US\$ 48 billion on average during 2000/04 to more than US\$ 150 billion per year in 2006/10, whereafter it declined to US\$ 114 billion per year in 2011/12. Its OFDI flows increased with the launch of the 'going out' (*zou chu qu*) or 'going global' (*zou xiang shi jie*) (Shambaugh, 2013: 174ff) and the 'dances with wolves' (*yu lang gong wu*) strategies (Tang et al., 2008: 38f) in the late 1990s, from US\$ 2.4 billion per year in 2000/04 to US\$ 40 billion per year in 2006/10, to reach a new all-time-high in 2012 of US\$ 77 billion. The outward stock of FDI has grown from US\$ 28 billion to US\$ 443 billion between 2000 and 2012. The O/I stock ratio in China amounted to 0.14 in 2000, grew to 0.25 in 2006, to reach about 0.50 in 2012.[1,2] While the majority of the Chinese OFDI initially was directed toward extraction of food, mineral and energy resources overseas, the rapidly growing trend, as observed by Chinese as well as foreign scholars, is to get access to foreign markets through acquiring a brand or technological competence, and at the same time improve quality of production and customer service at home

(Alon et al., 2009, 2012; Cui and Jiang, 2009; Deng, 2009; Luo et al., 2010; Söderman et al., 2008). This phenomenon can be seen as an element in the entering of a new stage in the Chinese manufacturing upgrading process, where deeper integration with foreign production is necessary, but, in terms of China's growing importance as a key actor in the global economy, and not only as being a hub of global manufacturing assembly, there are larger and more general implications to draw from this trend.

Since the 'going out' strategy was launched by the Chinese government more than a decade ago, the number of successful Chinese emerging multinationals, despite being latecomers in the global market, has accelerated at a high speed, with the most spectacular cases being found in the resource and energy sector, but to an increasing extent also within advanced manufacturing industries. Examples include Haier's greenfield investments in the US in 1999–2001, SAIC's acquisition of South Korean Ssangyong in 2004, Lenovo's taking over of IBM's PC business in 2005, the TCL–Thompson Electronics deal and Wanxiang Group's cross-border M&As in the US, Dalian Wanda's acquisition of AMC Theaters in 2012, and, most recently, Shuanghui International Holdings' US\$ 4.7 billion bid for American Smithfield Foods, the world's largest pork processor and hog producer, in 2013 (Barboza, 2013; Deng, 2008: 22ff; 2012: 143ff; Wu et al., 2012: 113ff). In aggregate these developments have called into question whether the process of internationalization among Chinese firms reveals a different pattern from what has been observed in other Asian emerging economies. In particular, the dominance of state-owned enterprises, the massive support from the public sector to finance OFDI activities, as well as the lower level of technology and managerial experiences compared to its Asian neighbours, have been put forward as new elements in the Chinese internationalization strategy (Buckley et al., 2007, 2008; Child and Rodrigues, 2005; Dunning, 2006; Gugler and Boie, 2009; Gugler and Fetscherin, 2010; Liu et al., 2005; Mathews, 2006; Morck et al., 2008; Nolan, 2001; 2012; Rugman and Li, 2007; Rui and Yip, 2008; Williamson and Raman, 2013).

However, the speed of development in the globalization of enterprises calls for a continuous revision and amendment of the existing literature. The cases referred to above do traditionally represent market upgrading through acquisition of superior technology abroad, where the buyers usually have been state-owned enterprises, and continued to be considered as Chinese, despite rapidly going global. There are much fewer examples where the acquisition of a foreign transnational corporation has been motivated by the objective to build up new production capacity under the foreign brand at home, mainly aimed at the domestic market, while keeping the global reputation of the acquired company and seeing the new domestic market only as a minor part of global sales, even though it is planned to grow in relative terms.[3] The example of Geely–Volvo Cars may therefore be harbinger of a new trend in China, where formally private and legally foreign enterprises are the acquirers, but where the financial support is mainly domestic and public.

11.3   The institutional framework behind the rise of Chinese foreign direct investment

11.3.1   Industrial co-development and technological upgrading

The hitherto few cases of acquisitions of global market shares in advanced foreign premium brands by private Chinese business actors, taking advantage of the mutual benefits with the political and administrative leadership in order to strengthen local domestic production and pave the way for further technology and knowledge transfers, are furthermore worthwhile to study from another viewpoint. China's recent history of strict state control over production and foreign trade and the lack of a solid, transparent and credible legal, institutional framework to cope with the dynamic development of market forces, rapid internationalization of previously dominantly domestic activities, combined with a pragmatic political attitude to wealth-building among its entrepreneurs and government officials, can in very simplified terms be seen as having been a successful model of economic transformation, technological upgrading and industrial co-development (Alon et al., 2009; Brandt and Thun, 2010; Breznitz and Murphree, 2011; Herrigel and Zeitlin, 2010; Peng et al., 2008; Ren et al., 2010; Steinfeld, 2004, 2010; Thun, 2006).

Private entrepreneurship mainly originated from the so-called town-and-village enterprises (TVEs). Since private enterprises with more than eight employees were not permitted until 1988, there was a growth of 'disguised' private firms, officially recorded as collective enterprises or public businesses. This phenomenon has been called the 'red hat' strategy (Li, 2012: 2; Yang, 2007). Thus, for a long period of market transition, there was a pragmatic coexistence of the public-owned and free private enterprise sectors (Li, 2012: 26). The 'red hat' firms were preferably located in the coastal provinces and in the special economic zones. When the government in 2002 announced a plan to 'eliminate all restrictive and discriminatory regulations that are not friendly towards private investment and private economic development in taxes, land-use, business start-ups, and imports and exports' (Li, 2012: 23f), this measure also paved the way for the opportunity to register a company outside Mainland China, for example, in Hong Kong, but still operate as a private Chinese firm. The number of officially registered private enterprises has subsequently soared at an accelerated pace. The 'red hat' strategy can be seen as a kind of a double entrepreneurship that enables the manipulation of institutional rules in an underdeveloped economy (Li, 2012: 27; Yang, 2007). In such a path-dependency perspective, this 'coexistence' approach may continue to be the mainstream strategy also favoured by the new generation of national political leadership and in the implementation of the current 12th Five-Year Plan, and the guidelines from the 18th National Congress of the Communist Party of China in November 2012, although there are numerous signs that counteract the sustainability of this model. With the use of the powerful state investment vehicle China Investment Corp. with its claimed value of almost US$ 500 billion, it is announced that there will be acquisitions of foreign assets amounting to US$ 560 billion during the current plan period 2011–2015.[4] A recent study has revealed the massive state subsidies to domestic industrial firms, which have further altered the competition pattern with foreign rivals, and facilitated opportunities to make foreign acquisitions (Haley and Haley, 2013).

11.3.2   Avoidance of the 'middle-income-trap'

The challenges in contemporary Chinese society to support the continuous upgrading of its manufacturing sector and at the same time complement the successful policy of export-orientation with the urgent need to back further OFDI, can be categorized along two entirely different, but coinciding and mutually interdependent external processes. The first of these is the avoidance of the 'middle-income-trap,' and, second is the new logics of transformative technology. The 'middle-income-trap' phenomenon is featured in a situation when a successful model of economic growth, built on physical labour and capital accumulation, reaches a level where the continued climbing upwards the value chain in the industrial system will rely more on technological innovation and advanced skills, and when the 'invisible' service content in the value-added process surpasses the physical manufacturing element.

China's transformation from a poor rural economy with an annual average per capita income of less than US$ 300 in the early 1980s to become an urbanized middle-income country with an average per capita GNI of US$ 5,400 at nominal market exchange rates and US$ 8,300 in PPP terms thirty years later, and, indeed, 50–100 percent higher levels in the larger cities along the coast, has subsequently forced the political leadership at the national level to gradually revise and reformulate its basic strategy of sustaining economic growth. This process can easily be observed by analyzing the messages in the consecutive five-year plans since the relaunch of the policy of the 'Four Modernizations' in the late 1970s, as well as the frequently updated and revised guidelines from the Communist Party. Even though the strategy of taking small and reticent reform steps has proved extremely successful in the past, it may now have reached a stage where much more fundamental changes have to be launched without losing political and economic control, both at the national and the local levels in the country, as well as the passive support from a growing urban well-educated and informed middle class.

It is fruitful in this context to contrast the approach of 'industrial co-development,' implying an ever closer integration of Chinese manufacturing into various forms of global and regional production networks, with a more inward-looking strategy, putting national interests in the forefront. The latter policy would be to subsequently reduce the dependence on foreign-invested enterprises and replace them with 'national champions,' controlled by a mix of private and public interests for mutual benefit. This would be in line with a consolidation of the legitimacy of the Party institutions in a highly transformative society.

11.3.3 Shift towards transformative technology and innovation

The second parallel challenge to the Chinese business model is of a more exogenous character, and can be derived from the shift toward transformative technology and innovation in Western advanced economies in general and in the US in particular.[5] The continuous upgrading of the production system in all sectors of manufacturing and services to cope with increasing domestic as well as foreign demand, will in itself require not only an entirely new thinking on innovation policy, protection of intellectual property rights, focus on quality control, maintenance, after-sales service, management competencies and so on. All these changes will inevitably call for a fundamentally different role for the administrative institutional framework – the quality of government and governance – at all levels in society. The accelerated process of continuous introduction of new technological logics, such as in so-called additive manufacturing, or 3D-printing, may be the end of the large-scale process manufacturing that formed the basis of China's economic success, and pave the way for 'reverse offshoring' back to the old industrial core countries, in order to come closer to the design laboratories and to final customers.

These 'threats' to the existing Chinese model, may, together with the risk to get stuck in the 'middle-income-trap,' also pave the way for an enhanced interest in China to support the acquisition of advanced foreign transnational companies to secure access to new technologies and manufacturing and services processes. At the same time, such a strategy will lead to a rising number of TNCs operating in China and overseas, but more or less dependent on direct and indirect control by the Chinese government.

11.3.4 Governmental policy shifts

One feature related to the gradual shift from strict government control of international economic relations, which is more apparent in China when compared to many other emerging economies in Asia, is the dichotomy of centralization and decentralization. The economic reform process in emerging economies will normally pave the way for the decentralization of decision-making and interpretation of rules and regulations surrounding business activities. In the case of China, the decentralization process can be seen to have created a set of government controls on at least three separate levels – the central, provincial and local government respectively, where the differences in exercising power are expressed in geographical/territorial supremacy rather than in the point at issue. Luo (2005) has formulated five specific features of shifts of governmental policy toward inward FDI, which are relevant as an empirical framework for this study. These are (1) the shift from entry intervention to operational interference; (2) the shift from overt control to covert intervention; (3) the shift from separation to convergence in relation to domestic policies; (4) the shift from regulatory homogeneity to regulatory heterogeneity; (5) the shift from policy rigidity to treatment elasticity (ibid.: 295f). Each of these shifts contains a number of specific operational measures, which are relevant for the analysis of the government's policies toward foreign investors, and can be compared to how a 'hybrid' firm is treated, and will be used as guidelines in the empirical case below.

Principally, the basic legal precondition for treating foreign companies in a market-based economic system should be equality, transparency and predictability. However, foreign corporations in many emerging economies with a strategy to attract FDI have normally been subject to special and differential treatment. The mainstream literature of the 1980s and 1990s mainly focused on the largely adverse relations between TNCs and host country governments, including high entry barriers, rigid control over mode of entry, restrictions toward foreign ownership, access to indigenous natural resources and transfer of generated profits back home. There are also numerous examples of host country governments who have systematically worked at attracting inward FDI, usually by offering more favourable business conditions to the foreign enterprise compared to domestic counterparts. These special rules can be temporary or valid until further notice; they might differ between different sectors of industry and different geographical regions in the host country. The recent experiences from China demonstrate further how special and differential treatment for foreign-owned enterprises gradually erodes in the direction of favouring the emergence of 'national champions,' while the dividing line between the 'foreign' and the 'domestic' has become more blurred (Kettunen, 2013). The remaining part of this chapter will thus be devoted to the question whether the transfer of ownership of Volvo Car Corp. from Sweden via the USA to China can fit into this changing institutional framework.

11.4   The Volvo Car experience[6]

11.4.1   The acquisition process

Volvo Car Corporation (VCC) was divested from the larger Swedish-based Volvo Group in 1999, and acquired by Ford Motor Corp. at the official price of US$ 6.5 billion. It was put on Ford's list of candidates for sales in 2009 in the aftermath of the deep crisis in the global economy, and the subsequent financial troubles of Ford.[7] After a long and strenuous process with many speculator bidders, the VCC was acquired in early 2010 by Zhejiang Geely Holding Group, a Chinese company listed in Hong Kong and majority-owned (51 percent) by a private businessman, Mr Li Shufu, at the price of only US$ 1.8 billion. The Group is incorporated in the Cayman Islands, and is the only major Chinese car manufacturer without formal ties to the state. It holds control of the passenger car brand Geely, headquartered in Hangzhou, Zhejiang Province, and has nine assembly plants in China and manufactures three product brands and ten major models, largely targeting the domestic market, but increasingly looking abroad with an export share of about 20 percent in 2012.[8] The total sales in 2012 of the brands in the Geely family, excluding Volvo, amounted to about 483,000 units, that is, slightly more than VCC's global sales. The acquisition of VCC was financed by a consortium of interests, which, except from the majority-holder, included an investment company owned by the City of Jiading, in the northwestern part of Shanghai district (12 percent) and a state asset operation within the City of Daqing, Heilongjiang Province (37 percent) (Figure 11.1). The new owners declared at an early stage that VCC planned for a rapid volume expansion of global production – from about 370,000 units annually in 2010 to 800,000 units in 2020, with production in China becoming a third main pillar in the geographical distribution of assembly, together with the existing main plants in Gothenburg, Sweden and Ghent in Belgium.

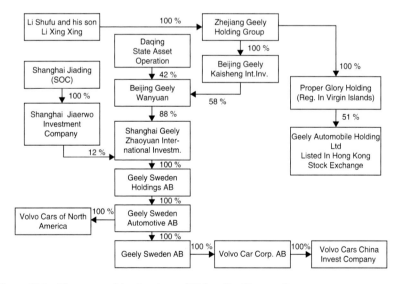

Figure 11.1   The ownership structure of Volvo Car Corporation
Source: Translated and adapted by the authors from original material in *Dagens Industri* (Swedish Business Daily), November 1, 2012.

The announced domestic sales target was set at 200,000 units in 2015, which is about 20 percent of China's predicted premium car segment. The close connection between the new shareholders and the location of VCC's planned activities in China was manifested in the fact that the headquarters of a new technology center, containing production and development, purchasing and design, was established in Jiading; the first assembly plant was to be set up at Chengdu in Sichuan Province, neighbouring an existing Geely plant, and that the planned second assembly should go to Daqing, formerly better known for oil production and petrochemical industries. Furthermore, it was decided to build a new engine plant, in the city of Zhangjiakou northwest of Beijing, in Hebei Province, intended to complement the existing main production facility in Skövde, Sweden[9] (see Figure 11.2). An office for general coordination, marketing and distribution was moreover set up in Pudong in central Shanghai. The optimal location for Chinese car manufacturing has traditionally been close to one of the larger cities at or near the coast, where the market potential is largest, and where the majority of suppliers are established. Foreign manufacturers have also favoured a location close to the coast in order to secure a smooth supply chain of imported parts and components. The 12th Five-Year Plan, 2011–2015, though, gives a clear indication of a shift of manufacturing production to more central provinces, which is why the decision to choose Chengdu and Daqing could be seen as

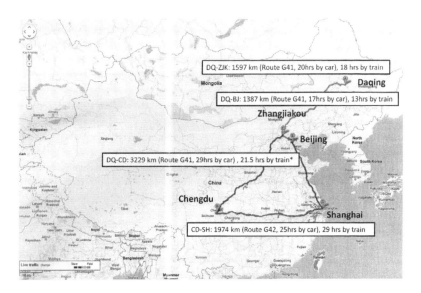

Figure 11.2 Location of the production and management units of Volvo Car Corporation in China: approximate distances between separate units
Note: Authors' own calculations.

a preconditional step for any company – Chinese or foreign – to be granted permission by the government body, NDRC (National Development and Reform Commission) to start new passenger car production. There has been a locational shift inland in recent years, not least to the populous Sichuan Province, among Chinese as well as foreign manufacturers. From this point of view, the location of the first Volvo plant in Chengdu is logical, as seen both from the government policy perspective and from the ambitions by the new owners. It should be noted that the formal permission to produce the first model (S60L) in the Chengdu plant was not given by the authorities until the last week of June 2013, three weeks after the official inauguration of the plant (Hedelin, 2013a).

11.4.2   The start of operations

The construction of the new assembly plant at Chengdu with a planned capacity of 120,000 units a year and 2,500 employees when reaching full capacity, began in 2011, and is expected to commence serial production in late 2013.[10] It is an integrated plant with a bodyshop, a paintshop, and a final assembly line. The time plan for the Daqing plant is more vague, with an expected start of operations in 2014 at the earliest, and with projected full capacity in 2017–2018. The local pressure to speed up the launch of the plant has been strong, though.[11] It should be noted that the total annual production capacity of the nine Geely plants in China is estimated at 600,000 units, that is, only two-thirds of capacity will be utilized. There was accordingly a technical possibility to produce Volvo cars in existing units – a decision that was avoided, presumably because of the necessity, at least in the beginning, to keep the Volvo and Geely brand separate, but also to meet the requirement of a Volvo plant in the home town of the second biggest owner, Daqing State Asset Operation.

By the time of the shift of ownership from Ford to Zhejiang Geely, VCC assembled cars for the China market in a joint plant (Chang'an Ford Mazda Automobile Corp.) at Chongqing together with different Ford and Mazda models. The production in 2012 amounted to 5,500 units, down from 17,000 units in 2011. This operation will cease with the opening up of production in Chengdu, and will also mark the end of the technical cooperation in a common platform with Ford, when VCC launches its new sovereign SPA (Scalable Product Architecture) in Chengdu. Other forms of technical cooperation with Ford in Europe will also be brought to an end during 2013. The SPA, which also will be launched in the European plants, permits a flexible adjustment to different models – in particular to the fact the Chinese versions are slightly longer than the European ones. At least two of the eight planned models from the new platform, and about 20 percent of the global production capacity, will be manufactured in the Chengdu plant.

VCC's share of the Chinese premium brand market is modest, and Volvo is, moreover, positioned in a niche of severe competition, both by domestic and other foreign brands.[12] A rapid growth of sales was reported in 2011, with an increase of 17,000 units to 47,000 from 30,000 in 2010. The sales for 2012, though, were a big disappointment with a decline of 11 percent to about 42,000 units, despite a general strong growth of sales in the premium segment, and a clear success of the main European competitors.[13] In light of the present figures, the previously announced targets to reach a sales volume of 200,000 units in China by 2015 had to be revised and pushed forward in time. The latest official target, stated in June 2013, is to reach this level by 2018. The board also announced a change of CEO in October 2012 to signal the seriousness of the failed sales targets in the company and the urgent need to realize the settled strategic objectives, and there have been a number of changes in remaining senior management, both in China and in Europe during 2012 and 2013, following the acute need to address the poor sales results and the subsequent red figures in the financial report of 2012. A recent study of state subsidies to private firms as revealed that Geely Automobile was by far the largest recipient, with US$ 141 million in 2011 or 51 percent of net profit.[14]

11.4.3   The ambiguity of 'in-betweenness'

The formal commercial relations between the Volvo and Geely brands remain uncertain. The official business strategy rhetoric of the VCC management, the Board of Directors, as well as by the main owner, is that '*Volvo is Volvo, and Geely is Geely*,' that is, that the two brands are completely separate in terms of product development, design, distribution, marketing and dealers.[15] However, within this general arrangement of complete sovereignty, there is room for considerable indirect coordination and cooperation, as has been already demonstrated by the close location of the VCC assembly plant in Chengdu in premises already occupied by Geely. Moreover, the suppliers' network is also subject to possible informal cooperation, as will be indicated below. The main owner, Chairman Li, caused further confusion when in an official interview he stated that Volvo was 'too Scandinavian' and needed to 'adapt better to Chinese consumer tastes,' This statement, though, was fervently retracted in another speech a few months later in connection with the inauguration of the Chengdu plant, when Li repeatedly underlined his passion for Scandinavian design and values, and that the mission of the Geely Group is to establish a global inclusive corporate culture in which national differences and particularities are acknowledged. He also said that Volvo should regain its past splendour, and that it was about 'time to let the tiger out of the cage' (Hedelin, 2013b). These uncertainties about Volvo's brand strategy related to the one of Geely illustrate very well the ambiguity of being 'in-between' a global and a Chinese-based company.

There are another two issues that particularly highlight the grey zone of being foreign, but at the same time being completely dependent on domestic political interests. First, apart from the existing tripartite ownership, is the long-term financing of the ambitious investment plan, including the roughly US$ 10 billion investment in the 2010–2015 period in SPA (Scalable Product Architecture) and VEA (Volvo Engine Architecture); second is the increasing demands from domestic political actors to forge a closer cooperation between Volvo and Geely in order to make Volvo more 'Chinese.'

Already at an early stage in the transformation process, VCC had concluded a Memorandum of Understanding with China Development Bank to evaluate financing of the business plan of the company, and in December 2012, the first loan agreement of €922 million was signed in order to refinance the current loans of the company. The security of the loan is in fact the company itself.[16] With this deal, the present thin 51/49-balance in favour of foreign private ownership, controlled by Chairman Li, may very well shift to the combined interests of the national level, represented by CDB, and the regional/local level of the present minority shareholders, Daqing State Asset Operation and Shanghai Jiaerwoo Investment Company. In such a case, the 'hybrid' status has changed shape, but until then, and in the preferred scenario, as seen from the viewpoint of VCC, in which sales will increase, and the company will return to profit, there will be no external intervention, but the ambiguity will remain.

The second issue regarding a closer judicial bond between VCC and Geely should be seen in light of the announcement by the national government in early 2012 regarding the procurement of cars for public officials at different levels. By deciding rules that excluded not only foreign brands, which was expected beforehand, but also Volvo, it became evident that VCC was not considered to be a domestic partner, eligible for national preferential treatment. The current sales target was partly dependent on the presumption that the large market in sales of official cars to public authorities, giving priority to domestic producers, should include Volvo. It was later officially confirmed that Volvo was not among the brands subject to special and differential treatment. This was not stated explicitly, but through establishing maximum procurement price levels that none of the foreign brands, including Volvo, could match. Thus, while VCC in Sweden is seen as a foreign company that operates in Sweden under Swedish law, it is considered to be a foreign company in China under Chinese law (Liang and Cao, 2012).

The next step in the increasingly complex dialogue regarding whether VCC is foreign or not, came after one year of the launch of the new company when the Chinese national government announced the requirement that Volvo China should be legally subject to a new 50/50 joint venture together with Geely, registered in China. This measure will limit the sovereignty of Volvo China as a part of Zhejiang Geely itself, since it introduces a new level between the formally foreign majority ownership of the latter company, and VCC's operations in China; furthermore, it will establish a stronger connection between Volvo China and the Geely brand than was originally anticipated.[17]

Another step in the further technical integration between the two brands was taken in February 2013 when it was announced that Geely would set up a new Research & Development Centre in Gothenburg with around 200 engineers, both from Sweden and China, and that it would be in full operation by the end of the year. The R&D Centre would develop a new modular architecture and set of components for future smaller cars, addressing the needs of both Volvo and Geely.[18] This venture may be the starting point for the launch of a joint production of small cars and/or electric cars under a common new brand, which, according to unconfirmed information, is planned close to Geely's headquarters in Hangzhou (Matson, 2013).

A further example of indirect cooperation between VCC and the Chinese government was the launch of the China-Sweden Research Centre for Traffic Safety in Beijing in December 2012 together with technological universities in Gothenburg (Chalmers) and Beijing. The Centre, which is also financed by the Swedish and Chinese governments, is a result of a Letter of Intent signed at the visit in Gothenburg by the then PM Wen Jiabao in April 2012.

11.4.4   Domestic vs export markets

One further issue is related to the establishment of an export platform based on Chinese production. This is a test of whether Volvo's brand image abroad will be affected by its production in China and would also shift the hybrid position toward becoming more 'Chinese.' Currently, the Chinese market accounts for roughly 10 percent of VCCs' global car sales, and the main part is served through imports, paying high duties with the same conditions as are applied to other foreign brands. The aim is to increase the present share of local content considerably, and in this respect VCC is treated as a foreign brand when interpreting the LCR (Local Content Requirement) rules. With plans to build up a substantial production capacity with overly ambitious sales targets until 2020, the strategy to use the Chinese plants to serve other Asian markets is logical. These measures are further facilitated by the realization of various regional free trade agreements, which give an advantage to export from China to, for example, ASEAN countries compared to shipment from Europe. An even more radical measure would be to serve the North American market from China. The US, which is the largest single market for Volvo, at present accounts for 16 percent of Volvo's sales, and there is no local production in North America despite the decade of integration with Ford. The prospects of a gradual shift of production from Europe to China can be seen as long-term matter of concern for a European manufacturer with a well-established brand image to protect. The '*Volvo is Volvo and Geely is Geely*' mantra has already began to be nibbled at through the number of cooperative projects launched within product development, purchasing and distribution. There is thus a subtle balance between the present 'hybrid' status on one hand, and the possible shift to become less foreign on the other.

11.4.5   Management and control

The deep interviews with various representatives of the company, both in Sweden and China, during 2010–2013 revealed that there is a strong element of perceived expectations and implicit requirements in the negotiations with government representatives at different levels, and furthermore an uncertainty concerning the ultimate agenda by the majority owner. Even though there is no official or formal requirement expressed by the government representative in a certain field, the fear that policies will be changed in the future is a sufficient reason for changing the corporate strategy to cope with the potential impacts of this unexpressed demand.

There has also been a high level of rotation in the executive management of the company. VCC is indirectly owned through three levels of Swedish listed holding companies, Geely Sweden Holdings AB, Geely Sweden Automotive AB and Geely Sweden AB (see Figure 11.1). The meetings with the multinationally constituted Board of Directors are in practice not led by Chairman Li, but by the (Swedish) Vice-Chairman, Mr Hans-Olov Olsson, formerly CEO of VCC before the divestment to Ford, and thereafter senior vice-president of Ford Motor Corp. The minority shareholders are not represented on the VCC board. Mr Stefan Jacoby, a German national, who was recruited to be the CEO after the Geely acquisition, previously had a long career within multinational automotive industries, including Mitsubishi and Volkswagen. Partly due to the disappointing results, he was replaced in October 2012 by a Swede, Mr Håkan Samuelsson, who by the time of the appointment was a member of the Board of Directors, but previously had pursued his career in the Swedish and German truck industry, including Scania and being CEO of MAN. The first CEO for the China operations, Mr Freeman Shen, recruited from the Geely organization, but having served previously in senior positions in a number of European and American companies, including Fiat, was in early 2013 replaced by Mr Lars Danielsson, a Swede with a pure Volvo background.

These changes in the top management of VCC as a whole, as in Volvo Cars China, can be interpreted as a message from the majority-owner to counterbalance the concerns of a gradual shift to become a pure Chinese company with a slow but steady absolute and relative decline of manufacturing operations in Europe, and an increasing dependence on Asia in general and China in particular for its survival in the hardening competition within the premium car segment. They symbolize the intricate balance that the majority-owner has to manage between the other main shareholders, as well as with the central government, represented by the NDRC, the Ministry of Industry and Information Technology (MIIT), and China Development Bank.

11.5   Summary and conclusion

This longitudinal study of how a company that is led and controlled by a private Chinese entrepreneur has acquired a well-reputed foreign TNC with limited operations and sales in China, in order to establish a stronghold at home through the building up of new production capacity in a new market segment, is a striking example of how a 'grey zone' is established between 'pure' domestic and 'pure' foreign companies in emerging markets. Zhejiang Geely Holding Group is headquartered in Hangzhou in Zhejiang Province, with production in different parts of China, and is in this respect a 'true' domestic company. On the other hand, it is listed in Hong Kong and incorporated in a Caribbean tax haven. The acquisition was realized through a kind of public–private partnership, involving a couple of public sector minority shareholders at the regional/local level in different parts of China, and supported by China Development Bank, which holds the key in the case of financial troubles caused by a high-risk expansion strategy in a market characterized by over-capacity and fierce competition in the premium car segment.

The arising of what in this chapter is tentatively labelled a 'hybrid' emerging market firm, which is treated differently from domestic as well as foreign TNCs, can be seen as a new phenomenon in the subsequent development of the Chinese-managed market economy. For the individual company in this grey zone, it adds an element of uncertainty and a situation of a 'liability of in-betweenness' to all other specific implicit or explicit rules and regulations that face a foreign company in China, and especially at a time when there is a clear trend toward a more strict and less favourable treatment of non-Chinese ventures in those manufacturing sectors where there are 'pure' domestic competitors and dedicated 'national champions,' which can be expected to complement and ultimately to replace the foreign firms. There are also limited opportunities to formally establish the special and differential treatment of a hybrid international from a 'pure' domestic company and a 'pure' foreign TNC.

The notion of a 'hybrid' emerging market firm is not clear-cut, however, and it has to be viewed from a dynamic, rather than a static perspective. As has been evident through the example of Geely and Volvo Cars, also confirming the general description of shifts in China's government policy toward inward FDI by Luo (2005), the grey zone between a pure foreign-owned enterprise and a private, domestic firm is not explicitly stated, but has to be tested through numerous disparate decisions, measures, regulations and formal legislation at both the national, the regional/provincial and the local level. The 'managed' location decisions of the new production capacity, as well as the lack of special and differential treatment when it comes to public procurement seem to support the opposition assumption that VCC cannot be seen as a hybrid, but has been treated similarly to other foreign companies. On the other hand, the apparent indirect financial support by the political leadership to a private majority-owner of a legally foreign company to implement the business plan in investments that exceed the initial acquisition cost by at least five to six times, gives support to the assumption that the Central Government has given Zhejiang Geely Holding Group a reassurance that the VCC acquisition must not fail, and that domestic public sector interests at the central, regional and local levels are prepared to take over the majority control if the present business plan is not complied with. This outcome is presumably an emergency exit, and it is likely that the Government aims at maintaining the subtle grey zone between pure foreign and domestic companies, thus having fostered a new 'hybrid' category.

A dynamic viewpoint, however, might be to see the hybrid status of an acquired foreign company as a soft transition phase before establishing direct control. Such a measure can be motivated by the apparent risk to damage the global reputation of a company, 90 percent of whose sales take place outside China, and where the prospects of future technology and knowledge transfer rely on continuous support and cooperation with employees in existing foreign plants. In this respect, the possible establishing of an export platform with the Chinese production as a base is a 'litmus test' of the role of the European plants, and, thus, the current, hybrid status or whether the grey zone between being foreign and domestic is merely a transition phase in the direction of making VCC a purely Chinese company, although under private ownership.

This chapter has on a more general level also dealt with new forms of government–firm relationships at different levels of government, as well as of the emerging market firm aiming for internationalization, following the theoretical starting points formulated in previous literature (Alon et al., 2012; Luo, 2005; Luo and Tung; 2007; Ramamurti, 2012; Williamson et al., 2013). In its rapid transition from a closed centrally planned economy via a period of open and experimental export-oriented and investor-friendly legislation to today's increasingly self-confident domestically oriented managerial system, China is an appropriate example to study for industrial co-development in international business. The aim was to investigate new varieties of the liability of foreignness and the liability of outsidership, by particularly focusing on a situation where the acquiring emerging market firm adopts the 'springboard' approach in the sense that the main ambition with the strategic asset-seeking investment abroad was to improve its competitive position at home. However, the acquirer does not belong to the traditional category of a state-owned enterprise or a private former 'red hat' firm, but was already incorporated and floated on a stock market outside the home country. The empirical case implies that this category of companies will become more common in the future with the further rise of outward FDI from emerging markets, but that it will in particular be frequent in China with its intricate mix of government control and market economy experimentation, and that it is consequently motivated to introduce such a new 'hybrid' category of emerging market multinationals in order to better describe and interpret this process.

Notes

1. All figures are from International Financial Statistics database of the International Monetary Fund, and from the annual UNCTAD World Investment Report, various years, complemented with official figures from China Ministry of Commerce (MOFCOM) regarding 2012.
2. These figures include the substantial amounts of 'round-tripping', i.e. OFDI directed at Hong Kong, Caribbean tax havens and elsewhere, which at a later stage are transformed into IFDI.
3. Lenovo's acquisition of IBM's PC business in 2005 provides an interesting example of the complexity in the categorization of being purely 'domestic' or 'foreign.' The roots of the deal are in the state institution of the Chinese Academy of Sciences and in the investment firm Legend Holdings. Since the IBM acquisition Lenovo has been run as a transnational foreign firm with double headquarters in China and USA, and with continuous expansion abroad. It acquired the German electronics firm Medion in 2011, entered a joint venture with Japanese NEC the same year, purchased Brazil's biggest computer firm, CCE, in 2012, and launched the 'Think' brand for the premium segment in 2013. Despite this impressive globalization, it is still considered to be a 'national champion,' heavily reliant as it is on the domestic Chinese market, being its main source of profits for financing overseas expansion (Deng, 2012: 143ff; The Economist, 2013a: 52f).
4. www.euronews.com/newswires/1846158-exclusive-china-wealth-fund-commerce-ministry-to-get-new-heads-sources/ [accessed March 7, 2013].
5. Many of the arguments put forward in the following paragraph are taken from Magnus (2012: 9).
6. All figures regarding sales and other facts are from the official websites of VCC: www.volvocar.com; www.geelyauto.com.hk; http://202.155.223.21/~geelmhk1/en/cb.html [accessed January 13, 2013]. The data and interpretations of factual information were gathered through deep interviews on several occasions with responsible purchasing managers in the VCC headquarters in Gothenburg, as well as in Jiading, the Pudong office, and Chengdu between September 2011 and February 2013. In addition, an interview was carried out with a senior representative of a Swedish TNC in another sector of manufacturing with long experience of production in China, in order to investigate whether there are major differences in the government–firm relationship on the basis of sectoral identity.
7. A thorough analysis of the disintegration process from Ford from an inside perspective is given by Schweizer and Hamberg Lagerström in the previous chapter of the present book.
8. For an extensive description of the development of Geely, as well as of the background to the acquisition of VCC, see also Fetscherin and Beuttenmuller, 2012: 380ff; Wu et al. 2012: 115ff.
9. See map, indicating the physical and time distances between the main units (Figure 11.2). This plant will initially only assemble engines, but will gradually develop into an integrated engine plant when the new four-cylinder turbocharged VEA engine (*Volvo Engine Architecture*) is launched.
10. The plant was officially opened in June 2013, and will commence serial production during the second half of the year, aiming at a production of about 1,500 units in 2013, and 30,000 units in 2014.
11. At the time of the writing (June 2013), the plant is physically completed, although not equipped, and local authorities have for some years been targeting potential

suppliers. According to unconfirmed information, manufacturing of outgoing SUV models, e.g. the XC90, will be located at the Daqing plant (Matson, 2013).
12. The segment is dominated by German BMW and Audi, followed by Mercedes and (now) Indian LandRover. Depending on the definition of the premium/luxury segment, Volvo's share can be estimated at 4 to 7 percent (2012 figures).
13. Based on preliminary sales figures: https://www.media.volvocars.com/global/enhanced/en-gb/Media/Preview.aspx?mediaid=47240, released January 7, 2013.
14. Fathom China, quoted by The Economist (2013b).
15. This statement was also confirmed in a personal meeting with Mr Li Shufu, September 15, 2010.
16. https://www.media.volvocars.com/global/enhanced/engb/Media/Preview.aspx?mediaid=47241 [accessed January 13, 2013].
17. China Daily, February 27, 2012. http://www.chinadaily.com.cn/bizchina/2012-02/27/content_14698973.htm [accessed June 19, 2013].
18. http://www.automotiveworld.com/news-releases/volvo-cars-and-geely-cooperate-in-new-rd-centre-in-gothenburg-sweden/ [accessed February 20, 2013].

References

Aggarwal, R. and Agmon, T. (1990) 'The International Success of Developing Country Firms: Role of Government-directed Comparative Advantage,' *Management International Review*, 30(2): 163–80.
Alon, I. and McIntyre, J.R. (eds) (2008) *Globalization of Chinese Enterprises* (Basingstoke: Palgrave Macmillan).
Alon, I., Fetscherin, M. and Gugler, P. (eds) (2012) *Chinese International Investments* (Basingstoke: Palgrave Macmillan).
Alon, I., Fetscherin, M. and Sardy, M. (2008) 'Geely Motors Case: The Internationalization of a Chinese Automotive Firm,' *International Journal of Chinese Culture and Management*, 1(4): 489–98.
Alon, I., Chang, J., Fetscherin, M., Lattemann, C. and McIntyre, J.R. (eds) (2009) *China Rules: Globalization and Political Transformation* (Basingstoke: Palgrave Macmillan).
Barboza, D. (2013) 'Chinese Bid for U.S. Pork Had Links to Wall Street,' *New York Times*, June 2, http://www.nytimes.com/2013/06/03/business/global/behind-the-chinese-bid-for-smithfield-foods.html?_r=0 [accessed June 2, 2013].
Brandt, L. and Thun, E. (2010) 'The Fight for the Middle: Upgrading, Competition, and Industrial Development in China,' *World Development*, 38(11): 1555–1574.
Breznitz, D. and Murphree, M. (2011) *Run of the Red Queen: Government, Innovation, Globalization and Economic Growth in China* (New Haven, CT: Yale University Press).
Buckley, P.J., Clegg, L.J., Cross, A.R., Lin, X., Voss, H. and Zheng, P. (2007) 'The Determinants of Chinese Outward FDI,' *Journal of International Business Studies*, 38(4): 499–518.
Buckley, P.J., Cross, A.R., Tan, H., Liu, X. and Voss, H. (2008) 'Historic and Emergent Trends in Chinese Outward Direct Investment,' *Management International Review*, 48(6): 715–748.
Cantwell, J. and Tolentino, P. (1990) *Technological Accumulation and Third World Multinationals* (London: Routledge).
Chaisse, J. and Gugler, P. (eds) (2009) *Expansion of Trade and FDI in Asia: Strategic and Policy Challenges* (New York: Routledge).
Chen, H., Hsu, C.-W. and Caskey, D. (2013) 'Internationalization of Taiwanese Manufacturing Firms: The Evolution of Subsidiary Mandates and Capabilities,' *Asian Business & Management*, 12(1): 37–60.

Chen, T.-J. (2006) 'Liability of Foreignness and Entry Mode Choice: Taiwanese Firms in Europe,' *Journal of Business Research*, 59(2): 288–294.

Child, J. and Rodrigues, B. (2005) 'The Internationalization of Chinese Firms,' *Management and Organization Review*, 1(3): 381–410.

Cuervo-Cazurra, A. (2012) 'Extending Theory by Analyzing Developing Country Multinational Companies: Solving the Goldilocks Debate,' *Global Strategy Journal*, 2(3): 41–47.

Cui, L. and Jiang, F. (2009) 'FDI Entry Mode Choice of Chinese Firms: A Strategic Behavior Perspective,' *Journal of World Business*, 44(4): 434–444.

Deng, P. (2008) 'Resources, Capability, and Outbound FDI from Chinese Companies,' in I. Alon and J.R. McIntyre (eds), *Globalization of Chinese Enterprises* (Basingstoke: Palgrave Macmillan): 17–30.

Deng, P. (2009) 'Why Do Chinese Firms Tend to Acquire Strategic Assets in International Expansion?,' *Journal of World Business*, 44(1): 74–84.

Deng, P. (2012) 'Effects of Absorptive Capacity on International Acquisitions of Chinese Firms,' in I. Alon, M. Fetscherin and P. Gugler (eds), *Chinese International Investments* (Basingstoke: Palgrave Macmillan): 137–153.

Dolles, H., Alvstam, C.G. and Ström, P. (2013) 'The Changing Competitive Landscape in Euro-Asia Business – Guest Editorial,'*Asian Business and Management*, 12(5): 499–502.

Dunning, J.H. (1998) 'Location and the Multinational Enterprise: A Neglected Factor,' *Journal of International Business Studies*, 29(1): 45–86.

Dunning, J.H. (2006) 'Comment on Dragon Multinationals: New Players in 21st Century Globalization,' *Asia-Pacific Journal of Management*, 23(2): 139–141.

Dunning, J.H. and Lundan, S.M. (2008) *Multinational Enterprises and the Global Economy*, 2nd ed. (Cheltenham: Edward Elgar).

The Economist (2013a) 'Chinese Industry – From Guard Shack to Global Giant: How Did Lenovo Become the World's Biggest Computer Company?,' January 12, http://www.economist.com/news/business/21569398-how-did-lenovo-become-worlds-biggest-computer-company-guard-shack-global-giant [accessed August 5, 2013].

The Economist (2013b) 'Perverse Advantage: A New Book Lays Out the Scale of China's Industrial Subsidies,' April 27, http://www.economist.com/news/finance-and-economics/21576680-new-book-lays-out-scale-chinas-industrial-subsidies-perverse-advantage [accessed June 25, 2013].

Ellingsen, G., Likumahuwa, W. and Nunnenkamp, P. (2006) 'Outward FDI by Singapore: A Different Animal?,' *Transnational Corporations*, 15(2): 1–40.

Fetscherin, M. and Beuttenmuller, P. (2012) 'Geely's Internationalization and Volvo's Acquisition,' in I. Alon, M. Fetscherin and P. Gugler (eds), *Chinese International Investments* (Basingstoke: Palgrave Macmillan): 376–390.

Gammeltoft, P., Barnard, H. and Madhok, A. (2010) 'Emerging Multinationals, Emerging Theory: Macro- and Micro-level Perspectives,' *Journal of International Management*, 16(2): 95–101.

Goh, S.K. and Wong, K.N. (2011) 'Malaysia's Outward FDI: The Effects of Market Size and Government Policy,' *Journal of Policy Modeling*, 33(3): 497–510.

Grosse, R. (ed.) (2005) *International Business and Government Relations in the 21st Century* (Cambridge: Cambridge University Press).

Gugler, P. and Boie, B. (2009) 'The Rise of Chinese MNEs,' in J. Chaisse and P. Gugler (eds), *Expansion of Trade and FDI in Asia: Strategic and Policy Challenges* (New York: Routledge): 25–57.

Gugler, P. and Fetscherin, M. (2010) 'The Role and Importance of the Chinese Government for Chinese Outward Foreign Direct Investments,' *AIB Insights*, 10(4): 12–15.

Haley, U.S.V. and Haley, G.T. (2013) *Subsidies to Chinese Industry: State Capitalism, Business Strategy and Trade Policy* (Oxford: Oxford University Press).

Hedelin, J. (2013a) 'Klart för produktion av volvobilar i Kina' [Green light for production of Volvo Cars in China], *Dagens Industri [Swedish Business Daily]*, July 2.

Hedelin, J. (2013b) 'Li Shufu tror på designen [Li Shufu believes in the design],' *Dagens Industri [Swedish Business Daily]*, June 7.

Hemmert, M. (2012) *Tiger Management: Korean Companies on World Markets* (Abingdon: Routledge).

Herrigel, G. and Zeitlin, J. (2010) 'Interfirm Relations in Global Manufacturing: Disintegrated Production and its Globalization,' in G. Morgan, J.L. Campbell, C. Crouch, O.K. Pedersen and R. Whitley (eds), *The Oxford Handbook of Comparative Institutional Analysis* (Oxford: Oxford University Press): 527–561.

Johanson, J. and Vahlne, J.-E. (2009) 'The Uppsala Internationalization Process Model Revisited: From Liability of Foreignness to Liability of Outsidership,' *Journal of International Business Studies*, 40(9): 1411–1431.

Kettunen, E. (2013) China's policy environment toward foreign companies: Implications to high tech sectors. *AI & Society. Journal of Knowledge, Culture and Communication*, Special Issue: Competition and Innovation for Smart and Creative Society. Published online 4 July 2013. DOI 10.1007/s00146-013-0466-y.

Lall, S. and Chen, E. (1983) *The New Multinationals: The Spread of Third World Enterprises* (New York: Wiley).

Li, H.Q. (2012) 'History and Development of Entrepreneurship in China,' in T. Zhang and R.R. Stough (eds), *Entrepreneurship and Economic Growth in China* (Singapore: World Scientific Publishing Co.): 13–34.

Liang D.-L. and Cao, H.-L. (2012) 'Identity Crisis Rattles Volvo's Chinese Owner: Buying the Swedish Firm Was Easy Part for Now Frustrated Executives,' *Caixin Online*, http://articles.marketwatch.com/2012-05-24/industries/31838035_1_geely-chairman-li-shufu-geely-and-volvo-chinese-government [accessed January 13, 2013].

Liu, X., Buck, T. and Chang, S. (2005) 'Chinese Economic Development, the Next Stage: Outward FDI?,' *International Business Review*, 14(1): 97–115.

Luo, Y. (2005) 'Shifts of Chinese Government Policies on Inbound Foreign Direct Investment,' in: R. Grosse (ed.), *International Business and Government Relations in the 21st Century* (Cambridge: Cambridge University Press): 295–313.

Luo, Y. and Rui, H. (2009) 'An Ambidexterity Perspective toward Multinational Enterprises from Emerging Economies,' *Academy of Management Perspective* 23(4): 49–70.

Luo, Y. and Tung, R.L. (2007) 'International Expansion of Emerging Market Enterprises: A Springboard Perspective,' *Journal of International Business Studies*, 38(4): 481–498.

Luo, Y., Xue, Q. and Han, B. (2010) 'How Emerging Market Governments Promote Outward FDI: Experience from China,' *Journal of World Business*, 45(1): 68–79.

Magnus, G. (2012) 'Why China is Losing its Lead as the Hub of Global Production,' *Financial Times*, September 14: 9.

Mathews, J.A. (2002) *Dragon Multinational: A New Model for Global Growth* (Oxford and New York: Oxford University Press).

Mathews, J.A. (2006) 'Dragon Multinationals: New Players in 21st Century Globalization,' *Asia-Pacific Journal of Management*, 23(1): 5–27.

Matson, H. (2013) 'Ny volvofabrik planeras i Kina [New Volvo plant is planned in China],' *Dagens Industri [Swedish Business Daily]*, July 3.

Miller, S.R. and Eden, L. (2006) 'Local Density and Foreign Subsidiary Performance,' *Academy of Management Journal*, 49(2): 341–355.

Miller, S.R., Thomas, D.E., Eden, L. and Hitt, M. (2008) 'Knee Deep in the Big Muddy: The Survival of Emerging Market Firms in Developed Markets,' *Management International Review*, 48(6): 645–666.

Morck, R., Yeung, B. and Zho, M. (2008) 'Perspectives on China's Outward Foreign Direct Investment,' *Journal of International Business Studies*, 39(3): 337–350.

Narula, R. (2012) 'Do We Need Different Frameworks to Explain Infant MNEs from Developing Countries?,' *Global Strategy Journal*, 2(3): 188–204.

Nolan, P. (2001) *China and the Global Economy* (Basingstoke: Palgrave Macmillan).

Nolan, P. (2012) *Is China Buying the World?* (London: Polity Press).

Pananond, P. (2013) 'Moving Along the Value Chain: Emerging Thai Multinationals in Globally Integrated Industries,' *Asian Business & Management*, 12(1): 85–114.

Peng, M.W., Wang, D. and Jiang, Y. (2008) 'An Institution-based View of International Business Strategy: A Focus on Emerging Economies,' *Journal of International Business Studies*, 39(5): 920–936.

Petersen, B. and Seifert Jr, R.E. (2013) *Liability of Ownership and Strategic Asset Seeking of Emerging Market Firms* (forthcoming).

Ramachandran, J. and Pant, A. (2010) 'The Liabilities of Origin: An Emerging Economy Perspective on the Costs of Doing Business Abroad,' in T.M. Devinney, T. Pedersen and L.-T. Tihanyi (eds), *Advances in International Management: The Past, Present and Future of International Business and Management*, 23 (New York: Emerald): 231–265.

Ramamurti, R. (2012) 'What is Really Different about Emerging Market MNEs?,' *Global Strategy Journal*, 2(1): 41–47.

Ramamurti, R. and Singh, J.V. (eds) (2009) *Emerging Multinationals in Emerging Markets* (Cambridge: Cambridge University Press).

Ren, B., Liang, H. and Zheng, Y. (2012) 'An Institutional Perspective and the Role of the State for Chinese OFDI,' in I. Alon, M. Fetscherin and P. Gugler (eds), *Chinese International Investments* (Basingstoke: Palgrave Macmillan): 11–37.

Rugman, A. (2009) 'Theoretical Aspects of MNEs from Emerging Markets,' in R. Ramamurti and J.V. Singh (eds) (2009), *Emerging Multinationals in Emerging Markets* (Cambridge: Cambridge University Press): 42–63.

Rugman, A.M. and Li, J. (2007) 'Will China's Multinationals Succeed Globally or Regionally?,' *European Management Journal*, 25(5): 333–343.

Rui, H. and Yip, G.S. (2008) 'Foreign Acquisitions by Chinese Firms: A Strategic Intent Perspective,' *Journal of World Business*, 43(2): 213–226.

Shambaugh, D. (2013) *China Goes Global: The Partial Power* (Oxford: Oxford University Press).

Schlunze, R.D., Agola, N.O. and Barber, W.W. (eds) (2012) *Spaces of International Economy and Management: Launching New Perspectives on Management and Geography* (Basingstoke: Palgrave Macmillan).

Schweizer, R. and Hamberg Lagerström, K. (2014) 'A Business Tale on Marriage, Divorce and Remarriage in the Corporate World: A Conceptual Framework of Firms' Disintegration Process,' in C.G. Alvstam, H. Dolles and P. Ström (eds), *Asian Inward and Outward FDI: New Challenges in the Global Economy* (Basingstoke: Palgrave Macmillan): 201–216.

Söderman, S., Jakobsson, A. and Solér, L. (2008) 'A Quest for Repositioning: The Emerging Internationalization of Chinese Companies,' *Asian Business & Management*, 7(1): 115–142.

Steinfeld, E. S. (2004) 'China's Shallow Integration: Networked Production and the New Challenges for Late Industrialization,' *World Development*, 32(11): 1971–1987.

Steinfeld, E.S. (2010) *Playing Our Game: Why China's Rise Doesn't Threaten the West* (Oxford: Oxford University Press).

Tang, F.C., Gao, X.D. and Li, Q. (2008) 'Knowledge Acquisition and Learning: Strategies in Globalization of China's Enterprises,' in I. Alon and J.R. McIntyre (eds), *Globalization of Chinese Enterprises* (Basingstoke: Palgrave Macmillan): 31–43.

Thun, E. (2006) *Changing Lanes in China: Foreign Direct Investment, Local Governments, and Auto Sector Development* (New York: Cambridge University Press).

Vahlne, J.-E. and Johanson, J. (2013) 'The Uppsala Model on Evolution of the Multinational Business Enterprise – From Internalization to Coordination of Networks,' *International Marketing Review*, 30(3): 189–210.

Wells, L. (1983) *Third World Multinationals: The Rise of Foreign Investments from Developing Countries* (Cambridge, MA: MIT Press).

Williamson, P.J. and Raman, A.P. (2013) 'Cross-border M&A and Competitive Advantage of Chinese EMNEs,' in P.J. Williamson, R. Ramamurti, A. Fleury and M.T. Leme Fleury (eds) (2013), *The Competitive Advantage of Emerging Market Multinationals* (Cambridge: Cambridge University Press): 260–277.

Williamson, P. and Zeng, M. (2009) 'Chinese Multinationals: Emerging through New Gateways,' in R. Ramamurti and J.V. Singh (eds), *Emerging Multinationals in Emerging Markets* (Cambridge: Cambridge University Press): 81–109.

Williamson, P.J., Ramamurti, R., Fleury, A. and Leme Fleury, M.T. (eds) (2013) *The Competitive Advantage of Emerging Market Multinationals* (Cambridge: Cambridge University Press).

Wu, X., Ding, W.-L. and Shi, Y.J. (2012) 'Motives and Patterns of Reverse FDI by Chinese Manufacturing Firms,' in I. Alon, M. Fetscherin and P. Gugler (eds), *Chinese International Investments* (Basingstoke: Palgrave Macmillan): 107–121.

Yang, K. (2007) *Entrepreneurship in China* (Aldershot: Ashgate).

Yeung, H.W.C. (ed.) (1999) *The Globalization of Business Firms from Emerging Economies* (Cheltenham: Edward Elgar).

Yeung, H.W.C. (2012) 'Foreword,' in R.D. Schlunze, N.O. Agola and W.W. Barber (eds), *Spaces of International Economy and Management: Launching New Perspectives on Management and Geography* (Basingstoke: Palgrave Macmillan): xiii–xix.

Yildiz, H.E. and Fey, C.F. (2012) 'The Liability of Foreignness Reconsidered: New Insights from the Alternative Research Context of Transforming Economies,' *International Business Review*, 21(2): 269–280.

Zaheer, S. (1995) 'Overcoming the Liability of Foreignness,' *The Academy of Management Journal*, 38(2): 341–363.

Zaheer, S. (2002) 'The Liability of Foreignness, Redux: A Commentary,' *Journal of International Management*, 8(3): 351–358.

Zaheer, S. and Mosakowski, E. (1997) 'The Dynamics of the Liability of Foreignness: A Global Study of Survival in Financial Services,' *Strategic Management Journal*, 18(6): 439–463.

Statistical sources

International Monetary Fund, *International Financial Statistics, Database*.

MOFCOM (Ministry of Commerce, People's Republic of China). http://english. mofcom.gov.cn/.

United Nations Conference for Trade and Development, *World Investment Report*, various issues. Geneva.

Interviews

Repeated personal interviews with middle and senior management representatives of Volvo Car Corporation, in Gothenburg and China (Pudong, Jiading, Chengdu), October 2011–February 2013.

Personal interview with a senior management representative of one of the major Swedish TNCs with outstanding experience of production in China, October 2012.

Personal communication with VCC Chairman Mr Li Shufu, Vice-Chairman Mr Hans-Olov Olsson, CEO, Mr Stefan Jacoby, Gothenburg, September 15, 2010.

Personal communication with senior management representatives at Geely's headquarters, Hangzhou, China, May 2011.

12
Concluding Remarks on Asian Inward and Outward FDI; New Challenges in the Global Economy

Claes G. Alvstam, Harald Dolles, and Patrik Ström

In this volume we have attempted to give a broad overview of the current scholarly debate around foreign direct investment (FDI) in emerging Asian countries, in which the main message has been to demonstrate that FDI flows – inward and outward – continuously take new directions, and change form incessantly. Despite several decades of multifaceted and successfully carried out research on FDI in different parts of the world – an endeavour that has broadened and deepened our knowledge of the complexities of international economic and political integration – reality has constantly impinged. Emerging market multinational enterprises feature new logics, and their activities are anchored in different institutional environments compared to the traditional firms, and demand accordingly new theoretical interpretations and explanations. The emerging market multinational enterprises should never be seen as a homogenous group, neither should companies from different Asian countries be scrutinized with the same glasses. Yet, there are indeed common aspects that motivate joint examination in the search for better explanation of past trends and enhanced predictability and probability of alternative future scenarios. The revealed heterogeneity between newly created multinational companies in various large emerging markets can also be seen as an appropriate starting point for the theoretical debate on intra-variations vs inner variations in the comparison with MNEs from the 'old industrial core' countries (for a recent successful example, see, for example, Williamson et al., 2013). It also raises the discussion of how and to what extent those companies increase competitive pressures, and one therefore needs to better understand the implications these pressures have on strategic development by competitors in Europe, Asia and in the rest of the world (for a recent publication, refer, for example, to Dolles, Alvstam and Ström, 2013).

There has been an ambition in this volume to capture and to elucidate aspects that have been less observed and assessed in the scholarly debate up to now. Some of these 'hidden dimensions' of foreign direct investment may turn out to be erroneous, misleading or insignificant in future developments, while others may contain the seed of an entirely novel interpretation of the transforming process of the continuous opening up of national economies, and the creation of larger common markets in Asia. One common theme in several contributions to this volume has been to put the limelight on new forms of invisible added values in physical production. While services as a compound phenomenon have attracted increasing attention, and value-added services have become more salient in recent research, much effort remains, theoretically, methodologically and empirically, to give the service content in physical production its proper role in the value chain. In particular, there is still, for historical and ideological reasons, a clear underrating of the true value of service production in China's economy, while in other Asian countries, for example, Japan, the service content in physical production has traditionally been included in the physical product, leaving little room for independent after-sales services and distribution. The examples taken in this volume of various 'hidden' types of value-added in services relate to the advantages of research cooperation, as in the chapters by Chie Iguchi et al., and the concept of talent development, described by Christian Schmidt and others. The view of the human resource factor in service development, and in the evaluation and measurement of service content, may in many aspects be a cultural phenomenon. Therefore, it is highly relevant, as in the chapter by Rolf Schlunze et al. to investigate how top managers representing different cultural backgrounds relate to each other, and how their different 'cosmologies' affect their priorities and decision-making regarding production, research and development, location, distribution, marketing, etc. – all aspects intrinsically woven together with visible effects in the form of trade and investment. These three chapters are also examples of the micro- or the human-cantered approach to international economic integration that should be given more attention in future research, not least in Asia. It is commendable that this route toward a more coherent focus on technology- and knowledge-transfers in the form of research cooperation, talent development and management experiences and practices across Asian borders is followed henceforth, not only in exchange with the advanced market economies in North America and Europe, but to a larger extent between Asian countries.

The focus on the higher levels of value-added in the service sector should not leave out those sectors that create larger volumes of manual labour, and which may have a more distinct impact on employment generation in remote areas than various types of professional business services, which more or less per definition act as centralizing forces to the main population conurbations. The tourist and leisure sector is a growing field within international business in the Asian context, due to the growth of a well-off middle class. Since tourism belongs to those sectors of services that are most decentralized, and are likely to give a quick indirect impact at the local level in terms of job creation, and multiplier effects in the form of infrastructure etc., this is a sector that also should attract broader research. The chapter by Andrew Staples in the volume, using an example of inward FDI to Northern Japan also illustrates a promising new research topic around foreign actors in the tourist industry, and the interconnectivity between tourism and other sectors, in services as well as in manufacturing.

There has been moreover a deliberate choice in this volume to further promote research related to the separate firm, on the basis that deep longitudinal studies of the spatial development of the single business enterprise can capture some of the subtle nuances and difficult-to-grasp environment that characterizes the strategic decision-making of the firm. This topic has often been frowned on, for many good reasons. The opportunities for good generalizations from single case studies are indeed limited, and it is tempting to get lost in the details. On the other hand, the company case study with focus on a particular issue makes a good complement to other research and contributes to reveal complex patterns that are difficult to trace by more conventional methods. There have recently been promising attempts to invigorate this research tradition in the Japanese context in a recent collection by Schlunze et al. (2012). The chapter by Sang-Chul Park and others in the present volume can be seen to follow this track through an attempt to find out the intrinsic key factors behind the immense global success of Samsung Electronics. In order to avoid the trap of incorporating too many parallel aspects in a longitudinal firm-level study, future research along this tradition should to a larger extent focus on decisive moments where corporate strategy takes a new direction, the role of the entrepreneur or decision-makers within, and to identify the specific environmental context within which the crossroad opportunity occurs. There are also too few attempts to complement the traditional use of external open sources with in-depth interviews with senior management in order to better interpret the underlying reasons behind key strategic changes. Even though the degree of openness toward independent researchers might vary between different countries and different industries, we would nevertheless argue that the qualitative approach has been underutilized in previous years and should be applied more often.

There is also a persistent gap between typical firm-level studies on one hand, and broader macro-oriented business-system approaches on the other. Despite the obvious fact that the international strategic management of the firm is to a large extent a function of the surrounding institutional framework of the firm, there is more to be done to highlight in which way this framework affects decision-making. By using the free trade agreement between Korea and EU as an example of a decisive event, calling for new business opportunities for Korean companies in the European single internal market and further opening the Korean market to FDI, Flora Bendt et al. offer in their chapter a framework of how the coupling between firm-level behaviour and changing business environments could be described and analyzed.

The chapter by Harald Dolles and Sten Söderman takes the perspective on how sponsoring of mega-events as a new marketing strategy works in an emerging market context. By taking a longitudinal approach in investigating advertising patterns of the Beijing Olympic Games sponsoring partners from the decision to award the Games to Beijing to the actual event of the Games the authors developed a unique data-set to indentify different marketing strategies by local as well as foreign companies. The research also highlights the challenges associated with sponsoring a mega-event like the Olympic Games in an emerging market. In 2008 the Tibetan uprising escalated and thousands of protesters and counter-protesters lined the planned route of the torch relay in London. As this and further protests happened shortly ahead of the Games and human-rights activists also started to criticize the sponsors of the Beijing Olympic Games for partnering with China, this constituted one of many issues creating uncertainty among existing sponsors and potential investors (the riots in Brazil ahead of and during the Confederations Cup – although starting with a different reasoning – might be just in line with the risk of awarding mega-events like the Olympic Games or the Football World Cup to an emerging economy). Another crucial issue that is revealed in this context in the chapter is the fact that sponsorship toward the Olympic Games in Beijing was not self-imposed, but government-appointed. The purpose of the government inviting companies to be sponsors may simply be a means of making them share the financial burden of the Beijing Olympic Games 2008. The authors therefore conclude that sponsorship in an emerging market context might serve different purposes compared to established markets, and that activating the sponsorship investment by designing a focused advertising strategy is therefore not necessarily needed, but would allow the leveraging of the investment.

A variant of the firm-level study, also applying a longitudinal approach, is exemplified by the two chapters by Roger Schweizer and Katarina Hamberg Lagerström, and Claes G. Alvstam and Inge Ivarsson respectively. The object of their attention is the transformation of the Swedish-based Volvo Car Corporation from ownership by American Ford Motor Corp. to Chinese Zhejiang Geely Holding Group. These chapters represent several fields that should be subject to future research activities. First, the neglected aspect of what happens during the disinvestment of an integrated company to a new owner, that is, where the partner becomes a competitor. While merger & acquisition (M&A) cases have attracted numerous efforts in international business research, the disintegration process implies equally important effects of company behaviour. The automotive industry is in this respect particularly relevant, due to the huge investment in product development and economies of scale related to common platform architecture. This implies that a disintegration will take many years to implement. In the case of Volvo and Ford, the joint production plant in China remains four years after the decision by Ford to put up Volvo for sale. This chapter is also an example of the use of rich qualitative interview data to follow the disintegration stages.

The chapter by Claes G. Alvstam and Inge Ivarsson, on the other hand, focuses on what has happened after the transformation of ownership. Theoretically it relates to the literature around the liability of foreignness and the liability of outsidership, as well as the debate around how emerging market multinationals use a 'springboard' approach to acquire well-known and prestigious brands abroad as well as the latest technology in order to improve their competitive advantage in the home market. The suggestion that a new category of 'in-between companies' or 'hybrids' is created, in which the acquired company is neither foreign nor domestic, is pending the attitude by the Chinese government at different levels to maintain such a twilight zone. Since it is argued that this is a new situation that has come to stay, it is crucial in future research regarding China's internationalization to follow closely the interaction between government and the owners, as well as identifying new cases when they appear. One particular aspect that is also represented in this volume through the chapter by Yu Zheng, is the relationship between headquarters and subsidiary in Chinese industry, where particular attention is paid to Japanese MNCs. It is in this respect crucial to assess whether the strategies adopted toward local subsidiaries are typical for Japanese management, or if they can be traced in other home countries as well.

The most challenging opportunity for future research regarding the gradual opening-up of Asian economies for inward and outward foreign direct investment should be to better integrate the global value-chain (GVC) approach into the present studies. The GVC reveals how the division of labour is fragmented into numerous tasks including physical and non-physical production; it can be used to demonstrate the spatial distribution of value-added, by mapping the nodes of production as well as the links between the production nodes. In the latter aspect, the logistical constraints and opportunities along the value-chain can be integrated into an analysis of geographical competitive advantages and factors behind changing advantages and disadvantages. This approach has been used in specific research contexts over the last two decades, but it is only recently that it has become more widely observed and accepted as an appropriate method to follow international investment. The latest annual *World Investment Report* published by UNCTAD (UNCTAD 2013) is the most apparent example of this trend, and it is commendable that the various angles to GVCs that are presented in this research report should be an inspiration for future ambitions to better understand the ongoing process of international economic integration and interaction, not least in Asia.

References

Dolles, H., Alvstam, C.G. and Ström, P. (2013) 'The Changing Competitive Landscape in Euro-Asia Business – Guest Editorial,'*Asian Business and Management*, 12(4): 499–502.

Schlunze, R.D., Agola, N.O. and Barber, W.W. (eds) (2012) *Spaces of International Economy and Management: Launching New Perspectives on Management and Geography* (Basingstoke: Palgrave Macmillan).

UNCTAD (2013) *World Investment Report. Global Value Chains: Investment and Trade for Development* (Geneva: United Nations Conference for Trade and Development).

Williamson, P.J., Ramamurti, R., Fleury, A. and Leme Fleury, M.T. (eds) (2013) *The Competitive Advantage of Emerging Market Multinationals* (Cambridge: Cambridge University Press).

Index

Abney, David, 53
academic conversation, standard model in, 115–16
action research, 120–2
adaptation
  to new realities, need for, 218–20
  product, 70
  of talent management, 105–8
additive manufacturing, 225
Adidas, 43, 58
advertising/advertisement, 39–41, 48–59
  patterns, of Beijing Olympic Games' sponsoring partners, 36–59
    findings and analysis, 48–57
    framework in research, applying, 45–7
    research framework, developing, 38–43
agent–owner conflict, 116
Aggreko, 43
Aifly, 44
Air China, 43
Akafuku, 121
American Chamber of Commerce, 140
American Corning Glass Works, 184
Ampherex, 185
Aokang, 44
Apple, 194
ASEAN, 3, 13, 24, 67, 232
ASEAN-10, 4
Asian Development Bank, 6
ASML, 193
Association Internationale des Etudiants en Sciences Economiques et Commerciales (AIESEC), 127, 128, 133n2
Aston Martin, 206
Atos Origin, 43
Audi, 54, 237n12

Bangladesh, 4
Bank of China, 43
BEIFA, 43

Beijing Automotive Industry Corporation (BAIC), 220
Beijing Olympic Games
  Beijing Organizing Committee for the Olympic Games (BOCOG), 43, 44, 47, 53, 58
  Global Television and Online Media Report, 36
  sponsoring partners, advertising patterns of, 36–59
    findings and analysis, 48–57
    framework in research, applying, 45–7
    research framework, developing, 38–43
  sponsorship levels, 43–4
Beijing Organizing Committee for the Olympic Games (BOCOG), 43, 44, 47, 53, 58
Beijing Yanjing Brewery Co. Ltd, 51–2
bhpbilliton, 43
brand(ing)
  association, 40, 41
  awareness, 40, 59
  co-branding, 37, 40–1, 48, 51–3
  contract, 42
  equity, 11, 37, 39–40, 42, 100
  image, 40, 180, 219, 232
  loyalty, 40
  value, 41
Brazil, 236n3, 246
  iron ore exploitation in, 1
  see also BRIC
BRIC, 88
  see also Brazil; China; India
Budweiser, 43, 51–2
bundling subsidiary strategy, 27–9

Capinfo, 44
capital, 160, 166
  human, 68, 87, 160–2, 167–8
  labour–management relationship, 167
  social, 118, 132, 162, 165, 168
capitalism, 157–9

chaebol, 13, 163, 165, 170, 196
Chang'an Ford Mazda Automobile
        Corp., 229
Chen Zhixin, 57
China
    Four Modernizations, policy of, 221,
        224
    institutional framework, 223–6
    internationalization process, 221–3
    multinational corporations in, 17–32
        global industrial structure and
            subsidiary upgrading, 21–2
        localization, as overarching
            corporate strategy, 23–5
        power structure, 20–1
        research methodology, 22–3
        subsidiary strategy, 19–20
    outward/inward FDI, trends and
        developments in, 2–3, 6–7
    physical production, service content
        in, 244
    talent identification, challenges of
        adapting, 100–1
    12th Five-Year Plan, 224, 228
    see also Beijing Olympic Games
    see also BRIC
    Zhejiang Geely Holding Group (Geely)
        acquisition of Volvo Car
            Corporations
        see Volvo Car Corporation (VCC),
            ownership transfer of
        see Ford Motor Cooperation
            (FMC), Volvo's acquisition by
            Geely

China Development Bank, 233, 234
China Investment Corp., 224
China Mobile, 43, 54
China-Sweden Research Centre for
        Traffic Safety, 232
Chinese National Library, 45
Chinese Olympic Committee (COC), 44
Chinese Olympic Team, 44
Citibank, 139
Citigroup, 148
civil society, role in South Korean
        institutions, 162
climbing subsidiary strategy, 26–7
CNC, 43
CNPC, 43

co-branding, 37, 40–1, 48, 51–3
Coca-Cola, 43
Code Division Multiple Access (CDMA),
        186
co-leadership, 127, 131, 132
    corporate, 118
    intercultural, 9
    networking, 128–9
    see also leadership
'coming-in' (*yin jin lai*) strategy, 221,
        224
competence
    -creating subsidiaries, 67, 68, 70, 71, 79
    -exploiting subsidiaries, 67, 68
    intercultural, 115, 118, 119
    transfer of, 212
Confucianism, 4, 168–72
cooperation agreements, 212, 213
coordinated market economies (CMEs),
        158
Corning Inc., 197n4
corporate culture, 91–2, 93, 103–9, 168,
        180, 186, 193, 219, 230
corporate governance
    in academic conversation, 115–16
    defined, 116
    by managers, 115–33
        co-leadership networking, 128–9
        cultural views on, 123–4
        mutual mechanism of, 124–5
        network, 125–8
        preference and network, 130–1
        practitioner's model, 115–16
Corporate Social Responsibility (CSR),
        116, 193
corporation
    branding, 42
    -centred advertising, 42
    image, 42, 48, 51–3
corruption, 171
Costco, 139
country-of-origin effect, 91
Crystal CG, 44
culture
    corporate, 91–2, 93, 103–9, 168, 180,
        186, 193, 219, 230
    defined, 92
    -free industries, R&D by MNEs in,
        70–1
    and leadership, 94–5

levels of, 92, 93
national, 91–2, 93, 101, 103, 105, 106, 109, 157
-specific industries, R&D by MNEs in, 71–2
and talent management, 91–4
views on corporate governance, 123–4

DaimlerChrysler, 204
Daio Paper, 121
Dalian Wanda
    acquisition of AMC Theaters, 222
    'dances with wolves' (*yu lang gong wu*) strategy, 221, 224
Danielsson, Lars, 233
Daqing State Asset Operation and Shanghai Jiaerwoo Investment Company, 231
Dayun, 44
delivery agreements, 212
Delta 1 project, 207, 208
demerger process, 202, 204–13
    disintegration phase, 209–13
    disintegration process, 202–3
    neglected phenomenon of, 203–4
    negotiation phase, 207–9
    pre-demerger phase, 205–7
Democratic Party of Japan (DPJ), 141
Der Floor, 44
disintegration phase, mergers and acquisitions, 209–13
disintegration process, mergers and acquisitions, 202–3
    neglected phenomenon of, 203–4
Doctoroff, Tom, 58
DRAMs, 185–6, 188
dynamic capabilities, of multinational enterprises, 67–9

eclectic paradigm, of internationalization process, 181
economic motives, of demerger process, 205
English First (EF), 44
enterprise resource planning (ERP), 190
entrepreneurship, 180, 186, 223
'environmental friendly factory', 30
Ericsson, 180, 194
Euro-Asia Management Studies Association (EAMSA), 7

European Business Council (EBC), 121
European Union (EU)
    free trade agreement with South Korea, 245
expatriate managers, 118–19
experiential learning, 183
extrafirm network, 115

Fairchild, 185
Fiat, 233
Five-Year Plan (China), 12th, 224, 228
fledging subsidiary strategy, 29–31
Ford Motor Cooperation (FMC)
    'One Ford' strategy, 206, 207
    ownership transfer to Volvo Car Corporation, 11, 12–13, 202, 204, 205, 212–13, 214, 220–1, 234, 235, 246
    Volvo's acquisition by Geely
        acquisition process, 226–8
        Delta 1 project, 207–8
        Delta 2 project, 209, 211–12, 213, 214
        demerger process, 205–13
        disintegration phase, 209–13
        domestic vs export markets, 232–3
        in-betweenness, ambiguity of, 230–2
        management and control, 233
        negotiation phase, 207–9
        pre-demerger phase, 205–7
        operations, 229–30
Foreign direct investment (FDI)
    flow patterns, in hybrid emerging market firms, 217–18
    inward, 1–7, 8, 10, 137–50, 166, 180, 219, 221, 226, 234, 243–7
        political economy of, 138–142
        role in economic revitalization, 137–50
        trends and developments in, 1–7
    outward, 1–7, 8–10, 13, 183, 195, 201, 218, 219, 221, 222, 224, 235, 243–7
        trends and developments in, 1–7
    positive effects of, 73–83
foreignness, liability of, 217, 220, 235, 247
France, 118
free trade agreement (FTA), 232
    EU–South Korea, 153–4, 173, 245

Geely, *see* Zhejiang Geely Holding
Group (Geely)
acquisition of Volvo Car Corporations
see Volvo Car Corporation (VCC),
ownership transfer of
see Ford Motor Cooperation (FMC),
Volvo's acquisition by Geely
Geely Sweden AB, 233
Geely Sweden AutomotiveAB, 233
Geely Sweden Holdings AB, 233
Gehua Ticketmaster Ticketing, 43
General Agreement on Tariffs and Trade
(GATT), 5
General Agreement of Trade in Services
(GATS), 5
General Electric (GE), 43, 180, 193
General Motors (GM), 202
General Telephone and Electronics
Corporation (GTE), 185
Germany, 95
coordinated market economy, 158
Ghosn, Carlos, 139
Global Business Manager (GBM) system,
191
global commodity chains, 21
Global Competitiveness Reports (World
Economic Forum), 167, 169
global industrial structure and subsidiary
upgrading, 21–2
global network, 129–30
global production networks, 5, 7, 21, 26
Global Product Manager (GPM) system,
191
global standardization, for talent
management, 105–8
global value chain (GVC) approach, 21,
247
'going global' (*zou xiang shi jie*) strategy,
221, 224
'going out' (*zou chu qu*) strategy, 221,
222, 224
Great Wall, 43
gross domestic product (GDP), 1, 2, 141,
166, 167

Haier, 43, 192, 222
Héng Yuán Xiáng, 43
Higashiyama Prince Hotel, *see* Niseko
Village
Hilton Hotels Corporation, 148

Hisense, 192
Hong Kong, 234, 236*n*2
industrial co-development, 223
outward/inward FDI, trends and
developments in, 2
HuáDi, 43
Huawei, 192, 202
human capital, 68, 87, 160–2, 167–8
human resource management (HRM),
89, 93, 94, 102, 103, 109, 224
Hummer, Sichuan Tengzhong
Heavy Industrial Machinery
Company's acquisition of, 202
hybrid emerging market firms, 217–35
adaptation to new realities, need for,
218–20
case study, 226–33
example, 220–1
FDI flow patterns in, 217–18; *see also*
Foreign direct investment
industrial co-development, 223–4
internationalization process, 221–3
middle-income-trap, avoidance of,
224–5
policy shifts, 225–6
shift towards transformative technology
and innovation, 225
technological upgrading, 223–4
hybrid managers, 119

IBM
personal computer business, Lenovo's
acquisition of, 11, 201, 222,
236*n*3
R&D investment portfolio, 188
Ikea, 139
in-betweenness, Ford's ownership
transfer to Volvo Car
Corporation, 217–18
ambiguity of, 230–2
India, 5, 13, 81
outward/inward FDI, 4
see also BRIC
individual development plans (IDP), 101
Indonesia, 2
industrial co-development, 223–4
Information Technologies,
Telecommunication, Consumer
Electronics and Entertainment
(ITTCE), 191

innovation, shift towards, 225
intercultural competence, 115, 119
International Investment Agreements
(IIAs), 6
internationalization
    behavioural or process-oriented view,
        182
    eclectic paradigm of, 181
    economic–strategic view, 181–2
    process theory of, 182
    resources-based view of, 181–2
    Uppsala model of, 182
International Monetary Fund (IMF),
    170
International Olympic Committee
    (IOC), 43
Investment Development Path (IDP)
    model, 2
inward foreign direct investment (IFDI,
    1–7, 8, 10, 137–50, 166, 180,
    219, 221, 226, 234, 243–7
    political economy of, 138–142
    role in economic revitalization,
        137–50
    trends and developments in, 1–7

Jacoby, Stefan, 233
Jaguar, Tata Motors' acquisition of, 202,
    206, 210, 213
Japan
    coordinated market economy, 158
    Democratic Party of Japan, 141
    foreign direct investment in, 137–51
        discussion, 149–50
        inbound, 1, 3–4, 5, 138, 140–1
        outbound, 1, 3–4, 5, 138
        political economy of, 138–42
        role in economic revitalization, 142
    hybrid emerging market firms in, 219
    Investment Development Path
        model, 2
    Keiretsu, 3
    physical production, service content
        in, 244
    Tokyo Stock Exchange (TSE), 139, 147
    Visit Japan campaign, 142
Japan External Trade Organization
    (JETRO), 3, 4, 140, 146, 150
Japan Investment Council, 139
Johnson & Johnson, 43

Kao
    dynamic capabilities of, 68
    knowledge-creation mechanisms of,
        74–83
    resource and development in, 71, 72
Keiretsu, 3
Kerry Oil & Grains, 43
knowledge-creation, by multinational
    enterprises, 65–84
Kodak, 43
Koizumi, Junichiro, 139, 141, 142
Kokuyo, 44
Korean Institute of Science and
    Technology (KIST), 185
Korea Semiconductor, 185

Land Rover, Tata Motors' acquisition of,
    202, 206, 210, 213
leadership, 117–18
    co-leadership, 9, 118, 127, 128–9, 131,
        132
    competencies, 94–5
    culture and, 93, 94–5
    defined, 117
    development, 91, 93–5, 98–109, 106
    skills, 88
    values to talent management,
        challenges of transferring,
        102–3
Lee Byung-Chull, 179, 195
Lee Kun-Hee, 179, 180, 185, 186, 190
    see also Samsung Electronics
leisure sector, 244
Lenovo, 43
    acquisition of IBM's personal
        computer business, 192, 201
Lewin, Kurt, 120
LG Electronics, 186, 192
Li, 233
liability
    of foreignness, 217, 220, 235, 247
    intercoder, 46
    of outsidership, 195, 196, 217, 220,
        235, 247
liberal market economies (LMEs), 158
Library of the Graduate School of
    Chinese Academy of Social
    Sciences (CASS), 45
Liby, 44
Lincoln, 206

Li Shufu, 227
    see also Volvo Car Corporation (VCC),
        ownership transfer of
Liu Xiang, 48
Livedoor, 121
Local Content Requirement (LCR) rules,
    232
localization, as overarching corporate
    strategy, 23–5
local network, in global city, 125–6
Lucky Goldstar, *see* LG Electronics

Mainland China, 2, 147, 221, 223
    see also China
Malaysia
    outward/inward FDI, 2, 221
    resource and development in, 70
management
    human resource, 89, 93, 94, 102, 103,
        109
    labour–management relationship, 167
    South Korean business system, 162–3,
        165–6
    supply chain, 190
    talent, *see* talent management

managers
    corporate, 155, 163
    expatriate, 118–19
    global, 9, 87
    global product, 191
    hybrid, 119
    and leadership education, 99
    motives, of demerger process, 206
    power of, 20–1
    rationale of business, 171
    talent development, 87–109
        adaptation of, 105–8
        analysis and discussion, 103–5
        culture and, 91–4
        data analysis, 95, 98
        data collection, 95, 98
        development, 91, 87–9, 98–100
        feature research, 109
        global standardization for, 105–8
        goals of, 89
        identification, 87–9, 91, 98–101
        implications of, 108–9
        phases of, 90
        research sample, 95, 96–7

theoretical research framework,
    89–90
transferring leadership values,
    challenges of, 102–3
Manulife, 43
Matsushita Denki, 184, 196
McDonalds, 43
means–objectives framework (sponsoring),
    37, 39, 45, 46, 50, 51
mega-sporting events, sponsoring for,
    36–8, 246
Memorandum of Understanding with
    China Development Bank, 231
MengNa, 43
mergers and acquisitions (M&A)
    cross-border, 11, 201, 222
    disintegration phase, 209–13
    large-scale, 3
    neglected phenomenon of, 203–4
    negotiation phase, 207–9
    out–in, 139
    pre-demerger phase, 205–7
Microsoft, 44
middle-income-trap, avoidance of,
    224–5
Ministry of Finance, South Korea, 166
Ministry of Industry and Information
    Technology (MIIT), 233
Ministry of Internal Affairs and
    Communications of Japan
    (MIC), 69
Mitsubishi, 233
Mondo, 44
Morgan Stanley, 151n8
Motorola, 185
multinational corporations (MNCs),
    17–32
    global talent identification and
        development, approaches to,
        98–100
    power structure in, 20–1
    subsidiary strategy within, 19–20
multinational enterprises (MNEs)
    dynamic capabilities of, 67–9
    intra-variations vs inner variations
        in, 243
    knowledge-creation by, 65–84
    R&D by
        in culture-free industries, 70–1
        in culture-specific industries, 71–2

Nanjing Automobile Group, 220
Nanoradio, 193
national culture, 91–2, 93, 101, 103,
    105, 106, 109, 157
National Development and Reform
    Commission (NDRC), 229, 233
National Olympic Committees (NOCs), 43
National Science Foundation Network
    (NFS), 69
National Shanghai Library, 45
nation-wide networking, 128
NEC, 184, 195
neglected phenomenon, of demerger/
    disintegration process, 203–4
negotiation phase, mergers and
    acquisitions, 207–9
nepotism, 171
Netherlands, The, 95
network(s/ing)
    closed business, 165
    co-leadership, 128–9
    extrafirm, 115
    global, 129–30
    local, in global city, 125–6
    nation-wide, 128
    and preference, 130–1
    South Korean business system, 162,
        165
Newauto, 44
NIE-tigers, 2
Niseko, 142–5
    comparison with Yubari, 144–5
    firms in, 146–9
        institutional investors, 147–8
        property development, sales and
            management, 146–7
        spillover effect, 148–9
    foreign direct investment in, 137,
        146–9
    foreign presence in, 143–4, 145
    Niseko Masterplan, 150
    overview of, 142–3
    see also Japan
Niseko Village, 147–8
Nissan, 139
Nokia, 180
North America
    automotive manufacturing transplants
        in, 1
Novartis, 204

Olsson, Hans-Olov, 233
Olympus, 121
Omega, 43
opportunities
    identification of, 183
    recognition of, 182–3
organizational motives, of demerger
    process, 205–6
organizational talent review (OTR), 91
Organization for Economic
    Co-operation and Development
    (OECD), 115, 167
Organizing Committees of the Olympic
    Games (OCOGs), 43
outsidership, liability of, 195, 196, 217,
    220, 235, 247
outward foreign direct investment
    (OFDI), 1–7, 8–10, 13, 183, 195,
    201, 218, 219, 221, 222, 224,
    235, 243–7
    trends and developments in, 1–7
ownership
    of South Korean business system, 162,
        163–5
    transfer of Volvo Car Corporation, 11,
        12–13, 202, 204, 205, 212–13,
        214, 220–1, 234, 235, 246
        acquisition process, 226–8
        Delta 1 project, 207–8
        Delta 2 project, 209, 211–12, 213,
            214
        demerger process, 205–13
        disintegration phase, 209–13
        domestic vs export markets, 232–3
        in-betweenness, ambiguity of,
            230–2
        management and control, 233
        negotiation phase, 207–9
        pre-demerger phase, 205–7
        operations, 229–30

Pakistan, 4
Panasonic, 43, 192
P&G
    dynamic capabilities of, 68
    knowledge-creation mechanisms of,
        74–83
    resource and development in, 71, 72
Philippines, 2
Philips Electronics, 192

physical production, service content in, 244
PICC, 43
policy shifts, 225–6
power structure, in multinational corporations, 20–1
practitioner's model, 115–16
pre-demerger phase, mergers and acquisitions, 205–7
Premier Automotive Group (PAG), 206
PricewaterhouseCoopers, 44
Prince Hotels, 147–8
process theory of internationalization, 182
product image, 42, 48, 51
product-orientated advertisement, 41–2

Qinxihe, 43

real estate investment trust (REIT), 147
regionalism, 171
region image, 42
relationship commitment decisions, 183
Renault, 139, 179
resource and development (R&D), 65–6
   decentralization of, 66
   laboratories, 69–70
   by multinational enterprises
      in culture-free industries, 70–1
      in culture-specific industries, 71–2
      knowledge-creation mechanisms, analysis of, 74–83
      research methodology of, 72–4
resources-based view framework, 181–2
'red hat' strategy, 223
return on investment (ROI), 115
revenue generation, 41
reverse engineering, 184, 196
reverse offshoring, 225
Ripplewood Holdings, 139
Royal, 43

Samsung Automobile Co. Ltd, 179, 245
Samsung Corning Precision Glass Joint Venture, 197n4
Samsung Corporation, 43, 179
Samsung Electro-Mechanics, 197n3
Samsung Electronics, 179–97
   Ericsson's business strategy, adoption of, 180
   financial crisis 1997 and, 179

Global Business Manager (GBM) system, 191
as global leader, 186–90
global leadership, maintaining, 191–4
global organizational structure, creation of, 190–1
Global Product Manager (GPM) system, 191
internationalization process, 181–3
   behavioural or process-oriented view, 182
   economic–strategic view, 181–2
   mission of, 180
   as national champion, 183–6
New Management Movement, 190
very large scale integration, 185
Samsung Group, 179, 185, 186, 190
Samsung Heavy Equipment Co. Ltd, 179–80
Samsung-Sanyo Electronics, 183, 184
Samsung-Sanyo Parts, 184
Samsung SDI, 197n2
Samsung Semiconductor, 185, 186
Samuelsson, Håkan, 233
Sanyo Electric, 183, 184, 195, 197n1, 3
Schenker, 43
search engine optimization (SEO), 148
Seibu Holdings, Inc., 147
service
   content, in physical production, 244
   value-added, 244
Shanghai Automotive Industry Corporation (SAIC), 222
Shared Delivery Model, 211
Shen, Freeman, 233
Shuanghui International Holdings, 222
Sichuan Tengzhong Heavy Industrial Machinery Company
   acquisition of Hummer, 202
SIEM, 121, 123
Singapore
   inward/outward foreign direct investment, 2, 4, 5, 221
   resource and development in, 70
single business enterprise, spatial development of, 245
Sinian, 43
Sinopec, 43
Skoda, 54
Skyworth, 192

small and medium-sized enterprises (SMEs), 162
Smithfield Foods, 222
Snickers, 43
social capital, 118, 132, 162, 165, 168
Sohu.com, 43
Sony, 180, 192
South Korea
  business system, 153–74
    analysis of, 160–3
    capitalism, varieties of, 157–9
    data analysis, 155–6
    data collection, 155
    delimitations, 156–7
    management, 162–3, 165–6
    networks, 162, 165
    ownership, 162, 163–5
  chaebol, 13, 163, 165, 170, 196
  civil society, role of, 162
  culture, 171–2
  free trade agreement with European Union, 245
  historical influences, 162, 170
  hybrid emerging market firms in, 219
  institutions
    capital, 160, 166
    human capital, 160–2, 167–8
    social capital, 162, 168
  inward/outward foreign direct investment, 221
    trends and developments in, 2, 4
  Ministry of Finance, South Korea, 166
  Samsung Electronics, *see* Samsung Electronics
  South Korean-German Chamber of Commerce and Industry, 155
  state, role of, 162, 168–9
South Korean-German Chamber of Commerce and Industry, 155
spillover effect, 148–9
sponsoring, 36–59, 246
  findings and analysis, 48–57, 246
  framework in research, applying, 45–7
  limitations of, 47–8
  for mega-sporting events, 36–8, 246
  research framework, developing, 38–43
  see also Beijing Olympic Games
'springboard' perspective, 217–20, 235, 247

Ssangyong, 222
Standard Operating Procedures (SOP), 116
Staples, 43
state, role in South Korean institutions, 162, 168–9
State Grid, 43
subsidiary(ies)
  competence-creating, 67, 68
  competence-exploiting, 67, 68
  strategy, 19–20, 25–31
    bundling strategy, 27–9
    climbing strategy, 26–7
    fledging strategy, 29–31
  upgrading, global industrial structure and, 21–2
Sumitomo Trading, 183, 184, 195
Sunglo, 44
supply chain management (SCM), 190
sustainable development, 146, 147, 150
Switzerland, 95

Taishan, 44
Taiwan
  hybrid emerging market firms in, 219
  inward/outward foreign direct investment, 221
  trends and developments in, 2
talent development, 244
Takahashi, Yoshiaki, 59
talent management, 87–109
  adaptation of, 105–8
  analysis and discussion, 103–5
  culture and, 91–4
  development, 91
    challenges to, 87–9
    global, MNCs' approaches to, 98–100
  feature research, 109
  global standardization for, 105–8
  goals of, 89
  identification, 91
    challenges to, 87–9
    to Chinese conditions, challenges of adapting, 100–1
    global, MNCs' approaches to, 98–100
  managerial implications in, 108–9

talent management – *continued*
  methodology
    data analysis, 95, 98
    data collection, 95, 98
    limitations, 95, 98
    research sample, 95, 96–7
  phases of, 90
  theoretical research framework, 89–90
  transferring leadership values to,
    challenges of, 102–3
Tata Motors, 202
  acquisition of Jaguar and Land Rover,
    202, 206, 210, 213
TCL–Thompson Electronics, 222
TechnoGym, 43
technological upgrading, 223–4
TEPCO, 121
Tesco, 139
Thai Chaereon Corporation (TCC),
    151n8
Thailand
  inward/outward foreign direct
    investment, 2, 221
  resource and development in, 70
3D-printing, 225
Tokyo Stock Exchange, 139, 147
TongYi, 43
Torok, Ken, 53
total quality control (TQC), 184
tourism, 244–5
town-and-village enterprises (TVEs), 223
transfer of competence, 212
transformative technology, shift
    towards, 225
transitional service agreements, 212
Transnational Service Agreements
    (TSAs), 212
Tsingtao Brewery Co. Ltd., 43, 51–3

UNCTAD, 6
Unilever
  dynamic capabilities of, 68
  knowledge-creation mechanisms of,
    74–83
  resource and development in, 72
Unipack, 44
United Parcel Service of America, Inc.
    (UPS), 53–4, 55
Uppsala model of internationalization,
    182

UPS, 43
USA, 95
  Ford Motor Cooperation (FMC)
    'One Ford' strategy, 206, 207
    ownership transfer to Volvo Car
      Corporation, 11, 12–13, 202,
      204, 205, 212–13, 214, 220–1,
      234, 235, 246
  liberal market economy, 158

Vietnam, 2
Visa, 43
Visit Japan campaign, 142
Vodafone, 139
Volkswagen (VW), 43, 54–7, 58, 233
Volvo Car Corporation (VCC),
      ownership transfer of, 11,
      12–13, 202, 204, 205, 212–13,
      214, 220–1, 234, 235, 246
  acquisition process, 226–8
  Delta 1 project, 207–8
  Delta 2 project, 209, 211–12, 213, 214
  demerger process
    disintegration phase, 209–13
    negotiation phase, 207–9
    pre-demerger phase, 205–7
  domestic vs export markets, 232–3
  in-betweenness, ambiguity of, 230–2
  management and control, 233
  operations, 229–30
  Scalable Product Architecture (SPA),
    229, 231
  Shared Delivery Model, 211
  structure, 227
  Volvo Engine Architecture (VEA), 231,
    236n9
Volvo Group, 179–80, 226

Wanxiang Group, 222
World Economic Forum (WEF)
  Global Competitiveness Reports, 167,
    169
World Investment Report, 247
World Trade Organization (WTO), 5,
    194

YADU, 43
Yanjing Beer, 43
YiLi Industrial Group Co., Ltd., 43,
    48–51, 52

Yuanpei Translation, 44
Yubari
    comparison with Niseko, 144–5
    financial collapse of, 142

Zara, 139
Zhang Fengyi, 54
Zhejiang Geely Holding Group
        (Geely)

acquisition of Volvo Car Corporations
    see Volvo Car Corporation (VCC),
        ownership transfer of
    see Ford Motor Cooperation (FMC),
        Volvo's acquisition by Geely
Geely Sweden AB, 233
Geely Sweden Automotive AB, 233
Geely Sweden Holdings AB, 233
ZTE, 192